Natural Law and the
Social Construction of Reality

Bernie Koenig

University Press of America,® Inc.
Dallas · Lanham · Boulder · New York · Oxford

Copyright © 2004 by
University Press of America,® Inc.
4501 Forbes Boulevard
Suite 200
Lanham, Maryland 20706
UPA Acquisitions Department (301) 459-3366

PO Box 317
Oxford
OX2 9RU, UK

All rights reserved
Printed in the United States of America
British Library Cataloging in Publication Information Available

Library of Congress Control Number: 2004104336
ISBN 0-7618-2903-2 (paperback : alk. ppr.)

∞™ The paper used in this publication meets the minimum
requirements of American National Standard for Information
Sciences—Permanence of Paper for Printed Library Materials,
ANSI Z39.48—1984

Contents

Preface		v
Acknowledgments		ix
Chapter 1	Natural Law and the Scientific Revolution	1
Chapter 2	Conceptual Revolutions	21
Chapter 3	John Locke, Natural Law and the Empiricist Tradition	51
Chapter 4	The Kantian Response	111
Chapter 5	The Postmodern Response	187
Chapter 6	Postmodern Science as Social Construct	259
Chapter 7	Conclusions	299
Appendix		313
Notes		325
Bibliography		333
Index		339

PREFACE

My interest in what I later learned was natural law theory dates from a 1963 television debate on the then recently-published *Eichmann in Jerusalem: A Report on the Banality of Evil* by Hannah Arendt. I was fascinated by the theme of the debate, which was how our views of human nature affect how we evaluate human behavior.

The debaters were Gustave Gilbert and Ernest van den Haag. Gilbert was the army psychologist at the Nuremberg trials and interviewed all the major war criminals. Two books came out of this experience: *Nuremberg Diary*, where the Nazis spoke for themselves and *The Psychology of Dictatorship*, his theoretical work in which he tried to explain how such a regime was possible. Van den Haag was a practicing psychoanalyst who had co-authored a text entitled *Passion and Social Constraint*.

I had just transferred from Manhattan School of Music to Long Island University and discovered that Gilbert was the chair of the psychology department and taught a course on the psychology of dictatorship in which he assigned his book. As soon as I had the prerequisites I took his course. Then the following Summer I took van den Haag's course at the New School for Social Research.

By this time I had taken a number of philosophy courses and had developed my analytical skills.

Gilbert was an adherent of humanistic psychology and believed that people were basically good and altruistic. Thus he had to do some convoluted reasoning to explain how Naziism developed and how someone like Eichmann could do what he did.

Van den Haag was a very conservative Freudian and held that under the right circumstances anyone is capable of anything.

As a young philosophy student I found Gilbert's position untenable on two grounds. First he really didn't argue for his position. He just stated it. Second, his explanation of what happened to was convoluted and ad hoc. I did not think that he actually explained anything and he did not do well in answering questions in class.

I found van den Haag's views a bit extreme on the other side. But he tried to give answers to questions and never resorted to authority.

I came away from these experiences believing that humanistic psychology was not so much a theory about how people behave but a belief about how we would like to think about ourselves. I also came away with healthy positive—yet skeptical—view of psychoanalytic theory. Van den Haag did a good job of explaining the theory although he was a bit too dogmatic in his presentations.

In my later studies of various psychological theorists, these views were confirmed and reinforced. Humanistic psychology was not in any sense a serious theory or explanation of human behavior, while too many psychoanalytical theorists were a bit too dogmatic. Yet, on methodological grounds, psychoanalysis, with all its faults, showed real explanatory power.

My views on the contextual nature of knowledge, and my finally understanding Kant on this issue date from a course I took with Robert Binkley at The University of Western Ontario on the philosophy of Wifrid Sellars. So many of the questions I had asked as a fledgling philosopher were answered in that course. This is not to say that this course answered all my questions, but it did give me a whole new perspective on philosophy. Needless to say, the work of Sellars has had a profound influence on me.

My views on the nature of feminism and on the difference between sex and gender come from my reading of Nancy Chodorow. Her work changed how I understood social relationships and the relation between social structures and our views on the nature of sexuality and on the nature of knowledge.

The origins of this book go back to the spring of 1983 when my colleague Harvey Brown asked me what I planned for the summer. I said I was going to sit down with Freud, get rid of the nonsense, and find the kernel of truth about his concept of a person and then look at the ethical implications of this view of personhood.

Harvey then asked if I would be willing to compare Freud to Aquinas. When I asked why, he said that I could then read the paper at the International Medieval Congress. So I began writing and came up with two papers. I read the first, "Natural Law and the Scientific Revolution", in 1984 and the second, "Freud and Aquinas on the Concept of a Person", in 1987. The first paper amounted to an outline of this book and the second paper provides the basis for discussions in chapter four.

In 1992 I was both a referee and commentator on Roland Puccetti's paper "Does the Universe Exist Because it Ought to?" at the Canadian Philosophical Association. The paper discussed the issue of axiarchism. In my reply I developed answers that the three different views of science would present. This work provided the foundation of the extended discussions of science in this book, which I was later able to develop when I taught a methodology course.

In 2001 Harvey Brown called and asked if I could read a paper on the theme of natural law in a human rights context. My "John Locke as a Natural Law Theorist" was the result and provides the basis of the beginning of chapter three. And in 2002 I read a paper entitled "Natural Diversity and the Unnaturalness of Aquinas", which provides the basis for parts of chapter five.

Through the book I make references to literature, both as a way of demonstrating various philosophical views and as examples of how art and science have certain similarities. In 2002 I read a paper based on these themes entitled "The Art and Science of Poetry" to the College Association on Language and Literacy.

And in the spring of 2002 I sat down and started to make sense of all this work, finally resulting in this book.

ACKNOWLEDGMENTS

I owe a great debt to Harvey Brown. Thanks to his encouragement I was able to work in this area and present my views to a professional audience. Needless to say, most of that audience disagreed with my views but also took them seriously. Comments and questions from those sessions led to this being a better book.

I would like to thank Bernard Hodgson for his encouraging comments on an earlier draft of the manuscript.

I also owe a great deal to May Lee-Jarvis for her editorial work. Like all great editors she translated "Academese" into English, yet kept it true to my original style.

And finally, I would like to applaud my students whose questions made me think more clearly about these issues.

Acknowledgments are due to three publishers for granting copyright permission to quote lengthy passages from their work. Thanks go to:

Harvard University Press for permission to quote from *In a Different Voice: Psychological Theory and Women's Development*, by Carol Gilligan, copyright 1982, 1993 by Carol Gilligan;

University of California Press, for permission to quote from *The Reproduction of Mothering: Psychoanalysis and the Sociology of Gender*, by Nancy Chodorow, copyright 1978 The Regents of the University of California;

Routledge/Taylor & Francis Books, Inc., copyright 2001, from *Feminist Science Studies*, edited by Maralee Mayberry, Banu Subramaniam and Lisa H. Weasel.

Chapter 1

NATURAL LAW AND THE SCIENTIFIC REVOLUTION

Two themes have dominated Western thought: the search for ultimate truth and the search for the place of humanity in the overall scheme of things. When these two themes are brought together we have a new subject called natural law. Briefly, natural law is the view that by discovering the natural order of the universe we will also come to discover or infer humanity's place in that universe. The quest for our place in the overall scheme of things—moral knowledge—leads to metaphysical or epistemological knowledge—scientific knowledge. Conversely, by beginning our search for metaphysical or epistemological knowledge we will discover moral knowledge. Thus, within the view of natural law, all forms of knowledge are interconnected.

This position is not the only view of natural law. For example, Alexander Passerin d'Entrèves, in his well-known and influential work, *Natural Law: An Introduction to Legal Philosophy* claims that natural law refers to human behavior and not to physical phenomena.[1] Yet through his discussions we see the relationships between a world view and a conception of behavior in the theorists he discusses. His conception of law, though, is legalistic and not scientific. My point is that the two, when they come from the same world view, are the same.

In a sense, most, if not all, religions and philosophical systems deal with these combinations of issues. What sets natural law apart from other systems of thought is how the investigations are undertaken and how the connections are justified. It is by emphasizing how the connections are justified that lead to natural law theory. For a moral theory to be considered a natural law theory the connections between the knowledge base—the natural order—and the moral or ethical concepts must be explicit. Thus, a religious teaching, which tries to explain the role of humanity within the role of overall creation, would be an example of a religious approach to natural law. But a religion which talks about God's will in the abstract and then presents moral teachings is not a religious approach to natural law since the connection is not explicit.

The same can be said for non-religious approaches to moral theory. If an explicit connection between a world-view and a moral view is established, as we can see in Locke and Kant, then we have a natural law approach to moral theory. But if there is no clear connection, or if there is a clear separation between fact and value, as we see in Hume, we do not have a natural law approach to moral theory.

I single out Hume here since he was the historical figure most responsible for the separation of fact and value. Until his work, most philosophers tried to connect fact and value, even if the connection was not explicit enough to be considered a natural law theory. A brief look at major historical figures will show this.

PLATO

We can see this combination of themes, along with a justification operating in Plato when, in *The Republic*, Socrates asks, "What is Justice?" The first attempt to answer this question is on an individual level: What is the just individual? But it is very quickly discovered that the question of justice cannot be answered on this level. So the question is taken to the next level: What is the just state? The just state reflects the virtues of wisdom, courage, temperance and justice. In political terms these virtues translate into the deliberative, productive and executive functions of governing. Justice here becomes understood as the unifying principle which operates when the other virtues work in harmony. Once this view of the state is established, Plato shows how these virtues are reflected in the individual. Individuals have a soul with three parts: appetite, reason and honor. Justice, on the personal level, occurs when all parts of the soul work in harmony.

Individuals mirror the social order. But the social order is made up of individuals. A just state will comprise just individuals. And just individuals will be the inhabitants of the just state. Now that the analysis has reached this step, the hard part begins. Wisdom and Justice must be properly defined in absolute terms. The definitions are discovered by looking for the functions in the perfect state.

Plato does this by arguing that each individuals, depending on their abilities, must find their proper place in the state. They will be aided in this task by the system of education set up by the state to ensure that justice prevails.

In determining how people will fit into the scheme of things Plato finds the need for leaders. Leaders must function as part of the state so they must be educated properly. Education is based on truth. Plato defines truth as knowledge of the eternal. Since this world is not eternal, but a changing phenomenon, truth must be about another level of existence. This is where Plato introduces his theory of forms or ideas. It is here that Plato's quest for moral knowledge leads to the quest for metaphysical knowledge.

Once Plato develops an understanding of metaphysical knowledge, he can use it to ensure that the leaders of the state will use this knowledge properly so that there will be a just state. Plato's view can be considered a natural law position because of how and where knowledge is found. As Francis M. Cornford points out

> The ideal state of man is the true state or man; for if men, who are in fact always imperfect, could reach perfection, they would only be realizing all that their nature aims at being and might conceivably be. Further, the realm of ideals is the real world, unchanging and eternal, which can be known by thought.[2]

Thus, by coming to learn the nature of justice, and how justice functions on the moral, epistemological and metaphysical levels, Plato establishes the ideal state. It is how these levels of knowledge are combined that makes Plato a natural law theorist.

ARISTOTLE

If Plato's ideal state can be considered a natural law theory, so can Aristotle's teleological view of the universe where all things strive to attain their potential in seeking the ultimate good or happiness. People strive for happiness which can be attained by realizing their natural potential.

Aristotle saw all things in nature as capable of movement. While things were capable of self movement, this self movement was usually caused by something external. An animal moves to get food, but does so because of the external stimulus of the food. People behave in much the same way. But, unlike other beings in nature, people are capable of reason.

Aristotle developed a complex view of causality to be able to explain movement. Things in nature have their true essences. These essences contain potentials. Movement is needed to attain or actualize these potentials. For this explanation Aristotle saw four stages or levels of causality. The formal cause explains how or why something has a specific form. The material cause explains why the object is made up of what it is. The efficient cause explains how the movement to actuality occurs. And the final cause explains how this goal is attained. In people, who can use reason, this ability is found in the efficient cause.

Aristotle also talked about the soul. But unlike Plato, the soul for Aristotle was not a separate entity that animated the body. Rather, for Aristotle, the term "soul" stood for the qualities which defined the essential characteristics of being a man. While Plato was a body-soul dualist, Aristotle was a monist.

Aristotle developed a very different view of persons than Plato. While Plato saw the soul as a separate entity which animated persons, Aristotle saw the soul as the properties that enabled a person to function as a human. In *De Anima* Aristotle argues that "there seems to be no case in which the soul can act or be acted upon without involving the body...."[3] (Aristotle, 537) Later he states that "...the soul must be a substance in the sense of the form of a natural body having life potentially within it. But substance is actuality, and thus soul is the actuality of a body..." (Aristotle, 555) Thus "...it indubitably follows that the souls is inseparable from its body,....." (Aristotle, 556) And he concludes that "The soul is the cause of the living body. The terms cause and source have many senses. But the soul is the cause of its body alike in all three senses which we explicitly recognize. It is (a) the source or origin of movement, it is (b) the end, it is ©) the essence of the whole living body." (Aristotle, 561)

While Aristotle saw people as deliberating and choosing, his description of human action had a causal flavor to it. On the one hand people appeared to act freely, on the other hand, human behavior was externally or teleologically caused. Aristotle's view of action is best summed up by Copleston.

> (I) The agent desires an end. (ii) The agent deliberates, seeing that B is a means to A (the end to be obtained), C the means to B and so on, until (iii) he perceives that some particular means near to the end, or remote from it, as the case may be, I something he can do here and now. (iv) The agent chooses this means that presents itself to him as practical...[4]

But what makes Aristotle's view a natural law view is that the good, or humanity's end or essence is part of nature. Thus ethics is derived from metaphysics. Aristotle's ethics are teleological in nature. All action is for a purpose. The main purpose may be human happiness or "the good". Indeed, in the table of contents of his *Nicomachean Ethics* Aristotle lists politics, which is related to ethics, as "The science of the good for man..."[5] We also see natural law themes in the Roman philosophers such as Cicero. And natural law is a hallmark of Christian thought. St. Augustine Christianized Plato in his *City of God*. But today, when one thinks of natural law theory, one thinks immediately of St. Thomas Aquinas.

THOMAS AQUINAS

On this issue, Aquinas' accomplishments are many. First, Aquinas must be seen as a great synthesizer. He took the work of the Greeks, Romans and early medievalists, found common themes which he sorted out and then, building on this work, developed a more comprehensive view of natural law. He then presented his views in a Christian framework, thereby setting the stage for all discussion of natural law for centuries. It is through Thomistic philosophy that this tradition has been kept alive.

Aquinas' position on natural law is complex. He sees the world as being governed by Divine Providence which produces God's law or Eternal law.

> ...law is nothing but a dictate of practical reason issued by a sovereign who governs a complete community. Granted that the world is ruled by divine providence...it is evident that the whole community of the universe is governed by God's mind. Therefore the ruling idea of things which exists in God as the effective sovereign of them all has the nature of law. Then since God's mind does not conceive in time, but has an eternal concept...it follows that this law should be called eternal.

> Since all things are regulated and measured by Eternal law...it is evident that all somehow share in it.

> ...intelligent creatures are ranked the more noble because they take part in Providence by their own providing for themselves

and others. Thus they join in and make their own the Eternal Reason through which they have their natural aptitudes for their due activity and purpose. Now this sharing in the Eternal Law by intelligent creatures is what we call "natural law".

...every agent acts on account of an end, and to be an end carries the meaning of to be good. Consequently the first principle for the practical reason is based on the meaning of good, namely that it is what all things seek after. And so this is the first command of law. "that good is to be sought and done, evil to be avoided"; all other commands of natural law are based on this. Accordingly, then, natural law commands extend to all doing or avoiding of things recognized by the practical reason of itself as being good.[6]

So we see a multi-layered view of law. Eternal law is Gods's plan for the universe. Natural law is the part of Eternal law in which mankind participates. Mankind comes to know Natural law through Divine laws as set out in God's words to mankind. Then we come to Human law where man must use his reason in order to deduce how to apply natural law to specific human conditions.

We also clearly see the Greek influence on Aquinas. His notion of eternal is very much influenced by Plato, as interpreted by St. Augustine. And his views on seeking the good, and human reason are Aristotelian. All through his work, where Aquinas speaks of "the philosopher," he is referring to Aristotle. For detailed discussions of Aristotle's influence on Aquinas see Copleston.

In order to develop human law and to understand what good is, it is necessary to have an understanding of human nature. So, Aquinas asks, what is a person? This discussion is based on 1a question 78. A person is a composite substance including both body and soul. Following Aristotle, Aquinas held that soul is the essence, body is the form. But, diverging from Aristotle, Aquinas argued that while the soul has functions for which the body is needed, it also maintains functions after bodily death. Those functions of the soul which survive death play an important role in Aquinas' metaphysics, which in turn influence his teleological view of the universe. But it is the functions of the complete body and soul which are directly important for his natural law theory.

Persons are the high point of creation, and, as such, exhibit everything from lower orders of creation to their own unique properties. First, we find that persons have a vegetative faculty, consisting of the powers defining basic life: nutrition, growth and reproduction. Next comes the sensitive faculty: the five external senses from which we gain knowledge of the world and the internal senses of imagination and reason which bring human qualities to what we have learned. Finally, there is the rational faculty, comprising the active and passive intellects which allow us to think and reason and make decisions.

Thus, persons function on a biological level, sense the world around them, interpret what they learn from their senses and then, by using their unique human properties, make decisions and act on the basis of what they have learned. Now this presents a fairly complex picture of persons. But when applied to his ethical theory Aquinas emphasizes the importance of the rational aspect of persons. This is so because of his teleological view of the universe and of the place of persons in that teleology. Reason is what makes people unique and gives them their moral sense. Aquinas' teleology moves towards the good.

> Of the actions a man performs those alone are properly called human which are characteristically his as a man. ...Consequently those actions alone which lie under his control are properly called human.

> Clearly all activities a power elicits come from it as shaped by its formal interest. And this, for the will, is being an end and good. Consequently all human acts must be for the sake of an end. (Aquinas, 1a 2ae q 1 a1)

> There are specific or individual ends, such as achieving something in a specific or individual case and there are ultimate ends. But even specific actions have their roots in the unified end. (Aquinas, 1a 2ae q1 a7) And this unified end is God.

> Well then, if we speak of the ultimate end with respect to the thing itself, then human and all other beings share it together, for God is the ultimate end for all things without exception. (Aquinas, 1a 2ae q1 a8)

Reaching this end brings happiness. While there are many forms and degrees of happiness, true happiness is equated with goodness, and goodness is found "not in anything created, but in God alone" (Aquinas, 1a2ae q2 a8).

Some of the specific ends are about satisfying bodily needs, other ends have to do with the soul.

Happiness has two phases, one incomplete, and possible in this life, the other completed and subsisting in the vision of God. As for the first, the body is clearly needed, for such happiness comes through the activity of mind, theoretical and practical, which cannot be performed without imagination, and this, as we have shown in the *Prima Pars* (Aquinas, 1a 84, 6 & 7) works on a bodily organ. And so the happiness open to us at present depends to some extent on the body (Aquinas, 1a 2ae q4 a5). But final happiness is for the soul in the afterlife (Aquinas, 1a 2ae q4 a8).

Happiness, a human goal, is attained by using reason as a basis of action. But Aquinas' discussion here is very Aristotelian. While he emphasizes the role reason plays in human action he also uses the Aristotelian language of causality.

Those things, however, which have some grasp of what an end implies are said to move themselves, because within them lies the source, not only of acting, but also of acting with a purpose. And since on both counts the principle is internal to them, their acts and motions are termed voluntary, which conveys the meaning of following a bent quite their own. It is in this sense that is it used by Aristotle, Nemesius, and Damascene: they define voluntary action as having its principle within the agent together with the added proviso that it is done with knowledge (Aquinas, 1a 2ae q6 a1).

> Though no part of the substance of an act, the final cause is capital because it moves the efficient cause. For this reason an act gets it species from its end above all (Aquinas, 1a2ae q7 a4).

It is this self movement that Aquinas refers to as willing. Persons are seen as self moving objects whose wills bring them, through deliberation, to their ends. (Aquinas, 1a2ae q9 a4)

Now let us look at this view. Men gain knowledge by using their senses. But there is much that the senses cannot come to know. This is where intellect comes in. It is by using our intellect we come to know the First Cause, which is God. And by coming to know God we come to know Divine law. We need to know divine law. By knowing what it is to be human, what our place in the universe is and how we participate in the universe, we come to know the Divine law. Then we are in a position to use our intellect by the use of practical reason to derive Human law from Divine law. Thus, for a complete theory of natural law we need to know the nature of the universe, human nature, the place of humanity in the overall scheme of things and how these things are all connected.

Much of what Aquinas says is based on two points. One is his view of the nature of the universe which was created by God for His purpose. The second is Aquinas' view of persons, for it is persons who, through their participation in the Eternal order, come to know, albeit imperfectly, what this Eternal order is.

An integral part of Aquinas' view is that values exist independently of humanity. Things are good because of the nature of creation, and moral or human values follow deductively from the nature of man and his place in the universe. Reason in people then becomes equated with the good since it is this ability to reason that allows people to know and to choose the good.

Aquinas is also aware of the realities of action. He acknowledges that actions are made in contexts, that motives change and that people are subject to the influence of external factors such as lust. But "Man is free to make his decisions. Otherwise counsels, precepts, prohibitions, rewards and punishments would all be pointless" (Aquinas, 1a q83 a1).

We have now taken a very brief look at natural law as it developed in the ancient and medieval worlds. We have seen that natural law is about finding connections between the nature of the universe and of humanity's place in that universe. This connection can be developed in either direction. We can start with a conception of persons and, by asking questions about actions and values, we can come to develop a world view. Or we can begin with a world view, a view of the nature of the universe, i.e., metaphysical or scientific knowledge, and deduce the role of persons in that world or universe.

NEW DEVELOPMENTS

Now we need to take a closer look at the concepts of a person and the metaphysics or world views of the theories we have just looked at. We must do so because if our understanding of the nature of the universe changes, or if our understanding of what a person is changes, our view of natural law must also change. And the views of the nature of the universe and of what a person is have drastically changed over the centuries. I shall begin by looking at the concept of a person.

The ancient and medieval thinkers we have looked at held a very different view of persons from the view we hold today. The main difference is in the area of individuation. This is not to say that there was any confusion over identifying one person from another. I am me and you are you. But personal identity included being part of a social order. For example, when asked his identity, the Greek man said, "I am Timon of Athens." The "of Athens" part of his name was not just a geographical identification but a part of his personal identification. This is because people did not see themselves as separate from their communities. Part of Timon's identity was as a member of Athenian society. His sense of self, his sense of values, his sense of his place in the universe came from his identification with his being a member of a clearly defined social order.

This explains why exile, rather than death, was the ultimate punishment. In death, especially if there was a belief in an afterlife, one kept one's identity. But in exile one lost one's identity since one lost one's sense of belonging. This point has been strengthened by the work on suicide by sociologist Emile Durkheim who showed there was a direct correlation between times of great social change and rates of suicide. He explained this relationship by arguing that when society is in flux, an individual can lose his or her moorings and become cast adrift. This loss of belonging leads to a loss of individual identity with the result being suicide.[7]

This view of group identity is exemplified by Greek drama. The plays written at that time were renderings of stories or myths known by all the people. Different playwrights simply emphasized different aspects of those stories. While much of today's literature is about not knowing the thoughts of other people this was not an issue in Greek drama. Everyone knew what everyone else was thinking. And to emphasize this point the on-stage chorus told us what the main characters were thinking. Today's notion of individual privacy of thought would be totally foreign to a person living in the ancient world.

This view of identity is enforced when reading Greek philosophers. One is struck by a lack of the term "person". This is why Plato was unable to develop an individual sense of justice. For Plato the individual was inseparable from the community. And this is why Aristotle, and Aquinas, following Aristotle's influence, used the language of causality in explaining human action. Thus, even though we used our rationality in decision making, our decisions and the actions which resulted from those decisions could only be understood as belonging to a social context.

. Changing views of personhood, with more emphasis on individuality, began to develop in the medieval period even before the time of Aquinas, but that development was limited. The concept of the individual as we understand it today built on the medieval view but quickly became the foundation of the new modern period. Three major events, over a period of about a century, with follow-up developments taking close to another century, cemented the modern concept of individualism. Our discussion will begin with a look at the monastery movement, the printing press, the protest of Martin Luther, and the Copernican presentation of the heliocentric view of the universe. These events were followed by astronomical observations by Galileo demonstrating the truth of Copernicus' view and, finally, Newton's theories of mechanics, gravity, and optics, which explained the heliocentric view of the universe.

All of these developments led to further philosophical discourse. Most of the issues raised in this context will provide the material for later chapters. Now let us look at the events that led to the developments of individualism.

THE INDIVIDUAL

The modern conception of individualism, where an individual has personal identity apart from any social context began to develop around the time of Aquinas. This point is very persuasively argued for by Colin Morris in his *The Discovery of the Individual 1050-1200*.[8]

Morris argues that the concept of individualism is present in Christianity, for Christianity is an inner religion which maintains a respect for humanity. But, following the influence of St. Paul, Christians learned to identify with Christ, and in so doing identified with other believers (Morris 1987, 11). This was largely the case through the early medieval period. However, from about 900 to 1050, as cities and trade grew and contact with others increased, people had to become more self-reliant. Also, political relationships depended greatly on the people in power maintaining the respect of their subjects. Thus personal qualities became important factors (Morris 1987, 26). The political turmoil also led to people being in a position of choosing their beliefs. Before, one held the views of one's tribe or one's town. Now people had to start choosing their own beliefs as they became exposed to more influences. This was also a time when Christians took the monastic life seriously. By turning inwards and by becoming concerned with their own salvation, their concept of individuation became stronger (Morris 1987, 32). This last point is reflected in the rediscovery of the Greek ideal "know thyself". The search for inner knowledge during this time period led to concerns about individual salvation and about evaluating individual actions from the standpoint of the actor's intentions, which, in turn, led to the formalizing of confession in the Catholic Church in 1215 (Morris 1987, 73).

This concern with inner knowledge paralleled the metaphysical debate at the between the realists and the nominalists. Such terms "individual" and "singular" were terms of logic, not of human reference (Morris 1987, 64). But as people were becoming concerned with their self identities, general questions arose with regard to the relationship between the individual and the class. I am a man and I exist. I belong to the class of men. Does the class of men exist? And can a class, or a universal, exist independently of its members?

The realists, influenced by Plato and Augustine, held that classes or universals were real, i.e., they did indeed exist independently of their members. This had a great deal to do with Plato's view of language. According to Plato if something could be named it must exist. Thus in a sentence such as "the table is brown" both the table and the brown existed. Their ideal forms existed, albeit on another level of existence. Nominalists, following Aristotelian thought, held that while the universals had names that is all they were. This is partly because Aristotle argued that predicates did not name things but described properties of the subject. The nominalists carried the Argument.

Most of these developments were taking place in what is now France. Indeed, historians talk of the twelfth century as the French Renaissance. At this time, as learning increased, and as the political structures changed, political and economic advisors became necessary. Also at this time we see major shifts in literature. We see references to "I" (Morris 1987, 68). But most importantly, because of the exposure to different beliefs and the challenges to accepted beliefs, the use of critical reason began to develop. Philosophers and theologians used reason to criticize beliefs they opposed and then used reason to show how their beliefs could be supported without resorting to faith alone. This is the source of the work of St. Anselm of Canterbury who tried to use logic alone to establish the existence of God.

All of these changes were reflected in the literary forms of the day. Monasticism led to the writing of personal confessions and letters to other monastics and friends. The best known of these are the works of Abelard. Because of an awareness of different views individuals were able to criticize the church. This led to the development of satire. Good examples are the works of Peter Damiani and Bernard of Cluny. This is also the first time we see references to courtly or romantic love in such works as *The Romance of the Rose* by Guillaume de Lorris and Jean de Meun. Many of these concerns were also reflected in the newly developing folk music of the troubadours. Archive records and the Musical Heritage Society have excellent recordings of this music.

Needless to say, all of these developments led to many changes within the church. Once a top-down all-inclusive institution, the church began to reflect more individual concerns. Morris sees this evident in how attitudes changed towards the passion of Christ. In earlier times Christ was depicted on the cross as still alive. At this time we start seeing the dead Christ. This signified a more compassionate and personal identification with Christ's suffering (Morris 1987, 140). Instead of being a symbol of the church, the passion of Christ now became a symbol of personal salvation. The result of all these changes made it

> possible to look at man either as a natural being or as a being designed for fellowship with God, whereas before the former could not be conceived separately from the latter. From this time onwards, the objective study of the natural order was possible, as was the idea of the secular state" (Morris 1987, 161)

This personal approach to religion was fostered by the development of the printing press in about 1440. Before the printing press was developed books were reproduced by hand, making them both expensive and scarce. Through the middle ages Bible stories were presented in churches through paintings and sculptures. Most people were illiterate, except for the clergy who controlled knowledge and kept the Catholic Church as a top-down institution. But with the printing press, more and more people could own their own Bibles, learn to read them, and learn to develop their own views of the nature of religious belief. This development of individual interpretations was the beginnings of the challenges for the Catholic Church. As Heinrich Wilhelm Wallau points out in his article on Gutenberg in the Catholic Encyclopedia

> The invention of Gutenberg should be classed with the greatest events in the history of the world. It caused a revolution in the development of culture. Equaled by hardly any other incident in the Christian Era. Facility in disseminating the treasure of the intellect was a necessary development of the sciences in modern times. Happening as it did just at the time when science was becoming more secularized and its cultivation no longer resigned almost

entirely to the monks, it may be said that the age was pregnant with this invention. Thus not only is Gutenberg's art inseparable from the progress of modern science, but it has also been an indispensable factor in the education of the people at large.[9]

It was this dissemination of knowledge in the context of a growing individualism that set the stage for the revolution in Christianity led by Martin Luther when he posted his 95 theses in 1517. Luther's concern was to address what he considered to be abuses of power within the Church. Needless to say, the church powers disagreed and this led Luther to spearhead a new approach to Christianity, one which "protested" against the top-down power structure of the Church and one which put more emphasis on the role of the individual and less on the authority of the church hierarchy.

Shortly more versions of the protest developed by such people as John Calvin. Of course, the development of the Church of England, which arose for a combination of personal and political reasons, surely could not have occurred at any time sooner, since Henry VIII needed a social, political, and religious context which would allow his challenge to the Catholic hierarchy to make sense.

THE COPERNICAN REVOLUTION

It was only a short generation from Luther to Nikolas Copernicus and the formulation of the heliocentric view of the universe, a view which challenged the Catholic claim that Earth, and therefore humankind, was at the center of the universe. This event, which is usually considered to be the first step in the so-called scientific revolution, led to a whole new way of looking that world, of then place of the world in the over all scheme of things, and of the place of humankind in this over all scheme.

To make better sense of this revolution we shall turn to looking at how metaphysical knowledge, or knowledge of the nature of the universe has changed. The major factor in this change is the occurrence of the scientific revolution of the sixteenth and seventeenth centuries. As characterized by historian of science Herbert Butterfield, the scientific revolution was brought about "by transpositions that were taking place inside the minds of the scientists themselves." This was so because the phenomena that these scientists were confronted with "required a different kind of thinking cap" since "the modern law of inertia is not the thing you would discover by mere photographic methods of observation."[10]

Natural Law, Science, and the Social Construction of Reality 15

So just what was this scientific revolution? Before this question is answered let us take a quick look at the scientific foundations of the ancient and medieval worlds. We have already seen Aristotle's view of causality. This was coupled with his view of physics. Aristotle, following in the footsteps of early Greek thinkers, saw everything as consisting of four basic elements: earth, the heaviest element, which moved to the center of the universe; water, the next heaviest, which sat on the earth; air which surrounded the earth; and fire which rose from the earth.

Each element had certain essential properties. In their various combinations the objects they comprised also had these properties. The behavior of all objects was explained in terms of how causality, in conjunction with the properties of objects, moved to attain actualities. Things made of earth tended to move to the centre of the universe while things made of fire tended to rise from the earth.

Using this system of physics, the second century BCE Egyptian astronomer Ptolemy explained the known movements of the wanderers in the sky —the planets. This Aristotelian Ptolemaic view of how the universe worked, later enforced by the church, dominated the world until the end of the medieval period.

As people became more self aware and began to investigate the world around them with a new critical faculty they began to see things that this old view could not explain. This was especially true with regard to the paths of the planets. The observed paths were seen as too complex for the planets to be revolving around the earth. Thus in 1543 Copernicus presented the hypothesis that the earth was one of these planets and all the planets revolved around the sun. By the turn of the new century Kepler had mathematically worked out the orbits of the planets. And in 1609 Galileo, using a telescope he built himself, observed the moons of Jupiter which presented a model for the workings of the solar system. The further importance of Galileo's discovery was to show that, contrary to the Catholic teaching that everything in the universe revolved around the Earth, objects in the heavens revolved around other objects in the heavens. Thus there was now proof of the heliocentric model of the universe, which took Earth and humankind out of the center.

These new developments raised as many questions as they answered. First these new claims totally undermined the Aristotelian Ptolemaic system. Because of so many unanswered questions, this new model of how the universe worked was not yet in a position to replace the old one. For example, if the earth moved, why didn't the people on the earth feel the motion? If the earth rotated why didn't people fall off the earth when it was upside down? And if Aristotelian causality could no longer explain movement, then by what force did the planets move? These questions may seem silly to us today, but they were very real for the people living then.

NEWTON

These questions led to a tremendous amount of work by natural philosophers. The answers were finally established in 1687 in Newton's *Principia*, or the *Principles of Mechanics*. This is where Newton presents his theory of gravity and the three laws of motion:

> 1. Every body continues in its state of rest or of uniform motion in a right line unless it is compelled to change that state by forces impressed upon it.
> 2. The change of motion is proportional to the motive force impressed and is made in the direction of the right line in which that force is impressed.
> 3. To every action there is always opposed an equal reaction; or, the mutual actions of two bodies upon each other are always equal and directed to contrary parts.[11]

Instead of all objects remaining at rest until moved by an external force, as was held by Aristotle, this new view had all objects in motion unless stopped by an external source. Thus, instead of the universe being passive, it was then understood that the universe was dynamic although it was also mechanistic. Newton explained gravity in terms of forces and attractions.

> If spheres be however dissimilar (as to density of matter and attractive force) in the same ratio onward from the center to the circumference, but everywhere similar at every given distance from the center, on all sides round about; and the attractive force of every point decreases as the square of the distance of the body attracted; I say that the whole force which one of these spheres attracts the other will be inversely proportional to the square of the distance of the centers (Newton 1965, 105).

Thus the planets stay in orbit around the sun because of the way they continuously attract each other.

In the twentieth century physics has made new developments. In

Natural Law, Science, and the Social Construction of Reality   17

discovering the nature of matter, physics has gone beyond the observable into the atomic realm. Matter is understood as being composed of atoms, which combine to form molecules. Newtonian mechanics does not work on the work the atomic level so a whole new field of mechanics, known as quantum mechanics has been developed.

The question that readers will be asking now, though, is what this work in physics has to do with moral theory The answer is "everything," for not only has our place in the universe changed but so has our understanding of how the universe works and, thereby, our understanding of our place in that universe. The major implication of the scientific revolution, as well as ongoing scientific and cosmological development today, is that the ancient and medieval views of the world and have been undermined and thereby rendered false. The new world view which started to develop in the wake of the scientific revolution presents a very different way of understanding the world, its place in the universe and our place in the scheme of things. The implication of this point is that we do not just re-evaluate the work of Plato, Aristotle and Aquinas to see what can be adapted to the new way of thinking. Rather we reject their entire work as having anything relevant to say to the world of today.

And what holds true for metaphysical knowledge also holds true for ethical knowledge. For the new way of thinking also leads to a new conception of what a person is and what the place of persons is in the overall scheme of things. This view of persons develops some of the points made above in regard to the discussion of individualism in Morris' work.

But what does it mean to say that one world view overthrows another, or that a new world view renders an old one false? A good example is a political analogy. A revolution involves the overthrow of an existing order and the establishing of a new order. This concept is understandable in politics when one form of government is replaced by another. In science the same process occurs: one world view replaces another. A political revolution results in people relating to government, and to each other, in different ways. For example, if a democracy replaces a dictatorship, people will have the opportunity of directly participating in the choice of a leader. And in so doing they will interact with each other in a more open manner. The same holds for a scientific revolution. Because our understanding of the world will be different we will see the world differently and we will understand interpersonal relationships or values differently.

To repeat the point, when the new view of the world replaced the old, not only did we learn that, appearances to the contrary, the Earth rotated round the sun, we also put knowledge on a more individual basis. The philosophers in the sixteenth and seventeenth centuries who responded to the challenges of the scientific revolution all saw the need to re-establish a basis for knowledge. The question was not whether or not we had knowledge —we did, even though what we knew was changing. But since the foundations of knowledge had been undermined, new foundations had to be built. Unlike the ancient and medieval foundations of knowledge which were built on a shared social structure, the new foundation was built on the observations of individuals.

One may ask if all of these changes happened rationally, or if there was another background factor that led to these changes. There was indeed such a factor —the black plague. The plague, which was largely caused by people overworking the land, allowed otherwise benign bacteria to multiply. As historian Andrew Nikiforuk argues,

Long before the plague, bacillus, fleas, rats and Genoese merchants all collided in Italy for their epic encounter, medieval society prepared for the disaster by inviting misery and famine into Europe's crowded household. Climate played a subtle role in this drama. Throughout the Middle Ages a run of long hot summers and short cool winters encouraged peasants to grow more crops and produce more peasants. This baby boom turned Europe into a fermenting test tube of bacteria as its population grew from 25 million well-fed souls in the year 700 to 75 million hungry ones in 1250. Humans rarely recognize their good fortune until they give it away.[12]

Nikiforuk goes on to describe the devastation of the plague. With many peasants dying, feudalism was destroyed. The shortage of labor led to enhanced wages for land workers, setting the stage for capitalism (Nikiforuk 1996, 64). This led to a need for merchants to travel to seek more customers (Nikiforuk 1996, 65). And the plague, by killing so many clerics, "seriously undermined Church authority" (Nikiforuk 1996, 68).

> The plague years altered human thinking not only about reproduction but also about Nature. Once revered, or at least respected, Nature was now an enemy to feared and tamed.... The plague's incredible die-offs conditioned people to seek mechanistic explanations for Nature's unpleasant visitations, with the hope that humankind could somehow fix or rework the environment or hammer it into submission.... After the plague, it's not really surprising that humans decided to trust machines more than Nature (Nikiforuk 1996, 75-76).

Thus a natural occurrence, helped along as it was by people, created conditions under which social and intellectual change occurred. The relationship between environment and culture will be discussed at length in chapter four.

A GLIMPSE AHEAD

Indeed, the history of philosophy from Descartes to Kant can be seen as the history of building this foundation. And, given development in science in the 20th century, a similar process is again underway.

In the first section of the book I look at the work of John Locke, who can be considered to be the embodiment of early modern thinking. He not only developed an individualistic theory of knowledge but he also developed an individualistic theory of politics. The two views are logically consistent and when taken together can be seen as an early modern attempt at a secular natural law theory.

I will then look carefully at the view of science which developed from Locke's work. In looking at some of the problems with this view I shall turn to the work of Immanual Kant, who can be seen as the founder of an alternative view of science. I shall then look at another attempt at natural law theory in the context of this view of science. This view is based on the work of Sigmund Freud.

Then, using two distinctive but decidedly modernist views of natural law, I will look at how different views can be compared. This will involve a detailed discussion of scientific and conceptual change.

Finally, by looking at criticisms of Freud in the context of our understanding of scientific change, I shall show how one strain of postmodern thought has developed, one which leads to both a third view of science and a corresponding view of persons. I will here raise issues as to whether or not there can be a postmodern natural law theory.

Chapter 2

CONCEPTUAL REVOLUTIONS

In the previous chapter we saw three different views of the world: Plato saw the world in terms of what could be named, with ultimate reality existing on a higher plane; Aristotle saw the world in terms of essences and functions; Aquinas saw the world as divine creation. Newton was mentioned, and in the next chapter we shall see that he saw the world as a machine, with God as the great engineer. In later chapters we will discuss further developments in how to view the world. The argument of this book is one of context and change. Knowledge arises in a context and when that context changes, so does our knowledge. Whatever changes occur cause us to re-evaluate what we thought we knew and look at that old knowledge in the new context. If the change is drastic enough we find ourselves abandoning the old knowledge. If the change in not that drastic we may try to reconcile the two bodies of knowledge. The questions that arise here are how to tell when two bodies of knowledge are compatible or when a new body of knowledge must replace the old. If we thought we once knew something, how can we now say that we no longer know it? This applies to our knowledge of the physical world and our knowledge of morality. Indeed, since natural law theory is about the relationship between both bodies of knowledge—how one is dependent on the other—the same questions that apply to our knowledge of the physical world apply to our body of moral knowledge, for if one changes, so must the other.

THOMAS KUHN

We will begin our look at these issues with the work of Thomas Kuhn's influential book *The Structure of Scientific Revolutions*.[13] Kuhn began his career in physics but was soon struck by problems in the history of science. His knowledge of the history of science led him to ask why the natural sciences had a greater acceptance than other disciplines when there was just as much disagreement among its practitioners as in other disciplines.

Kuhn's argument begins with a discussion of history and the role that textbooks play in purveying scientific knowledge. He argues that the aim of textbooks is persuasion and pedagogy. Such texts reflect a concept of science that is designed to teach a specific approach to the subject:— an approach which reflects the views of the scientific establishment. But as Kuhn states, such textbooks have as much to do with how science is actually done as reading a travel brochure has to do with actually going somewhere (Kuhn, 1962 1). In other words, standard texts present an idealized version of the subject, designed to introduce students to the fraternity of practicing scientists. But science does not work in the rational, systematic way that textbooks describe.

Textbooks present science as progressing in an orderly manner with new knowledge being added to old knowledge. But such changes do not take place in such an orderly fashion. So the historian of science must ask difficult questions about the nature of scientific discovery and of scientific change (Kuhn, 1962 2). For example, we know something about the discovery of oxygen, but when was it actually discovered? And by whom? These are real questions because the discovery of oxygen did not occur as a result of one experiment. A lot of work by a lot of people set the stage for the discovery. Even then it is not clear how to identify the actual moment of discovery. The reasons for these problems will be discussed later. But the answers lie in looking how science goes through changes.

In order to answer these questions Kuhn makes a distinction between normal science and revolutionary science. Normal science is the everyday puzzle solving of working scientists. Revolutionary science is the establishing of a new way of doing science or a new theoretical framework or "paradigm" of what science is, how it should be done and what the problems or puzzles to be solved will be. Normal science is understood as research firmly based upon one or more past scientific achievements that a particular scientific community acknowledges for a time as supplying the foundation for its further practice. (Kuhn, 1962 10) A paradigm is simply an example of such a practice. The real historical questions have to deal with how paradigms are established and how they, in turn, lead to the establishment of normal science.

The establishment of a paradigm is essential for the doing of science since it is the paradigm that gives meaning to the facts. Without a paradigm all science would be is a collection of random facts without any connections or explanations (Kuhn, 1962 15). In other words, it would not be science. Fact collecting only makes sense in a context, for it is the context,—the paradigm—which tells the scientist what kinds of facts to look for and what will or will not be a scientifically significant fact.

Most sciences begin without paradigms, but with some problem, no matter how ill-defined it might be. Pre-paradigm scientists collect information in the hope they will find what they need in order to solve their puzzles. As they collect this information, as it starts to make sense, and as they begin to put the pieces together—not unlike dumping out the pieces to a jigsaw puzzle, only we do not know if all the pieces to the puzzle are in the box or if all the pieces come from the same puzzle—they establish a framework that clearly defines the nature of the problems they are working on. This framework becomes, in Kuhn's language, the paradigm which establishes what these scientists are doing and how they should be doing it. And the paradigm becomes "an object for further articulation and specification under new or more stringent conditions".(Kuhn, 1962 23) These new conditions set the stage for normal science or puzzle solving, i.e., filling out the paradigm or figuring out which pieces actually belong to the puzzle and how and why they fit together.

So, now that we have some idea as to what a paradigm is, let us see if we can begin to fill it out. This is where Kuhn points out the problems with the notion of discovery. The search for new information, or the need to establish a new paradigm, is usually the result of some anomaly that requires explanation, i.e., something is not the way it is supposed to be. This is where Kuhn gets into the problems around trying to understand the discovery of oxygen. As he points out, at least three different people could lay claim to being the discoverer of oxygen: Swedish apothecary C.W. Scheele, British scientist Joseph Priestley and French scientist Antoine Lavoisier. Scheele's claim is usually denied since he published his findings after the others had already published theirs. Priestley identified nitrous oxide as a result of his work on mercury vapors in 1774. And Lavoisier actually identified oxygen in 1775, probably as a result of Priestley's work. At issue here is who actually discovered oxygen and when it was discovered. Lavoisier could not have made his discovery without the prior work of Priestley. But Priestley did not actually discover oxygen and disagreed with Lavoisier's claims about the nature of oxygen. Kuhn argues that to ask such questions is incorrect. Discovery is not the sort of process that can be identified in the way the questions imply. It is a process in which members of a scientific community who agree on the problems facing them all work on solving the puzzle. This notion of community is important for it highlights the nature of a paradigm. In a sense the paradigm defines the community since all scientists working within the same paradigm share the same concerns; that is, they agree on what the problems are and why they are problems. On this view it does not make sense to say that oxygen was discovered if it means that the discovery has to be pinpointed. Of course, oxygen was indeed discovered. Kuhn argues that discovery involves an extended "process of assimilation" (Kuhn, 1962 56). The point here is that the scientific community recognized the problem. This led to work being done by a number of people. And the results of experiments in one area led to work in other areas, and so on until the problem was solved. The whole process is the answer to when the discovery was made. The problem—the anomaly—would not have existed if these scientists were not working within an accepted paradigm.

Now we have seen that scientists work within paradigms and that these paradigms give significance to the work that is being done. Once a paradigm is in place—once scientists agree on what the problems facing them are—and once they begin to generate some experimental successes they must generate theories, or more general explanations, of the data they have accumulated. The question that Kuhn asks is how such theories or explanations can arise from normal science (Kuhn, 1962 66-67). The answer can be found in the role that anomalies play in the scientific enterprise. When scientists become aware of anomalies they know something is wrong with the current explanation of how the world works. First one such anomaly will be seen; then others. This process will lead to a general awareness that the existing view can no longer do the job it was designed for. This view may not be a full-fledged paradigm—it may just be a collection of unorganized or unsystematic views, or it may be a full-fledged paradigm which can no longer account for the data now being discovered. In any case a new paradigm or explanatory mechanism must be developed in order to explain the newly discovered phenomena. As Kuhn states

> On this point historical evidence is, I think, entirely unequivocal. The state of Ptolemaic astronomy was a scandal before Copernicus' announcement. Galileo's contributions to

the study of motion depended closely upon difficulties discovered in Aristotle's theory by scholastic critics. Newton's new theory of light and color originated in the discovery that none of the existing pre-paradigm theories would account for the length of the spectrum, and the wave theory that replaced Newton's was announced in the midst of growing concern about anomalies in the relation of diffraction and polarization effects to Newton's theory. Thermodynamics was born from the collision of two existing nineteenth century physical theories, and quantum mechanics from a variety of difficulties surrounding black-body radiation, specific heats, and the photoelectric effect (Kuhn, 1962 67).

The point here is failure of the old views is what leads to the development of a new theory or paradigm. But this raises two new questions. One has to do with reinterpreting old knowledge and the other has to do with how to set up this new paradigm since it may be possible that more than one model will do the job. In other words, how do we choose between competing solutions to a given problem?

The first question raises most of the issues in the philosophy of science with regard to the role that observation plays in science. Traditional empiricism, which was developed by Locke and Hume in response to the successes of Newton, maintained that knowledge was obtained by observation or experience but that we had to use logic or reason to be able to tell the difference between illusion and reality. When apparently insoluble problems arose with regard to justifying knowledge claims on this model, Kant developed a view which held that all observations were done within categories. Kuhn takes a kind of neo-Kantian position in that he substitutes changing paradigms for Kant's fixed categories. These issues will be discussed in greater detail later in this chapter. But for now the important point is that all observations are theory or context-laden. This means that the kinds of things we look for, and how we interpret what we find, are determined by the theory or paradigm that is being used to guide the observations. When scientists start finding things they are not supposed to be finding, or when they do not find what they are supposed to find, in Kuhn's language, they are in a crisis situation. The solution to the crisis is to develop a new paradigm. This will then lead to the reinterpretation of old data. It may even ignore certain data which only had significance in terms of the old paradigm.

But, one might ask, what about our observations. We saw certain things. Are we now to say that we no longer see those things? The answer is "yes and no". We no longer see those things. We see new things with new relationships as interpreted through the lens of the new paradigm. We see the sun move round the Earth but we now know that the Earth moves round the sun. We see the same thing but we make different sense of it or we reinterpret it. The discovery of oxygen is a good example of this. Before oxygen was discovered all kinds of hypotheses were made about the *ether*, the airlike fluid that everything was contained in. But once oxygen was discovered and scientists realized that the ether did not exist, new explanations of old phenomena were developed. Thus metals increase in weight when burned not because they absorb part of the ether, but because air, and its components such as oxygen, has weight and the combustion process leads to the oxygen being combined with the molecular structure of the metals.

The point here is that observational tests cannot always be developed to help us reinterpret old data nor to help us choose between competing explanations. Thus, the two questions about reinterpreting old data and choosing competing explanations are really two aspects of the same issue, which is how to establish a new paradigm.

This issue is not just a scientific or philosophical question. It has to do with how people think and with how well entrenched the old view is. For example, even if the old view yields all kinds of anomalies and is in tremendous crisis, it will not be abandoned unless there is a clear alternative. And if the old view, with all its problems, is still liked, or is still well entrenched in how people think, it will be difficult to develop an alternative. The final decision, according to Kuhn, is always made with more in mind than just a comparison of how a new paradigm compares to the observed world. The decision to accept a new paradigm

> is always based upon more than a comparison of that theory with the world. The decision to reject one paradigm is always simultaneously the decision to accept another, and the judgement leading to that decision involves the comparison of both paradigms with nature and with each other (Kuhn, 1962 77).

The point here is that the crisis must be resolved so that people can return to some kind of normalcy. When a good alternative becomes available it will be used to replace the old paradigm. It may not be the best possible solution but it will be a solution. Picking the best paradigm is not the primary issue; resolving the crisis is.

Once this issue has been properly understood we have to take a new look at just what constitutes a scientific revolution. Or as Kuhn puts it, "what are scientific revolutions, and what is their function in scientific development?" (Kuhn, 1962 91). The major issues here are that when a crisis is resolved and a new paradigm is established we find that the new paradigm may not necessarily include all of the data from the old one, or it may do so in a different way making the two paradigms not directly comparable. The implication here is that science does not develop in an orderly cumulative fashion but these paradigm changes or revolutions bring about a change in the way we understand the world and our place in it.

So how do choose between paradigms? Such choices cannot always be made on purely rational or scientific grounds. Other factors will play a role in such decisions. The most important will be the desire to resolve the crisis. Any solution is better than none. But there will be those who do not want to relinquish the old paradigm for any number of reasons. Some of these reasons may be due to their place of privilege in the old order which be lost in the new order, or that they thought they knew what the world was about and what their place in it was, even if there were problems. Better the devil you know than the angel you do not know.

An example of the first reason was the reaction of the Church to the claims of Galileo. These claims directly challenged the authority of the church, so the Church fought Galileo and used its power to get him to recant. An example of the second reason is the reluctance of some physicists to give up Newtonian mechanics in favor of relativity theory. They claim that Newtonian mechanics are a subset of relativity theory, even though the two are incompatible and relativity theory has been demonstrated to be superior in that it can explain not only everything Newtonian mechanics can, albeit in a different way, but also a whole range of atomic and subatomic phenomena that Newtonian theory cannot.

In both cases, and in any situation that can be called a revolution, one view overthrows or replaces another. This new view is not continuous with the old even though it was developed in the first place to solve problems that occurred in that old view. The reason those problems occurred was that the old view could not account for or explain such phenomena. That is why a new view had to be developed. In accounting for these new phenomena, the new paradigm changes how we understand the world in which we live. This raises again an issue discussed above. Do we now see things differently or do we just understand what we see differently? Kuhn's answer is the latter. Kuhn asks

> But is sensory experience fixed and neutral? Are theories simply man-made interpretations of given data? The epistemological viewpoint that has most often guided Western philosophy for three centuries dictates an immediate and unequivocal Yes! In the absence of a developed alternative, I find it impossible to relinquish entirely that viewpoint. Yet it no longer functions effectively, and the attempts to make it do so through the introduction of a neutral language of observations now seems to me hopeless (Kuhn, 1962 125).

So, while Kuhn knows that the old empiricist approach to epistemology and the philosophy of science has become untenable he cannot entirely give it up. He knows this view has become untenable because of his analysis of the history of science. But that very analysis does not let him give it up yet since there is no new view to replace it. At least there was no such view at the time he wrote his book. As we shall see later in this chapter such a view has been developed. Indeed, it was being developed at the very time Kuhn was writing. This view is a form of neo-Kantianism known as scientific realism or concept realism. In brief, this view holds that the category or the conceptual framework—the paradigm—through which we investigate the world determines what is real.

Kuhn comes close to that view in his comments on how investigations presuppose a paradigm. His point is not that we actually perceive differently but that we see the same things through the filters of different paradigms. He uses the pendulum as an example. Everyone observing a pendulum sees something moving back and forth. But their explanations of what they see will be different. Aristotle would see a "constrained fall", where the pendulum's natural affinity to fall is being prevented by something else. Newton would see an example of what would become his laws of motion. Thus their respective understanding of what they see would be different and not directly comparable even if they reported the same visual experiences.

Kuhn refers to various discussions of perception from psychologists about how we can learn to see things differently. The most well known of these examples is the various figure/ground experiments taken from gestalt psychology. Do we see a vase or a face? It depends on what we see first or on our prior experience. But we can learn to see both figures. Kuhn leaves this issue open. We shall return to it later when we look at other views of scientific change.

In his conclusions Kuhn returns to a discussion of science textbooks. His purpose here is to explain why scientific revolutions, which are so significant, are not usually recognized by scientists and by nonscientists. Kuhn argues that textbooks

> address themselves to an already articulated body of problems, data and theory, most often to the particular set of paradigms to which the scientific community is committed at the time they are written. Textbooks aim to communicate the vocabulary and syntax of a contemporary scientific language (Kuhn, 1962 135).

They do this because textbooks "record the outcome of past revolutions and thus display the bases of the current normal scientific tradition." This is important because textbooks become the "pedagogic vehicles for the perpetuation of normal science" (Kuhn, 1962 136). In so doing they disguise the revolutions that took place. In turn, this invisibility of revolutions perpetuates the old view that such events do not occur and that science proceeds in an orderly, cumulative manner. It is as if the scientists themselves do not see what they are doing as revolutionary. It takes an analysis of the scientific enterprise by historians and philosophers to put the scientific enterprise into perspective. But philosophers can miss some of the important points as well, as Kuhn points out in his brief discussion of Sir Karl Popper.

One of the developments of the empiricist view of knowledge led to the development of "the principle of verification" which held that for a statement to be meaningful—to be capable of being determined to be true or false—one had to set down the criteria for how that statement could be verified. Usually this process required that one be able to find positive data—hence the label "positivism. There are problems with this criterion in that it can be too limiting and it is too easy to ignore data which does not confirm one's view.

In order to correct this problem, Popper developed the principle of falsifiability, which states that before one performs an experiment one must be able to state what kinds of evidence will count against one's views. If one cannot do so, then one's views have no real empirical content.

Kuhn points out that verification is important to science because "it picks out the most viable among the actual alternatives in a particular historical situation"(Kuhn, 1962 145). Popper developed the principle of falsification to insure that scientists did not just rely uncritically on positive evidence to support their views. But Popper went on, in discussion of conjectures and refutations, to leave out the process of verification altogether. And he developed such a strong sense of falsification that any or every test of a hypothesis could undermine it.

Kuhn argues that Popper's position is too strong. One could argue that Popper errs in the mirror image way he accuses the positivists of erring. The positivists' problem was that their view of verification was too limiting. In the mirror image, Popper's view of falsification is too limiting. Both processes are needed in the scientific enterprise. Kuhn goes on to argue that Popper's view of falsification is not unlike the role that anomalies play in science. When a hypothesis has been falsified we do not reject it completely; rather we acknowledge that there is a problem with the hypothesis and that a crisis may be looming. We cannot accept Popper's view because if we were to reject a hypothesis or a theory every time a piece of falsifying data came along we would never be able to get any scientific enterprise off the ground.

It is now time to review what Kuhn has said about scientific change. His view is that changes in science occur when an existing view can no longer explain phenomena that it should be able to explain. So a new set of hypotheses is presented. As these new views gain acceptance through success because they see things differently than did the old view, we have a revolution. The new view has displaces the old, and we say that the relationship between these two views is one of incommensurability because they explain the world differently. Both views look at the world

> and what they see has not changed. But in some areas they see different things, and they see them in different relations to one another. That is why a law that cannot be demonstrated to one group of scientists may occasionally seem intuitively obvious to another (Kuhn, 1962 149).

> And the switch from one paradigm to another will not always be made on purely rational grounds. One just has to come to see how the new view works and why it is better than the old view. Or sometimes it has to be made on the basis of future promise. Sometimes it is a decision that is made on faith (Kuhn, 1962 157).

Kuhn's work has been criticized. Most of the criticism has been from the point of view of the old paradigm of science and is therefore irrelevant to Kuhn's arguments. Indeed, one might argue that the kinds of arguments presented against Kuhn from the old view of science simply go to prove Kuhn's position. These arguments are based on the view that science is a rational, cumulative enterprise. Indeed, in his response to his critics, Kuhn says that he is tempted to posit two Thomas Kuhns. First, there is Kuhn # 1, the author of *The Structure of Scientific Revolutions* and the essays in the volume under discussion, *Criticism and the Growth of Knowledge* [14]. Then there is Kuhn # 2 who is the author of another book of the same title. It is the book written by Kuhn # 2 that is discussed by all but one of the contributors to this volume.

PAUL FEYERABEND

We will also offer some criticism of Kuhn. This will come from the other two views that will be discussed in this chapter. The first of these philosophers is Paul Feyerabend. This discussion will be based on his book *Against Method*.[15] Feyerabend picks up where Kuhn leaves off. Kuhn acknowledged that the ways in which we choose between competing paradigms or theoretical frameworks is not always completely rational, but it is always guided by the need to solve a crisis. Feyerabend concentrates not only on the notion that such choices are not completely rational but also that we sometimes do not even have good reasons for our choices. Feyerabend does not use the language of problem-solving or crisis-solving. He sees competing views all over the place and wonders why some of those views have been abandoned. He cites such views as witchcraft and voodoo as legitimate explanation frameworks or paradigms that have been abandoned for no good reason.

His argument is based on the underlying view that there can be many different ways to explain the nature of the universe and our place in it. Any one may be sufficient. Perhaps all of them are up to the task of providing us with a workable explanatory framework or paradigm. He sees no reason why any number of them should not be usable at any one time. This view leads him to what he calls an anarchistic or *dadaistic* view of science. Anarchism is the view that "anything goes". And that more than one thing can go at the same time. Feyerabend sees anarchism as true democracy with all views having equal weight. He uses the *dada* label because of the negative connotations that are associated with anarchism. A *dadaist* is one who takes things lightly, not seriously (Feyerabend, 1975 21).

Theoretical anarchism or theoretical dadaism is a more

productive view than the traditional rational views of science because they are not as limiting and take all alternative views seriously. The only way to democratize science is to be anarchistic. He argues that it is not desirable to support a tradition that is held together by strict rules since these rules are exclusionary and they limit the use of the individual scientist's imagination and thereby limit possible solutions to our problems. (Feyerabend, 1975 19-20) Thus, in science, as in other aspects of life, anything goes (Feyerabend, 1975 23). Feyerabend begins his argument by stating that the scientific revolution "occurred only because some thinkers either decided not to be bound by certain 'obvious' methodological rules, or because they *unwittingly* broke them." He then goes on to argue that such rule breaking is "*absolutely necessary* for the growth of knowledge."(Feyerabend, 1975 23).

Feyerabend acknowledges an intellectual debt to Karl Popper but argues that Popper maintains a too narrow view of rationality. Of course falsifiability, or counterinduction, as Feyerabend calls it, is necessary for doing science. But Popper's view of falsifiability is too limiting. Here, Feyerabend might agree with Kuhn, but he takes his argument in a different direction. He asks if counterinduction is more reasonable than induction and, if so, when should it be used.

First he acknowledges that counterinduction can be used to refute theories but that evidence that could be used to do the refuting can only be discovered by developing an alternative theory. This is so because all observation is theory laden and alternative data must come from some other theoretical context. Thus the only way to properly falsify a theory (or hypothesis or paradigm) is to present an alternative theory (or hypothesis or paradigm). To just look for falsifying data is insufficient, for if one looks for it in the context of the theory one is working in one will not find it. Thus one cannot just adopt the principle of falsifiability. One must adopt a complete pluralistic methodology. A major implication of this view is that science is no longer concerned with truth but with making "the weaker case the stronger." It does not matter what the case is. If it can be made stronger than its rivals then it is the best case.

It is in this context that Feyerabend talks about such alternative ways of explaining the nature of the world and our place in it. Views like witchcraft and voodoo are not mere superstitions but alternative explanatory models. In many cases such models are surpassed not because the newer models are better but because the newer models are sold more effectively. Such views may be more logically or internally consistent than the theories that have replaced them. But for all kinds of reasons, with logic perhaps being the least important, these views have been replaced.

Feyerabend acknowledges that a theory should not be replaced unless there are pressing reasons to do so and the only such reason is if the theory disagrees with the facts. But since facts are theory-laden—a theory determines what the facts are—the only way one can say that a particular theory does not fit the facts is if one is referring to facts according to another theory. The only way one can make sense of this argument is if the alternative theory overlaps the original. In this way one could say that both theories, at least to some extent, are trying to explain the same facts. Otherwise there will be two competing theories which explain two different sets of facts. And if the theories are incommensurable then the facts must also be. To prove this point Feyerabend looks at the history of science. He argues that such important historical figures such as Galileo and Newton made their cases this way. Indeed, he argues that these figures knew that their theories had significant problems with them but they pushed them anyhow.

Feyerabend argues that Galileo used "propaganda" and "psychological tricks" to make his case.

> These tricks are very successful—they lead him to victory. But they obscure the new attitude towards experience that is in the making, and postpone for centuries the possibility of a reasonable philosophy. They obscure the fact that the experience on which Galileo wants to base the Copernican view is nothing but the result of his own fertile imagination, that it has been invented. They do this by insinuating that the new results which emerge are known and conceded by all, and need only be called to our attention to appear as the most obvious expression of the truth. (Feyerabend, 1975 81)

Feyerabend quotes Galileo at length to show how he gets us to "recall" or "remember" certain "facts". But we cannot do so since these are not facts that we have known. They are new facts which Galileo sees as proving his theory. The best example has to do with the dropping of a stone from a tower. If the Earth moved then one would think that the stone would move to show this. But the stone falls in a straight line. Galileo develops a complex argument to show that the empirical consequences of the competing theories are the same whether the Earth moves or not. He argues that if the Earth did not move the stone would drop in a straight line. But then he argues that if the Earth did move the dropping stone would move along with it. Thus he developed an ad hoc relativistic hypothesis to make the facts fit his theory. And because he can explain other things with his theory he puts it all together in such a way that we accept the whole package.

Another example is the telescope. We know how certain things look on Earth. When we magnify them we see the same things, only larger. And when we look at the night sky we can identify certain planets and stars. We do this by their location and by their magnitude or brightness. But with the telescope the magnitudes are different from what they appear to be with the unaided eye. One could just as easily argue that at such distances the telescope distorts such images. But Galileo successfully argues that since the telescope presents accurate images from a distance on Earth it must also do so from the sky. It is our eyes that cannot see accurately at those distances. The point here is that there was no way of empirically deciding the issue. This is compounded because in Galileo's time there was no newly developed theory of optics which would account for what was seen through the telescope. Thus, while ultimately Galileo may have been correct, he gets us to accept his views by means other than good logical or good scientific reasons.

Feyerabend's point here is that one could not completely accept Galileo's view any other way unless he presented a completely new world view that could be compared to the old one. And even if Galileo had presented such a view there is no reason why anyone should accept it. They would still have to be sold on the idea that this new world view was better, whatever "better" means in this context. For if the two views are incommensurable it would make no sense to call one better than the other. While the scientific enterprise may use reason it may not be based on reason, since to develop a new way of looking at the world requires breaking out of the old one. If the old way is based on some kind of reason then the beginnings of the new one must be seen as a break with reason. As Feyerabend states "Copernicanism and other 'rational' views exist today only because reason was overruled at some time in their past." (Feyerabend, 1975 155) Putting the point this way is interesting, given Kant's influence on Feyerabend. One of the more important commentators on Kant is P.F. Strawson who states in the preface to *The Bounds of Sense* that Kant draws the bounds of sense in two ways and in a third way he transverses them when he attempts to "extend beyond the limits of experience the use of natural concepts..."[16]

The best way to conclude this section on Feyerabend is to present his own summary.

> When the "Pythagorean idea" of the motion of the earth was revived by Copernicus it met with difficulties that exceeded those encountered by contemporary Ptolemaic astronomy. Strictly speaking, one had to regard it as refuted. Galileo, who was convinced of the truth of the Copernican view and who did not share the quite common, though by no means universal, belief in a stable experience, looked for new kinds of fact which might support Copernicus and still be acceptable to all. He obtained such facts in two different ways: first, by the invention of his telescope which changed the sensory core of everyday experience and replaced it by puzzling and unexplained phenomena; and second, by his principle of relativity and his dynamics which changed its conceptual components. Neither the telescopic phenomena nor the new ideas of motion were acceptable to common sense (or to the Aristotelians). Besides, the associated theories could easily be shown to be false. Yet these false theories, these unacceptable phenomena, are distorted by Galileo and are converted into strong support of Copernicus. The whole rich reservoir of the everyday experience and of the intuition of his readers is utilized in the argument, but the facts they are invited to recall are arranged in a new way, approximations are made, known effects are omitted, different conceptual lines are drawn, so that a new kind of experience arises, manufactured almost out of thin air. This new experience is then solidified by insinuating that the reader has been familiar with it all the time. It is solidified and soon accepted as gospel truth, despite the fact that its conceptual components are incomparably more speculative than are the conceptual components of common sense (Feyerabend, 1975 160-161).

Thus science progresses by all kinds of methods. If Galileo had followed the so-called rules or logic of discovery or the philosophical procedures which are designed to test theories, he would never have developed his views. This is what Feyerabend means when he says that for science to progress it has to break the bounds of reason. To demand strict criteria for verification or falsification would be to destroy the scientific enterprise. Since science develops in irrational ways and its findings really cannot be demonstrated to be true on objective external grounds, Feyerabend concludes that science is very much like a myth. It serves the same purpose: explanation of our world and our place in it.

Now let us take a comparative look at Kuhn and Feyerabend. There is a great deal of similarity between the two views and there are some significant disagreements. Let us look at the similarities first. Both views hold that observation is theory-laden and that so-called facts are relative to a theory or paradigm. They agree that new theories or paradigms are accepted for reasons other than logical ones and that science does not progress in an orderly manner. They agree that new theories or paradigms are developed because of some crisis or problem with the old way of understanding the world. But they disagree on the nature of the problem and how and why a new theory or paradigm gets developed and replaces the old one.

The main disagreement between these two views appears to be on the issue of reason. Kuhn acknowledges that reason is not always the deciding factor in adopting a new theory or paradigm but does not know how to abandon reason altogether. The crisis in the old view that led to the development of the new view was discovered by reason. Once a problem is discovered the most important thing is getting a solution. Thus factors other than reason come into play only after reason has identified a problem. And then, presumably, reason will return once a new paradigm is in place. Of course, since notions like "truth" and "fact" are theory-laden what constitutes reason in the new paradigm may not have constituted reason in the old paradigm. But some semblance of reason will be utilized.

Kuhn acknowledges that since different paradigms are incommensurable they cannot be directly compared to each other. But they can be compared in some limited ways, especially with regard to which view has fewer problems with it. That is, which view would still have a crisis within it and which view appears to be able to resolve the crisis. Thus, even though the new paradigm is incommensurable with the old one, and therefore science or knowledge does not progress in an orderly manner, both views become related to each other with regard to how they respectively resolve the crisis at hand. The view offering the best solution wins.

Feyerabend acknowledges that new theories develop because of problems with the old ones, but because of his more complete relativism he creates a problem for himself. There were problems with the old view, which was why a new view was developed. But Feyerabend is not clear why the old view developed the problems it did since, according to the way Feyerabend argues, it would appear that some creative thinkers in the old view would have been able to develop a series of ad hoc hypotheses to explain the apparent anomalies and would then have been able to convince everyone that the old view was still viable. While Feyerabend gives a thorough historical analysis of how Galileo got his view to be accepted he does not provide an analysis of why a new view had to be developed in the first place. This point is compounded by Feyerabend's methodological pluralism. He states that we have to constantly proffer alternative views with regard to explaining how the world works. The reason for this is to achieve the best or most complete or most sellable view. But he does not justify the need to do so. To use an old saw, "if it ain't broke, don't fix it." If people do not think they need to change their outlook, or if they do not think there is a crisis, or even if there is one and thinkers are able to provide proper ad hoc hypotheses to keep the old view sellable, Feyerabend provides no reasons—he does not do a good selling job—on why we need to keep looking for new explanatory models. That is unless he really believes in some notion of scientific progress. And if he does, his views are just a radicalization of Popper's views. Recall that Popper believed that knowledge advanced by the process of trial and error—conjecture and refutation. If Feyerabend cannot persuade us as to why we should continue to proffer conjectures which are designed to refute or replace established views in the light of his pluralism then we should be content with the views that we have and only look for alternative views when such views are needed. That only occurs when the old view cannot explain phenomena that it should be able to explain, i.e., when there is a crisis with that view.

Let us look at this issue with a mundane example. I own a ten-year old car. I have maintained it well and it still runs great. I like the car and think of it as an old friend. I am not a technology buff so I do not care about many of the new innovations in the automotive field. I have taken skid control courses so I do not need anti-lock breaks. I have installed heavy-duty seat belts so I do not need air bags. I like working on the car so I do not need computer-controlled engine management systems. The only problem I have is that since the car is so old replacement parts are no longer being made so if something fails I either have to have a new part made or improvise something—provide an ad hoc solution.

Now Kuhn would say that I might have a crisis looming for if a number of major parts go all at once the car may not be repairable, in which case I will need a new car. Feyerabend would want me to get a new car immediately and would try to do a good selling job on me. But he will not be able to convince me to get rid of my old car. On his view I should still be able to improvise parts and rebuild things even if these rebuilt parts are not built to the same specifications as the original parts. I would have an ad hoc car. On his criteria that would be acceptable. I would only need a new car if I were not even able to develop such ad hoc repairs to the old car. This would constitute a crisis. But this would be a crisis in a Kuhnian sense.

Indeed, we can push this point even further so that Feyerabend's methodological pluralism requires me to buy a car, then sell it right away and buy a new car, sell it and buy a new car, ad infinitum. But if I keep doing this I will never keep a car long enough to see if it does the job it was bought for. The point here is that Feyerabend is too quick to explain how new views are developed without really explaining why the old view has to be abandoned. It is as if he indeed believes in some sense of scientific progress, even if this progress is discontinuous.

WILFRID SELLARS

The conclusion I have reached here is that Kuhn gives a more complete analysis of why a new view has to be developed while Feyerabend gives a more complete analysis of how the new view becomes established. In both cases factors other than reason or good scientific practice are the main reasons for the development and acceptance of new views. But many questions still have not been answered with regard to how the new view develops the way it does and why people are prepared to buy this new view. After all, it is a marketplace truism that one really cannot be sold something one does not want. One has to want something; a good salesperson will try to convince you that what is being shown to you is what you want. So the main question that still has to be answered is why people believe they need a new theory or paradigm. To help us answer this question we shall look at the work of Wilfrid Sellars.

Sellars approaches the issue from a different perspective than Kuhn and Feyerabend. He looks at the issue from the standpoint of categorical changes in the history of philosophy. In this sense he is closer to Kant than either Kuhn or Feyerabend. He talks about the original image of man in the world, the manifest or common sense image of man in the world and the scientific image of man in the world.[17] Sellars sees things in terms of images since he sees philosophy as the subject that tries to make sense of other subjects, to get things to "hang together." And the thing that makes everything else hang together is our sense of self or our concept of a person. This is the case since it is we who are doing the making sense. We try to make sense of the world around us and of our place in that world in terms of how we understand ourselves. Of course, as we learn about the world and apply that knowledge to ourselves, we will end up changing our sense of who and what we are. So Sellars also sees our knowledge as changing and, as we have seen from our discussions in the previous chapter, he also holds that truth is relative to an image or conceptual framework.

Before continuing with the argument let me take a moment for some terminological clarification. Kuhn uses the term "paradigm" in much the same way Feyerabend uses the term "theory". The equivalent terms for Sellars would be "image" or "conceptual framework". Sellars' primary definition of theories is that they explain why individual objects obey general laws. Feyerabend sees theories as general explanatory models. And the general explanatory model for Kuhn is the paradigm. Sellars' original image of man in the world is similar to Kuhn's pre-paradigmatic view. Individuals have pieces of information but there is nothing to make sense of these individual pieces and there is no basis for critical evaluation of the bits and pieces. It is only when a paradigm or a conceptual framework develops that people can start putting the bits and pieces together in the hope that they will complete the puzzle or the image. And as they try to put the pieces together they begin to ask critical questions as to whether or not specific pieces belong in the puzzle or what the puzzle is supposed to look like and how they are supposed to go about finding missing pieces. In short, one begins to develop a methodology only in the context of a framework or paradigm.

In a more specific sense the original image was one in which persons saw everything in terms of personhood. That is, all objects were personified. The manifest image of man in the world is our common sense image of ourselves. It is the image that philosophers from Plato on have been concerned with understanding. It is the image in which persons separate themselves from other objects and "depersonalize" them. In the original image being a tree was "a way of being a person" (Sellars, 1963 10) while in the manifest image this belief changed. And when man in the original image stopped thinking of what man in the manifest image calls trees as persons, "the change was more radical than a change in belief; it was a change in category." (Sellars, 1963 10)

For Sellars this manifest or common sense image includes the science of Galileo and Newton. This is so because their science still explained manifest or directly observable things in terms we could understand. Two points need to be made here. One has to do with the apparent duality of persons and the second has to do with the development of theoretical or unobservable scientific entities. Persons are physical beings who interact with the physical world and whose bodies obey the laws of physics; for example, when pushed a person will fall. But persons are conceived of as capable of rational thought and free decision-making. It is this duality that became translated into an ontological mind/body dualism. The psychological theory of behaviorism tried to explain the so-called mental phenomena in physical terms and is thereby a manifest image explanation of personhood. Thus the manifest or common sense image of the world is based on the observable world and explanations of that world have to be couched in terms that relate directly to those objects.

What Sellars calls the scientific image is an image of the world in which the behaviors or properties of common sense objects are explained in terms of unobservable or theoretical entities. This move from the common sense perceptible object to the scientific theoretical object is another categorical change. In the scientific image the behavior of persons is explained in terms from biology and physics. In physics, all matter is understood as being made up of atoms and molecules. In biology, persons are seen as beings with complex neurophysiological systems. So we explain the biological aspects of persons in biological or neurophysiological terms but then we explain the neurophysiology in molecular terms. Thus persons become scientific entities.

The manifest and scientific images are two competing images of man in the world. But Sellars points out that the contrast he is concerned with is not between a scientific and an unscientific view of the world

> but between that conception which limits itself to what correlational techniques can tell us about perceptible and introspective events and that which postulates imperceptible objects and events for the purpose of explaining correlations among perceptibles....Our contrast then, is between two ideal constructs: (a) the correlational and categorical refinement of the "original image", which refinement I am calling the manifest image; (b) the image derived from the fruits of postulational theory construction which I am calling the scientific image. (Sellars, 1963 19)

The main point here is that the scientific image develops out of the manifest image in the same way that the manifest image developed out of the original image. In trying to make sense of the original image men constructed the manifest image. In trying to explain the manifest image we are in the process of constructing a scientific image of ourselves.

Natural Law, Science, and the Social Construction of Reality 41

Thus although methodologically a development *within* the manifest image, the scientific image presents itself as a *rival* image. From its point of view the manifest image on which it rests is an "inadequate" (in principle) likeness of a reality which first finds its adequate (in principle) likeness in the scientific image. I say "in principle" because the scientific image is still in the process of coming into being...(Sellars, 1963 20).

This last quote gives us the clue we need to answer the questions posed above with regard to the relationship between images or paradigms or theories and why we should adopt a new one. The new view is developed because of problems in the old one. The new view is constructed in order to solve the crisis that existed in the old view. That is the connection between the old view and the new. We accept the new view because it solves the crisis in the old view. If there are rival solutions we choose the one which best solves the crisis in the old view in terms that come closest to it. Thus a form of reason does operate in our choices even if it is not the reason of so-called scientific method. It is the reason of pragmatism.

Let us look at this issue in terms of that new car. I really do not want to buy a new car. Feyerabend would want me to a buy a new car as soon as there is any kind of problem with the one I have. He may even insist I buy a new one before I have a problem since the new one will be a better car. Kuhn would suggest I buy a new car when the old one shows signs of completely breaking down. There is no point in buying a new car before the old one becomes close to being unusable, but I should buy the new car before the old one completely dies so I will not be stuck without transportation. But Kuhn gives me no help as to how to go about buying that new car. Sellars would agree with Kuhn that I should start thinking about a new car before the old one becomes unusable. But Sellars provides help in how to make that choice. When looking for a new car, if I was satisfied with the old one, I should look for a car that does its job in a new way but in a way that I can connect to how the old one did the job. In other words, I will buy a replacement for the old car that most closely resembles it, recognizing, of course, that I am buying a different kind of vehicle in a context that is different from the one in which I bought the original car. So while I make a categorical or paradigm shift I can still make a connection between the old and new cars, or between the old and new images. The choice may not use so-called scientific reason. Rather it uses personal choice with pragmatic considerations.

Another example, which may do a better job of illustrating the relationship between paradigms or frameworks, is that of a house.

Let us say it is the year 1200 and our ancestors have just built a beautiful state-of-the-art stone castle. The castle has stamped earth floors, thick stone walls, windows, and huge fire pits for heating and cooking. In later years descendants of the builders add such things as running water, sewage flows, and heating ducts. Later descendants add electricity, garages, central heating and air conditioning. Then we add telephones, televisions, computers, and internet hookups.

When we see the castle from the outside it may still look like the building from 1200, but when we enter we know we are inside a 21st century building and not a 13th century building. What has happened is that the house has been transformed or reconstructed. Each generation of owners added something to, or took something away from, the original house, thereby changing it. The house underwent a paradigm shift or an image change and is no longer the house it started out as. We relate to this house in a totally different way than the original owners related to it. And we relate to it differently than if we were living in the unchanged house. We would not want to live in the original house. We live in it now because it is a different house.

This is why we adopt the scientific image. We do so because it was developed to explain the manifest image. But in so doing a new image was constructed in much the same way our new house was constructed. The theoretical entities, which were postulated to explain the behavior of the manifest image, become the new objects of the scientific image. Thus my chair supports my weight not because it is made of solid objects but because it is made of atoms and molecules. And this new image, when completed, will be incommensurable with the old one.

CULTURE AS A PARADIGM

Another good way of looking at the relationship between paradigms or images is to look at comparative cultures. Think of one person traveling to a foreign country where the language and customs may be different. Or think of a person trying to learn a language that is structured differently from his own—say English and Chinese. Or think of an anthropologist going to study a very different culture.

People living in a culture share a way of looking at the world. By looking at some of the methodological issues involved in understanding how cultures work we will get a better idea of how paradigms or images work. Let us begin by defining culture. *The Random House Dictionary*, in different editions over the years has the same definition, supplied by a sociologist. Culture has more than one definition. The sociological definition is "the sum total of ways of living built up by a group of human beings and transmitted from one generation to another." The sum total of things includes such things as language, values, and artifacts. These artifacts or arts reflect another definition of culture. We often think of culture in artistic terms. We say that a person who is knowledgeable about the arts is cultured. The arts include such activities as painting, sculpture, music, literature and dance.

This double definition brings out a point about how we separate ourselves from our cultural contexts. By separating the arts from the rest of our culture we become divorced from what we are. Because we have created a complex culture which has lost sight of its roots, we identify culture not with the forms of our lives and with our mores but with our artifacts. Thus one is not cultured—one does not fully fit into a society—unless one is versed in the products or artifacts of the culture. In sociology there is a distinction made between the professed values of a group and the values that are actually practiced. These latter values or norms are the salient or the operational ones. They determine how members of a culture make decisions and react to crises. For example our society claims to favor so-called family values and holds that children are to be highly regarded. Yet most decisions appear to be made based on economic considerations even if such considerations place families under hardship. For example, over the two decades from 1970 to 1990 costs rose significantly, and the production of individual workers, partly due to automation, has increased, yet wages in real terms have decreased. This has put burdens on families so that in order to meet the same needs two incomes are needed when one had previously been sufficient. So both mother and father work. But no provisions are made for day care and mothers are made to feel guilty for not staying at home.

Thus while we *say* we believe in family values, in fact we do not. Family values take a back seat to economic values. While family values are the professed values of our society economic values are the salient values. This provides a good example of how we value our artifacts over ourselves. We must act in a way which is good for the economy even if doing so will be bad for ourselves and our family life. We let our artifacts control us instead of controlling them.

This discussion raises two issues. One is the separation of people from their culture and the second is how culture takes on a life of its own.

These are actually two aspects of the same issue since the fact that cultures can take on a life of their own is what allows people to become alienated from their cultures. The analogy to scientific revolutions should be fairly obvious. When paradigms or images change, people who do not make the conceptual changes necessary to move into the new image become alienated from that image and end up fighting a rearguard action to try to reinstate the old values. The Catholic Church's fight against Galileo is a prime example of the rise of reactionary movements based on old values in reaction to the revolution in thought that is taking place.

Let us return to the nature of culture so we can see why culture can take on a life of its own. Culture is everything we do. It is our form of life. The fact that we go to work in the ways we do, that our families are structured the way they are, that we have the educational system that we have, that we have the kinds of laws and penal systems that we have and that we act according a set of values or norms that we learn from birth and, for the most part, do not challenge unless there is a crisis, all define our culture. In short, how we act in the ways we do reflects and defines our culture.

We can set up an analogy between a culture and a paradigm or image in the sense that our culture is such a paradigm or image. Just as the individual entities of a scientific theory act in the way they do because of how they are constructed, people behave in the ways they do because of the kinds of entities they are. A theory explains why chairs hold my weight and a culture explains why I participate in the social world in the ways I do. My behavior in terms of how I go to work, raise my children, entertain myself, and so on can all be explained in terms of the fact that I live in a culture with a certain set of institutions. It is as if these social institutions exist independently of me. And this is exactly what is meant by cultural materialism: cultures can be talked about and studied as if they were actual entities in the world just as chairs and tables are entities in the world.

It is because culture has these properties that we can identify certain ways of doing things as belonging to different cultures. We can say that certain behaviors are clearly American or Canadian or French or Chinese or German. Each society has evolved its own institutions and ways of doing things. Each society reflects a slightly different image of man in the world. For sociologists and anthropologists, questions regarding the relationships between these different cultures arise. For example, is Chinese translatable into English or German? And what of multicultural societies? Are they comparable to people living in a situation where more than one image is operable? And if so, do these people move back and forth between images or do they try to blend them? A good way to look at these issues is from an example presented by Jamake Highwater in his book *The Primal Mind*[18]. When the white man first came to the new world in large ocean-going vessels the natives here saw them not as boats but as floating islands. Boats were canoes, small vessels for local transportation. Islands were floating land masses on which people lived. The Europeans lived on their vessels so they were seen as floating islands and not as boats. What we have here is not the simple task of expanding the native concept of "boat" because the concept of a boat is entrenched in the culture. The language reflects that culture—how the Native Americans understood the world. With the coming of the Europeans the Native Americans were forced to change how they saw their world. Things they never conceived of were thrust upon them and this exposure to such things caused a crisis in their world view. A number of strategies presented themselves. One would be to adopt the European world view. Another would be to try to make sense of the European view in their own terms. A third option would be to try to combine the two views.

Initially the concepts of floating island and boat are not translatable: They stand for different kinds of things and reflect different images of man in the world. But as the Native Americans became used to seeing such new things they learned to refer to them in their own terms. Eventually the concept of "boat" changed and was able to encompass both the canoe and the floating island. This was possible because of the floating nature of the floating island. One looked at the same thing from a different perspective and thereby categorized it differently.

In another Canadian example, when we look at the sky we see a constellation of stars we call the Big Dipper. When Inuit people look at the same constellation, as Norman Hallendy shows in his book *Inuksuit*, they see the Great Caribou[19]. (Illustration after Hallendy, 2000)

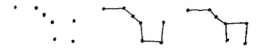

Two different groups of people look at the same thing, agree on the seven stars, but disagree on the picture it makes. The difference comes from their different cultures. Westerners tend to see things in terms of things; Inuit tend to see things in terms of their environments.

Let us relate these discussions to our point above. What happens when we try to translate one language to another? How often are we told that certain terms cannot be literally translated? How many times are we told that to translate from one language to another is to torture the language? The point here is that it is not always possible to translate one language to another just as it is not possible to understand a foreign culture from the standpoint of one's own.

What can be done is to learn the other language so that one can go back and forth between the two. One will not always be translating; one will literally be going back and forth between two ways of speaking. Eventually what might happen is that the speaker develops a new language which is a mix of the two. For example in French-speaking Quebec there is a "language" known as *Franglais*; a mixture of English and French. Native French speakers learn enough English words to get by in English parts of Quebec but they do not adopt the English attitude towards things. Thus Franglais is not a true mingling of languages. French Canadians maintain their cultural identity while adapting to the English presence in their lives. They maintain their own paradigm or image of their place in the world while acknowledging that there is another such image, that of English Canadians. And English Canadians know that there is more than one English view of the world since Canadian policy is multicultural. People are encouraged to maintain the customs they bring to Canada as long as they do not break the main laws or customs of the country. Thus Canada is a real laboratory for the mixing of images. Sometimes this creates very real problems since each group sees its concerns as more important than the concerns of another group. Since these concerns are incommensurable, there is no way of talking to each other.

Different cultures reflect different ways of looking at the world and these different ways can be incommensurable. They reflect different paradigms or images of the world. When two cultures come into contact all kinds of problems arise. Since the two cultures reflect different images it may not be possible to translate one language into the other. But members of each group can learn to participate in the culture of the other group so that both images become understandable if not comparable. In a sense what we have here is a Feyerabendian situation. Many different cultures (theories, images) are being presented at the same time. All of them appear to be doing a good job so there is no way to choose which one is better. People in one culture may find they prefer living in another culture and adopt or convert to that culture. Or, over time, some practices of some cultures may no longer make sense and may be abandoned.

But what can happen is that representatives of the different cultures all start making claims about the same kinds of things. For example, each culture wants government funding to pursue its concerns. There is only so much money so the government has to make choices as to which projects it will fund. Representatives of the different cultures will each try to convince the government their project is worth funding.

The government people are representative of a culture as well. They are not neutral even if they present that pretense. Some of them may belong to some of the groups who are applying for funding. Some may not belong to any group that is applying for funding. But they all belong to some group so whatever decisions they make will be made in the context of a culture, of an image. What we then have here is a set of competing images. The difference in this example is that different and incommensurable images are making claims about the same thing. Once this happens, once they leave their limited domains, and set themselves up to make claims about the same kinds of things that other groups make claims about, the claims and the proposed solutions become directly comparable. At that point a solution will be reached which appears to solve the problem in terms of how the problem is stated. If it is stated in terms of government criteria then the government can look at all the claims and make rational choices with regard to their criteria. If there is no such set of criteria then each group not only gets to present its case but also gets to argue why their needs are more worthy of the grant than another group's needs. When this happens direct comparisons can be made. Such comparisons will not be easy since the concerns will be so different.

The philosophical point here is that when different scientific theories or images compete for acceptance they are judged on how well they solve the perceived problems. The choices are pragmatic and there will be resistance to those choices. But eventually one view will prevail. That will be the view that appears to solve the problems at hand, or that at least appears to be able to solve those problems. But in the case of cultures, one may not always prevail, but solutions to problems that are shared by different cultures can be solved in this way.

In sociology there is a distinction between the dominant culture and subcultures. Subcultures have different values than does the dominant culture, but members of subcultures have to live within the confines of the dominant culture. Practices which may have been acceptable at home may be criminal here. The point of this distinction is that the above process takes place in that kind of context. One can see the dominant culture as the existing paradigm and in different areas of that paradigm specific theories are being challenged by the subcultures. Some specific challenges may be acceptable. At first no one will notice any problems with the dominant culture. It will appear to absorb these changes. But eventually after enough of these changes have been made it may appear that the dominant culture is in crisis and may need to be abandoned.

The point of this diversion into the problems of multiculturalism is that cultures have a life of their own. Different cultures reflect different views of how people relate to the world. As long as one view is not challenged, there is no problem. There also is no problem with many cultures co-existing. But once they start making demands on shared space—on things which are comparable—something has to give. This point can be made with our old house analogy. Let us imagine a descendent of a very old family who has inherited the family home, discussed above, which originally dates from the 13th century. This person and his contemporary family believe in maintaining traditions so they try to maintain the home in as pure a way as possible. Because of this maintaining of tradition, they see themselves in a very real sense as living in medieval times. Thus the they see themselves as medievalists. That is, they see the world as a person living in that time sees saw the world. For them Thomas Aquinas is a contemporary thinker.

But the world has changed and there is a modern world outside their doorstep, a world in which this family participates on a daily basis: they go to work, they go to school, they go shopping, they participate in contemporary political discussions and so on. Thus the modern world has entered their medieval home. Over the years the home has been updated. It now has running water, electricity, central heating, dual glass and insulation, telephones, televisions and so on.

Two points need to be made here. First, even if no changes have been made to the house and it is still preserved in its medieval authenticity, the occupants must leave the house and function in the modern world. At best, the occupants lead a split life, moving between two different worlds, the medieval and the modern. If they can live this way, fine. But by participating in the modern world they have accepted, whether they like it or not, the technology of the modern world, and in so doing they have accepted the modern scientific view of the world, since it is that view of the world which has made modern technology possible.

The second point has to do with the house if it has been altered. Such alterations bring the modern world into the house and thereby alter it so that it is no longer the house it originally was. Of course, from an ontological standpoint it is the same house since one can trace the house through its history. Yet from a conceptual standpoint the house is different because of all the changes that have occurred—it has undergone a revolution. The occupants cannot have it both ways. Either they live in the modern world or they live in the medieval world. By remodeling the house and/or by accepting the inventions of the modern world, the occupants have accepted the modern world. Of course, there is nothing wrong with treating one's home as a refuge from the pressures of everyday life. In this sense we can say that this family has created a kind of subculture which they practice at home. But such an attitude, or such a participation in a subculture, does not prevent one from accepting the fact that one is committed to the new scientific framework which represents the dominant culture.

To put this point differently, the encroachment of the modern world into the medieval home and/or the need of these medievalists to participate in the modern world creates a crisis in the medieval view. This forces the people to accept that they must begin to see themselves as modernists and their home as both a refuge from the everyday world and a link to the past. But they can no longer say they live in the past.

A GLIMPSE AHEAD

We have come a long way. We now have some idea as to the nature of scientific change and of the relationships between competing paradigms or images or theories. New images or paradigms are developed because of problems in the existing images or paradigms. But when those problems are solved the result is not a fixed old image but a shiny new one, which will explain things differently. We will have bought a new a car and we will have remodeled our old homes.

In the following chapters we will be going through the process of test driving new cars and of remodeling or reconstructing our homes. We have a long journey with many winding roads and backtracks and we will have to buy a whole lot of construction materials. But it will be one great experience.

Chapter 3

JOHN LOCKE, NATURAL LAW AND THE EMPIRICIST TRADITION

There were many responses to the challenges of the scientific revolution. The first important systematic response was that of René Descartes. His approach reflected the new status of the individual trying to cope with a changing social structure.

Since one of the results of the scientific revolution was the overthrow of old knowledge, all new knowledge claims were put in doubt. So Descartes undertook a systematic doubt. He was to doubt everything until he came up with something that could not be doubted. And, with this undoubtable beginning, he would deduce other things which then would be known with certainty.

What he found that could not be doubted was his own existence. If I am doing the doubting I must exist. *Cogito ergo sum*—I think therefore I exist[20]—has become part of our consciousness. But it was a revelation in the 17th century. And it provided an individualist basis for knowledge. For while I could not doubt my own existence I could still doubt the existence of other things and persons until I obtained good reasons for accepting their existence. I could also doubt the existence of my body, since one of the lessons of the scientific revolution was that our senses could not always be trusted. But it was the existence of my thinking capacity, my mind, that could not be doubted.

From Descartes we have a legacy of a strong individualistic basis for knowledge and a strong distinction between body and mind. The importance of this combination of individualistic foundation of knowledge and mind body dualism was that it led to a whole new set of issues concerning knowledge of other minds. The knowledge that I have may be different from yours. And since I cannot know the contents of your mind and you cannot know the contents of mine we have to find some common ground so that we can communicate.

Historically, knowledge was based on a combination of

observation and reasoning. At times logic was seen as more important than perception; at other times perception was seen as more important than reasoning. Since one of the implications of the scientific revolution was that our senses could not always be trusted—things were not always as they appeared to be—Descartes relied on logic to solve problems when logic contradicted our observations. Although he went a long way in the process of finding a modern foundation for knowledge, he is seen as not having succeeded since his reliance on reason or logic led to a dead end. If another thinker found a different item which could not be doubted and then deduced a different set of knowable facts, and the reasoning of both were logically valid, there was no way to decide which view was correct.

An interesting way to see the world from a Cartesian standpoint would be to read the early attempts at fiction writing, which began to appear shortly after Descartes' death in 1650. These took the form of letters. This was because the letter objectified the subjective thoughts of the writer. That is, it took the writer's personal thoughts, which were not observable by anyone else, and made them publicly observable. The earliest of these epistolary novels were presented as real correspondences, not as fictional works because they were attempts at a new literary form and by making them appear to be real their sense of objectivity was enhanced.

For a good discussion of these early attempts at novel writing, and for a good sampling of them, see *The Novel in Letters* edited by Natascha Wurzbach[21]. Throughout this section I will use literature as examples of the new developments in philosophical and scientific thinking.

JOHN LOCKE I: SOCIAL CONTRACT

Since the Cartesian approach led to a dead end another approach had to be taken. This was to be a reliance on observation. This time, however, observations would be done in a scientific manner with logic as a test. The first important figure here was John Locke who, in many ways, embodied the thought of the period. His views were influential in England and were a major factor behind the French Revolution and in the Constitution of The United States of America. He not only developed an individualist theory of knowledge in response to the work of Newton but also developed a political and ethical theory with an individualist basis. Together these theories become a modern approach to natural law. The works involved are *An Essay Concerning The True Original, Extent and*

End of Civil Government[22], and *An Essay Concerning Human Understanding*[23]. Both were published in the same period but we shall start with the work on Civil Government as it was begun much earlier.

The theme of Locke's work on government espouses the concept of a social contract. Like any other contract, this implies that the contractees have agreed to the terms of the contract—that the governed have agreed to the terms under which they are governed. This, in turn, shows that this kind of political contract is based on liberty and justice, as opposed to force.

Locke's view of a social contract had its roots in three areas. The first was Aristotle's politics which made a distinction between a ruler or a king and a tyrant. This distinction allowed the people to hold the king accountable to them. The second was the heritage of Roman law which put binding strictures on the ruler. And the third was the Bible, especially the Old Testament where David made a covenant with his people[24].

It should be pointed out that Locke's religion was not the religion of Aquinas. Locke was a good modern Protestant Puritan. Protestantism could be seen as the religion of the early modern era in the same way that Catholicism was the religion of the medieval era. Each religion embodied the value structures of its respective time and place. To elaborate this point we shall take a very short side trip into the world of sociology.

The roots of sociology can be found in the 18th century, although sociology as a subject in itself did not develop until well into the 19th. There are two reasons for this. First there is the old adage: "if it ain't broke, don't fix it. In this context it means that as long as society functions no one really thinks about the role of the social structure as it affects our identities or how we do what we what we do. Rather it was the major social upheavals brought about by the industrial revolution that led to a look at the structure of a social order, why and how it changes, and how those changes affect the people living in a changing society. The second reason sociology started when it did was because, as a result of the scientific revolution, there was a method which could be used for such inquiries.

One of the most important lessons to be learned from sociology is that everything connects. A society is made up of a number of social institutions—family structures, courtship rites, education structures, legal structures, economic structures, and so on. When one of these structures or institutions undergoes a change there will be corresponding changes in all the others. Different accounts of how these institutions are connected, why the changes occur, and how new social structures are formed reflect the different schools of sociology.

It is because of the interconnectedness of all aspects of society that we can label different periods and cultures. In the medieval period people saw themselves as members of their social order and this social order included the economic, religious and family structures of the time.

With the coming of the scientific revolution and the new individualism, society changed. Catholicism was universal in outlook and Catholics saw themselves as part of this universal order. One's moral worth was seen in terms of how one lived and fulfilled one's obligations to one's society and to the church. Also, in the medieval period, most people were not literate and depended on the church for all instruction. Thus the church controlled the lives of the people by controlling their access to information and knowledge.

Protestantism developed a new set of values which focused on individual belief. One's moral worth was now seen, to some extent, in terms of one's material worth. The foundation of morality moved to the individual who began to see him or herself as an individual and not solely as a member of a social order. Thus capitalism and Protestantism developed together and reinforced each other. This view has been demonstrated by Max Weber.

Weber's argument begins with a distinction between religions based on reason and magic. Magical systems are usually based on authoritarian models with those in power controlling the access to magic, much like the Catholic Church. In such systems individuals do not have access to magic nor even to understanding how the magic works. Thus they cannot plan their lives in any rational way since magic can always intervene. One cannot carry on rational economic activity if one does not understand how one's society works. "Very different is the rational state in which alone modern capitalism can flourish. Its basis is an expert officialdom and rational law"[25].

Weber points out that the modern rational state has its foundation in Roman law. And it is law that provides the structure in which a regulated economic life can function. (Weber, 1994 52) It was in this context that Protestantism flourished. The Protestant Reformation challenged the authority of the church and the idea of a universal morality for everyone with advantages for the leaders. Along with this challenge other things were challenged as well.

> The other-worldly asceticism came to an end. Sternly religious characters who had previously gone into monasteries now had to practice their religion in the life of

the world. For such an asceticism within the world the ascetic dogmas of Protestantism created an adequate ethics. Celibacy was not required as marriage was viewed simply as an institution for the rational bringing up of children. Poverty was not required, but the pursuit of riches must not lead one astray into reckless enjoyment. (Weber, 1994 55)

> It is true that the acquisition of wealth, attributed to piety, led to a dilemma in all respects similar to that into which the medieval monasteries constantly fell: the religious guild led to wealth, wealth led to fall from grace, and this led again to the necessity of re-constitution. Calvinism sought to avoid this difficulty through the idea that man was only an administrator of what God had given him; it condemned enjoyment, yet permitted no flight from the world but rather regarded working together, with its rational discipline, as the religious task of the individual. Out of this system of thought came our word "calling" which is known only to the languages influenced by the Protestant translations of the Bible. It expresses the value placed upon rational activity carried on according to the rational capitalistic principle, as the fulfilment of a God-given task. (Weber, 1994 56)

The import of this discussion is that as the modern state began to develop, and as the individual developed a clearer sense of self and of the ability to use reason, religion changed in the same way. This new religion embodied the value structure which reflected the new rationality and individualism. This is how Protestantism and capitalism go together like the proverbial horse and carriage. And this is the context in which John Locke worked out the details of his social contract.

Locke begins by defining political power as

> a right of making laws with penalties of death, and consequently all less penalties, for the regulating and preserving of property and of employing the force of the community, in the execution of such laws, and in the defense of the commonwealth from foreign injury; and all this only for the public good (Locke, 1960 4)

To understand the nature of this power "we must consider, what state all men are naturally in, and that is, a state of perfect freedom to order their actions, and dispose of their possessions and persons, as they think fit, within the bounds of the law of nature, without asking leave, or depending upon the will of any other man." (Locke, 1960 4)

But this freedom in a state of nature is not a state of license since

> The state of nature has a law of nature to govern it, which obliges every one, and reason, which is that law, teaches all mankind, who will but consult it, that being all equal and independent, no one ought to harm another in his life, health, liberty, or possessions. (Locke, 1960 5)

And this law of nature

> would, as all other laws that concern men in this world, be in vain, if there were nobody that in the state of nature had a power to execute that law, and thereby preserve the innocent and restrain offenders. And if any one in the state of nature may punish another for any evil he has done, every one may do so: for in that state of perfect equality where naturally there is no superiority or jurisdiction of one over another, what any may do in prosecution of that law, everyone must needs have a right to do.

Thus, in the state of nature, "one man comes by power over another; but yet no absolute or arbitrary power,..."(Locke, 1960 6.)

And this balance of power or contract works because "Men living together according to reason without a common superior on earth, with authority to judge between them, are properly in the state of nature." (Locke, 1960 13)

So people are free in a state of nature. This natural state of freedom implies everyone is equal to everyone else. The concept of the social contract here stems from the this natural freedom and human reason that allow people in the state of nature to act responsibly and to use the implications of the state of nature to punish those who break these laws. Thus the concepts of equality and freedom, and the need to maintain them, imply a set of ethical principles or laws which are understood by people in the state of nature through the use of their reason. These principles or laws imply the concept of responsibility: if I break the law I can be punished. And anyone in the state of nature with me is in a position to carry out the punishment since that person is my equal and his reason tells him what his powers are with regard to being part of a social contract.

It is not that people in a state of nature sit down together and write a contract, but rather that by using their reason they come to understand the implications and limits of individual liberty and the responsibilities that go along with this liberty. Adherence to the contract is implied by one's behavior.

So people find themselves in a state of nature characterized by individual freedom This not only implies that one can do whatever one wants to do but also implies limitations on that freedom, since every free individual must respect the freedom of every other free individual. By using one's reason to do so, one agrees to the social contract.

When in a state of nature people have to survive. People require food and shelter. So they work the land. And this work gives them rights or privileges over the land. Work is what gives value to the land and one's work is rewarded with title to the land. Thus "the condition of human life, which requires labor and materials to work on, necessarily introduce private possessions." (Locke, 1960 22) The organization that develops around working and defending property and sharing one's produce heralds the beginnings of modern society. The community, as sanctioned by its individual members, becomes the arbiter of disputes (Locke, 1960 50) and this organization becomes the basis of civil government which must be authorized by the individual members of that society. And once such a political organization is established

> this puts men out of a state of nature into that of a commonwealth, by setting up a judge on earth with authority to determine all the controversies and redress the injuries that may happen to any member of the commonwealth; which judge is the legislative or magistrates appointed by it. And wherever there are any number of men, however associated, that have no such decisive power to appeal to, there they are still in the state of nature. (Locke, 1960 52)

When men enter into a commonwealth and leave the state of nature the principles of individual freedom found in the state of nature limit the powers that can be exercised by the commonwealth. Legislative or judicial powers are to be used to enforce liberty and redress transgressions against that liberty. For "every man. by consenting with others to make one body politic under one government, puts himself under an obligation to everyone of that society to submit to the determination of the majority..." (Locke, 1960 57) But, if men are free in a state of nature, the question remains as to why anyone would be willing to give up this freedom to join a commonwealth and to be governed by the majority. The answer is

> that though in the state of nature he hath such a right, yet the enjoyment of it is very uncertain and constantly exposed to the invasion of others; for all being kings as much as he, every man his equal, and the greater part no strict observers of equity and justice, the enjoyment of the property he has in this state is very unsafe, very insecure. This makes him willing to quit this condition which, however free, is full of fears and continual dangers; and 'tis not without reason that he seeks out and is willing to join in society with others who are already united, or have a mind to unite for the mutual preservation of their lives, liberties, and estates, which I call by the general name, property. (Locke, 1960 73)

Thus the purpose of civil government is protection. People leave the state of nature and enter into a civil contract, based on the principles found in nature which form the basis of the social contract, in order to protect what they have achieved in the state of nature. In other words, once people begin amassing wealth they leave the state of nature and enter into a commonwealth where they create a civil government in order to protect that newfound wealth and the freedom that goes with it.

Let us sum up Locke's position. He began with an individualist view of society that, as we saw from Max Weber, came from the development of Protestantism, which developed in tandem with capitalism. In Locke we saw how individuals working the land create private property, which, of course, is the basis of capitalism. And then we saw how the need to protect one's life, liberty and property leads to the creation of civil government, which must always be accountable to the governed in accordance with the laws of nature. Here we see the beginnings of the concept of government of the people, by the people and for the people.

To put this summation differently, we see a natural law position here in that all aspects of life connect and the connection is based on Locke's understanding of the state of nature. Thus, because of how things are in the state of nature, and given the nature of man, we find that individualism—man's natural state—leads to value structures and social organizations that are designed to protect this individualism and the accomplishments of individuals. Thus we have an individualist social contract, a form of government accountable to, and for the protection of, its individual members, the amassing of individual wealth, and a religion which embeds these values. In combining all of these factors we see how we associate individualism, capitalism and democracy. This combination of value structures and this view of human nature gives us a Lockean view of natural law.

JOHN LOCKE II: THEORY OF KNOWLEDGE

Now, in keeping with the theme of this book, we shall look at Locke's theory of knowledge and see how his views of individualism in value theory are paralleled by his views as to how we acquire knowledge of the world in which we live. In order to understand Locke's views here we will first take a very brief look at the work of Isaac Newton, who influenced Locke.

Even though Locke was religious, and his views on nature were entrenched in his Protestantism, his views on human rationality and government provided the basis for a secular foundation of ethics and politics, thus fulfilling the promise pointed out by Morris referred to in the Introduction. Yet, people were loath to give up on religion altogether. This problem was solved by Newton's work, since in his science people saw the workings of God. As John Herman Randall Jr. points out, Newtonian Science

> furnished a "Nature" fully as effective as the earlier "will of God." It had, in fact, at last demonstrated what the will of God really was; and what it demonstrated was that the Divine Will had decreed a mechanism that worked automatically without further interference.[26]

This automatic mechanism was, of course, Newton's laws of motion coupled with his explanation of gravity—a combination that explained the workings of the universe and answered most of the questions posed by the scientific revolution. God becomes revealed in His creation through our understanding of the workings of the universe. God becomes the great engineer.

Another important aspect of Newton's work was his views on perception. The issue of determining reality from illusion became important. Newton developed what has become known as a causal theory of perception.

> When a man views an object...the light which comes from the several points of the object is refracted by the transparent skins and humors of the eye...as to converge and meet again in so many points in the bottom of the eye, and there to paint the picture of the object upon the skin...with which the bottom of the eye is covered...and these pictures, propagated by motion along the fibres of the optic nerves in the brain, are the cause of vision.[27]

Thus what we perceive is based not only on what is there to be seen but also on how the light reflected from what we see is refracted and how that refracted light is interpreted by our senses and our brains.

Newton also reflected on the methodological implications of his work. In his *Philosophiae Naturalis Principia Mathematica,* he said that "We are to admit no more causes of natural things than such as are both true and sufficient to explain their appearances."

Newton states this "since the qualities of bodies are only known to us by experiments, we are to hold for universal all such as universally agree with experiments ,..."[28] Thus we learn about the properties of objects through experience and experiment, which is a form of experience. Newton then states that "..this is the foundation of all philosophy." (Thayer, 1953 4) Elsewhere Newton continues

> ....For the best and safest method of philosophizing seems to be, first, to inquire diligently into the properties of things and to establish those properties by experiments, and to proceed later to hypotheses for the explanations of things themselves. For hypotheses ought to be applied only in the explanation of the properties of things and not made use of in determining them; except in so far as they may furnish experiments. (Thayer, 1953 5-6)

Newton's work demonstrated that we have knowledge and, to some extent, how we get that knowledge. The role of the philosopher is to provide the foundation on which that knowledge is built and thereby to show how that knowledge is possible. So we now turn to Locke's *Essay Concerning Human Understanding.*

Locke is concerned with the concept of "understanding" since it this capacity that sets men apart from other sensible things. And this understanding contains ideas which form the basis of our knowledge. To see what we have knowledge of we have to understand what ideas are and where they come from. "To this I answer, in one word, from EXPERIENCE." (Locke, 1961 10) Experience comes in two varieties. The first is observation which has to do with our perception of the world through our senses, so Locke refers to this form of experience as SENSATION. The second form of experience comes from REFLECTION on the workings or the contents of our minds. These contents come from sensation. Thus the basis of all knowledge comes from observing or sensing the world and from reflecting on what we have sensed. It is important to emphasize here that the observations, experiences and ideas

Locke is talking about are those of individuals. Knowledge of the world is based on my, or your, observations, experiences and ideas.

Ideas are initially simple. That is, they are about one clear and distinct thing. But we can put ideas together to come up with complex ideas which can be about things that themselves cannot be experienced. Also, simple ideas come to us through one sense. However, it is possible for ideas about the same object to come to us through more than one sense. Such ideas would also be complex. We can touch and see and smell something at the same time. We can then combine one or two or three of these sensations with other sensations and come up with ideas that have no basis in the observable world. Such ideas are the products of our reflection.

Using this view Locke argues against the concept of innate or native ideas. Descartes, for example, argued that since we have ideas of things which we cannot observe, and which are greater than our imaginations, such as our idea of God, such ideas must be innate. But Locke argues that using our reflective abilities we can put together such ideas. Thus simple ideas become the basis of all knowledge.

But what are these ideas about? In other words, what do we have knowledge of? Following Newton's view of perception, Locke argues that our ideas are about the qualities of objects. He distinguishes between primary and secondary qualities of objects. Primary qualities are qualities or properties of the objects in question, such as solidity, shape, form, extension and motion. Secondary qualities "are nothing in the objects themselves, but powers to produce various sensations in us by their primary qualities..." (Locke, 1961 25).

For example, let us look at what happens when we place a stick in water. When it is not in the water the stick is straight. When it is put in water it appears bent. This is because, following Newton, we know that the light is refracted by the water differently than the light which comes to our eyes directly from the stick. The stick itself is straight, yet we experience it as being bent. A second example is that of different people putting their hands in a tub of water. Some people will say the water is warm, others will say it is cool. So what is the property of the water? Clearly, based on these diverse experiences we cannot answer that question.

From such subjective or individual disparities Locke argues that only the primary qualities are real and the secondary qualities we experience are based on those experiences. If we were to turn off the light that allows us to see the bent stick, we would no longer see the stick. Yet we could still touch it. The stick exists. And because of its primary qualities the stick has the power to cause us to experience sensations of it. But those sensations or secondary qualities do not exist on their own. They are dependent on the primary qualities of the object. Thus, sensation provides us at best with knowledge of how things appear to us. Sensation provides us only with the beginnings of knowledge. In order to attain true knowledge of the objects we experience we must use reason. And our reasoning is based on the contents of our experiences, our ideas. We must develop complex ideas, we must compare and abstract them, and we must come up with conclusions that are consistent with a range of experiences.

Another way of putting the above point is to say that we take our individual experiences, reason about them, compare our reasonings with those of other people and then construct a view of the nature of the objects in question. Thus, knowledge begins with individual experience but develops into conclusions based on shared experiences.

Now, again following Newton, perceiving is a passive undertaking. We open our eyes and reflected light reaches them thereby presenting to us the secondary qualities of the objects before us. But thinking about these objects—developing simple ideas into complex ones—is an active undertaking. And by reflecting on this active property of our minds we develop the concepts of the will and of volition. Locke defines the will as the power of the mind which directs action. (Locke, 1961 43) And when this action is performed without reference to a prior action we say such an action is voluntary. Such voluntary action involves the suspension of the causal process initiated by the passive receptivity of the mind. In other words, by using our reflective capabilities we break the chain of cause and effect. For it is during this suspension of cause and effect that we can reason and decide how we are going to respond to a situation.

It is because of concerns about how persons think that Locke had to confront the whole issue of personhood. Locke begins this discussion with a distinction between "man" and "person". "A man is identifiable by appearance and a participation of the same continued life" (Locke, 1961 66) but a person has subjective qualities as well. These subjective qualities include all the things we associate with being human: the ability to think, feel, make rational decisions, and to be self-aware or conscious. Consciousness is the hallmark of self-identity. It is by being aware of ourselves that we can identify ourselves. It is by being able to reflect on what we do—to be able to perceive ourselves—that we can have knowledge of ourselves. And this implies that if we are aware of ourselves, if we are conscious, then we must be able to know that we know something.

Locke uses such terms as "body", "mind" and "soul" somewhat imprecisely. It would appear that mind is part of soul. Body is the substantive part of the person, soul the personal part which contains the functions associated with mind. Thus a person must be a dualistic substance of united soul and body, with the unifying force being consciousness. For it is self-awareness that allows me to know that I am same person I was in the past. And consciousness becomes the test of our knowledge of the world around us. When we perceive the world our knowledge of what we perceive is a factor of our ideas, our reasoning and our awareness. Our ideas, since they can be products of our imagination, especially when we combine various simple and complex ideas, will always exceed what we can actually know. But we can never have knowledge of something we cannot have an idea of.

Truth, or our understanding of what actually exists, is determined by coherence with our ideas and a "conformity" (Locke, 1961 92) between our ideas and what they represent. In this way have a way of determining whether or not an observation is accurate or if what we are seeing is in fact they way it should be. In other words, if an observation does not conform to what we already know should be the case we have good grounds for believing we are seeing an illusion. And by using our awareness and our ideas we not only have knowledge of the world but we also have mathematical knowledge and, more importantly for our purposes, moral knowledge.

As Locke demonstrates, we have mathematical knowledge since, if our knowledge of mathematical figures begins with ideas, we know, for example, the qualities of a triangle for certain. And when we actually observe a triangle in the world, if the real triangle conforms to the ideal triangle, we will then have certain knowledge of the qualities of the real triangle. In the same way that we have mathematical knowledge we have moral knowledge.

> For certainty being but the perception of the agreement or disagreement of our ideas, and demonstration nothing but the perception of such agreement, by the intervention of other ideas or mediums; our moral ideas, as well as mathematical, being archetypes themselves, and so adequate and complete ideas; all the agreement or disagreement which we shall find in them will produce real knowledge, as well as in mathematical figures. (Locke, 1961 94)

This last passage is extremely important but also very unclear. Locke does not elaborate on what he means by mathematical knowledge being archetypes, and the literature is limited. But we must make some kind of sense of it since a large of Locke's, and my, argument is based on this passage.

We do have knowledge, both of mathematics and of morals. The question here is what form this knowledge takes. We know Locke does not believe in innate ideas or in Platonic forms. We know that, for Locke, knowledge begins with experience. We also know that we can put simple ideas together to create complex ideas and concepts.

So let us imagine that what Locke is doing here is taking the concept of "triangle" which has a specific definition. Locke can say that he has an idea of a triangle. In Kuhnian language we can say that Locke has a paradigm example of what the perfect triangle is. So whenever he sees a three-sided object Locke immediately knows it must be a triangle.

The same holds for moral knowledge. We learn moral knowledge through experience, whether it is from our parents or from attending church. We formulate ideals of this knowledge so, when we find ourselves in various situations, we immediately know what is the moral thing to do.

In one sense, then, mathematical and moral knowledge is based on experience. But in another sense it is based on reason. This can be seen as an anticipation of the Kantian concept of synthetic a priori knowledge—knowledge which is both based on experience and therefore synthetic, and a fixed category that exists prior to experience and which makes sense of the experience. This concept will be discussed at great length in the next chapter.

Thus Locke's conception of moral knowledge is a combination of individual experiences put into a category which makes sense of those individual experiences. This conclusion strengthens Locke's position as a natural law theorist since it places moral knowledge on a par with mathematical knowledge, which is also based on experience but which also yields necessary conclusions.

So we come full circle. We began with man in a state of nature. The intellect begins as passive with man receiving impressions from the world around him. From these impressions he develops ideas about the world and his place in it. Reflecting on these ideas and how they relate to the world leads to the development of reason and self-awareness, qualities needed for survival in the state of nature. When he begins to acquire possessions and to encounter other people he learns how to develop a set of rules to maintain those possessions and to get along with other people. And this understanding of the world in which he lives leads to further contemplation of the kind of being he is. This in turn leads to the conclusion that he has moral knowledge.

This complete circle, and not just his social contract, constitutes Locke's natural law theory. For it is his epistemology and psychology which provide the foundation, or the explanation, of how we have the knowledge we need to enter into and to justify such a contract.

A good way to understand the Lockean view of the world would be to read *Robinson Crusoe* and *Moll Flanders* by Daniel Defoe. Today *Robinson Crusoe* is seen as a children's adventure story, but it is much more than that. Most historians of the novel consider it to be the first real attempt at novel writing. It was the first attempt at first person narrative fiction with a "novel", i.e., unknown, ending. What we see in this novel is the world according to John Locke.

Crusoe comes from a society with a social contract in force. He is shipwrecked and thereby returned to a state of nature. In this state of nature he uses his ideas to visualize what kind of living conditions he should have and then attempts to construct something that, given the materials at hand, can best approximate that ideal. He meets Friday, a person living in a true state of nature. They soon establish a set of rules or an understanding, i.e., a social contract, between them. Friday's lack of knowledge of the Christian God is seen as an illustration of Locke's views against innate ideas. And, finally, when Crusoe is rescued, the first thing he asks about is the status of his accounts, illustrating Locke's capitalism.

While Crusoe is an individual on an actual island in the middle of the sea, Moll Flanders is an individual who is cast alone in the sea of English society. She is the child of a woman in prison. In England this is her problem, but as she states at the beginning of her tale, in a neighboring country orphans such as herself would be looked after until they are capable of looking after themselves. This passage shows the still existent Catholic communal values operating in France, while protestant individualism has taken over in England. This theme of contrasting values is seen throughout the novel as Moll becomes involved in all kinds of questionable behavior. But at the end, because the circumstances were not of her making, and she only did what was available to her in order to survive, she is repentant and rewarded. Thus, though Defoe clearly illustrates the world according to Locke, one can wonder if indeed he approved of this new way of looking at the world. As we saw in Locke's politics, social contracts bestow rights on those who participate in the contract. But what of those who do not enter into a contract but are affected by that contract? Should not the contractors insure that such persons are looked after? Indeed, would not this inclusion exemplify what is meant by "community"?

DAVID HUME

Locke's views were criticized and developed. Since my purpose here is to show how certain themes developed I will not present a detailed criticism of Locke's views. Such criticisms will be implicit, and sometimes explicit, in the following discussions of how other views developed. My main concern here is to show how Locke's empiricism developed, which I shall do by looking at another British empiricist, David Hume, and at the implications of these developments, using his *An Inquiry Concerning Human Understanding*. This was written just fifty years after Locke's *Essay*.

Hume's discussion of impressions and ideas is similar to Locke's, but in his discussion of abstract ideas Hume introduces another concept which has great importance. He argues that for impressions to result in ideas we have to understand the concept of cause and effect. It is because of this relationship that we can say there is a connection between impressions and ideas, for the impressions are the cause and the ideas are the effect. A cause is not just the event that results in something else happening, it also can be understood as something with the power to bring about a specific effect[29] We shall return to Hume's discussion of causality later.

In his discussion of ideas, Hume argues that when we start to associate a number of similar things into one category we develop an abstract idea. In this, his position is not dissimilar from Locke's. But then, Hume asks, when we think of a triangle, for example, which kind of triangle do we think of? Obviously we only think of one triangle when many triangles would fit the bill. Thus, "some ideas are particular in their nature, but general in their representation." (Hume, 1967 22) And "all abstract ideas are really nothing but particular ones, consider'd in a certain light."(Hume, 1967 34)

What lets us pick the particular triangle, or the particular table, that we pick has to do with custom. There is no necessity here since more than one item would do. Any particular item can be used to stand for a class of items. We just pick the ones we are comfortable picking, since those are the ones that do the job. Thus we establish a custom. And we

practice this custom until it becomes a habit. (Hume, 1967 20-21)
We must also remember that Hume accepted Newton's view on perception. Each act of perception is separate. We unify a series of perceptions by how we associate ideas and develop customs and habits, but we do not perceive that unity. This holds not just for our observations of a series of events but of time itself. Each moment is a unique event perceived individually. We impose unity on those observations. (Hume, 1967 30-31) In this context, where each act of perception is a unique event, and where our knowledge of the existence of objects is dependent on our ability to observe them, and by our imposing continuity over a series of acts, Hume looks at the concept of causality. Hume acknowledges that the concept of causality implies the concept of necessity. To say that A caused B is to state that B could not have happened without A having happened first. When we say that we have experienced that the occurrence of A always appears to result in the occurrence of B we imply that there is some quality in A which produces B. And since we always see these two events together we infer that the connection between A and B is a necessary one. (Hume, 1967 73-78) This is so because, given our understanding of events, we know that every event must have a cause. (Hume, 1967 82) But we do not actually perceive a cause. Causality is a process we impose on a series of events. We always associate A with B. We see A occur. Then we see B occur. Given our understanding of A and B we conclude from the constant association that A causes B. Thus, causality is derived or inferred from the relationship of contiguity and is enhanced by the notions of custom and habit.

Now, since we do not actually perceive causality, and since we know that things do not happen by themselves we infer that every event has a cause. But since we cannot know the future as we have not as yet observed it, it is possible that the future will not resemble the past. It is possible that in the future we will observe A and will not observe B following A. The point here is that we have no real grounds to go beyond our observations. As Hume forcefully puts the point "Objects have no discoverable connexion together; nor is it from any other principle but custom operating upon the imagination , that we can draw any inference from the appearance of one to the existence of another." (Hume, 1967 103) So when we predict future events such predictions can only be made in a probabilistic manner. While we may have good grounds for "believing" the future will resemble the past we cannot "know" that it will since knowledge is based on observation. This is so because we "frequently meet with instances to the contrary" that "What we have found once to follow from any object, we conclude will for ever follow from it." (Hume, 1967 131) Hume defines a belief as "a lively idea related to or associated with a present impression." (Hume, 1967 96) In other words, a belief is a product of the imagination based on the combination of ideas and impressions already in the mind. The conclusion to be reached from this discussion is that ultimately all knowledge is based on probabilistic beliefs. And this probabilistic belief basis of knowledge leads Hume to a general position of skepticism.

A skeptic is a person who holds the view that we cannot be sure about anything. Or, that we really do not know anything. But, if pushed, the skeptic would have to admit that either we know that we do not know anything, in which case we do at least know something; or that we probably know things but we just cannot justify that knowledge. Hume is a skeptic of the second version. He acknowledges that since we are always observing the world and are receiving visual impressions, we have knowledge. But this knowledge of the world is not about the things in the world but about the impressions we have of them. Since all the connections we make between our observations, including our knowledge of cause and effect, are based on custom and habit, and because we do not know that the future will resemble the past, we have no way of justifying our knowledge claims. (Hume, 1967 186-189)

An excellent definition of skepticism comes from Bertrand Russell, a 20th century British philosopher working in the tradition of Hume.

> The scepticism I advocate amounts to only this (1) that when the experts are agreed, the opposite position cannot be held to be certain; (2) that when they are not agreed, no opinion can be regarded as certain by a non-expert; and (3) that when they all hold that no sufficient grounds for a positive opinion exist, the ordinary man would do well to suspend his judgment.[30]

But we must act and we must assume certain things are true. A major implication of skepticism is that we must separate reason from our senses. We can reason, and logic stands on its own. We reason about the impressions in our minds. But a chain of reasoning can be developed in such a way that loses touch with its starting point. We will return to this point later.

There are two more points that need to be made about Hume. The first has to do with his view of persons. When we observe ourselves we run into the same problems that we run into when we observe anything else. We observe a series of impressions. But any continuity of ourselves is imposed on those impressions by custom and habit. Thus our knowledge of ourselves is as flimsy as our knowledge of anything else. Personal identity "is merely a quality which we attribute to them (perceptions), because of the union of their ideas in the imagination, when we reflect upon them." (Hume, 1967 260) So I not only cannot justify my knowledge claims about the world, I also cannot justify my knowledge claims about myself. Of course, I "know" who I am. I just cannot prove it.

The last point to be discussed here is Hume's views on values. The theme of book two of the *Treatise* is about how the passions are the motivators of action. It is in this context that Hume's discussion of values takes place. Given Hume's views on perception we know that our knowledge comes from impressions. We then reason about those impressions. But since reason alone can have no influence on human action (Hume, 1967 413-415), values cannot be derived from reason. (Hume, 1967 457) And since reason is the determining factor in deciding if a knowledge claim is true or false, reason cannot be used to determine the truth or falsity of value claims. (Hume, 1967 458) The implication of this point is to separate fact from value.

A good way to understand.....the world according.....to Hume....is to read.....*Tristram Shandy* by Laurence Sterne.....This book is written.....in short phrases.....like this....to reflect.....Hume's views on perception......Each perception.....or each thought.....is a separate event....with no necessary connection. Chapters can be in the wrong order.....or they may be in the correct order but......they can be numbered incorrectly. The book is hilarious.....if at times.....difficult to read.

Let us take a look at where we are. We saw that Locke developed an individualistic ethic and an individualistic epistemology which supported the individualistic ethic. And, since his ethical views were based on his understanding of the natural order of things, or of man's place in the state of nature, we see Locke's position as a natural law position. Then Hume took Locke's individualistic empiricism to its limits. And by doing so he showed that this approach to epistemology cannot do the job Locke wanted done. This individualistic epistemology is not able to offer support for Locke's social contract. Indeed, since Hume's position leads to a form of skepticism, this individualistic approach to empiricism cannot provide a foundation to Newtonian physics either.

What has happened over the years since Locke and Hume wrote

is that Hume has prevailed in many ways. Because of his separation of fact from value it has been easy to maintain Lockean views on ethics and politics while trying to come to grips with Hume's arguments on the foundations of knowledge. But developing this combination has undermined the natural law status of Locke's position since it no longer has an epistemological foundation. Indeed, one can characterize the modern era as a fragmented one in which views in different areas exist independently with no attempt being made to try to show how epistemology should be used to offer a foundation to an ethical theory.

EMPIRICISM IN THE 20TH CENTURY

While the Lockean puritanical capitalist democratic minimalist state has become the dominant ethical and political ideology in the western world, epistemologists have been trying to come to grips with Humean skepticism. Due to the great success of Newtonian science, not just in its ability to explain the workings of the universe, but also in the technological developments that became possible because of those theoretical accomplishments, the view of science associated with Locke and Hume that developed in the light of Newton's work became the dominant philosophy of science from the 18th century to the present day.

This success was spurred by the development of Darwinian biology, which gave us a new way of looking at the place of humanity in the world, and, in the 20th century, the Theory of Relativity and quantum mechanics, the combination of which seemed to offer solutions to problems that classical Newtonian theory could not solve. Initially Newtonian theory was seen as being a special case of relativity theory, though, as we shall see later, this is not now the case. But the developments in relativity theory and quantum mechanics were seen by many as the triumph of science. Not only could we explain the workings of the common sense objects in the world but now we also had explanations for an understanding of our place in the universe.

Epistemologists, and philosophers of science, who are epistemological specialists, are still trying to develop an empiricist foundation for science. This is so because it appears clear that scientific knowledge is attained by empirical means through the use of experimentation.

I will now set forth what Kuhn would call a textbook presentation of a Humean approach to the philosophy of science as it has developed through the 20th century.

When one thinks of science, just what is included in such a thought? Most people think of science as a systematic way of gathering knowledge. The knowledge that is gathered in a scientific manner can be said to be objective, value-free, and once shown to be true it will always be true. By "objective" we mean something that is known independently of any one person's concerns. When something can be shown to be objective it has been shown to be true for everyone. By "value-free" we mean that regardless of what a scientist believed before beginning an investigation, the findings must speak for themselves and one's personal views cannot interfere with the scientific endeavor. Indeed, because of the objective nature of scientific investigation, a scientist's own values are capable of being eliminated from consideration. And once something can be scientifically demonstrated as true, that fact must always be regarded as true since the nature of truth does not change.

Now, if further asked what science is, most people would say that science explains things. For example, we know that if we drop something it will fall, but when asked why it falls we might not be able to give the answer. Science, by investigating the nature of gravity, is able to explain why the dropped object falls. Or we know that when someone is sick you call the doctor. And when the doctor properly diagnoses what is wrong, she will prescribe a medicine that will cure the patient. You don't know why the medicine cured the patient, but the doctor will be able to explain to you exactly what the disease is, what the medicine does and why the medicine does what it does.

Let us look more closely at the nature of an explanation. We shall begin with something basic. Why does a chair, which weighs only a couple of kilograms, hold up a person who weighs fifty times as much? Someone might say it is because of the spirits that live in the chair. The spirits of the chair give the chair its properties.

Now, what would be your response to such a comment? The first thing you might want is some kind of definition. Just what is meant by a spirit? Let us say that the person who believes this says that a spirit is intangible and invisible, that is it has no substance and it can't be seen, but it is there, just the way a poison gas that can't be seen or tasted can kill someone. The spirit believer says that he knows the spirit must be in each chair because the chair can hold so much weight. At this point you agree that he knows it is there because of the consequences, just like he knows the poison is there. But, you say, there is a difference. The poison can be detected. Once the symptoms have been described, the poison can be tested for. But can we test for the chair spirit? Can we cut apart the chair and find some evidence of a spirit in the chair? If this cannot be done it no longer makes sense to talk about chair spirits.

Before continuing on with whether or not we can find a chair spirit we need to take a detour into the philosophy of language, for it becomes very important to be clear on what we are talking about and how our language is related to what we are looking for.

Language is made up of syntax, semantics and pragmatics. Syntax is about the structural aspects of language, for example, the fact that English sentences have a subject and a predicate; semantics is about meaning; and pragmatics has to do with contextual usage. For example, take the sentence "the grass is green." It is syntactically well formed; we know what the words in the sentence mean; i.e., we know what they stand for; and we know where to look to see if this sentence is in fact true.

However we had a problem with the claim about the chair spirit for a number of reasons. First, we may not have been sure we understood the sentence. Second, even if we did understand it we might not be sure as to what a spirit would look like. And finally, we were unable to find a situation where we could discover if the statement was true. Thus we say that the statement about the chair spirit could not be verified. And therefore the statement has no meaning. Finding the conditions under which a statement can be determined to be true are associated with meaning or semantics.

Now let us look at a general claim made in logical language. This view of putting claims in logical form to see if truth values can be applied to them comes from Bertrand Russell's theory of descriptions[31]. Let us say that something exists and this thing has certain properties. We say that X exists and has properties a, b, c and d. To give this form some substance let us say that unicorns exist and that they are white, one-horned, good to people and good for the environment. Let us also assume that we know what a unicorn is and that we would recognize one if we found it. But then we search and search but do not find any. Thus the claims about unicorns are false.

Then say that someone claims that unicorns are black, not white. This claim will also be false. So the question becomes how two opposite claims can be made about the same thing. In other words, how can something be both one thing and its opposite at the same time? The answer, of course, is that it cannot. So, what are our options? We can say that since there are no unicorns, all claims about unicorns are false. Or we can say that since there are no unicorns, claims about them are not semantically meaningful. This is another way of saying that since claims about unicorns are not verifiable they are meaningless even though they appear to be meaningful. Or we can say that since there are no such things, claims about them are not syntactically or semantically well formed. That is, we really cannot make claims about them. This response to Russell is influenced by P. F. Strawson's response "On Referring"[32].

Another example would be "The subway car gave birth to twins". While this sentence appears to be well formed, it is in fact nonsense, because subway cars are not the kinds of things that give birth. This is an example of a category mistake, since we are predicating something belonging to one category—things that give birth—onto another incompatible category—subway cars.

In all cases there is a strong connection between what is said, what can be said, and what we discover to exist. If claims have no semantic connection or correspondence with things in the world, they are not verifiable because they are not syntactically or semantically meaningful. This connecting of language with observation with regard to truth claims is known as the semantic theory of truth. It is also known as the principle of verification, where, for a sentence to be meaningful, one must have some conception of how to demonstrate the truth or falsity of that sentence. Thus, on an empiricist view of science, one must have a theory of meaning before one can undertake any investigation, and one must be able to state under what conditions one can find the appropriate data so that the meaningful sentence can be demonstrated to be true or false. Thus meaning and truth are tied together.

Before we go on, let us take a closer look at what was we have just discussed. We first asked for a definition of something. What was meant by the terms that were introduced to the discussion? Then, once everyone was clear about that definition, some kind of evidence was asked for. This evidence was asked for in two ways. First we looked for the evidence in a positive way. Can we directly observe this evidence? Can we directly observe the chair spirit? As we saw, we couldn't do this because of the way in which the spirit was defined. Then we looked for evidence by implication. In the case of the poison we were able to reason back from the effects of the poison. Then we could look for the poison. But with the chair spirit this was not possible. Even when we saw the effects of the spirit we were not able to demonstrate that it was really there. When this happens—when the spirit cannot be identified either way—we must conclude that the hypothesis about the chair spirit will not lead us to any conclusion and we must look for another explanation of why chairs can do what they do.

POSITIVISM

So, how are we to find such an explanation? First we must be clear on what we mean by a chair. We must also be clear on what we want to know. We can define a chair as an object made out of various materials such as wood and metal, which has a general shape and which is used for the activity we call sitting.

Once we are clear as to what we are studying, we can begin to observe how chairs are used, how they are made and how different manufacturing techniques and materials can affect the capabilities of the chair. We can see that, for example, metal chairs can support more weight than wood chairs can, that hard wood chairs can support more weight than soft wood chairs and that certain shapes of chairs can support more weight than other shapes when both chairs are made out of the same materials.

The next step in our investigation would be to look into the properties of the materials. It might be important to know what some of the properties of the various woods and metals are. It might also be important as to why the different shapes of chairs work so differently. This is where things get interesting. We have lots of observed information or data, but what does it all mean and how does it help us to explain why chairs do what they do?

According to the view of science under discussion, explanations can be made by using known laws of nature and by **deducing** specific conditions from the laws. A **law of nature** is a statement which is general or universal in nature. For example, consider the law of gravity which says that if something is dropped, it will fall. This is always the case, unless some specific condition is stated, such as that something will not fall if dropped in space where there is no gravity. When we deduce something we start with a general statement and go to a specific statement. An example of a deduction is:

> When dropped, all things fall
> The book was dropped
> Therefore the book fell.

What such deductive reasoning does is to show that a specific object belongs to a class or category of objects. The technical term is **argument**. An argument present reasons for a point of view. The statements in an argument are called **premises** and the result is the **conclusion**. When the conclusion of an argument is used in a more general way, such as a background premise in a more general argument, it is called a **proposition**. **Logic** can be defined as the science of reasoning and states the rules which allow us to make deductions. **Deduction** is a form of logic. Later in this chapter we will meet another form of logic called **induction**. Now, let us get back to explanations. These take the same form as the deduction. For example we can say that the chair I am sitting on is capable of holding a person weighing 200 kilograms. We can explain this by stating that all chairs that are made the way this chair is made can support over 200 kilograms. We know that this chair is made the same as the other chairs. Therefore, we know that this chair can hold 200 kilograms. And this explanation is given more strength because we have also investigated the properties of the materials that were used in manufacturing the chair. These investigations told us about the properties of wood and metal so we have an understanding of why metal is stronger than wood.

But, one might say, nothing here has really been explained. All that has been done is to categorize something. We know what a chair is and we know that a chair will support a lot of weight. To then say that this chair belongs to the category of chairs doesn't tell us anything. What we want to know is why chairs can hold the amount of weight they do.

To answer this question we must be able to talk about the properties of the materials that are used in chair manufacture and we must be able to talk about what happens when different shapes are used. In order to do these things, we must go beyond the realm of the directly observable data and even beyond the realm of learning from logical inference. We must go into the realm of unobservable data. That is, in order to explain observable phenomena, we have to **postulate** entities or forces we cannot directly observe. To postulate something is to assume that it is there. We say that such and such must exist, otherwise the object in question cannot do what we observe it to do.

When we postulate things, we don't just use our imagination, although imagination can certainly be used. Mainly, though, we postulate entities that we understand or that we believe to exist from other scientific investigations.

Let us leave chairs for a moment and take a look at how unobservable entities enter into an explanation. Let us begin with a common concept—causality. We think we know what it means when we say that something caused something else. But can we really explain it? Can we really explain what we mean when we say that thunder is caused by lightning? Or that a lack of vitamin C causes scurvy? Let us look at these examples in turn. Remember, Hume believed that causality was a necessary connection but that the actual cause could not be observed and was explained in terms of constant conjunction.

What does it mean to say that lightning causes thunder? We hear thunder after we see lightning. We learn to associate the two things. Whenever we see lightning we can always say that we know we will hear thunder shortly thereafter. If we don't hear thunder then we say it is because the lightning is too far away for the sound of the thunder to reach us. But we know, because we saw the lightning, there must be thunder somewhere.

We don't see or hear causes. We see or hear (we sense) the lightning and thunder. Because we come to associate the two, we begin to say that you can't have one without the other. Then we say that because of one thing happening, the other thing must happen. Then we say that the second thing—the thunder—is a result of the first thing—the lightning—occurring.

But this is still not enough. We really don't know if lightning can occur without thunder following. Nor do we really know if thunder can occur without lightning first occurring. In order to answer these questions we must inquire into the nature of lightning and thunder. That is, we must try to discover the natures of lightning and thunder.

Upon investigation, we discover that lightning is a form of electricity. Of course the nature of electricity is another subject, but let us, for the moment, assume we have some idea as to what electricity is. We know from our other researches into the nature of electricity that an electrical charge has a great deal of force or energy behind it. In our laboratory, we set up an experiment. We get a large airtight jar, something like a large fish tank or terrarium and put air in it. We then introduce an electrical charge—lightning—into the tank so we can observe what effect it will have on the air. The process is photographed so whatever occurs can be carefully studied later. The photos show us that the electricity appeared to burn the air. Masses of air were heated and the heat caused the air to expand very quickly. This rapid expansion of masses of air is what we hear as thunder. These sounds could be detected by a sensitive sound meter. So now we know that lighting causes thunder and we know why.

To put this explanation into deductive form should be easy. We find our law of nature: lightning causes thunder. We observe lightning, so we can conclude that thunder will occur. But as soon as we state our law of nature we must define all the key terms in that law. Thus we must first state what lightning is, what thunder is, and under what conditions they occur. Then we add the conditions which exist at the time of the instance we want to explain. Then we add the next parts of the explanation. The whole explanation will then look something like this:

> Whenever lightning is seen, thunder will follow.
> Lightning is an electrical charge.
> When an electrical charge is put through the air, air masses expand
> This expansion of air is noisy.
> Lightning was just seen.
> Therefore thunder will shortly be heard.

Now let us look at how the lack of vitamin C causes scurvy. This is not so clear cut. The story of the discovery goes that sailors who did not have access to fresh foods on long journeys came down with scurvy. By a process of trial and error it was discovered that when the sailors ate foods with vitamin C they were quickly cured. So, to prevent scurvy, all ships coming from England were required to carry limes on board for the sailors.

One of the difficulties in determining the cause of scurvy was that not everyone who did not get vitamin C got scurvy. Or at least they didn't get it within the same time frame. This discrepancy led to another factor that was to be included in the nature of an explanation. This factor was a distinction between two kinds of conditions which must be present if one event is to cause another. These are called necessary and sufficient conditions. A necessary condition is a condition or a set of circumstances which must obtain if the expected result is to happen. But sometimes the necessary condition needs help. If the necessary condition isn't enough to do the job, any other conditions that are needed to make the necessary condition work are called sufficient conditions. So someone who doesn't get a proper dose of vitamin C may not get scurvy right away because his overall health may be better than his mates' health, or because his metabolism works differently so that his body still retains some of the vitamin C he ate before he left on his journey, and so on.

The important point here is that, just like with the thunder and lightning example, in order to explain one thing, you have to know all kinds of other things. Thus knowing what to know, and what kinds of things to look for is a very important part of the scientific enterprise.

Now that we have some idea as what a **cause** is, it is important not to confuse a cause with a **correlation**. This is when two events or things appear together and it appears that one caused the other. However, on closer inspection one will, hopefully, see that the two items in question are both caused by something else. Explanations by correlation, as opposed to explanations by cause, are unfortunately quite common. They appear most frequently in explanations of various illnesses or behavioral patterns.

Now we return to our chair. The remaining questions regarding the nature of chairs have to do with understanding the properties of the materials used in making chairs and in understanding how the different shapes can effect how the chairs work.

Upon investigation we learn that different woods have different properties. Some woods are harder than others and can support more weight. But some soft woods can flex and thereby hold more weight than might at first be believed. As a result of experimenting on wood scientists start to talk about different properties in more abstract terms. We start to hear such terms as "stress" and "structure" and "support". A chair can support weight because the materials used in its construction create a structure which can accept certain stresses and can thereby support the weight.

This last sentence doesn't appear to say anything. But in fact it says a great deal once we know how those key terms are being used. We can't see stresses but we can see how different structures can handle different amounts of weight. This is when all materials are the same. The fact that these different shapes work differently is said to be due to the stresses that each shape can handle. We can't see stress, but we can use the term to name an effect of changing the shape of a chair. We can then define stress in terms of how much weight a certain shape can hold before breaking. So "stress" becomes understood in functional terms. But in order to properly understand how stress functions we must further understand the nature of the material that the chair is built with.

If you have studied matter in your natural science class you will know something about atomic theory. I will briefly discuss this, then I will explain what a theory is according to this view of science.

According to atomic theory materials such as wood and metal, which appear to be solid, are in fact made of countless numbers of atoms, which form into molecules. These molecules come together and are held in place by what has been called the **strong nuclear force**. The term "nuclear" is used because atoms are believed to be made up of a centre or a nucleus and various electrically charged particles called electrons. Atoms containing different numbers of electrons have different properties but all atoms have one nucleus, hence the term "nuclear". Atoms combine to form molecules. The properties of the material formed by the combining of molecules are determined by the kinds of atoms that make up those molecules. Atoms with more electrons produce materials denser or stronger materials than those formed by atoms with fewer electrons. So though the chair you are sitting on looks like a solid object, it is really made up of a swarm of countless numbers of atoms which are held together by the force generated by their motion. So, not only is the chair not solid, it is also constantly in motion. Now, atoms and molecules cannot be directly observed. When the concept of atoms was first postulated, atoms could not even be indirectly observed. So how could such entities come to be postulated? In order to answer this question we will have to understand what a theory is.

We have already had some discussion of theories in the previous chapter and so we know there is more than one view of what a theory is. All views agree that a theory is a form of scientific explanation which uses postulated unobservable entities to explain directly observable phenomena. These entities don't just come from nowhere. Their properties reflect the way in which scientists already understand the behavior of the object in question, and the postulated entities are usually given properties which reflect the general knowledge that scientists take with them to their specific tasks. The different views of theories disagree most on the nature and status of these entities. In this chapter we will just look at views developed in the Humean positivist tradition. Also, there is a long tradition which distinguishes illusion from reality. Scientists know that in order to explain what we see we often must go beyond appearances to see what the thing is really like.

The model of what an atom would actually look like was derived from the solar system. The solar system has a number of planets circling round the sun in orbits which are maintained by gravity. The gravitational force is created by the size of the planets and their distance from each other. Since the atom was conceived of as a nucleus with electrons, the solar system provided the basis for depicting what an atom would look like. So postulated entities and their properties are based on knowledge that scientists already have.

The fact that unobservable entities have come to play such a significant role in scientific explanations has caused problems for scientists. If science is to be objective and if scientific knowledge is to be demonstrable then the goal of science should be to either eliminate the need for all unobservable entities or for scientists to be able to show that, at least indirectly, there is good reason to suppose these postulated, unobservable entities really exist. Such entities are shown to exist by implication. This method was used to show that a colorless, odorless poison was used to kill someone. We already know that there is such a poison. So when it has been suspected of use, we need a test to show that the symptoms induced by the poison are present. If they are present, it is safe to conclude that the poison was in fact used. This hold true for atoms also. For a good discussion of these issues see Carl G. Hempel "The Theoretician's Dilemma: A study in the Logic of Theory Construction."[33]

If metals and woods are made of certain kinds of atoms then the woods or metals should behave in certain ways. This is where the fun begins. We need to set up an **experiment** to see if our **hypothesis** is correct. An experiment is a kind of test to see if our understanding of the object in question is correct. We set up the experiment and make a **prediction** as to its outcome. If the experiment turns out the way we predicted we say that we have gained new knowledge about the object. If the experiment does not come out as predicted, on this view of science, we will simply go back to the drawing board and try to come up with either new experiments which will hopefully show us what we want to know, or we must revise our hypothesis regarding the nature of the object we are investigating.

A hypothesis is a kind of educated guess regarding what is being investigated. Most of you have heard the term "hypothetical question". This is a question concerning a set of circumstances which could occur even if they have not as yet actually occurred. A hypothesis is an educated guess about the possible characteristics of the object in question. These characteristics are regarded as hypothetical because we cannot directly observe them and because we are still investigating them. Once we complete our experiments and learn that our guesses were correct, we no longer call such claims hypothetical. But, even though our experiments turned out as we predicted based on our hypothesis, because we are still basing our knowledge of the objects in question on the use of unobservable, postulated entities, such knowledge must be, on this view of science, called **theoretical knowledge**.

Now let us look at what a theoretical explanation of why a chair can support so much weight would look like. From our investigations we know that the wood or metal that is used in the manufacture of the chair has a certain atomic structure. Because of this atomic structure the wood or metal is capable of supporting a certain amount of weight. We know from our researches that additional stress factors come into play when the wood or metal is formed in certain configurations. So pieces of wood that would normally support, say, three or four times their weight by themselves can now support many times that weight when put into certain configurations because the individual parts in the configuration support each other thereby creating a whole new item that has powers greater than the sum of its individual parts.

With this background information we return to the deductive explanation presented above which starts with the general statement that all chairs are able to support many times their weight. That explanation still holds. The theoretical knowledge is used to support that explanation. When the term "chair" is used in the explanation, the theoretical information we have learned about chairs and the materials used to make them is understood as part of the meaning of the word. Thus, when the statement "All chairs support many times their weight" is used in the explanation, we are really saying "All chairs made of wood or metal which have specific atomic structures and are capable of specific stresses and which are manufactured in specified ways so that they have greater stress factors can support many times their weight."

This is the basic view of science known as **positivism**, so named because it is a view based on positive evidence for a claim as being the primary factor in gaining a scientific understanding of natural phenomena. The view presented here is just a sketch: a complete discussion of this view of science would fill a short book of its own. But here are some references to help fill out this view.

The principle of verification has a long history. In the 20th century the background can be found in Ludwig Wittgenstein and the Vienna Circle, a group of philosophers who tried to develop a contemporary empiricist philosophy of science through the 1920s and 1930s, including Rudolf Carnap and their British expositor A.J. Ayer.[34]

Before we leave positivism a couple of things need to be mentioned. There are two very important distinctions in everyday use because of the influence of positivism. And there are some serious problems with this account of science. The two distinctions are between **fact and value** and between **pure and applied science**. The distinction between fact and value seems to reflect common sense. After all, whether I like something or not has no bearing on what it is. It is a fact that the pass was intercepted. It is my value judgment, depending on which team I am rooting for, as to whether I approve or disapprove of the interception. In my case, since I am not a sports fan and I don't care who wins, I will always approve of a good play.

This is a much more complex distinction than one that is simply used to evaluate daily activities. It is a fact that science learns about the world. But how that knowledge is used is a different story. For example, science learns about the nature of electricity and how to use it. We may or may not decide to place a value on this knowledge. And if we do place a value on it, we can do so in many ways. We can use such knowledge for entertainment systems or for weapons systems. And so the fact/value distinction actually leads to the pure/applied science distinction.

Pure scientists can work on whatever interests them in the hope of discovering laws of nature or at least of coming to understand some of the complex data we encounter in our environment. But how this knowledge is to be used is of no direct interest to the pure scientist. Decisions regarding the application of this knowledge are not up to her, but are open to anyone in a position to make and act upon them. The consequences of these distinctions are that a technology industry has developed totally independently of the research industry. Frequently this is not a problem since many of the conveniences we have are a result of applying the findings of science to the practical sphere. A negative consequence, though, is that the scientists who discovered the relevant knowledge become divorced from inventions that use that knowledge. This can result in either inappropriate or incomplete uses of the knowledge. Another problem relates to correlational explanations. Because we often think certain ways about certain things, i.e., we believe before we undertake an investigation that A causes B, so that when we find the two things occurring together, we, often too hastily, conclude that A in fact does cause B. If we had investigated more closely, we would have seen that both A and B are caused by something else. Such conclusions are often arrived at in medical or social research. So, while these two distinctions have had a long and major influence on scientific thinking, these distinctions pose problems, and, in recent years, have come under strong attack. Now we must take a look at the implications of this view of science for both the concept of a person—the theory of psychology that developed using this method—and for ethical theory.

PSYCHOLOGY

One of the implications of this view of science is how it has been used in the social sciences. The social sciences, especially psychology, have been trying to attain scientific respectability. One way that is seen to attain this is to present findings in some empirically quantifiable manner. In sociology and economics this is done with the use of statistics. In psychology it is done by studying only overt behavior, and by either denying that such things as emotions and feelings exist or by saying that they exist but are irrelevant to the study of psychology, or that they are the products of behavior. This approach to psychology is called, obviously, behaviorism. This view began at the end of the nineteenth century with the work of Pavlov and continued into the 20th century in the work of Watson and Skinner.

My purpose here is not to present an outline of this view of psychology but to develop a chain of reasoning that led to the development of this view of psychology. Pavlov's original research was in trying to understand the workings of the digestive system.[35]

While performing experiments on the digestive processes of animals Pavlov noted certain behavioral patterns in his experimental animals. One such pattern was that the sound of the experimenter's footsteps coming towards the animal activated its salivary response. Pavlov performed a variety of experiments on animals including varying the stimulation to the animals and then measuring the saliva outputs. He then correlated the relationship between the strength of the stimulus and the salivary response. For example, Pavlov would bring food to a dog and at the same time introduce another factor such as a tuning fork. After a number of such performances, Pavlov would just ring the tuning fork but would produce no food. This experiment was varied by changing the pitch of the tuning fork and by changing how many times the fork was rung before the food was omitted. The animals, upon hearing the tuning fork, would salivate in anticipation of the food, even though no food was brought. The conclusion that Pavlov drew from these experiments was that the animals learned to associate the secondary stimulus—the tuning fork—with the primary stimulus—the food—and would therefore respond to the secondary stimulus if even if the food were not presented.

Pavlov could have used Lockean or Humean language to explain the associations or learning processes he observed. But since Pavlov was a biologist he used biological language to explain these behavioral patterns, which he understood in neurological terms. Thus he considered the production of saliva at the introduction of food or other stimulus as a reflex action. Such a response to food is an unlearned reflex. But the introduction of the secondary factor involved learning on the part of the animal. Thus Pavlov called the salivary response to the tuning fork a learned or conditioned reflex.

We are all familiar with reflexes. When a doctor performs a physical exam one of the things she does is hit the patient lightly just below the knee with a hammer. If all is well with the nerves and muscles, the knee will jerk upwards. The hitting of the knee is the stimulus and the jerking of the leg is the response. In this situation, the person has no control over what happens. The process is completely neurological. Now when doctors repeatedly test patients, the patient learns to anticipate what the doctor is going to do. When the patient has been asked to cover his eyes and is hit on the knee his leg will jerk up. Sometimes the patient's knee will jerk up without being hit because the patient has anticipated the blow. In other words, the patient has made an association between the situation and what usually happens in that situation. This behavior is a learned or conditioned response, in much the same way that the dog responded to the tuning fork.

A conditioned reflex is defined as a learned behavioral pattern based on a history of an association between a stimulus or cause and a response or effect. The results of Pavlov's experiments led to the view that such procedures could be generalized and that all behavior, whether of animals or of humans, could be explained by using this stimulus-response model and that complex behavior patterns could be broken down in laboratories. In other words, the study of behavior could be put on a scientific basis and could be studied in a laboratory just the way biology can be studied. Carefully controlled experiments could be developed to show how people learn their behavioral patterns, then the results from such experiments could be generalized into a comprehensive theory of human learning and a complete picture of human behavior would hopefully emerge from this process. Thus, according to Pavlov, all human behavior, no matter how complex or no matter how creative it appears, no matter what we do or how we do it, is all based on the same principles as the dog who learned to salivate when it heard the tuning fork in anticipation of being brought its dinner.

This line of thought was continued by John Watson[36]. He began working with children at a psychiatric centre in Baltimore. He would observe newborn infants' reflex and emotional reactions. Behaviors such as sneezing, yawning and coughing were reflex behaviors. Reactions such as fear, rage and love were classified as emotions. Watson's goal was to show that these so-called emotional responses were simply learned responses to specific stimuli. He found that fear, for example, would be brought about by a sudden noise or a sudden loss of support. Rage would be brought about by sudden restraint, and love would be brought about by stroking or fondling.

Watson then used these results to attack the notion of innate

Natural Law, Science, and the Social Construction of Reality 85

fears. The infants he worked with showed no innate fears of fire or dark or of animals. All such fears, Watson concluded, were learned. In 1919 Watson undertook to see whether or not a fear could be conditioned in a human infant under controlled circumstances. His subject was eleven month old Albert B. or "Little Albert" and this experiment became one of the best known experiments in psychology.

Albert B. did not appear to have any fears except one. He reacted badly to loud noises. So Watson set up an experiment to use this fear to teach Little Albert other fears. Watson introduced a rabbit to Albert and then made a loud noise. Soon Albert started associating the rabbit, which he had not been afraid of, with the noise, which he was afraid of. Soon he began to exhibit fear of the rabbit. Then this fear became generalized. He started to fear all animals, men with beards, and fur coats. At this time Albert's mother took him from the hospital and no follow-up work could be done. But this experiment received wide discussion. Watson claimed it proved his thesis that all human behaviors, even emotions, are learned.

This line of thought was developed further by B.F. Skinner[37]. His work is built on the concept of the conditioned reflex and of the behaviorist view of learning. But he also realized that much behavior is goal oriented. We do certain things in order to achieve other things and in so doing we act on or operate on our environment.

Skinner found that when placed in a situation, in order to learn their way about, laboratory rats begin making what appeared to be arbitrary responses. He started to reward certain of these responses, thereby reinforcing them. Since the animal was operating on its environment, and since Skinner was modifying that behavior, he called this form of conditioning **operant conditioning**.

Skinner used this approach to attempt to explain human behavior as well. He went on to explain phenomena such as free will and self-consciousness as illusions, calling them nothing more than learned responses.

So, when we apply a strict empiricist methodology to the study of human behavior we must study only those phenomena which can be observed. Anything which cannot be observed becomes understood as either not existing at all or as a by-product of what can be observed.

ETHICAL THEORY

As we saw in our discussion of Hume, the passions became the basis for ethics, and ethics became separated from knowledge. Yet Hume wrote on ethics. He discussed all the relevant issues of ethics such as virtue and justice. But, like a good empiricist, Hume was not presenting a theory of morality—a prescription of how to act or why one should act in a certain way. Hume's *An Enquiry Concerning the Principles of Morals* can be seen as a descriptive analysis of the operating moral principles at Hume's time. Hume, and also Bentham and Mill, who will be discussed below, all spoke of the science of morals. By this they meant that they were doing empirical science by investigating the principles in use at the time and would thereby discover what morality was about. In this, these philosophers were following what they understood as the scientific method developed by Newton. One observes and analyzes. The "science of morals" is about discovering the hows and whys of moral reasoning, not about creating a moral theory. But, of course, in providing such an analysis, Hume, and Bentham and Mill, did indeed present the basis of a moral theory. Thus, by separating fact from value, by disconnecting moral values from a society's knowledge base, empiricism created a new subject in which the scientific method was used to investigate how and why people acted morally.

HUME

While it would be incorrect to say that Hume had answers to all the questions, two themes run through his section on principles of morals. One is that there is no foundation or ultimate principle to morality and the second is that we learn our moral principles through custom and habit—through participating in our society and through education.

Morality is seen to be about human happiness. Justice is needed to insure human happiness, as is a government to protect people.

> Thus we seem, upon the whole, to have attained a knowledge of the force of that principle here insisted upon, and can determine what degree of esteem or moral approbation may result from reflections on public interest and utility.[38]

The principle of utility becomes the basis for justice.

> In common life, we may observe, that the circumstance of utility is always appealed to; nor is it supposed, that a greater eulogy can be given to any man, than to display his usefulness to the public, and enumerate the services, which he has performed to mankind and society (Hume 259)

Like all good British empiricists of the day he believed that everything began with the individual, but unlike other empiricists he not believe that we began our moral questions from the standpoint of self-love which

> Is a principle in human nature of such extensive energy, and in the interest of each individual is, in general, so closely connected with that of the community, that those philosophers were excusable, who fancied that all our concern for the public might be resolved into a concern for our own happiness and preservation.

For we find that private concerns can be at odds with public concerns.

> We surely take into consideration the happiness and misery of others, in weighing the several motives of action, and incline to the former, where no private regards draw us to seek our own promotion or advantage by the injury of our fellow creatures. And if the principles of humanity are capable, in many instances, of influencing our actions, they must, at all times, have some authority over our sentiments, and give us a general approbation of what is useful to society, and blame of what is dangerous or pernicious (Hume 264-265).

The overall principle that Hume sees as fulfilling this role is that of **utility**. Clearly, Hume is concerned with actions and their consequences. Reason clearly plays a large part in Hume's thinking. But ultimately everything is about an action's usefulness for bringing about some good for society. This usefulness overcomes self-interest, especially when self-interest is in conflict with the public interest or the public good.

So while the passions lead us to act, reason, in the service of usefulness to the common good, keeps us from acting against that good.

Hume did not greatly elaborate on the principle. Since he was analyzing how people in fact reasoned about morality he knew that his audience understood the principle of utility, so he did not have to elaborate on it. It would seem that the principle of utility was an acceptable operating principle in British society and all Hume had to do was show how it operated.

BENTHAM

But that was not enough. The principle needed both elaboration and defense. These tasks were undertaken by the next generation of British empiricists, Jeremy Bentham, whose life overlapped Hume's, and Bentham's protégé, John Stuart Mill. Bentham was concerned with elucidating the principle of utility and show how it forms the basis of not only morality but also of legality, since legality should be based on morality.

Like all British empiricists of his day Bentham begins by discussing the role of individual in relation to the state or community. His position is that "The community is a fictitious body, composed of the individual persons who are considered as constituting as it were its members. The interest of the community then is, what?—the sum of the interests of the several members who compose it."[39]

But the main part of his work is to explain and analyze the principle of utility, which is the "principle which approves or disapproves of every action whatsoever, according to the tendency which it appears to have to augment or diminish the happiness of the party whose interest is in question..." (Bentham 319)

The principle of utility is all about maximizing pleasure and avoiding pain. The title of chapter three of his work is "Of the Four Sanctions or Sources of Pain or Pleasure." These four sources are "the physical, the political, the moral, and the religious:..." (Bentham). These are the sources from which pleasure and pain flow. The purpose of moral theory and of legislation is to understand these sources so that principles and legislation can be enacted or enforced to maximize pleasure and avoid pain.

Bentham then goes on to show how we can make choices. After all, when choosing between actions we must choose which action will yield the greater pleasure. So Bentham develops a method of measuring pleasures and pains. By applying this schema we can scientifically decide which actions will yield the greatest pleasures. We must look at intensity, duration, certainty and the propinquity of the pleasure.

So we want to act in a manner that will yield the most intense and longest-lasting pleasure—one we believe will result in obtaining this pleasure—one in which the results are near at hand.

Now Bentham is aware that our actions affect other people, for that is ultimately what moral theory is about: how our pursuits of pleasure affect other people. The main way in which the consequences of our actions can be measured in this regard is through our intention. Actions have consequences and these consequences are understood in terms of the agent's motives and intentions.

For example, let us suppose that shooting guns gives me great pleasure. Scaring people gives me great pleasure. I know that I must not harm other people since that will interfere with their pursuits of pleasure. Indeed, insuring that one person does not harm another is a main principle in the utilitarian basis of legislation. The role of the state is to protect the individual citizens. One person may not harm another in the pursuit of happiness. Harming another would be a negative on Bentham's scale of measurement.

But I take my shotgun to school and shoot it off in class. I aim at the ceiling since I don't want to harm anyone. My intent is to have some fun without causing harm. But some debris falls on a student and harms him. I am charged and taken to court. If I had intended to harm the student I would have been charged with assault or even with attempted murder, but since the injury was incidental— it was not intentional— I am charged with something less serious. My action still resulted in negative consequences for which I am responsible, but these consequences are to be understood in terms of what I set out to do and why I set out to do it. The important point for Bentham is that when we act we should be aware of the possible consequences, since full awareness— the use of reason— is part of the moral decision-making process. The pursuit of pleasure in moral terms must be seen as a rational pursuit. It is the use of rationality in the pursuit of pleasure that makes the pursuit a moral enterprise.

MILL

And now we turn to John Stuart Mill whose work can be seen as an elaboration and defense of both Bentham's work in particular and of the principle of utility in general.

Mill calls the principle of utility the "greatest happiness principle"[40] since according to the principle "actions are right in proportion as they tend to promote happiness, wrong as they tend to produce the reverse of happiness." (Mill 347) Happiness is understood in terms of pleasure and the absence of pain. But for Mill, as for Bentham, pleasure is understood in terms of awareness and the use of the intellect. It is not just base pleasures that people seek but higher ones which require the use of human intelligence. Thus Mill states: "It is better to be a human being dissatisfied than a pig satisfied; better to be Socrates dissatisfied than a fool satisfied. And if the fool or the pig are of a different opinion, it is because they only know their own side of the question. The other party to the comparison knows both sides." (Mill 348)

Mill is a bit more concerned with social context than Hume or Bentham. He states that utilitarian morality recognizes that there is pleasure in one's sacrifices for others, especially if this personal sacrifice brings about a greater good for more people. Indeed, a later formulation of the principle of utility is that when making a choice between alternative actions, one should make the choice that will bring about the greatest good for the greatest number of people.

And, ultimately, Like Hume and Bentham, Mill relies on reason for the justification of the principle of utility.

> We have now, then, an answer to the question of what sort of proof the principle of utility is susceptible. If the opinion which I have now stated is psychologically true— if human nature is so constituted as to desire nothing which is not either a part of happiness or a means of happiness— we can have no other proof, and we require no other, that these are the only things desirable. If so, happiness is the sole end of human action, and the promotion of it the test by which to judge of all human conduct; from whence it necessarily follows that it must be the criterion of morality, since a part is included in the whole. (Mill 365)

Utilitarianism is actually a fairly complex view of morality. It begins with the pursuit of happiness but uses reason to determine just what happiness is. Happiness does not mean satisfying one's basic desires willy-nilly. One must use reason to determine these desires and one must act in accordance with how one's actions affect other people. The higher the degree of happiness the better the action.

We have seen in the discussion of Hume, Bentham and Mill that the principle of utility is the actual operating principle for morality in their respective societies. All three philosophers claimed to be doing moral science. That is, they investigated the principles that people actually use to justify their moral behavior. While these philosophers separated fact from value in the way that philosophers from Plato to Locke did not, they still used the methods scientists and philosophers used for determining truth and applied them to the study of morality. So instead of coming up with principles that people ought to use to determine whether an action would be moral, these philosophers investigated what principles people actually use to justify their morality.

Thus the principle of utility is very much like Newton's law of gravity. In both cases we have an empirically discovered principle which explains a form of behavior. In Newton's case physics explains why solid objects behave the way they do. The Earth, which is bigger than the apple exerts a greater force, which is why the apple falls. In moral theory terms, the principle of utility explains why people make the kinds of choices they do in the moral realm. I choose an action which will bring about the greatest good. I determine the greatest good by analyzing the context, the role of other people and my motives and intentions. I use the schema of intensity to determine which alternative open to me is the best. And then I act. Thus making a moral decision involves something akin to using the scientific method. One puts forward an hypothesis to be tested or a possible course of action to be investigated. The role of reason is the same: to see how one's proposal can turn out. Will my experiment yield the results I hope for? Will my action yield the results I hope for?

So, even though these thinkers separated fact from value in the ways in which Aquinas and Locke connected them, these empiricist utilitarians did not divorce the methods for determining fact from the methods for determining value. Thus one could conclude that for the utilitarians statements of moral value have the force of statements of fact since the same kinds of methods were used to determine them. Morality, then, is a science just like physics. Basic principles or laws are discovered to explain the workings of specific cases. The chair holds my weight because of how it is constructed. The action is morally right because of the happiness it results in.

Now utilitarianism is alive and well, though it has undergone many changes. In trying to determine how to apply utilitarian theory two views have developed. One is called **act utilitarianism** and the other is **rule utilitarianism**. The principle behind rule utilitarianism is that in order to properly make moral judgments one must follow some general principle. The rule or principle will guide the person as to which choice to make. The principle behind act utilitarianism is that when contemplating an action, one must determine which course of action will bring about the greatest good for the greatest number. In each situation different factors may come into play so an overriding principle cannot be employed to determine which choice to make.

Adherents of rule utilitarianism argue that without a set of rules or principles there is no way to guarantee that the greatest good will be attained. Adherents of act utilitarianism argue that principles are too confining and one would need a whole set of principles which would tell people when various rules can be broken or bent. Adherents of rule utilitarianism have gotten bogged down in developing such second-order rules while adherents of act utilitarianism have been involved in developing two issues. One is in response to a criticism of utilitarianism which asks that if one must bring about the greatest good for the greatest number, whether one can sacrifice an innocent person for that greatest good. The second issue has to do with developing a test or definition of an "act" so that one knows how to properly choose a course of action. For a more complete discussion of these issues see *Morality and Utility* by Jan Narveson.[41]

The innocent person case has been widely discussed and there are various examples, from publicly executing an innocent person accused of a crime in order to insure overall public safety and confidence that crime does not pay, to killing a person who has a disease so that the blood can be used to develop a serum that will cure others who have that disease, to sacrificing a person whose situation is preventing a number of other people from being saved from some kind of disaster.

At issue here is when an individual takes precedence over a group. If, as we originally saw, utilitarianism was developed as an individualistic approach to ethical theory, then the answer is that a group is made up of individuals and therefore an individual cannot take precedence over a group. As Narveson points out what he calls the *General Principle of Duty* "no act of harming another person can be justified by reference to the benefit of others." (Narveson, 1967 161). He continues: "Given that a desire to harm someone ought always to be discounted, and to be suppressed whenever the bearer doesn't do so himself, it follows that we are never justified in harming an innocent in order to benefit others " (Narveson, 1967 164).

We must apply this principle consistently, and in doing so we must look at the context of our actions. For what act utilitarianism still needs is a test for each action. How is an actor to know whether his or her action is moral? It is one thing to believe that the action in question will bring about the greatest good, but how does one test for consistency?

If utilitarianism is an individualistic theory, and if we reject rule utilitarianism because we cannot find ways to develop rules which would still reflect the individual nature of utilitarianism, how do we set up a general test? The answer is in developing a principle of universality.

In the next chapter we will see another, more limiting, version of universality as developed by Imannuel Kant. But here, since utilitarianism is concerned with the consequences of action, we look to generalizing about those consequences. This discussion will be based on the work of

R.M. Hare[42].

Hare represents another development in moral theory. In the 20th century, following the later work of Ludwig Wittgenstein, philosophers became concerned with the nature of language. Above we met Russell and Strawson and saw that the importance of we describe things. In the realm of ethics what became important was understanding how ethical language was used. The two main concepts in ethical theory are "descriptive" and "prescriptive." In our discussions so far we have been using both with little analysis. Briefly, a descriptive analysis of ethical language follows the Humean tradition in seeing how people talk about ethics and in then clarifying such language so that it is used in a consistent manner. Prescriptive language tells us what we ought to do. It prescribes our behavior.

By analyzing how we use ethical language, and by showing how that language works, we come to understand the important concepts in ethical theory. We see where they come from and what their force is and we can then see how to properly apply them.

The task that Hare sets for himself in Freedom and Reason is to analyze the concept of "universality" or "universalizability." Moral judgments have both descriptive and prescriptive aspects. We describe moral behavior in a number of ways. When we say, "killing is bad" we are describing a situation. We are saying that, in our society, we hold a belief that life is valuable and that it is wrong for one person to take the life of another person. But included in this *description* of our behavior and beliefs is a *prescription* which tells us that we should not kill. Hare's task is to show what in the description leads to the prescription and what the characteristics of the prescription are.

When we say, "the desk is brown," we are using terms in the language and we are applying the rules of the language in much the way that Carnap did with scientific language. The word "desk" stands for a class of objects and the word "brown" stands for a class of color properties. So when we say, "the desk is brown" we are using words as they are used to describe a class of objects in the world.

To ensure that we always use terms correctly, Hare shows that there is a sense of universality built in to language. Thus whenever I use the word "desk" or the word "brown" correctly I do so because of the properties of the objects in question. In other words, I am using these terms in a consistent (universal) manner.

Hare argues that moral language operates in the same way as descriptive language. When I say, "X is good" "I am committed to calling any X like it good" (Hare, 1965 15). But because of the prescriptive nature of moral language descriptions imply prescriptions. To say "killing is bad" or "pleasure is good" involves not just a description but also involves a prescription. When one universally describes something accurately, one is then committed to acting in accordance with the prescription.

This last point brings up an issue that has been a part of moral theory since Hume: whether or not an "ought" can be derived from an "is." Hume argued that it could not, and this has been the common view. Just because something is the case does not mean that it ought to be the case. But what Hare has shown is that, because of the prescriptive nature of moral language, descriptions of behavior as good or bad imply prescriptions. Hare believes he avoids the "is/ought" fallacy since the descriptive meaning of moral terms is only one part of their meaning. Since moral terms also have prescriptive meanings, by properly using a moral term to describe a situation does not by itself lead to the conclusion that one ought to behave in that manner. This last inference is made because the terms also have prescriptive meanings. Thus we do not derive an "ought" from an "is". Rather the "ought" is already part of the meaning of the moral term. By looking at its descriptive meaning we are insuring that we are using the term correctly. But we are also looking at the prescriptive meaning of the term. If moral terms did not have this prescriptive meaning, then, by making prescriptive inferences from the descriptive meaning of the term we would be committing the fallacy of deriving an "ought" from an "is."

This is where the importance of the notion of universalizability comes in. When I say that "this is a good action" as argued above, it means that I am committed to saying that all actions of this kind are good. Since consequences are the primary determining factor in evaluating an action, though intent and motive also play a part, when we generalize or universalize actions we are in fact saying that since the consequences of my actions are good, all actions which bring about these consequences are good.

But we live in a pluralistic world and what may be a good set of consequences for me may not be a good set of consequences for you. If I clean someone out in a card game, it is good for me but not good for the person who lost. Or, more generally, since two people may have opposing interests, the outcome of an action may be considered good by one person and not good by the other. Putting the issue this way is important since we are looking at ethics from an individualistic point of view. So the question becomes how an individual can generalize or universalize his or her actions or the consequences of those actions.

The answer involves putting oneself in the position of the persons affected by one's actions. The actor must ask whether he or she would be prepared to accept those consequences if he or she were on the receiving end. The test case here is that of a fanatic. Let us look at the logic of the position of someone who believes that certain kinds of people are inferior beings and must be killed. Or let us make the weaker case where the belief is that such persons cannot have full rights and must remain second-class citizens.

Person X believes in such practices and belongs to an organization that actively pursues such policies. Let us say that such an organization comes into power and begins implementing such policies. Then it is discovered that the ancestry os person X belongs to this so-called inferior group. If person X is consistent he has two options: if he does not believe that he should be subject to second class citizenship or execution then he must change his beliefs accordingly and no longer espouse such discriminatory views or else he must submit himself to the authorities so he can be subjected to those consequences. Hare argues for the unlikelihood of that happening so he discounts fanaticism as being justified by any moral argument. But, this position is weak, for a true believer can act in this manner.

Hare's position is interesting and worth pursuing, but, as stated in his work, it falls short of providing the answers we want. Recall our discussion of Bentham and Mill who argued that it would be wrong to prevent someone from achieving their ends. While this claim is not very strong, it can be used against a fanatic in that all persons have a right to pursue their own happiness. Of course, a fanatic would deny that members of the group being discriminated against are somehow not full-fledged humans. One may argue against this point when the fanatic agrees to be treated in the discriminatory manner. But it is not strong enough to prevent the fanatic from offering a defense that meets the moral criteria set out by Hare.

Utilitarianism has had a long history and can probably overcome these criticisms. Indeed, we will meet utilitarianism again in chapter five. But before we leave this chapter we must look at another ethical view that developed in the empiricist tradition, namely in the logical positivist context. The name of this view is emotivism, and we will begin with the work of A. J. Ayer.

Recall our discussion of the verification principle of meaning above. For a statement to have meaning it must have some empirical content. We must be able to know how to apply the statement to the world so that we can determine whether the statement is true or false. If the statement in question cannot be shown to be true or false the statement has no meaning. It is just a bunch of words that look like a sentence but in fact is not a sentence. It may be syntactically well formed but it will be semantically meaningless. This is the analysis that Ayer brings to moral language. He argues that moral statements "are not in the literal sense significant, but are simply expressions of emotion which can be neither true nor false" (Ayer, 1952 103).

He goes on to argue that, on a strict empiricist view, a treatise on ethics should make no pronouncements but should just give an analysis of ethical terms (Ayer, 1952 103). He then admits "that the fundamental ethical concepts are unanalysable, inasmuch as there is no criterion by which one can test the validity of the judgments in which they occur" (Ayer, 1952 107). So when someone says, "you stole the money and stealing is wrong," the second part of the claim— that stealing is wrong— adds no information to the empirical claim of what happened. Indeed, one can say that, "you stole the money and stealing is good." It appears that these two claims contradict each other but since there are no empirical data that can decide the issue, the evaluative claims add no information to the discussion. Therefore such claims are empirically meaningless. Such claims reflect the feelings of the speaker. (Ayer, 1952 107)

Now ethical terms not only express feeling but are designed to arouse feeling in others, and they are designed to stimulate action.

Indeed some of them are used in such a way bas to give the sentences in which they occur the effect of commands. Thus the sentence "You ought to tell the truth" may be regarded both as the expression of a certain sort of ethical feeling about truthfulness and as the expression of the command "tell the truth." (Ayer, 1952 108)

So, if ethical terms have no cognitive content but only emotional content, of what significance is any ethical or moral discourse? This question has a number of dimensions. First, people like Ayer and others who espouse such a view lived in a society and, we can assume, lived within the rules of that society. Ayer had a long and distinguished career as a philosophy professor at Oxford. One never heard about scandals or inappropriate behavior. So we can conclude that Ayer was a moral person. Thus there must be more to moral discourse than just emotion or persuasion. Ayer does not deny that people have moral beliefs or that people should behave morally. His concern was to present an analysis of moral language given the logical positivist criterion of meaning. Since one can hold contradictory views on ethical issues, and since ethical terms add nothing to the empirical description of a situation, Ayer concludes that ethical terms have no cognitive content and are therefore meaningless.

Yet people espouse such beliefs and live by them. Moral issues, for Ayer, become the subject of psychology, sociology or theology (Ayer, 1952 112). People have moral views and act in accordance with them. Most people would defend their views and would hold that their views have content. Ayer would not entirely disagree. His point, though, is that when we apply philosophical analysis to moral language we come up empty because of the nature of that language and because of the criterion of meaning being applied. If another criterion were to be applied we may find that moral language has meaning, whether this meaning comes from religion or law or social pressures.

We have come a long way. This chapter began with a discussion of John Locke. I argued that Locke is a natural law theorist since his theory of knowledge and his ethical views support each other. But when looking at developments in his theory of knowledge, especially as developed by David Hume, we saw a separation of fact from value. This separation led to science and ethics developing independently of each other in one sense, but where the same techniques that were used in science were applied to the study of values. Instead of showing how our knowledge of the natural order (science) is connected to our knowledge of our place in that order (ethics) empiricists saw ethics as another subject to study, thereby severing the connection between knowledge and values.

But values exist. And natural law theory marches on. In the following chapters we will meet two other versions of natural law theory. Before we meet them we must show what is wrong with the view of science that has been explained in this chapter.

PROBLEMS WITH POSITIVISM

There are three problem areas I shall discuss here— the three most problematic areas for the positivist view. The first has to do with understanding the concept of a law of nature. The second has to do with explanations in which the needed information is not all available. And the third has to do with the concept of theory and the way in which the postulated unobservable or theoretical entities are used in explanations.

As we discussed above, a law of nature is a general or universal statement covering all instances of a range of phenomena. The problem that arises is how such knowledge was attained. If the basis of knowledge is observation, and if we only observe one thing at a time, even if we investigate fully all the properties of those things we observe, how do get into a position of being able to say something about all such entities?

Above we learned a little bit about deductive logic, where we reasoned from a general statement to a specific case. Now we shall have a short visit with **inductive** logic, the form of logic where we reason from the specific to the general. A true inductive argument proceeds from the singular to the general: this swan is white; that swan is white; the other swan is white. Therefore all swans are white.

As we have seen , inductive arguments are problematic because future observations can always render them false. But, as we have also seen, they can be used since the concepts used in such arguments are general and so they do serve a purpose in helping to formulate hypotheses for further investigation. The following story illustrates these points. A woman gets a promotion which involves a lot of business travel. While away she develops a nagging doubt regarding her husband's behavior so she hires a private eye to watch him when she is away. On her return the investigator says there is no problem. But her doubt persists so she keeps the investigator on. This pattern goes on for months with the same results. The investigator says that there is no point in continuing the case. He is convinced that there is enough evidence to conclude that there is no basis for her doubt. But her doubt persists and she keeps the investigator on the case. To make a long story short— this story should go on for a long time to give the feel of a long investigation— one night the investigator does indeed have something to report. That night her husband went out to dinner with some of his co-workers. This was not unusual. But at the restaurant they were seated next to a table of women. The people at both tables got friendly and they started dancing with one another. Her husband appeared to get very chummy with one of the women. They left together and went to his home. They had a nightcap and continued dancing. Their dancing became amorous and they started to head for the stairs. The investigator, being completely familiar with the house, went round the back where there was a tree overlooking the bedroom. When he climbed up he saw the two of them in the bedroom in a state of partial undress. Then the lights were turned out. "That nagging doubt!" yelled the woman. "Now I'll never know for sure."

I hope you found this story amusing. But, if you did, why did you laugh? The reason the punch line works is because you **know** what happened. But do you really? The point is that if knowledge is based on directly observable evidence, then the crucial piece of evidence was not seen, only inferred. And while in almost all cases the inference would be correct, it remains possible that the relationship was not consummated. The husband could have found out he was being followed and planned this whole thing to get back at his wife for not trusting him or because he is a real joker. We may have a high probability for concluding that we know what happened, but we cannot hold that conclusion with certainty. And that is the problem of induction. In science we can, and often must, continue with our work on the basis of such probabilities. But in human affairs, especially in legal or moral matters, where we believe that someone is innocent until proven guilty, we must withhold action.

Inductive and deductive logic, especially when arguments are put into symbolic or mathematical terms, are known as **formal logic**. That is because there are formal or standard rules that can be applied to test the validity of such arguments. But much reasoning is done in everyday language and uses less formal rules. Such argument forms are known as **informal logic** because their validity has more to do with the ways in which we use language, the assumptions we make about the things we are arguing about and the concepts we use regarding how we understand the things we argue about and their relationships to one another.

The story above is a good example of that. On a formal basis we saw that the reasoning of the woman was correct: her doubt must remain. But most readers will say that is nonsense— we know what happened. Well, we really don't know, but given our understanding of human behavior, and given the conditions under which that behavior was taking place, the inference that we know what happened seems to be justified.

So let us return to our chairs. We look at one chair and observe its properties. Then we look at another chair and observe its properties. We continue looking at chairs until we get to a point where we believe that we have observed enough chairs to make a general statement about the whole category of chairs. Of course we know that the **possibility** remains that we will come across something that we would classify as a chair but which does not behave in the way in which all other chairs we have observed have behaved. A possibility is simply something that can happen, though, of course, it may never happen. A **contradiction** is a case of opposites. I say yes and you say no. Thus you have contradicted me. As long as no contradiction of a limited logical kind can occur, anything remains possible. Thus it is possible for there to be life on the moon, but given our understanding of the conditions needed for life to survive, it is not very likely that there is life on the moon. When something is possible but we are not sure of how likely it is we say it is or isn't very **probable**.

Probability will be discussed shortly. So while it is possible, it is not very probable that there is life on the moon.

Now to return to the problem at hand. If observation is the basis of knowledge and if we observe single cases, it seems somewhat arbitrary to decide when enough cases have been observed to make a generalization out of those observations, one that can be used in future explanations, one that can be given the status of a law of nature, one that is supposed to be considered as true, and once considered true it is always supposed to be considered to be true. This view of science claims that scientific explanations are deductive, but this is not really true since the basis for the deduction, the general statement the deduction starts with, was arrived at inductively.

Incomplete explanations are not really a problem as such, but they are a problem for the positivist theory of science since this view would like to be able to present all explanations in proper deductive form. Most of you will have heard of probability from weather forecasts. Tomorrow there is a 75% chance of showers. Chance in this context means the same thing as probability. What such a forecast or prediction means is that there are too many factors involved to predict more accurately. If the prevailing winds keep up their strength then it will definitely rain. But there is a front of warmer air near the lakes. Usually when such a situation happens the warmer air will slow down the cooler, moister air, thereby delaying the showers until the next day.

Or, if the winds from behind that warmer air strengthen, then the cooler moister air could be moved off our map and it won't rain at all. Since all of the factors in the weather situation are basically understood, but because there are so many factors that can influence our weather, it becomes very difficult to say with precision what our weather will be. This is because in the past when all such weather systems were observed, there was no set pattern as to how they would behave. Thus, predictions about the weather can only be made in a **probabilistic** manner. But weather forecasting is only one area of science which must use probabilistic explanations. In nuclear physics, probabilistic explanations are used all the time. So probabilistic explanations are only a problem for this view of science because adherents of this view believe that probabilistic explanations are somehow incomplete and that full, deductive explanations are the standard which must be met.

Now for the third and most serious problem for positivistic science: what to do with those theoretical unobservable postulated entities. Traditionally, the problem has been put as follows. The problem of the two tables comes from physicist Arthur Eddington[43]. The chair that I sit on when I write is a solid three-dimensional object made of steel, aluminum, foam and wool. But according to physics it made up of swarms of countless atoms of different types and is anything but solid. So which is the real chair? The positivistic view of science wants to be able to explain the chair that is made of metal and fabric since that is how we encounter the object. The postulated atoms are used to explain the properties of the chair, but it is not that chair I sit on. The problem is compounded when positivists insist that science must be based on observation. Thus, even though it must be acknowledged that these unobservable entities exist—if they were held not to exist they then could not be used in the explanation—many scientists do not like the idea of such entities playing such a prominent role in scientific explanations.

Another way these scientists think about this problem is that by allowing the existence of such entities they are saying that, in some sense, both chairs exist, but on different levels of existence. Problems of this nature that led to the view of theories called **instrumentalism**, which was very popular among both philosophers and physicists, especially in the 1920s and 1930s. Physicists such as Ernst Mach, Percy Bridgeman, Henri Poincaré and Arthur Eddington were all instrumentalists. On this view theories, or our scientific chairs, are viewed as instruments used for the purposes of calculations and explanations. And once we no longer need the instrument we can discard it. Thus, on this view we do not speak of the truth or falsity of theories or the existence of theoretical entities. It is this view which has led to the word "theory" becoming so misused. As we have seen, a theory is a scientific explanation which relies on unobservable entities such as atoms to explain the behavior of observable entities such as chairs and tables. But because of the instrumentalist view, the word "theory" has taken on two technically incorrect usages.

The first incorrect use of "theory" is when someone says, "But it is only a theory." This implies that theoretical explanations are not as good as other kinds of explanations but that theories, perhaps because they use entities which cannot be directly observed, are somehow to be contrasted with fact. As we shall shortly see, this is a totally incorrect characterization of what a theory is. But the instrumentalist view of science allows for this interpretation.

The second incorrect usage of "theory" is when, for example, the detective says, "I have a theory as to who did it." The detective has a hypothesis, not a theory. He has a good idea, but does not yet know. But since the instrumentalist view of theories allows them to be confused with hypothetical knowledge, this confusion is easy to make.

Instrumentalism proved to be an unsatisfactory solution to the problem. On the one hand entities were postulated to explain something. On the other hand these entities were not given real status. So these entities, on this view, really did not explain anything. But instrumentalism posed a more serious threat to the scientific enterprise. Recall the discussion of Copernicus and Galileo in the introduction. As scientists, they saw their work as explaining how the universe really worked, but because this explanation challenged the Church's view of how the universe worked, the Church threatened both thinkers with imprisonment if they did not recant. In both cases the Church held the view that the theories of Copernicus and Galileo could be accepted as instruments for calculation but not as truth[44]. By allowing this move the Church rendered the truth of science irrelevant. The Church was the arbiter of truth; science just provided instruments to allow us to make calculations regarding observable phenomena. The philosophical point here is that in this way science becomes irrelevant. It ends up being about nothing. The only conclusion that can be acceptable to the scientific enterprise is that the scientific or theoretical entities, which are postulated in order to explain observable phenomena, must be considered to exist, hence the "realism" of this view of science.

This discussion of instrumentalism is based on the work of Karl Popper and Wilfrid Sellars[45]

CRITICISMS OF BEHAVIORISM

As we saw above, behaviorism is the psychology that reflects the positivist approach to science. We have just seen serious criticisms of the theory of positivism as a view of science. Now let us look at specific criticisms of how positivism has been applied in the field of psychology.

Today, behaviorism is on the wane. Very few therapists use these methods exclusively. They are still popular in psychiatric hospitals and in various other institutions for people with behavioral problems. The enclosed structure of the hospital or institution provides an excellent setting for the use of behavioral techniques. The therapist can control all aspects of the patient's environment. Medications can be used and controlled as needed. A strict behavioral program of rewards and punishments can be employed without any interference from unexpected sources. And, as Hamlet would say, there is the rub. For without the controlled structures, these techniques do not work very well. All too often patients start behaving as if completely cured while still in the institution, but very shortly after they have been released— that is very shortly after the controlled structures have been removed— they start reverting back to exhibiting the original behaviors that got them into the institution in the first place. Thus, behavior therapy or behavior modification can only work when all factors can be controlled.

This negative result led to much re-theorizing on the part of behaviorists. They started to modify their own theories and offer reasons why this negative result occurred. They basically said that what was done in the institution was correct but since they had not been able to anticipate all of the situations a person could be in, what was needed was follow-up therapy that reflected the actual situations the people found themselves in. And such therapy should take place in a community setting rather than in an institution.

But the problem would not go away. For this method of therapy only dealt with problems already encountered. It appeared difficult to condition someone to react in a certain way to a situation which the person had not yet experienced. In other words, behavior therapy does not seem to allow for generalizing from one instance to similar instances. And it does not appear to be able to deal with anticipating how a person should behave under different kinds of conditions not yet experienced. These failures in practice led to criticisms of the theory itself. Some of these criticisms are complex and more philosophical than psychological because they deal with the underlying assumptions of the theory. In other words, these criticisms attack the positivist theory of science and the concept of a person that behaviorists hold.

The first criticism is interesting. It says that if behaviorism is correct, and all of our behavior is simply learned responses, we should not be able to formulate such a theory about ourselves, because if we can formulate such a theory, it implies that we have stepped out of our conditioned structure to be able to see ourselves in it. Thus, the very fact that we can formulate a theory about ourselves in this way proves that the theory is false because the theory itself says we should not be able to do so.

The point of this criticism is that the behaviorist concept of a person is false. We are more than just the sum of our conditioned responses. We are capable of becoming aware that we have been conditioned and we are capable of becoming aware of the factors that influence our behavior. And once we are aware of these factors, it becomes logically possible, if not factually possible, to alter our responses ourselves. And if we can do this, we must have some sense of self-awareness, or consciousness, something that behaviorism says we do not have. Thus if we have capacities that a theory says we cannot have, the theory must be false. This point is actually well illustrated in Skinner's own novel, *Walden Two*[46] where Skinner hopes to create a perfect society by conditioning everyone to respond properly. But the question that is never asked, let alone answered, is who conditions the conditioners. This question is not asked because it cannot be answered. And this point clearly shows the weakness of the theory.

So, the faults of behaviorism show us that we are self-aware or conscious beings. While some aspects of our behavior may be explained by conditioning or structured learning, we are capable of more than just behaving at that level. Our ability to think and theorize shows us we are more complex beings than behaviorism allows. The area of language learning and usage is one that highlights much of the criticism of behaviorism. While this is not the place to go into a whole discussion of the philosophy of language— what language is, how it is structured and how it is used to convey information— or even a thorough discussion of the psychology of language— the ways in which language is learned— we must touch on some points of both topics.

Recall the discussion of Watson's view of language and thinking above. He unsuccessfully tried to show that thinking was some kind of inner speech. The relationship between thought and language has virtually always been a concern of philosophers and psychologists. And to look at thought as a form of inner speech is not such a silly idea. Watson's idea did not lead anywhere because of his narrow conception of speech and thought. Remember, behaviorists do not allow unobservable entities to enter into their explanations. So something as unobservable as thinking had to be explained in terms of something observable, such as speech. This was just a kind of reversal of what previous thinkers had done.

In the past some kind of dualistic view of persons was the dominant one. Mind and body were two separate but connected substances. Mental phenomena were seen as coming first. Recall our discussion of Descartes above, where "I" referred to the thinking capacity of the person. To a Cartesian who considered the question, speech would have been seen as the public form of thinking. As we saw, there were good reasons to abandon the Cartesian view of personhood. So, where does that leave us? On the one hand we have rejected making thought the basis for speech, and on the other hand we have rejected making speech the basis for thought. This is like the old question: which came first, the chicken or the egg? So, which did come first, thought or speech? The answer to this latter question is the same answer we give to the chicken-egg question. When you get a situation that appears to be unanswerable it is probably because you are asking the wrong question. Rather than ask which came first, we should be asking about the relationship between thought and speech. The answer comes from philosophy, not psychology.

In 1956 the American philosopher Wilfrid Sellars, gave a series of very influential lectures in England[47], in which he argued, among other things, that while we must use a form of methodological behaviorism in order to begin to understand the relationship between language and thought, we have to then introduce theoretical terms and concepts into our account so that we can complete our picture. The theoretical concepts, must, of course, be tied to what has been observed because these theoretical concepts will be used to explain what has been observed. Sellars has been one of the more important developers of the concept realist view of science.

Sellars is a neo-Kantian, and as such accepts the fact that we think in terms of concepts or theoretical frameworks. Because we think in terms of concepts, thoughts probably exist before speech. Speech is public thought. But if we didn't have the capacity or the structure for speech, we would not be able to think. Therefore thought is a form of private or inner speech. Thus the two go together like the proverbial horse and carriage. We speak because we can think but we think because we have the ability to speak. Therefore it is incorrect to ask which comes first. And any view which tries to separate thought from speech must be mistaken.

The next important step in the criticism of the behaviorist approach comes from Harvard University professor of linguistics, Noam Chomsky[48]. One of his most famous papers is a review of Skinner's book *Verbal Behaviour*[49] in which Skinner applies his view of stimulus-response operant conditioning to show how children learn language. Chomsky rips into Skinner's work with glee. He begins by stating that we really do not know how children acquire language, but to say that the stimulus-response method of learning explains anything is to do nothing but to put a new label on an old mystery. What is needed is to understand the child's capacity for learning language. This must include an understanding of the structure of language as well, so that we know what it is that the child is learning.

According to Noam Chomsky, language has a complex structure which enables someone who has learned only a little bit of a language to generate new sentences in that language and to transform the words and structures he or she knows in many ways to create new structures. He argues that the capacity to do this must be inborn. Thus he refers to his view as Cartesian. But he is not a true Cartesian and only uses this label because it was Descartes who argued in favor of innate ideas. Chomsky does not believe that we are born with specific innate ideas, but he does argue convincingly that we are born with certain abilities or capacities. This actually makes Chomsky more Kantian than Cartesian.

In his review of Skinner, Chomsky shows that if Skinner were correct and that operant conditioning were the way in which we acquired language, because of its closed structure, we would not be able to use language in creative ways or to generate new sentences in new contexts. Chomsky presents this as a logical point, much in the same way as I argued above about behaviorism not being able to account for the ability to theorize about behaviorism. To go beyond the theoretical limits of a theory is to render that theory false. By being able to formulate a theory that says that all of our behavior is based on operant conditioning is to break out of the conditioning. Thus, in the same way, in order to be able to use language in new and creative ways is to go beyond the limits of the theory and to render it false.

Before leaving this chapter I want to address another problem with this view. As we have seen with the way in which positivist empiricism has developed, most of the qualities we think of as human have been denied. Thus, instead of saying that people are rational beings capable of emotion, all non-observable phenomena are explained away. This is the case in the social sciences as well as psychology. In economics, for example, following Locke, Adam Smith provided a value-laden account of the developing marketplace. He talked about supply and demand and the role of wages and profits. However, capitalists today who talk about Smith clearly have not read him since he truly believed that big was not better and that there had to be checks and balances in the economy to insure that everyone was able to participate and benefit from the marketplace. Let us look briefly at Smith's work.

Smith talks about the community and how individuals develop concerns for others through the development of the notion of sympathy. Following his good friend Hume, Smith acknowledges that one person cannot feel the pains of another, but we can judge another person's misfortunes through a comparison to our own pains. "...by changing places in fancy with the sufferer, that we come either to conceive or be affected by what he feels...."[50]. And when trying to understand another person's viewpoint Smith argues that "(T)o approve of another man's opinions is to adopt those opinions, and to adopt them is to approve of them. (Smith 70)."

Smith is famous for his notion of the "invisible hand." This was not a fancy but a belief in the rationality of nature, that nature was a self-regulating entity or process, and that since people in the state of nature had the use of reason, people would come to sympathize or identify with others and act accordingly. Thus the title of his work *The Theory of Moral Sentiments* is to be taken seriously. The fact that we have sentiments regarding other people limits our actions towards them. Not everything is permissible.

Now, in his other work, *The Wealth of Nations*, Smith argues that we act from the standpoint of self-interest. He acknowledges that people act in social contexts and that

> man has almost constant occasion for the help of his brethren, and it is in vain for him to expect it from their benevolence only. He will be more likely to prevail if he can interest their self-love in his favor and show them that it is for their own advantage to do for him what he requires of them[51].

Thus, even though we are alone in a state of nature, the correct use of reason will create a self-regulating system. To illustrate this point let us look at a good example of a social contract: the process of negotiating a labor contract.

Adam Smith saw markets as relatively small and manageable, which is why the invisible hand could work. But today in a world of multi-national businesses new methods of maintaining the rationality of the market place must be developed. As businesses get bigger, the power of employees must also increase. In keeping with the notions of the invisible hand and of the social contract, workers must enter into a new social contract with employers. Since businesses are large, the workers must also reflect this size and organize. Thus the whole notion of labor unions— workers getting together in their own social contract so they can deal with employers on the employers' terms. Big begets big. Thus the invisible hand works. New forms of social organization develop to maintain the working of the market place. For big business to oppose the notion of workers' unions would be to oppose the notion of the invisible hand— the rationality of the market place. For businesses to oppose labor unions would be immoral since it is through these unions that the social contract of the market place is maintained.

Let us use the notion of the labor contract as an example of the wider social contract. By looking at such a contract we can see how rationality and morality are maintained in the marketplace. For a real contract to be in force, both sides must have equal power. This power comes partly from numbers but it should mainly come from the rational aspects of how the market works. Thus both sides will respect each other and recognize the position of the other.

Workers have one thing to bargain with: their labor. Employers have one thing to bargain with: compensation for that labor. So workers and employers enter into a contract. Workers will do so much work for so much compensation. Employers want to limit the amount of compensation because they want to maximize profit, but, since these employers are good contract theorists, they realize they have to treat employees fairly, so wages must be high enough for the workers to participate in the economy. Workers want to be paid as much as possible so they will ask for a large compensation package, but being the good contract theorists they are, they will limit their demands to one that will not jeopardize the viability of the business. So the workers will come away from the bargaining table with a contract that specifies how much work is expected of them and how much they will be compensated for that work. To ask a worker to do more than is specified in the contract would be to break the contract.

All too often we hear that workers are lazy, that they are not prepared to work hard. This frequently means that the employer is asking a worker to do something outside the conditions of the contract. Given the nature of the contract, the worker must refuse, unless additional compensation is offered. This is so because the contract is based on moral principles that both sides have agreed to. Any breach of the contract, no matter how trivial, should be seen as immoral. Workers are not lazy. They just do not want to be exploited.

But business did not adhere to the conclusions of Smith and others such as David Ricardo. Instead the early capitalists started to fight the various checks and balances and tried to control the workings of the economy. Thus, within a century of Smith writing on how the market *should* work, we see Karl Marx's damning account of how the market was in fact working, which was not how Smith envisaged it. Marx used Smith's work to develop an alternative model which turned Smith's model on its head.

But in both cases people immediately used these different models in ways the originators did not intend. Without going into details here—

that would involve another chapter— I want to make the point that by denying the important aspects of what we are and by only talking in abstractions about ourselves, we developed a language and a value system where the abstraction became more important than the individual.

Thus capitalism, when combined with utilitarianism and implemented by the people in control of the system led to a view where the abstraction as seen by the people in charge of the situation was all that mattered. Individual people did not matter, only "the economy" mattered. Checks and balances did not matter and were often seen as harming the economy. Thus it was acceptable to implement harsh policies for the good of the economy even if those policies harmed the very people the economy was supposed to help. Treating the economy in this abstract manner leads to economics becoming a value-laden non-empirical undertaking that is practiced in almost cultlike fashion. These practices can be seen operating today in the guise of "monetarism" where money matters, but people don't. Internationally these policies are being implemented in an ideological manner— in a manner where the principle is important but the individual facts are not—by institutions such as the World Bank and the International Monetary Fund.

The point here is simple. By denying the very things we should be studying we create a world that is not very hospitable for us.

To conclude this point, and this section, the positivist view of science has had a long history and has come to grips with most of the problems facing it. But its insistence on limiting the realm of science to the directly observable presented difficulties which would not go away. I shall now turn to an alternative view of science which arose partly out of dealing with the problems confronted by positivism.

Chapter 4

THE KANTIAN RESPONSE

Historically, the philosopher who set the stage for answering Hume's concerns was Immanuel Kant. Brought up in the rationalist speculative traditions of Descartes, Leibniz and Christian Wolff, Kant was very knowledgeable about Newton's work. But it was Hume's work that changed the direction of Kant's thinking. "I openly confess my recollection of David Hume was the very thing which many years ago first interrupted my dogmatic slumber and gave my investigations in the field of speculative philosophy a quite new direction."[52] Kant sees Hume as having correctly begun his investigations with the concept of causality, but in so doing he "challenged reason" by taking the notion that we cannot reason in an *a priori* manner from observations alone to the point that we cannot reason in an *a priori* manner at all (Kant, 1950 5-6).

The reason Hume reached this conclusion, according to Kant, was that he did not look beyond experience. But if Hume had envisaged our problem in all its universality, he would never have been guilty of this statement, so destructive of all pure philosophy. For he would then have recognized that, according to his own argument, pure mathematics, as certainly containing *a priori* synthetic propositions, would also not be possible; from such an assertion his good sense would have saved him[53]. Kant's main concern in the *Critique* was to show that there is an *a priori* component to empirical knowledge. We will look at Kant's main arguments in so far as they attempt to answer Hume and to set the foundations for an alternative view of science, while taking into account the three issues stated above. Some working definitions are in order. An *a priori* truth is true prior to or without any observation or empirical content. An *a posteriori* truth is true as a result of empirical observation. An **analytical** statement is true because the predicate adds no new knowledge to the subject; i.e., the subject already contains the information in the predicate. A **synthetic** statement in one in which the predicate amplifies or adds to our knowledge of the subject.

Kant hoped to show that our knowledge of the world was of a synthetic *a priori* nature. This was so, because, even though his empiricist predecessors began their inquiries with an attempt to demonstrate how scientific knowledge could be justified, due to of the way in which they limited their investigations to what could be observed they ended up being concerned with seeing if knowledge was possible. Since we had knowledge Kant realized that their approach was incorrect. So he returned to the original issue of how to justify that knowledge. (Kant, 1950 B19-20)

Kant agrees with the empiricists that knowledge begins with experience, but he goes on to argue that it does not all arise out of experience. This is so because we have to be in a position to know what it is that we are observing (Kant, 1950 B1). While we open our eyes and receive impressions the observation itself does not give us knowledge of what we perceive. Some aspect of our understanding must be at work to interpret those impressions so that we are in a position to say we have gained knowledge from them. This is especially the case when talking about concepts which involve necessary connections, such as causality, or the primary characteristics of objects, such as shape and extension. The point here is that embedded in the concept of causality is the concept of necessity. (Kant, 1950 B4-5) If we remove the empirical aspects of an object we have observed the space that object occupied still remains because our observations of objects include their primary properties. (Kant, 1950 B5) We know this not through observation but because of the *a priori* nature of our faculties of understanding. In other words, because of the way in which we understand what we perceive, we take to those observations a structure that makes sense of those them. This structure exists prior to our observations and provides the basis for the synthetic *a priori* nature of our knowledge.

To put this point in context with regard to Hume's position, causality is not justified on the basis of custom and habit but on the way in which we understand our perceptions. Thus causality becomes justified as a way of understanding how the world works. So the problem becomes, for Kant, how to explain the nature of our reasoning processes. He does this by talking about our *intuition*. Intuition takes place only in so far as the object is given to us. "Objects are *given* to us by means of sensibility, and it alone yields us *intuitions*; they are *thought* through the understanding, and from the understanding arise *concepts*." (Kant, 1950 A19) Observation takes place in space and time. But space and time do not exist as independent entities. They create the context in which we observe. Space and time are transcendental *a priori* concepts which allow us to perceive the world they way we do.

Kant goes on to argue that knowledge is the result of a complex process which involves our observing appearances of objects and making sense of them in a transcendental *a priori* context. It is this way we come to have knowledge of ourselves. For when we observe ourselves we do not see a Humean bundle of sensations but a unified manifold of consciousness. (Kant, 1950 B68) This process, which gives us knowledge, is guided by logic. And logic can be treated in a twofold manner. There is the logic of the general which "contains the absolutely necessary rules of thought without which there can be no employment of the understanding." And there is the logic of the special employment of the understanding which "contains the rules of correct thinking as regards certain kinds of objects." (Kant, 1950 A52 B76) So we get knowledge of the world by opening our eyes, by receiving impressions, and by making sense of them in an *a priori* manner because of how our reasoning faculty works. Our observations give us *a posteriori* knowledge which we state in synthetic terms. But due to the *a priori* way in which we make sense of this *a posteriori* knowledge it is true in a synthetic *a priori* manner. Because of the inseparable relationship between what we see and how we see it

> Without sensibility no object would be given to us, without understanding no object would be thought. Thoughts without content are empty, intuitions without concepts are blind (Kant, 1950 A51 B75).

Thus, though we have objective synthetic *a priori* knowledge of the world, this knowledge is only of the phenomenal or of the appearances of objects. Because of the way we perceive and because of how our understanding interprets our impressions we do not know what objects are like in themselves. Kant calls this level of being in themselves the *noumenal* realm, while what we see is the *phenomenal* realm. We know the *noumenal* realm exists since we know we have knowledge of objects in the world. But we do not know the nature of this *noumenal* world since it is closed to our observations.

To conclude this brief discussion of Kant, we see that he overcame Hume's skeptical conclusions. But he did so at a price.

Knowledge is not just based on observation but is also based on how we perceive and think about the world. Hume's custom and habit have now become the workings of the human mind and the categories with which we think about the world. We do not just see chairs and tables—we see impressions which we have to interpret as chairs and tables. It is our understanding and the concepts we use that turn observations into knowledge. And since this understanding works in an *a priori* manner, we avoid the problem of induction because of how we think about the world. Of course, the world can still offer surprises and the future may not resemble the past. But because of how we think we do not have to arrive at a skeptical conclusion. We have knowledge and we know why we have knowledge. Future observations will be interpreted in the same way. And if the future does not resemble the past, we will just have to revise what we know. But we will not have to challenge the fact that we do have knowledge.

One final point should be made here. By showing that perceptions and their conceptual interpretation are inseparable we see the historical foundation of the view of science known as "concept realism". In other words, it is the concepts we use to make sense of things that structure our knowledge. While Kant believed that Newtonian mechanics was the truth about how the universe worked, he believed that the concepts or categories of thought he identified were the categories that had to be used to attain that truth. However, as we shall see, partly because of the scientific revolution, we know that as we continue our investigations we learn new things about the workings of the universe. And this new knowledge may lead to another scientific revolution. As we expand our knowledge we may also expand or change our categories or concepts. And if we change the concepts we use to identify things in the world, we will be seeing a different world. We will return to this point in greater detail later, both in this chapter and in the next chapter.

But first we must look at Kant's ethical theory. In a strict sense Kant cannot be considered a natural law theorist since he did not apply his theory of knowledge to his theory of ethics. What he did was to apply the same concept of reason to both. In the *Critique of Practical Reason* Kant argued that practical reason works in the same way that pure reason works in that only "reason can determine maxims of the will"[54]. And the *Critique of Judgment*[55] shows how we apply these principles to practical questions. And he then applies this practical reason to ethical theory in the *Foundations of the Metaphysics of Morals*, saying that we "must concede that the ground of obligation here must not be sought in the nature of man or in the circumstances in which he is placed, but sought *a priori* solely in the concepts of pure reason..."[56]

A priori concepts of morality are about obligation and about the human will. Thus it is not sufficient that people act in accordance with duty or law, they must act "for the sake of the law." (Kant, 1959 6) And what makes an action good is not its consequences but the goodness of the will of the person doing the willing. (Kant, 1959 10) Ultimately, duty is expressed in terms of imperatives. "The conception of an objective principle, so far as it constrains a will, is a command (of reason) and the formula of this command is called an imperative" (Kant, 1959 30). There are hypothetical imperatives which deal with practical situations but if an action is to be "thought of as good in itself, and hence as necessary in a will which of itself conforms to reason as the principle of this will, the imperative is categorical." (Kant, 1959 31)

Recall that for Kant when we have a concept of something we have knowledge of that thing. So if we know what a person is, we know that all objects we identify as persons have those qualities. This knowledge implies a concern or respect for persons. And that, of course, is what morality is all about: our relations with other people. So Kant formulates the categorical imperative in different ways to reflect this view. The first formulation is: "Act as though the maxim of your action were by your will to become a universal law of nature."(Kant, 1959 39) The second formulation is: "Act so that you treat humanity, whether in your own person or in that of another, always as an end and never as a means only."(Kant, 1959 47) We see here a position similar to that of Hare as discussed in the first chapter, but with a big difference. The first formulation is the basis for Hare's principle of universalizability. But Kant's second formulation appears to solve the problems associated with Hare's view. This is obvious in the case of the fanatic. As we saw with Hare, if the fanatic were consistent we could have no argument that would oppose him. But Kant allows us to oppose the fanatic on the grounds that he would be using other persons as a means to an end and not as ends in themselves. Thus on Kant's view we can act against the fanatic. To reiterate, this is because Kantian epistemology gives us content with our concepts where the Humean view, which Hare's position is based on, does not.

Unfortunately, because Kant still formulated his categorical imperative in individualistic terms, the fanatic can say that from a specific viewpoint others are not full-fledged persons and therefore the imperative does not apply.

But Kant and Hume would agree on the important role that reason plays in ethical theory, though they may disagree as to what that role is. My point here is that there is more in common between Hume and Kant than we see at first glance. Both begin their investigations from the standpoint of the individual. Both reflect the influence of Newton. And even though Kant's epistemology, by putting concept and content together, paves the road for denying the distinction between fact and value which Hume strongly maintains, in his ethical theory Kant maintains that distinction. Both thinkers, even though they provide the respective foundations for different views of science, are modernist individualists. See my "Response to Wilson"[57] where I argue that Hume's custom and habit can be interpreted in a Kantian light. In other words, our customs and habits, when seen in a cultural context, provide content for our concepts since we learn them together.

With regard to broader ethical questions such as the relationship between capitalism and democracy we can see similarities between Kant and Locke. Both views start from the individualistic standpoint. With Locke's social contract we saw that each individual defined his interests and pursued them. The main moral issues were about acknowledging the equal interests of others. But on the Kantian view, since we begin by recognizing others as moral equals, we begin by acknowledging responsibilities to others. So both Locke and Kant can be capitalists, but they would be capitalists with a difference. Locke's capitalist would be concerned with maximizing his profit while paying workers what the market would bear. Kant would recognize that businesses have responsibilities to their workers and perhaps even to the society at large which allows them to operate. And, in turn, this view might allow the society to define how businesses can operate. This is because of the fact that business is a social institution and business decisions would still be guided by the categorical imperative.

The famous French novel *Les Liaisons Dangereuses* by Choderlos de Laclos is an early novel that reflects the Kantian world-view where we see a person reflecting on her own identity. Also, the novels of Jane Austen are considered by Ian Watt to be the best solution of the narrative problems set by the early writers who reflected either the empiricist or rationalist approach. Austen accomplished this by the use of an objective narrator. (Watt, 1970 310)

Kantian conceptualizing and abstract theorizing changed the way in which science could be done. Recall Newton's concerns about forming hypotheses. He was concerned that if his work were seen as too abstract it would look very much like religious theorizing, thus he had to stay close to the observed facts. By the time Kant wrote, science had become well established although the philosophical questions regarding how knowledge was possible were still being discussed. So, with science firmly behind him, Kant could theorize on a grand scale without worrying about bringing back pre-scientific religion. This in its turn allowed for the great theorizing of Darwin and even the theorizing and speculating of Freud. And, so, to look at the scientific implications of Kant's philosophy, we now turn to the work of these two thinkers .

DARWIN

Today we are all familiar with the theory of evolution. All too many people, though, still use language like "but it is only a theory," especially if they are not prepared to accept the truth of evolution. Given our understanding of biology and of paleontology—indeed, of our scientific framework or paradigm—there is no denying the truth of evolution. However, there is some disagreement regarding the explanation of the process of evolution. In this sense, the theory of evolution is still undergoing revision. But even if we do not have a complete explanation of the process, there is still no denying the facts which include all the observations made by Darwin regarding the variations of species in different locations. These are catalogued and discussed in Darwin's *Origin of Species*[58]. In addition to this information we have the existence of various vestigial organs in humans such as our fingernails, which are the descendants of claws, and our tailbone . We have knowledge of comparative anatomy which shows the relatedness of many species as well as variations within a species. We have the fossil record of extinct species and, today, we have a knowledge of genetics and heredity which demonstrate these various similarities. Indeed, the genome mapping process has shown the incredible similarity between species. There is approximately a 98.7% similarity in the genetic makeup of humans and chimpanzees. Even more astounding is that there is a 50% similarity between humans and earthworms. This clearly shows the biological relationship among all life forms.

The story of evolution begins with Darwin's work, *The Origin of Species*, first published in 1859. The formulation of this work dates back to 1837 when Darwin returned from his voyage on the Beagle where he had the opportunity to observe various life forms in different habitats. He noticed that the same species of bird or animal often showed variations in appearance in different geographical locales. The beaks of birds frequently differed in shape and/or size, or coloring was different. Darwin came up with the notion of adaptability to environment very quickly but it took him a long time to develop the explanation or theory of natural selection. Thus, *Origin* is written in Kuhnian fashion, as a reconstruction of the thinking process.

In retrospect Darwin's achievements are even greater than one could imagine because he was working with a very limited knowledge base. In his second chapter he admitted that he did not have a precise definition of "species", and he did not have a knowledge of the mechanisms of heredity. Yet, the science of the day did have general notions of these concepts. Knowing that species are differentiated and knowing that there is such a thing as heredity, Darwin proceeded to use these concepts to explain the variations in species he found in both nature and domesticated animals and plants.

In chapter three Darwin introduces his concept of "the struggle for existence." This term, which has been misused and misunderstood, was meant simply to express the observation that more beings are born than can survive (Darwin 75). Factors in survival include the available food supply and the ability to adapt to a changing environment. Darwin saw this struggle in the capitalist terms of his day and spoke in terms of competition for resources. The individuals who survived were the fittest. It is this process of survival and adaptation that Darwin called "natural selection."

> Natural Selection acts exclusively by the preservation and accumulation of Variations, which are beneficial under the organic and inorganic conditions to which each creature is exposed at all periods of life. The ultimate result is that each creature tends to become more and more improved in relation to its conditions. This improvement inevitably leads to the gradual advancement of the organization of the greater number of living beings throughout the world (Darwin 122).

Darwin knew that sex played a role in inheritance but the knowledge of the day did not understand the biological mechanisms of heredity. It is a real Kuhnian irony that just a few years after Darwin wrote *Origin* Gregor Mendel actually discovered the laws of inheritance, but the scientific community of the day neither understood what Mendel was saying nor saw the significance of his discovery. The paradigm of the day

Natural Law, Science, and the Social Construction of Reality 119

was not ready to accept Mendel's work.

Mendel developed a statistical method for determining the heredity of characteristics. As Nobel laureate François states, "The symbolic interpretation of the results in some way becomes the hinge between theory and experiment. It permits hypotheses to be formulated easily from the observed distributions; and it leads to predictions which can then be experimentally tested (Jacob, 1976 205). Jacob goes on to show that when Mendel first presented his views to a scientific body the audience was "surprised that arithmetic and calculation of probabilities entered into the question of heredity,...."(Jacob, 1976 208). It was some thirty five years after Mendel published his work that statistics was becoming understood and his work was "rediscovered." This rediscovery led to the development of the science of genetics as we understand it today. Just think how much more powerful Darwin's arguments would have been if they had been supported by Mendel's explanation of the mechanisms of heredity through the process of sexual selection. Thus, when Mendel's work is combined with Darwin's, a more thorough account of evolution is the result.

In this context Ernst Haeckel developed Mendel's work and made the claim that "Ontogeny recapitulates Phylogeny." **Ontogeny** refers to the pattern of the development of a species. **Phylogeny** refers to the history of the development of that species. If we look at the development of the human embryo we see it going through various stages. It develops the reptilian brain, it has gills to survive in the amniotic fluid, and so on. Thus the development of the human embryo involves going through the development—the evolution—of the human species. While this view has been modified it still holds. A current redefinition of the principle states that "it is more appropriate to suggest that existing related forms diverge from a more generalized embryonic form into distinctive adult forms during development."[59] Another way of putting this point is that

> ...the genetic development program has no way of eliminating the ancestral stages of development and is forced to modify them during the subsequent steps of development in order to make them suitable for the new life-form of the organism. The anlage of the ancestral organ now serves as a somatic program for the ensuing development of the restructured organ. What is recapitulated are always particular structures, but never the whole adult form of the ancestor.[60]

The biological evidence of today, thanks to developments in

genetics and embryology, confirm the general facts of evolution. But other questions remain. Darwin believed that natural selection was the only process of evolution and that the process worked slowly over time. Yet various fossil records seem to indicate that evolution can also occur quickly. This is especially the case in areas near water. Lynn Margulis[61] has demonstrated that for changes to occur additional oxygen is needed since cell evolution is a form of biochemical change. More oxygen and a greater variety of food—more changes in the biochemical environment—occur near water than inland. But another one of those Kuhnian ironies happens here. In 1960 Sir Alister Hardy published an article in *The New Scientist* suggesting that human evolution occurred on some coastal area rather than according to the received view that humans evolved in the jungle or near the jungle to adapt to a changed food gathering environment[62]. However, his work was ignored. Margulis does not mention it , yet, if anything, Hardy's hypothesis supports her conclusions. Even now his work is not readily discussed, except by feminist writers commenting on evolution.

Hardy's main points are that humans are virtually hairless (except for the hair on their heads) relative to our closest cousins, the apes. She concluded that the hairline developed to reflect a swimming body—that our erect bodies, and the hair on our heads but not on our bodies, reflected a species who spent a lot of time wading in water. These points are developed by Elaine Morgan in her 1971 book *The Descent of Woman*[63] Morgan's main point is to account for the role of women in the evolutionary process. The role of women and the changing view of science is a topic for the next chapter.

At this point we can conclude that evolution is a fact even if there are disputes about the theory—the explanation of the process of evolution. Evolutionary theory can be seen as an excellent example of Kantian philosophy in that Darwin theorized beyond directly observable data in order to make sense of that data. As the theory has developed we see how it adapts to new information, especially when some aspect is demonstrated to be false. We have also seen how the concept of paradigms or frameworks sometimes operated to prevent developments in the theory. But in any case the fact of evolution cannot be denied.

FREUD

Psychoanalysis also has roots in the latter part of the nineteenth century but is very much a contemporary theory. It was first developed by

Sigmund Freud at the end of the 19th century. He began doing work on the nervous system and was very much influenced by the work of Darwin and Helmholz. As a result of these influences he saw humans as dynamic biological beings and wanted to be able to understand how these beings functioned in neurological terms. However, his work with patients led him to develop the psychoanalytic process as it is still widely practiced today. His early concern was with the way our biological makeup worked so that we could become self-aware beings capable of rational action? Due to the antisemitism of Vienna at that time, Freud was denied a promotion at the university, so to support himself he was forced to enter private practice as a physician with his specialty the treatment of nervous disorders. The development of psychoanalysis is an excellent example of the concept realist view of science at work. In Vienna Freud was exposed to neo-Kantian philosophy. He was influenced by Franz Brentano and was quite familiar with the work of the English philosophers and psychologists. He even translated some of John Stuart Mill's work into German. Freud began his theorizing as a result of problems he saw in his patients. He then turned his analysis on himself. This self-analysis was the basis for his book *The Interpretation of Dreams*, published in 1900. Over the years he modified his views as new evidence in the form of patients' problems presented itself. He revised his early work significantly, with the result that some people like to distinguish between the early and the late Freud. See for example Peter Gay's biography, *Freud: A Life for our Time*, where he titles the whole section of the book dealing with Freud's later work as "Revisions."[64] One very important reason psychoanalysis became so popular, influential and long-lasting is that the theory developed out of actual medical practice. Whenever Freud or one of his followers theorized about some aspect of human behavior, the theorizing almost always arose out of actual practice and the write-up of the theory was always supported by clinical evidence.

And, as we shall see, Freud developed a complex theory of psychology which relied on all kinds of unobservable entities and processes to explain observable behaviors. Also, since his theorizing came directly out of clinical practice, we can see Freud as following the concept realist view in not making a distinction between fact/value and pure and applied science. All theorizing and evaluating was done directly from clinical experience. Since Freud wrote so much and was constantly revising his work, and because he made important contributions to all facets of psychology, the best way to present his work in a short introduction is to do it systematically rather than historically.

During his long career Freud was concerned with five basic issues:

1. Finding a biological basis for explaining human behavior
2. Understanding the various specific neurotic symptoms he discovered in his patients
3. Developing a complete concept of a person so that the individual symptoms could be understood in context
4. Developing a method for alleviating the symptoms and for curing the underlying disease
5. Understanding how civilization is possible and what its effects are on individual behavior.

As we have seen, Freud began his career as a neurologist. One of the underlying assumptions that he held throughout his career was that behavior was explainable in biological terms. In 1895 he wrote *Project for a Scientific Psychology*, a work which was not published until 1950. He argued that there are neurological networks for providing internal stimuli, neurological networks for providing the reception of external stimuli and neurological networks for providing interaction between internal and external stimuli. These networks were at the basis of behavior. Using his training as a scientist and his work as a physician, Freud developed a view of psychological disorders as a form of disease which could be treated and cured. In order to cure a viral infection we must not only alleviate the symptoms but we must also kill the virus. That is we must eliminate the cause of the symptoms. In order to cure neurotic behavior we must not only alleviate the behavioral symptoms but we must eliminate the cause of those symptoms. Thus Freud employed a medical model of disease which he applied to psychology.

The discussion above brings out a very important distinction between cause and symptom. The symptom may be alleviated but the patient may not be cured because the underlying cause that gives rise to the symptoms may still be present and we may shortly see a new set of symptoms in the patient. Many critics of behaviorism, especially those influenced by another view of psychology, such as psychoanalysis, see behaviorism as only changing the symptoms of a problem by altering a person's behavior, arguing that unless the cause of those symptoms is dealt with, the person will soon exhibit a new set of symptoms. Behaviorists try to explain this away, but their inability to deal properly with this point is one of the factors that led to the demise of behaviorism. Interesting questions for behaviorists arise in this context. Where are all the conditioned behaviors stored? Where are all the things persons have learned? This answer is obvious—since they are not conscious, they must be unconscious.[65] The important point here for Freud is that to trade one set of symptoms for another, even if the second set of symptoms allows the patient to function better that he could originally, is still not to cure the patient. And it is a cure we are looking for.

Hysteria was an illness that was highly prevalent in the early days of Freud's career. Freud traveled to Paris to study with Charcot, who had made important strides in the understanding of hysteria by using hypnosis. Freud was initially greatly influenced by Charcot and used hypnosis early in his practice. Another important influence was H. Bernheim whose *De la Suggestion et de ses applications a la therapeutique* held the maxim "suggestion is everything". Bernheim's book was published in Paris in 1886 and this maxim is quoted by Freud in his discussion of Frau Emmy von N. in *Studies in Hysteria*[66]. At this time Freud was collaborating with Dr. Josef Breuer who also used hypnosis in trying to treat hysteria. In 1895 they jointly published *Studies in Hysteria*. This text contains five case studies, one by Breuer and four by Freud. They begin by using hypnosis to discover the underlying causes of the symptoms and suggestions to eliminate them. But, as Freud soon came to realize, this method had its limitations in that it all too often only eased a symptom instead of getting rid of the cause. He also had some difficulties with hypnotizing patients. At first he thought it was because he did not have the proper technique but later he came to realize that, even if this were the case, hypnotism and suggestion were not the answer to curing hysteria.

These doctors were beginning to learn that the secrets to understanding the nature of the illnesses lay in uncovering the causes buried in the patients' memories. By getting the patients to talk under hypnosis with their guards let down, information was given that was not given in a normal state. This information was the basis for the kinds of suggestions Breuer and Freud gave their patients. But this method proved to be insufficient in that two problems arose. One was the above-mentioned problem of replacing one set of symptoms with another. The second was that even under hypnosis patients did not always yield the needed information. It was this last problem that led Freud on his investigations of the unconscious and the mechanisms of repression. These investigations led to the development of the methods of cure we now call psychoanalysis. Thus the idea of the "talking cure" was still valid but instead of using information gained under hypnosis and then suggesting how the patient should alter her behavior, Freud came to realize that the patient had to be made aware of the causal factors in her past that led to the present day symptoms. In so doing the patient will offer resistance because these memories are painful, which is why they were repressed in the first place. It was the realization of these repressed memories in conjunction with the triggering event that led to the curing of the neurosis.

We see almost all of the major themes in psychoanalysis presented here. But it took the better part of the next thirty years to develop the proper explanations of how the unconscious worked and what its relation to consciousness was. It was during this process that Freud developed his views on sexuality. We shall look at these issues in turn.

The discussion of the unconscious will be based on three of Freud's works.[67] Freud defines "conscious" as "the conception which is present to our consciousness and of which we are aware..."(Freud, 1912 49). "Unconscious" is defined in terms of latent conceptions and memory.(Freud, 1912 49) The unconscious is dynamic because unconscious ideas have an effect on us and/or can become conscious.(Freud, 1912 50) It is the active unconscious that is revealed by the process of psychoanalysis. (Freud, 1912 51) Thus

> Unconsciousness is a regular and inevitable phase in the processes constituting our mental activity; every mental act begins as an unconscious one, and it may either remain so or go on developing into consciousness, according as it meets resistance or not (Freud, 1912 53).

The postulation of the existence of the unconscious is justified from clinical evidence and

> because the data of consciousness are exceedingly defective; both in healthy and in sick persons mental acts are often in process which can be explained only by presupposing other acts, of which consciousness yields no evidence.(Freud, 1915 116-117)

Freud continues that it is the unconscious which yields connections between otherwise seemingly unconnected conscious events. His argument then takes a decidedly Kantian turn. We have a concept of personhood that tells us that all persons have thinking and feeling capacities, so our perceptions of others in the light of this concept gives us knowledge of other persons. Or, as Freud puts it, "we impute to everyone else our own constitution and therefore also our consciousness, and that this identification is a necessary condition of understanding in us." (Freud, 1915 119) This point holds for our unconscious thoughts as well. Just as Kant warned us not to overlook the fact that our perception is subjectively conditioned and must not be regarded as identical with the phenomena perceived but never really discerned, so psychoanalysis bids us not to set conscious perception in the place of the unconscious mental process which is its object (Freud, 1915 121). And the unconscious contains

> on the one hand, processes which are merely latent, temporarily unconscious, but which differ in no other respect from conscious ones and, on the other hand, processes such as those which have undergone repression, which if they came into consciousness must stand out in the crudest contrast to the conscious mind. (Freud, 1915 122)

The unconscious is a complex mechanism. It is not only made up of latent and repressed thoughts but also contains our basic biological drives and instincts as well as our social conditioning and our moral ideals—our consciences. This is where Freud's famous id and superego come in. Throughout the modern era the basic assumption about humanity is that we are conscious rational beings. With all that Freud has to say about biological determinism and his causal model of explaining behavior, he still maintains this view, even if as an ideal. After all, one must remember that the behaviors that Freud explained were the neurotic behaviors of his patients. He did not have to explain normal behavior even though he had to understand it so he could treat abnormal behavior and have a model of normalcy to be attained. This normal rational conscious part of our personalities is known as the ego.

> It is to this ego that consciousness is attached; the ego controls the approaches to motility—that is, to the discharge of excitations into the external world; it is the mental agency which supervises all its own constituent processes, and which goes to sleep at night, though even then it exercises the censorship on dreams. From this ego proceed the repressions, too, by means of which it is sought to exclude certain trends in the mind not merely from consciousness but also from other forms of effectiveness and activity. (Freud, 1962A 7)

But not all of the ego is conscious. Part of the ego itself is unconscious and works to control and communicate with other components of the unconscious.

We are born as ids. But since we are human we quickly begin to develop our egos. And as we explore the world and are conditioned to behave by our parents and by the norms under which our society functions we begin to develop a built-in monitor—our consciences. This is the super ego. The super ego becomes not just a conscience but literally the superego or ego ideal. Our egos tell us who we are. Our superegos tell who we think we should be. (Freud, 1962A Chapter 3)

Let us explain this in more common sense terms. We are born. Being human means we have a basic biological makeup. We need to survive. We need to explore our environments to discover how we can survive. In this exploring, and in our maturing, we develop a sense of self. And as we behave and test what we can and cannot do we are controlled or punished or rewarded. In this way we learn our limits. We learn what we can and cannot do. We learn to develop a sense of expectations from the people around us.

The unconscious reasoning process goes something like this. I see something I really want. My id says, "go for it". My superego says, "you can't have it". My ego looks at the situation and sees under what conditions I may be able to satisfy my desire, even if this satisfaction is with some substitute. If my ego is weak, either the id will dominate, in which case I become an impulsive person with little or no self-control, or the superego will dominate and I will become an obsessive or highly repressed person who is afraid to act. The purpose of psychoanalysis is to "enable the ego to achieve a progressive conquest of the id." (Freud, 1962A 46)

Now we must look at Freud's views on sexuality since they pervade his views on both personhood and the nature of culture. In his Introductory Lectures, Freud asks his audience to think about what "sexual" means. His answer is that "Everything connected with the difference between the two sexes is perhaps the only way of hitting the mark:..[68] He continues

> In the popular view, which is sufficient for all practical purposes in ordinary life, sexual is something which combines references to the difference between the sexes, to pleasurable excitement and gratification, to the reproductive function, and to the idea of impropriety and the necessity for

concealment. (Freud, 1960 313)

He goes on to argue that this view in not sufficient for science. It is necessary to look at the role of sexuality in our personal and social development and how it pervades all aspects of our lives. He begins by looking at the new concept of childhood sexuality and points out that it would be absurd to think that children have no sexual life before puberty, that they

> suddenly acquire these things in the years between twelve and fourteen would be, apart from any observations at all, biologically just as improbable, indeed nonsensical, as to suppose they are born without genital organs which first begin to sprout at the age of puberty.(Freud, 1960 320)

Freud makes two points here. One is that it is a mistake to equate only sexuality with reproduction. The second is that because of our biological makeup, pleasures that we experience in childhood form the basis of our adult pleasures, which, of course, are sexual in nature. So the infant who finds pleasure in nursing develops a desire to suck on other things, thus the mouth becomes an *erotogenic* zone and the sucking pleasure becomes *a sexual one*. (Freud, 1960 322) This is so because

> Sucking for nourishment becomes the point of departure from which the whole sexual life develops, the unattainable prototype of every later sexual satisfaction, The desire to suck includes within it the desire for the mother's breast, which is therefore the first object of sexual desire;...(Freud, 1960 322).

More generally, because everything we do reflects sexuality, in one way or another every stage of development also reflects this sexuality. Freud draws an analogy between a seed and a plant and a child and an adult. The material for the plant is already contained in the seed, as are adult tendencies in the child. The basic stuff, as it were, is already there. It just has to be developed. And how it is developed will depend on the sexual health of the adult.

Children go through various stages of development and at each one the objects of their explorations change. As children become more aware of their bodies they explore them; as they become more aware of their environments they explore them. All of this exploring comes together at then time of puberty when children go through what Freud calls the

Oedipal stage. Basically, this is the stage when the child becomes sexually aware in an adult sense. At this stage, the parent of the opposite sex becomes the child's first mature sexual object. Boys develop a sexual desire for their mothers and girls for their fathers.

      As it turns out there are significant differences between how boys and girls mature. Freud saw masculinity as the dominant sex and the penis as the dominant sex organ. Men can develop sexual insecurities which are reflected in what Freud saw as a castration complex where men feared they would either literally or symbolically lose their organ while women envied the male role and the male organ. For Freud biology was the determining factor in how sexuality affected social roles. His views on this were strong enough for him to state "anatomy is destiny."[69] .180

      How one gets through this stage of development provides the basis for one's sexual relationships for life. If the child does not mature properly he or she will spend his or her adult life looking to satisfy the immature desire for the opposite sex parent and will probably never be satisfied since no one can quite measure up to image of the parent in question. If the person has not properly matured during his or her earlier stages, the object of sexual desire may be fixated at an earlier stage of development. This lack of maturation is the foundation for adults seeking sexual gratification with children. Psychologically speaking these adults are still children, but they are children with adult needs and drives. Also, when siblings are born, the competition for the parent heats up—how the parent expresses and handles this can lead to dysfunctions in the family as well. If the parent did not get through this stage of development properly, problems stemming from that stage can surface in this context. Thus a parent can develop serious neuroses with regard to his or her children, which, in turn, will lead to neuroses developing in the children.

      The point here is that we are sexual beings and if we deny this we create problems for ourselves in our dealings with just about everyone and everything we come into contact with. As the clinical work in psychoanalysis has demonstrated, adult neurotic symptoms are brought on by a an event that happens now, but the person reacts in that way because of how he or she was brought up originally. Children who are not permitted to explore will not develop proper attitudes to themselves and their sexuality and their superegos will dominate their personalities. If no restrictions are placed on children they will become impulsive and their ids will dominate. For the ego to remain in charge children have to be allowed to explore, but they also have to be made aware of the limits of what is permissible or when it is permissible. To understand these limits we have to understand the social context of behavior. So we now turn to Freud's views on the nature of civilization.

Freud begins his investigations by trying to understand the basis of various rituals which reflect a culture's symbolism. This symbolism, usually an animal, is called a totem. This totem is not only a symbol of a group of people—a clan or a horde—but the people also see themselves as descended from this animal. They are one with this animal and consider it sacred, so all kinds of taboos develop around the treatment of the living animals. For example, killing such an animal is punishable by death. But under certain conditions when the clan works as one, ritual killings are permitted. Since Freud saw parallels between this kind of behavior and neurotic behavior he attempted to use psychoanalytic methods to determine how this totemic structure developed. [70]

This whole issue of how social structures develop is important to Freud, since most of his work is in the area of individual psychology. Even in his later life, and running all through his work in culture and civilization, there is the view that the social order is made up of individuals. So the ways in which individuals come together to share values, beliefs and social taboos becomes extremely important. In this work Freud relies heavily on the work of William Robertson Smith's 1889 work *Religion of the Semites*. The point that Smith makes is that since sacrifice implies a divinity, "it was a question of arguing back from a comparatively high phase of religious ritual to the lowest one, that is, to totemism." (Freud, 1962B 132-133)

Sacrifice was the essential ritualistic feature in totemic religions. It was a public occasion in which "individuals rose joyously above their own interests and stressed the mutual dependence existing between one another and their god."(Freud, 1962B 134) The ritual eating of the sacrifice created a bond among the participants creating a kinship relationship. And this kinship relationship, which predates family life, provided the foundation for family life and all the rules, rituals and taboos found therein. (Freud, 1962B 135)

Freud compares this information to the modern family. He sees the totemic animal as a substitute for the father:

> This tallies with the contradictory fact that, though the killing of the animal is as a rule forbidden, yet its killing becomes a festive occasion—the fact that it is killed and yet mourned. The ambivalent emotional attitude, which to this day characterizes the father-complex in our children and which

> often persists into adult life, seems to extend to the totem animal in its capacity as a substitute for the father (Freud, 1962B 141)

So let us imagine the state of nature. In a state of nature men fight for survival. Freud's state of nature is not unlike that of Locke's, though it may be a bit more brutal, where the basic kinds of social organization probably consisted of bands of males, all of whom had equal rights.

> One day the brothers who had been driven out came together, killed and devoured their father and so made an end of the patriarchal horde. United, they had the courage to do and succeeded in doing what would have been impossible for them individually....Cannibal savages as they were, it goes without saying that they devoured their victim as well as killing him....The totem meal, which is perhaps mankind's earliest festival, would thus be a repetition and a commemoration of this memorable and criminal deed, which was the beginning of so many things—of social organization, of moral restrictions and of religion. (Freud, 1962B 141-142)

These developments occurred because the contradictory feelings that the crime aroused led to a sense of remorse, which in turn led to a sense of guilt. The memory of the dead became stronger than the living father. What was prohibited by the strength of the father in life was now prohibited by the sons out of their guilt. In so doing

> They thus created out of their filial sense of guilt the two fundamental taboos of totemism, which for the very reason inevitably corresponded to the two repressed wishes of the oedipus complex. Whoever contravened those taboos became guilty of the only two crimes with which primitive society concerned itself. (Freud, 1962B 143)

These two crimes were murder and incest. Thus the basis of civilization is guilt and from guilt comes the prohibition of the crimes that led to that guilt. That murder should be one of these crimes is obvious. It reflects remorse over a deed which could not be undone. Incest is a bit more complex, however. Since the first object of a child's sexual awareness is the opposite-sex parent, one of the benefits of killing the father would be sexual access to his women, the brothers' mothers. Here we see the basis of the Oedipal stage when the child develops sexual awareness and the opposite sex. By actually doing something to satisfy that desire, and by developing a sense of guilt because of it, such behavior must become taboo.

To see how this notion of guilt works in modern society we turn to Freud's last word on the subject, *Civilization and its Discontents*[71]

Now that we understand how civilization can be established we must look at the problems that living in civilization create. Given Freud's views regarding the biological basis of behavior, with personal and genetic survival being the two strongest drives, we see what Freud calls the pleasure principle as the basic program of life. (Freud, 1969 13) This is important since in the state of nature we have no artificial constraints on our behavior whereas in civilization we do. Indeed, this point can sum up the theme of Freud's work here. We need civilization to have an orderly way of satisfying our needs, but the constraints that civilization put on us create frustrations. The healthy person must find a path between the two.

We can develop an analogy between civilization and the individual here. Just as the healthy ego must control the opposing forces of the id and superego, the healthy person must control the opposing forces of his desires and of the constraints of civilization. In the state of nature we are threatened with our own mortality and with the forces of nature. But in civilization we are also threatened from our relations with other people. All of the benefits that we gain from living in civilization are opposed by the constraints of having to live with other people. In this sense Freud anticipated Jean Paul Sartre's famous dictum: other people are hell. This is the theme of Sartre's play *No Exit*. Freud would perhaps add that other people can also be heaven. Thus living in civilization puts us between heaven and hell. As Freud says

> A good part of the struggles of mankind centre round the single task of finding accommodation —one, that is, that will bring happiness—between the claim of the individual and the culture claims of the group; and one of the problems that touches the fate of humanity is whether such an accommodation can be reached by means of some particular form of civilization or whether this conflict is irreconcilable. (Freud, 1969 33)

When people enter into a social order the social order takes on a life of its own and makes demands on its members that may not have been anticipated at the outset. Such demands may be seen as psychologically unrealistic, thereby creating the negative aspects of civilization. (Freud, 1969 45-48) These affect us because of the way we are brought up in that civilization. These precepts or values are taught to us and become part of us. Indeed, we internalize them without realizing it and these social values become part of our superegos.(Freud, 1969 60-62) By internalizing social values the social order utilizes our consciences—our sense of guilt—to behave accordingly. This guilt is based on a kind of fear. In a state of nature we know what we fear: natural elements and rivals who are stronger than we are. In society we still fear authority, but the reason we fear it is because that fear has been internalized.(Freud, 1969 64) We really fear our superegos. Guilt makes the world go round because everyone in the world has internalized that guilt.

Life is based on the pleasure principle. But a lot of life is destructive, which is why Freud, in his later life, postulated a death instinct alongside the life instinct. This was presented in 1920 in *Beyond the Pleasure Principle*[72]. Just as he saw individuals engaged in a struggle between achieving individual happiness and dealing with social restrictions, he saw societies functioning in the same way. We know that individual aggression comes from unresolved or repressed desires. The energy has to be released somehow. If there is no allowable social outlet, or if the individual is too repressed, the energy will escape in an irrational manner. How it will escape will depend on the individual psychological makeup of the person in question. Depending on how one was brought up—how one resolved his oedipus complex—one will rape, murder, commit incest or just go on some kind of rampage. And what happens on the individual level can also happen on the collective or social level. If a whole society is repressed it can express its collective frustration in collective action, which can take the form of internal aggression such as rioting or external aggression such as war. Wars, of course, are about conquest and territory and principles, but the fact that men are capable of fighting wars has to do with their basic biological and psychological makeups. A society can only go to war if its members are capable of warlike behavior.

Recall how civilization leads to the internalization of values. These values are internalized by individuals who may have all kinds of unresolved conflicts—from guilt feelings to unresolved oedipal concerns. If these unresolved conflicts are endemic then members of the society, utilizing their internalized social values, will try to resolve these conflicts in the same way. If they identify with their society as individuals identify with their families, they become capable of collective action. This can be a war against another society in the same way a family may use aggression against another family or an individual may use aggression against another individual. Thus, in a very real sense, on this Freudian view, societies go to war because of such things as unresolved oedipal complexes.

Now it is time to sum up. We began this discussion with the Kantian view of science and of personhood. Then we presented the contemporary view of neo-Kantian science called concept realism. This was followed by the work of Sigmund Freud as the natural law flag bearer of this view. Freud's view can be seen as a natural law view since he presents a view of science and uses that view of science to develop a view of personhood. This is a naturalistic one in that Freud begins with a biological view of personhood as a person exists in a state of nature, then shows how that person develops in a social context. He ends by showing how civilization is possible and how the foundation of a civilization carries the seeds of its own possible destruction.

A good illustration of the Freudian model at work is in William Golding's novel *The Lord of The Flies* in which we see a group of young boys left on an island to avoid being affected by the war that the adults are fighting. They form into groups and create a totemic society, the totem being the head of a wild pig they have killed. At the end of the novel when the adults come to rescue them we see the adults in uniform with their battleship in the harbor. This illustrates that the primitive totemic society the boys have created on the island with its tribal warfare is not significantly different from the adult civilization with its sophisticated war machines. The veneer of civilization is very thin indeed.

So we see the psychoanalytic view of personhood as a very complex one. We see the Kantian concept realist view at work in that in many ways it is the unconscious functioning that really defines who a person is. To put this in Kantian terms, the ego or conscious world is the phenomenal world and the underlying unconscious world is the noumenal world. But since we have theoretical knowledge of the unconscious—of the noumenal—Freud has gone beyond the Kantian view. The philosophical implications of this point will be discussed later in this chapter.

He also follows this view with regard to causality. While he tries to explain everything in causal terms his arguments are not purely deductive but are what I above called conceptual. In therapy every patient is different and the ways that information is brought out are different. Thus, while explanations of neurotic symptoms are causal, they are narrative relative to specific cases.[73] For a discussion of this issue see Sherwood, Michael, *The Logic of Explanation in Psychoanalysis*. Freud was also a good methodologist in that he constantly held his views up to public scrutiny and constantly revised his views in the light of clinical evidence.

More importantly, psychoanalysis, while it was the invention of one person, became a whole movement or school of thought where practitioners would criticize the work of others. In this sense it is an ongoing developing way of looking at the place of humanity in the overall scheme of things. The first major critique of Freud's work came from his own disciple, Carl Gustave Jung, who developed a different view of the workings of the unconscious.[74] Karen Horney also challenged Freud's view of women as well as his methods of treatment, stressing adaptability instead of cure.[75]

ANTHROPOLOGY

Darwin and Freud influenced many other thinkers in different fields. Some of these influences led to interesting developments in these fields, which, in turn, led to further criticisms of Freud. We shall now look at how views on the nature of civilization have developed by two anthropologists in this context. We shall begin with the work of Robin Fox. Fox uses Freud's views on incest to begin his anthropological view of this issue. Fox begins by stating that his book "can be seen as an attempt to rewrite Freud's *Totem and Taboo* with a half century of hindsight."[76] (ix) Freud is important here because "It was the pursuit of incest as the root problem of social evolution that linked Freud to the anthropologists." (Fox, 1980 2) But in looking at Freud's work, and the work of virtually all anthropologists who have written on the subject, Fox thinks they asked the wrong question. By putting the question in terms of why there is a horror or universal taboo against incest they were actually begging the question, for posing the issue in those terms assumed that such attitudes and practices were the case. But such is not the case. So, perhaps, the question should be asked in terms of why humans do not commit much incest or of why humans do not want to commit much incest, or of why, if humans don't commit much incest, they are hard on those who do.(Fox, 1980 9)

Asking the questions in those terms not only begs the issue but ignores the relationship between nature and culture. This is important for two reasons. First, forms of incest do exist in nature and in some human societies. So the real question has to deal with where and when it may or may not be appropriate. Second, in culture incest is linked with exogamy—marrying outside one's group. Fox wants to know why we can explain why most societies ban marriages with close relatives but why we cannot or do not explain the ban on sexual relations with the same relatives, especially since "there are countless examples of relatives forbidden in marriage with whom sex is not forbidden..." He goes on to argue that

> We are certainly going to see that exogamy and incest *are* linked, but they are linked, as Freud thought they were linked—in the process of evolution. (Fox, 1980 12)

Fox concludes that the questions that must be asked regarding incest, then, are not those to do with the taboos but those that try to account for such behavior in evolutionary or biological terms. We can say that, from an evolutionary standpoint, humans are "'naturally' non-incestuous" (Fox, 1980 14), but given this we then have to explain how this naturalness leads to cultural taboos. Fox sees the issue more in terms of why do we favor exogamy rather than why we fear and ban incest.

He begins his argument by looking at how various human societies organize themselves to avoid incest or promote exogamy. He sees here how socialization mixes with biology to create such mechanisms. In his early work on kinship he concluded that

> The intensity of heterosexual attraction between co-socialized children after puberty is inversely proportionate to the intensity of heterosexual activity between them before puberty. (Fox, 1980 50)

And, following a study by Joseph Shepher of marriage patterns on kibbutzim in Israel, which showed that out of 2,769 marriages there were none between people who had been raised together to the age of six, Fox would amend the previous statement to read "between them before the age of 6." (Fox, 1980 50)

The point here is that such social conditioning occurs early in life. The implication of this conditioning being complete at such a young age—essentially the same age that Freud saw the basic personality of the child as being set—provides evidence for Freud's primal horde. Fox goes on to argue that something like Freud's primal horde must have taken place with the results contributing to the development of incest avoidance mechanisms between parents and children. (Fox, 1980 61)

Here the argument takes an interesting turn. We tend to think in terms of small families and specific genetic lines. This was not always so, especially in a horde, no matter how small that horde would have been. Fox sees the issue not just in terms of who is related but in terms of future relationships. If my opposite sex sibling is going to be a mother in my society I will stay away from her. But if she is not going to have that role the incest taboo may not apply. Referring to Jack Goody's studies on lineage, the general rule is not to not sleep with related women but "do not sleep with those women who are reproducing the lineage for you." (Fox, 1980 65)

This issue of reproducing lineage raises the issue of kinship relations for such relations determine who will or will not be in one's reproductive lineage. Different kinship relationships will define lineage differently, but all kinship relations have such definitions and all have rules regarding incest and exogamy. While Freud was definitely on to something with his primal horde myth it may not have happened the way he suggested it did. This is especially the case since Freud was always trying to show that his findings were universal in character. Anthropology has shown that on the one hand there are numerous social structures and that each social organization solves its problems in different ways, and on the other hand even though there are numerous social organizations with different solutions to their problems, there is a similarity of problems to be solved. So there may have been many such hordes with each dealing with the problem in a different way. But all of the hordes would have had to deal with the same problem. Fox rewrites Freud's myth as follows:

> In the beginning the sons were kept from the women of the horde by the fathers, and much as they would have liked to, the sons did not kill the fathers but simply withdrew from sexual competition with them. The frustration of their sexual drives was so intense it was frightening to them, so that when the fathers died (or were driven out) the sons could not face sexuality with the women. Their sexual interest in them was so intense, however, that while they took other people's sisters to bed, they acted out the fantasy of having children by their own sisters. They claimed the sisters' children as their own and denied the genitor any part in the process. Thus at one stroke they eliminated the fathers both as authorities and as sexual rivals. (Fox, 1980 73)

Here it is fear of their own motives rather than horror over their deeds that leads to the structure of taboos.

It is not only the psycho-anthropology of Freud that forms much of the underpinnings of Fox's view but also the biological evolutionary views of Darwin. Fox sees the explanations for what Freud described as a possible outcome or outcomes of the natural selection process. This brings us back to Freud's uncompleted attempt to explain behavior in biological terms. Freud was influenced by Darwin, as is Fox. To establish that such issues as incest and exogamy are natural solutions to natural problems, Fox turns to studies of primate behavior. He looks at the social organizations of gorillas and chimpanzees and finds that though these animals have different social organizations most if not all of these differences can be attributed to the environmental niche in which they live. How they live, how and where they get their food and how they have to protect their young in that context are the determining factors of social organization. But in one way or another all of these groups of apes exhibit exogamous behavior.

In these social organizations there are differences. Multi-male groups have enduring kinship groups while single male systems have permanent polygamous families. Fox finds that in different groups there are enduring ties based on relatedness and enduring ties based on lasting mating relationships. But in primates they do not exist together as they do in humans. To see how our biological inheritance developed into a purely human behavior pattern we must look at the evolution of the brain.

The focus of this is how the evolution of the human brain changed primate behavior and which aspects of primate behavior were kept. The point here is, of course, the point of evolution. More evolved species still reflect their biological inheritances, thus studying our nearest biological relatives gives us an idea of where we came from and what biological traits we inherited, while at the same time seeing how and why we differ The main area of difference in brain structures between humans and other apes is in the frontal lobes and in a larger brain, with brain size understood not in terms of mere size but in the ratio of brain size to body weight . This larger brain allowed humans to monitor their environments and learn to make decisions not just on emotional or instinctive responses but with the use of reason. (Fox, 1980 111) This capacity allows humans to be more adaptable to changing situations. Thus

> the more complex and crucial the information the animal has to deal with--that is the more complex and dangerous the social situation it finds itself in--the more it will have to

develop the capacity to equilibriate in order to survive. And the capacity to equilibriate lies in the complex relationship between the newer and older parts of the brain—between the limbic system, which is the source of emotions and which we share with all mammals, and the new parts of the cortex which are so greatly expanded in the primates (Fox, 1980 112). Fox quotes from the work of M.R. Chance "Social Behaviour and Primate Evolution", and "Nature and Special Features of the Instinctive Social Bond of Primates". We therefore conclude that the ascent of man has been due in part to a competition for social position...in which success was rewarded by a breeding premium, and that at some time in the past, a group of primates, by virtue of their preeminent adaptation to this element and consequent cortical enlargement, became preadapted for the full exploitation of the mammalian cortex. (Fox, 1980 116-117).

This means that if we go back to our horde we see the basic conflict arising out of a combination of social status, or the lack thereof, and of the competition for the best mates. A lesson of evolution is that something like this happened among primates as well as humans. Thus primates adopted various social structures as solutions to their concerns. These solutions were primarily explained in terms of the relationship between a food supply and the way in which the population lived in that environment. So we see one solution for primates who live on the plain and another for primates who live in the jungle. However, humans with their larger brains, taking this biological inheritance along with their new-found awareness, moved concerns of sexuality from the purely biological to the emotional. Thus the seat of sexuality for humans is in the mind, which is why we react so strongly to it. It is this evolutionary development which allows for the Freudian notions of guilt to control our social organization.

The question remaining is what event in history led to this development? Fox's answer is that "The brain began its upward march at about the same time as the earliest evidence of systematic large-scale hunting." (Fox, 1980 129) One important aspect of evolutionary theory is that for changes to survive there must be an open niche. Fox sees this niche for the big carnivore hunter. As he puts it: "Nature had a vacancy; man applied for the job." (Fox, 1980 131) Once in the job man developed to better grow into the job. Fox presents the work of Philip Thompson which makes the point that there is a predictable ratio between the size of a carnivore's prey, the length of its infancy, the size of its brain and the size of its body. (Fox, 1980 131) Fox goes on to argue that as the hunter's brain increases, so does the size of his prey. Smaller hunters compensate by attacking "in a body." Thus "social carnivores" such as humans can attack prey larger than themselves while freeing brain capacity for other functions. Thus, there is plenty of brain capacity "left over for things other than the hunting of large prey, even if this is what the large brain is needed for in the first "(Fox, 1980 131-132)

These additional brain functions were what later allowed for the development of language and the ability to develop complex tools and greater social complexity. And this greater social complexity led to the conditions described by Freud in his primal horde story. Thus the social condition of man is a direct result of his biological evolution.

So the question now becomes how man controls inbreeding. Part of the answer—indeed a great part of the answer—comes from our evolutionary past from which we inherited nature's tendency to outbreed. But because of our larger brain and the social complexity of human life we have to find other pieces to complete the puzzle. This is where Freud's story enters the picture. Man had to learn how to control his hostile impulses, especially those directed towards other men and not prey. By turning these impulses inwards man develops a fantasy life—an unconscious life. And these biological and unconscious controls go to work shaping man's social and personality structures. Thus, while our biological inheritance may be the source of our exogamic and anti-incestuous behavior, because of our larger brains and capacity for abstract thought and self-awareness we needed other forms of restraint to prevent us from squandering our inheritance. The results of these additional psychological behavioral restraints take the form of kinship relationships and sex-related social roles. Kinship systems are not just about the nuclear families of today. They are about "relationships set up between people who exchange spouses according to a set of rules." (Fox, 1980 140) There can be many such sets of rules or organizations. But whatever the rules, limitations are placed on individual choices. And these limitations are enforced by our biological heritage and by Freudian guilt.

And out of kinship relationships, in the context of hunting, come sex roles. Men and women take on specific social roles. While Fox does not use the term we can see Freud's "anatomy is destiny" surfacing here.

> The male-female division of labor has to do with vegetable foods, which the women gather, and animal protein obtained by the men...The trading of these products is essential to the diet of the omnivorous animal...The trading of these products

of "labor" between the males and the females, is probably at the root of a truly human society...Men no longer needed women for sex only, and women no longer needed men for protection only, but each had a vested interest in the *products of each other's labor*....The hunting way of life radically altered the *content* of social relations in the band, even if the general *structure* stayed the same (Fox, 1980 143).

In this context what kinship does is to set up the procedures and rules for who could mate with whom. As a result rules regarding incest and exogamy become entrenched in the culture. And once a stable culture is established men can concentrate on developing their newly developed mental capacities.

The point that Fox makes here is that men developed language and began to exert control over their environments. But these mental capacities are still part of what it is to be human in full biological evolutionary sense. The mind is simply an evolutionary product which developed to fill the niche provided for by man's larger brain. Thus, psychology is really a development of biology and anthropology. No wonder Fox is so influenced by Freud and why he can conclude that

> we learn easily to be uneasy about incest and categories and throw ourselves readily into the business of exogamy and exchange is not because of a fear of because these things were the pattern of our evolution, and our bodies, minds, and dire consequences or reprisals or even because of rational foresight or anything but that we are the kind of creature that evolved to do these things social Behaviour are these things--are the living, physical memory of them. We reproduce what produced us; there is no other way (Fox, 1980 197)

In an earlier work, which set the stage for his work discussed here Fox argues that if the proverbial Adam and Eve were put where they could survive and breed in isolation ,

> they would eventually produce a society that would be likely to have: laws about property, its inheritance and exchange; rules about incest and marriage; customs of taboo and avoidance; methods of settling disputes with a minimum of bloodshed; beliefs about the supernatural and practices relating to it; a system of social status and methods of indicating it; initiation rituals for young men; courtship

practices, including the adornment of females; systems of symbolic bodily adornment generally; certain activities and associations set aside for men from which women are excluded; gambling of some kind; a tool and weapon making industry; myths and legends; dancing; adultery; homicide; kinship groups; schizophrenia; psychoses and neuroses; and various practitioners to take advantage of or cure these (depending on how they are viewed)...In short, the new Adam and Eve would ...produce...a recognizable human culture and society....All these things would be there because man is the kind of animal that does these kinds of things.[77]

These days we hear a great deal about incest, usually of the parent-child variety. If this behavior is so unnatural, according to the views presented here, how can this behavior be so widespread? The only answer I can proffer is that we have created a culture which, at least from a sexual standpoint, is unnatural. In Freudian terms, we have a culture in which we do not allow our sexuality to mature properly and where so many people focus their sexuality at the level of their own sexual immaturity. In Darwinian terms we have developed a culture which has ceased to be adaptive to its environment. By divorcing our sexuality from our cultural and physical environments we have lost its proper focus. Thus, if Fox is correct in arguing that incest is unnatural, then any society in which incest occurs on a measurable scale must be, in some sense, an unnatural society. "Unnatural" here simply means that we are trying to force ourselves to live in ways which deny our basic natures.

We shall now turn to the work on the origins of culture by another Freud-influenced anthropologist, Marvin Harris.[78] We will see the Freudian position re-interpreted here. Harris notes that cultures take many diverse forms, but that the forms that culture takes are not just the results of chance.

> I think there is an intelligible process that governs the maintenance of common cultural forms, initiates changes, and determines their transformations along parallel or divergent paths. The heart of this process is the tendency to intensify production (Harris, 1977 4).

Harris sees increased food production as a response to various threats to a culture. Such threats include changes in climates, people migrations and competition for resources. Harris goes on to argue that such intensification, while initially successful, ends up always being counterproductive since "it leads inevitably to the depletion of the environment and the lowering of the efficiency of production". (Harris, 1977 4) Since this is always the result, Harris wants to know why people always choose this alternative. It should be pointed out that for all our supposed sophistication this is still the way we seem to do things today. But Harris' theorizing begins with less sophisticated cultures.

The answer has to do with increasing population. The main reason a culture needs to increase production is to feed itself. As the population increases so must food production. The theme that runs through Harris' work is that the forms cultures take depend largely, if not entirely, on the relationship between population and physical environment. This can take many forms, depending on climate and available resources. But the bottom line, so to speak, is how the physical environment can support the population living in it and how that population harvests what the environment has to offer. Thus the initial problem for early civilization was balancing population with food supply. If populations increased then food supplies had to increase. If food supplies could not increase then either populations had to be reduced or new sources of food supplies had to be found. If new sources of supply could not be found population control was the only alternative. Fertility could be controlled with diet. Harris shows that low fertility is linked with diets which are high in protein and low in carbohydrates. High protein allows the mother to nurse longer thereby delaying her fertile period (Harris, 1977 16).

When birth control methods fail, more drastic methods such as abortion and infanticide were used. How these problems were solved, given the physical realities of the environment, determined the form the culture would take.

Most early cultures were hunter-gatherers. Or perhaps a more accurate label would be gatherer-hunter since more of the food supply tended to come from gathering than hunting. But soon many cultures turned to agriculture. The main reason for the shift from gatherer-hunter to agriculture had to do with the depletion of animal protein sources. Harris does not see agriculture as a step forward in cultural evolution. Indeed he argues that the gatherer-hunter lifestyle was advantageous in that it provided the same amount of food for a lot less work, as long as the food was available. The point is that gatherer-hunters switch to agriculture is cost/benefit. "The idea of agriculture is useless when you can get all the meat and vegetables you want from a few hours of hunting and collecting per week." (Harris, 1977 26)

Agricultural cultures take various forms. Just because a group begins to cultivate some of its food supply does not necessarily mean that this group will establish a permanent farming village. This depends on the number of people and the nature of the other resources available to them. So people can form all kinds of cultures and live in all kinds of settings. The determining factors will always be the relationship between the population and the available food supply. Thus biological survival and reproduction are the determining factors in the structure of a culture.

When cultures compete for a food supply they go to war. This was the case for gatherer-hunters as well as for farmers. But gatherer-hunter warfare was not as vicious as warfare between agricultural communities. This was so for a number of reasons. One had to do with the permanence of such communities. Feuds could develop over generations. Also, a sense of ownership of territory made the defense of that territory stronger. Such communities were larger, thereby increasing the scale of the conflict. (Harris, 1977 35) But if the balance between populations and food supply is the social or political cause of war we still want to know why individuals are capable of such behavior.

Harris, following Ashley Montagu[79] argues that "There are no drives or instincts or predispositions in human beings to kill other human beings on the battlefield, although under certain conditions they can easily be taught to do so." (Harris, 1977 37)

So why do we do so? In order to answer this question Harris looks at questions of fertility. After all, if populations could be controlled there would be little or no need to compete for dwindling food supplies. Thus, fertility is the key. In a group consisting of one man and ten women there could be ten births. If there were ten men and ten women there still would be only ten births. And in a group with ten men and one woman there would be only one birth. Thus "the number of women determines the rate of fertility." (Harris, 1977 39) This fact, in times of overpopulation and/or dwindling food supplies, or especially in times of war due to these causes, leads to the creation of a strong patriarchal social structure and the devaluing of women. The extreme form that this takes is female infanticide. This is so because the group needs both more defenders and fewer people. Thus Harris argues

> that without reproductive pressure neither warfare nor female infanticide would have become widespread and that the conjunction of the two represents a savage but uniquely effective solution to the Malthusian dilemma. (Harris, 1977 41)

This explains a lot of other factors with regard to the social roles of men and women. For example, even during warfare when there is no serious lack of food women are more highly valued.

> After all, women can do most of the things men can do, and they alone can bear and nurse infants...Anthropologists have been misled about women's labor value by the fact that among hunter-collectors women have never been observed to hunt large animals. This does not prove that the observed division of labor naturally follows from the brawn of the male or from the supposed need for women to stick close to the campfire, to cook, and to nurse the children. Men on the average may be heavier, stronger, and faster runners than women, but in favorable habitats there are few production processes in which these physiological features make men more decisively effective than women...Women hunters could easily substitute for men without reducing the supply of high-quality protein. And several recent studies have shown that among horticulturists women provide more calories and proteins in the form of food plants and small animals even if they don't hunt big game...The explanation for the near-universal exclusion of women from big game hunting appears to lie in the practice of warfare, the male-supremacist sex roles which arise in conjunction with warfare, and the practice of female infanticide—all of which ultimately derive from the attempt to solve the problem of reproductive pressure. (Harris, 1977 42)

Thus "if the whole system is to function smoothly, no woman can be permitted to get the idea that she is as worthy and powerful as any man." (Harris, 1977 43)

The underlying theme here is that the forms cultures take depend on the relationship between food supply and population. Implied in Harris' work is that the respective roles of men and women are dependent on whatever the solution to the problem will be. Thus, unlike Freud, who saw that "anatomy was destiny" Harris would hold that social and sexual roles are dependent on the nature of the culture and its relationship to its physical environment. To develop this point further let us look at a recent study by anthropologist Patricia Draper who spent time studying the !Kung tribe in South West Africa.[80] Draper compared the ways jobs were divided along sexual lines in two groups of !Kung. One group still lives as hunter-gatherers in the Kalahari and the other has established a more sedentary lifestyle living by farming and animal husbandry with a bit of gathering. Both groups are of the same generation and therefore can be used as controls for each other. The group that has become sedentary reflects a different division of labor than does the hunter-gatherer group.

> Features of sedentary life that appear to be related to a decrease in women's autonomy and influence are: increasing rigidity in sex-typing of adult work; more permanent attachment of the individual to a particular place and group of people; dissimilar childhood socialization for boys and girls; decrease in the mobility of women as contrasted with men; changing nature of women's subsistence contribution; richer material inventory with implications for women's work; tendency for men to have greater access to and control over such important resources as domestic animals, knowledge of Bantu language and culture, wage work; male entrance into extra-village politics; settlement pattern; and increasing household privacy. (Draper in Reiter, 1975)

While the hunter-gatherers appear to be least sexist society known.

> Features which promote egalitarianism between the sexes include women's subsistence contribution and the control women retain over the food they have gathered; the requisites of foraging in the Kalahari which entail a similar degree of mobility for both sexes; the lack of rigidity in sex-typing of many adult activities, including domestic chores and aspects of child socialization; the cultural sanction against physical expression of aggression; the small group size; and the nature of the settlement pattern. (Draper in Reiter, 1975)

Now let us return to Harris and his comments on Freud. These comments are made in the above context of warfare and sex roles. The important point here, as we have just seen, is that the secondary role of women is not their natural role but one forced upon them by the conditions of warfare. Harris notes that Freudians have long been aware of the links between warfare and sex roles "but they have inverted the causal arrow and derived warfare from male aggressiveness rather than male aggressiveness from warfare." (Harris, 1977 64) Of Freud's view, which we stated above, Harris says that while it might appear to be "sheer poppycock, anthropological research has shown that there is a widespread if not universal occurrence of psychodynamic patterns that resemble

Oedipal strivings." Harris goes on to say that Freud was on to something. "What is poppycock is the idea that the Oedipal situation is caused by human nature rather than by human cultures."(Harris, 1977 65)

Reinterpreting Freudian theory in the light of this anthropological approach, Harris concludes that "The Oedipus complex was not the cause of war; war was the cause of the Oedipus complex (keeping in mind that war itself was not a first cause but a derivative of the attempt to control ecological and reproductive pressures" (Harris, 1977 65-66).

The main difference between Harris and Freud could be that Freud saw society as the product of individuals while Harris sees individuals as the product of their cultures. And the main differences between Fox and Harris could be traced to a similar source. Fox stays closer to Freud than Harris does. Fox also relies more on biology. He sees human culture in psycho-biological terms, with the psychology the result of biological evolution. Harris also sees biological evolution as the basis of human culture, but he sees how the development of culture led to a change in the nature of the beast. To use Fox' language, as the human brain evolved, the nature of human culture changed. This change was not just quantitative, as Fox appears to argue; it was also qualitative. The new cultural forms had as much influence on biology as biology had on culture. As we have seen, Fox acknowledges the interplay between biology and culture but he keeps the causal arrows running in the same direction. Cultural changes are always a result of biological changes. Harris sees how causal arrows can change direction. Biological evolution led to changes in human culture, but these changes in culture could have led to changes in how humans further evolved. Thus in Harris' work we see a greater interplay between culture and nature; while Fox acknowledges both factors, he sees less interaction. So Fox can maintain that anatomy is destiny, but Harris would not maintain so strong a position.

As we have also seen, in many respects there are greater similarities between the works of these two anthropologists than differences. These similarities have to do with their emphasis on the underlying factors that make us what we are. They both look to biology and psychology for their explanations of human behavior. Thus they are good concept realists in that people really are their noumenal selves; their biological and psychological inheritances. The not-directly-observable factors are what are needed to explain the observable forms of human behavior. And we have seen that both of these anthropologists take psychology seriously, but not in the same way.

One issue that can be raised here is the notion of human

consciousness. Freud believed normal humans were conscious but neurotics were controlled by their unresolved unconscious conflicts. Fox stated that the mind develops out of evolutionary pressures. He remains a Freudian, so perhaps he would accept Freud's view on consciousness. Harris does not address the issue directly but his discussions of behavior imply consciousness. The point I want to make here is that if humans are capable of conscious thought, and can therefore behave in a rational manner, even if the kinds of choices they make may be limited by their biological and psychological makeup, humans can then make some, albeit limited, choices as to the kinds of social orders they want to live in. Of course, we may find that even though we choose to live in certain ways, these ways will not work because of our biological and psychological inheritances.

SCIENCE IMPLICATIONS

Now that we have seen examples of Kantian thought as it has been used in science, we must look at the philosophical implications of this practice. We have seen how Kantian thought leads to knowledge, now we have to look at the issues which show us how that knowledge is possible. Let us begin with a look at the problems with the positivist view stated above. As discussed above, a law of nature is a general or universal statement covering all instances of a range of phenomena. The problem that arises is how such knowledge was attained. If the basis of knowledge is observation and if we only observe one thing at a time, even if we investigate fully all the properties of those things we observe, how do we get into a position of being able to say something about all such entities?

So let us return to our chairs. We look at one chair and observe its properties, then we look at another chair and observe its properties, and so on until we get to a point where we believe that we have observed enough chairs to make a general statement about the whole category of chairs. Of course we know that the possibility remains that we will come across something that we would classify as a chair but which does not behave in the way in which all other chairs we have observed have behaved.

If observation is the basis of knowledge and if we observe single cases, it seems somewhat arbitrary to decide when enough cases have been observed to make a generalization out of those observations, one which can be used in future explanations, which can given the status of a law of nature, which is supposed to be considered as true and, once considered true, is always supposed to be considered to be true. Thus, though this view of science claims that scientific explanations are deductive, this is not really true since the basis for the deduction, the general statement the deduction starts with, was arrived at inductively. On a Kantian view this problem is avoided since our thought processes follow a deductive pattern.

Another important consequence of positivism is that a sharp distinction has been made between fact and theory. Facts are things which can be directly observed but theoretical entities such as atoms cannot be directly observed. So, in some sense, explanations using theoretical entities are not as good as explanations using only direct observation statements. Thus theories are somehow placed on a lower plane than facts. This is nonsense, as we have seen, for theories are used as part of a factual explanation. But, because of the way in which positivism thinks about theories, it has brought this problem on itself.

To conclude this point, the positivist view of science has had a long history and has come to grips with most of the problems facing it, but its insistence on limiting the realm of science to the directly observable presented difficulties which would not go away. I shall now turn to an alternative view of science which arose partly out of dealing with the problems confronted by positivism.

As stated above I shall call this view of science "concept realism". The term "realism" is stressed because of the importance this view places on the postulated entities being real. The term "conceptual" is used because the way in which we use concepts in our thinking, and the relationship between thought and perception, is extremely important to this view.

Let us return to our chair. We still want to know why an object which weighs so little can hold so much. So of course we will observe chairs and we will investigate the properties of the materials used in the manufacture of the chair. But it will be pointed out that when we begin making our observations we do not do so in a vacuum. We make our observations in a context or a framework created by the way in which we formulate our problem. This context, which reflects our concepts and our prior understanding or explanations of the relevant phenomena, plays an active role in how we define our problem and in what and how we look for. The implication of this point is that all observation is concept or theory-laden. The earliest discussion of theory-laden observations comes from the work of Sir Karl Popper who introduced the concept in his first major work, *The Logic of Scientific Discovery*.[81]

Sellars and Feyerabend develop this issue in ways that Popper would strongly disagree with. And there is significant disagreement between Sellars and Feyerabend as well. Some of these disagreements will be touched on in this chapter. This insight has far reaching consequences: it has an effect on how we conceive of the role that perception plays in the gathering of our knowledge, it has an effect on how we think about things and affects how we perceive and classify them, it has an effect on how we think about what an experiment is, and it has an effect on how we conceive of "objectivity". Thus, on this view, while science is still objective, it may not be objective in the same way that positivism is objective. But perhaps the most far-reaching effect of this view is the role that values play in the scientific enterprise.

The first question that was asked was whether or not scientists, in their role as scientists, in a positivistic context, ever made value judgments regarding their work. The answer to this question, given by Richard Rudner, a positivist theorist, was a resounding yes.[82] Even positivist scientists make value judgments in the course of their work. When confronted by more than one hypothesis they must decide which one looks more promising to work on. When dealing with probabilities they must weigh the data and make value judgments regarding what may be more probable. And, ultimately, they must make judgments regarding the overall value of their work. Of course, the actual work of the scientists will remain objective. But values clearly play a role in determining how a scientist will proceed with her work.

The next question dealt with the nature of these value judgments. It was argued that the nature of the value judgments made by a scientist is determined by the nature of the problem she is working on. It is the scientist's interest in certain things, and the reasons that led her to be interested in such things—the way in which the scientist conceives of the problem she is working on—that determine how she will set up her experiments, weight various hypotheses and evaluate tentative findings. Thus, science is not value-free. But in order to make sure that science remains objective, new criteria for objectivity have to be developed.

As we saw in our discussion above about the chair spirit it is pretty easy to find or to interpret data to support one's view. While we did away with seriously considering the spirit hypothesis, we never really disproved it. We just showed that there were good reasons for abandoning it. And then we were able to present another hypothesis for which very good evidence was demonstrated. The point to be made here is that evidence in support of a hypothesis is not sufficient to prove the hypothesis correct. Something stronger is needed. The principle that one must be able to state the positive evidence supporting one's hypothesis is called the principle of verification. The stronger principle that was developed to solve the problem described here as developed by Popper is called the principle of falsifiability. This states that for a hypothesis to be considered worthy of investigation we must not only be in a position to state the evidence that will count as verifying the hypothesis but we must also be able to state the kinds of evidence that will be able to show that the hypothesis can be demonstrated to be false. This does not mean that the hypothesis must be proved false. If that were the case then we would have no scientific knowledge. But we must have some idea as to what would count against our hypothesis. Otherwise we can just find the data to support something, no matter how ridiculous it is.

What does it mean to say that a hypothesis must be falsifiable? Let us begin with some very basic examples. If I say it is raining, all of us can go to the window to look outside. We can all see if it is raining or not. If it is raining, what I said is correct. If it is not raining, what I said is false. But what if I were then to say that I didn't just mean here, but that my statement was general in nature. Thus as long as it is raining somewhere I am correct. Your response would be that such a statement on my part is cheating. Either I should have said that *that* was what I meant originally, or else by adding such a qualification I was in fact making my statement empty of any factual content because I would not let any evidence count against my statement. Indeed, by offering such qualifications, I have made my statement irrelevant to any evidence, positive or negative. As such, my statement, while it looks like a statement made about a possible condition in the world, is in fact just a bunch of words which do not describe anything.

Using the principle of falsification makes doing science more difficult than simply relying on the principle of verification. For in formulating hypotheses we must not only make predictions regarding what we hope will happen as a result of an experiment, but we must also be able to state what could make the experiment go wrong and try to understand why it could go wrong. The point of using the principle of falsification as well as the principle of verification is to insure that one's values can be overcome and that experiments are set up to accurately test the hypothesis and not just to demonstrate what was already believed. Thus, even though a scientist's values play a role in determining what she decides to study, how she will study it and how she will set up her experiments, by having to state what kinds of data will count against her hypothesis, the scientist's personal values can be overcome and objectivity is maintained. This is especially highlighted when the results of the experiments are made public so that other scientists can see if the results can be duplicated.

Now on this view, as was implied by the above discussion, the role of the experiment changes. On the positivist view an experiment was performed in order to gain new knowledge. It was a way of demonstrating whether a prediction based on the original hypothesis would turn out to be true. If the experiment were successful the scientist would say that new knowledge had been gained. If the experiment proved to be unsuccessful, the scientist could shrug off the results by saying that the particular line of reasoning which led to that particular prediction was unfruitful and should be abandoned. But the unsuccessful experiment would not necessarily have any negative bearing on the original hypothesis. Not so on this alternative view of science. On this view an experiment is regarded as a test of the hypothesis. The prediction being tested was derived from the original hypothesis and is thus directly connected to it. The prediction was made based on the understanding of the hypothesis and its possible implications. Included in the prediction must be the kinds of data that will count as verifying it and those that will count as falsifying it. If the experiment is successful we say that, while we have verified the results and have gained this knowledge which before the experiment was only guessed at, in a more important sense we have successfully tested the hypothesis.

If, on the other hand, the experiment turns out badly, we have not only not gained the knowledge we thought we should, but also we must investigate why our reasoning led us astray. In this way we are led back to checking out the hypothesis from which the predictions were made.

This last point opens up another issue regarding the way in which scientific knowledge is to be characterized. If a hypothesis which has previously been demonstrated to be true can, in the future, be shown to be false, then we must revise our whole conception of what knowledge is. Of course, no hypothesis may ever in fact be shown to be false after it has been accepted as true. But, given the implications of using the principle of falsification, it becomes possible that a well-accepted hypothesis can later be shown to be false. In fact, this has happened in the history of science. At one time it was held that the Earth was at the centre of the universe and that the planets and the sun revolved around it. Observations confirmed this view as did predictions based upon it. But as knowledge increased the old hypothesis could not explain much of the newly discovered data. So a new set of hypotheses had to be developed to explain the new data and to account for the old, though the old data had to be accounted for in new ways. One could no longer explain the orbit of Mars in old ways because the old ways had Mars orbiting around Earth instead of around the Sun.

So how does this concept realist view of science characterize scientific knowledge? First of all, knowledge is still based on experience. Thus we still need to look for positive evidence. But all observing is done within a framework or a context formed by the nature of the problems being investigated, one that reflects the values of the scientist and of the society in which she works. Thus the nature of objectivity must change. Scientific knowledge is objective because it can be tested and publicly demonstrated and the results achieved by one scientist can be duplicated by another. But scientific knowledge is not entirely value-free and scientific knowledge is fallible. That is, even though we now know something to be true, it can in the future be shown to be false. Popper responds to this point with his view of theories as a kind of net. We cast out a net and see what we find. When we examine our catch we redesign the net to avoid picking up what we do not want and to try to pick up things that we missed. In this way, by constantly refining our conceptual tools we will, hopefully, develop a theory which will explain everything we want explained.

A very important point in understanding this view of science has to do with the nature of how language is interpreted and how this view of language affects how advocates of this view understand logic. This discussion will lead us to briefly look at deductive and inductive logic again. We will then look at this view's position on the nature of theoretical entities. Recall the problem we had with the positivist view regarding laws of nature. Laws of nature were considered to be general statements from which deductions could be made. But these laws were developed inductively. Thus, though positivism appeared to be deductive in nature, in fact it was not. And since any inductive principle could be shown to be wrong with a new piece of contrary evidence, positivism could not really account for scientific knowledge being timelessly true.

Now, the principle behind induction is that we perceive one item at a time. Once we have perceived numerous instances of something we generalize about that thing. So we observe one chair, then we observe another chair, and a third and so on until we can generalize about the category of chairs. This new view says that in order to first recognize what a chair is we have to have an understanding of the category of "chair". The word "chair" refers to individual chairs and also to the category of "chairs". So when we observe one chair we have already categorized it. By learning language we learn both categories and how to identify individual members of each category. We have seen this point made by Locke, Hume and Kant in different ways. "Chair" refers both to the individual object and to the category of objects. For a contemporary discussion of the issue see Wilfrid Sellars, *Science and Metaphysics: Variations on Kantian Themes*.[83] Sellars calls such terms distributive singular terms. So we do not have to observe millions of chairs before we can generalize about chairs. To recognize that something is a chair is to have already generalized about chairs. Thus, on this view, reasoning about chairs can be said to be deductive right from the start. But this would not be quite accurate. Rather than use such terms as "deductive" and "inductive", adherents of this view prefer the term "conceptual". Thinking about things proceeds as one develops further understanding of a concept. Based on this understanding, one forms hypotheses which will be tested. Indeed, it has been argued that the only way in which science progresses is by putting forward new hypotheses and then trying to refute them by seeing if they can be falsified. This is Popper's view in *Conjectures and Refutations*.[84]

Language is used to convey knowledge about the world. Whether one says that the Earth is in the centre of the universe or that it is not in the centre of the universe, there should be some way of deciding which is correct. Science is that method. By analyzing concepts, by investigating consequences, by performing experiments and by carefully observing the phenomena in question we can, hopefully, decide between truth and falsity. Truth, then, becomes, at least in part, a function of language. Truth is expressed in language and is arrived at through investigation. A statement is true because the sentence which expresses the truth is well-formed according to the rules of the grammar of the language in question and because the words in the sentence are correctly used to refer to objects in the world which can be observed, or at least whose existence can be inferred by indirect observation. How we speak about the world and how we perceive the world are closely linked. In other words, as we learn to speak we are also learning how to categorize, and, therefore, we are learning how to perceive the world. This is why the principle of falsification is so important. If we learn to speak and perceive in the same way, we can all too easily just assume our generalizations are correct. So we must constantly be on our guard to overcome assumptions about the world which may be built into the way in which concepts are used in our language.

This is especially important when talking about unobservable entities. When we talk about atoms or molecules or forces we have to have some idea of what we are talking about and why we are talking about such things. On this view the reasons for postulating such entities is the same as on the positivist view—we want to explain observable phenomena. But in order to do so we must go beyond the directly observable. When we say that a chair supports our weight because the materials that the chair is made of have a certain atomic structure, we are in effect saying that the atomic chair is the way the chair really is. The entities were postulated to explain observable characteristics of the chair. The chair has these characteristics because it has this atomic structure. Therefore, the chair is made up of these atomic structures. It is these entities we refer to when explaining the properties of the chair. Thus language gives us the clue that these entities are considered real as soon as we postulate them.

We see the Kantian influence at work here, even if we are not using Kantian language. We observe things in terms of concepts or categories and we test our explanations against our knowledge. Thus it should not be any surprise that contemporary philosophers of science have come up with new formulations of Kantian themes. Wilfrid Sellars, for example, defends a version of the *synthetic a priori*. In order to understand Sellars' argument we have to introduce the concept of "language games" as presented by Ludwig Wittgenstein[85]. Language follows rules. It is the rules of language that allow us to communicate. We utter noises and those noises stand for objects in the world. We learn language in a social context. As we learn the language we can communicate with others. We understand each other because we all learn the same rules in the same way in that social context, just as we learn the rules of a game as we learn how to play it.

We learn that "green" stands for a certain visual property of such objects as grass, trees, cars, walls, and so on. Let us say I call something green and someone else calls it blue. So we have a disagreement. There are a number of ways we can resolve this disagreement. First we must make sure we are perceiving the same color. Then we must see if the mistake is semantic—am I using the word "green" to stand for something that the rules of the game say should be called "blue"? Or is the other person using the word "blue" to stand for what the rules say should be called "green"? Once this is sorted out we should agree on what we are talking about. It is possible we may have learned some of the rules incorrectly.

Now here comes Sellars' point. If the rules determine how language is used, then in a specific game the individual words and sentences are being used in a way that is necessarily determined by those rules. This necessity gives an *a priori* character to language. But, and here

Natural Law, Science, and the Social Construction of Reality   155

is the second part, the rules of the game can change. Thus the game itself is synthetic. If we were to change the game, or at least to change the main rules of the game we would use language differently. To push this point, the truth of a statement depends on the structure of the language. Change the language and we change what we say is true. So the semantic theory of truth takes on a neo-Kantian synthetic *a priori* flavor. (Sellars, 1963, chapter 10).

Continuing on neo-Kantian themes, Sellars gives an interesting twist to the Kantian distinction between the phenomenal and noumenal worlds. The phenomenal world is the world that is presented to our senses. This is Locke's and Hume's world of secondary qualities. The noumenal world is the substratum, the underlying reality, Locke's and Hume's primary qualities. What modern science has done is to make the noumenal world knowable to us. The atomic structures which underlie our observed reality can be seen as these primary qualities. Thus the theoretical world of modern science is the Lockean and Humean level of primary qualities and the Kantian noumenal world. (Sellars, 1968, chapter 2).

So when I say, "This is a chair," I *know* I am correct since I know I am using the terms in the sentence correctly. We learn language socially as we interact with objects in the world and hear how language is spoken by those around us. Thus knowledge is public. If we all learn the same language the same way we all have the same knowledge of the world. We all see the same things since we all have the same concepts which categorize what we see. This is what makes science possible.

To return to our discussion of theoretical objects, the real chair is the theoretical one. Theoretical statements, even though they refer to entities which are not directly observable, are nevertheless statements about the world, and must be considered as being true or false just like any other statement. So the gap between fact and theory is completely eliminated.

Let us take a look at the way concept realism sees the relationship between laws and theories in an explanation. Recall that according to positivism, theoretical statements were used as background information regarding the nature of the materials used in the chairs. But the heart of the explanation referred to the observable properties of the chairs. On this view, laws of nature are derived partly by observation and partly by concept analysis. We observe chairs, but we also try to fully understand the category or concept of "chair". What theories do is

> explain empirical laws by explaining why observable things obey to the extent they do, these empirical laws; that is

> theyexplain why individual objects of various kinds and in various circumstances in the observation framework behave in those ways in which it has been inductively established that they do behave. Roughly, it is because a gas is—in some sense of 'is'—a cloud of molecules which are behaving in certain theoretically defined ways, that it obeys the empirical Boyle Charles law. (Sellars, 1963 121)

Thus it is a law of nature that chairs of a certain design, made of a certain combination of materials can support so much weight. This has been confirmed and tested. But rather than just have the theoretical information sitting in the background, on this view we are told that the reason why the chair can support that weight is because the chair's materials have the atomic structure they have. It is because the materials of the chair have the atomic structures they have that the chair has the properties it has.

The difference between hypothesis and theory must be emphasized again here. An hypothesis is an educated guess generated by the available evidence. A theory is an explanation. This confusion derives from the positivist view which put hypotheses and theories in the same category.

To sum up this view let us look at the relationship between hypotheses, laws and theories. All scientific investigation begins with a problem. This problem arises in a context. We then formulate possible solutions to the problem. These possible solutions, or educated guesses, are called hypotheses. Given our general understanding of the issues involved and given our understanding of the context in which the problem arose we choose the hypothesis which appears to be the most promising to lead to a solution. We then begin our investigations to see if we can verify this hypothesis. Along the way we use existing laws of nature, or we find a new range of phenomena and find we must formulate a new law of nature. Then we take all the information we have and set up a deductive explanation. In the course of our investigations we found that we had to make various guesses at what the nature of our problem was. That is, we had to postulate unobservable entities and processes in order to make sense of what we observed. Thus we formulate a theory to explain why what we observe obeys the laws it does. The theory comes from our understanding of things but then becomes the defining factor of our understanding. So when we say that observations are theory-laden, we are saying that what we see and how we interpret what we see are determined by the concepts we use that are embedded in, or that make up, the theoretical framework we use to explain the behavior of the phenomena that we observe.

Concept realism is a more complex view of science than positivism. It also includes references to many other subjects. And finally, this view of science must account for the fact that we perceive objects as solid when science tells us they are not. Thus, even to do physics, we have to touch on psychology.

Now let us tie up a few loose ends. Science is a human undertaking that reflects human values and concerns. Indeed, many of the problems we investigate scientifically arise from everyday life situations. And the way in which we investigate them may reflect our personal values and concerns. All investigations begin with a problem. We don't just start investigating. We have to have some sense of what we are investigating and why we are investigating it.

We begin our investigations by observing the phenomena in question. Because our language works with concepts, we already begin to categorize items as we observe them individually. We then formulate generalizations about these classes of items. We then investigate the properties they are made of and how they are used. In order to explain why they behave in the ways observed, we postulate theoretical entities. Since these entities are directly related to what has been observed and since we talk about them in the same way we talk about observable entities, and because the entities are used to explain the behavior of the observed entities, these entities are said to exist in the same way that observable entities exist. We then realize that because these entities explain why the chairs behave the way they do, these entities are what really make up the chair. Theories, then, are true statements about the world. They explain why things behave in the way they do. They explain why categories of objects obey the observed laws of nature.

A theory can be more than just a limited statement regarding the atomic structure of some materials. One can talk about, say, the theory of relativity. In this case we have a very general theory which is made up of laws, and specific theories. The theory of relativity tries to explain why the other theories explain what they do. Now over time we can learn new things or we can come to see old things in new ways. Thus, even if something has been demonstrated as true, it may someday be shown to be false. Thus we say that scientific knowledge is fallible.

How does this view deal with the distinctions between fact and value and between pure and applied science? Because of the way in which problems arise and how they are investigated, this view denies both distinctions. Of course, adherents of this view acknowledge that people use these distinctions, and these distinctions have become imbedded in our culture. But they also argue that these distinctions must be abandoned for they have been shown to be false.

The distinction between fact and value goes by the boards as soon as we realize that what we call facts reflect our language and the way in which we perceive the world. When we make a factual judgment we apply certain conceptual criteria. When we make a value judgment we do the same thing. We think we are expressing an opinion but we are really applying a set of criteria to a situation.

The same goes for the pure/applied distinction. Of course there are people who just work with technology designing new tv sets or computers, for example, and there are people who just work in the theoretical aspects of electronic design. But both workers are essentially dealing with a set of problems arising from practical concerns. In many areas of research, especially in medicine, the practical results come from the so-called pure research while most of the so-called practical or applied research just keeps repeating variations on what is already known. Facts and values work together to lead us to see what we want to investigate. Then we investigate. The findings of the pure investigations should determine how the results are applied.

Science is a rational activity. That means that science should be guided by reason. But since science is a human undertaking, done in human conditions, various factors can intrude on the scientific enterprise. For example, superstitions or cultural myths can often determine what should or should not be studied, or how it should be studied. Intolerances of various pressure groups in society can try to influence institutions that do science with regard to what kinds of things should be studied. Since most science today is done in universities, politics can play a great role in project funding. Science done in industry isn't so much concerned with truth but with better products. Many other factors can influence how science is done. But, hopefully, the rationality of the enterprise will prevail.

Finally, what is involved in doing science in the Kantian concept realist approach as opposed to the Humean positivist approach? The main difference is that on this view we see the importance of developing theoretical explanatory schemes and then inferring our next steps from that theoretical structure. The theory, or the explanation, is what is important on this model for it is the explanation which makes the connections between facts and even determines what is a fact.

Here I would like to recommend some interesting works of fiction that illustrate the relationships between logic and the way science is done. A good way to study logic informally is to read mystery novels. Here one can see the relationship between the gathering of evidence and the use of reasoning. Basically, there are three ways of characterizing such relationships. The first is typified by Sherlock Holmes. Holmes investigates a crime by letting the evidence speak for itself. Of course, in order to know what the evidence says, he must already have an idea of what to look for and how to interpret what he finds. This is why he spends so much time performing experiments. Holmes is the archetypical empiricist. The second view is best typified by the stories of Edgar Allen Poe, where his detective sees no need to do serious investigations. All he needs is a complete description of what happened and he is able to deduce the results. Poe's detective, Dupin, is the archetypical rationalist. The third view is best typified by the stories of Georges Simenon, whose Inspector Maigret examines the scene, forms a hypothesis which leads to the next step in the investigation, and so on. Maigret has even been known to admit that he could be wrong. Simenon is the archetypical realist. This last approach has led to what is now known as the procedural approach to detective stories. One of the best series is the 87th Precinct series by Ed McBain.

ETHICAL IMPLICATIONS

We now return to our discussion of the implications of our biological-social-individualistic view of persons. It is in raising such questions that we see this kind of biological, psychological and anthropological work as becoming the basis of a natural law theory. For such work shows humanity in its state of nature and it shows the relationship between humankind and that state of nature. In other words, by understanding what kinds of beings we are—what we are capable of and what we are not capable of—we can prescribe certain kinds of living conditions that will maximize our humanity and make it easier to live in our environments.

Thus, perhaps, Darwin and Freud started more than they thought. Not only did they try to explain human behavior, they also laid the foundations for a value theory which would make the most of that explanation.

We will return to this topic shortly. But first let us look back at the views expressed in this chapter and at the views about values that come out of them. We shall begin with a very brief look at Kant's views on moral theory. This look will be brief since Kant cannot be considered as a natural law theorist. Instead of using his view of knowledge as a basis for investigating the nature of human behavior he returned to his views on pure reason and argued that pure reason must be at the foundation of moral theory in the same way it must be at the foundation of epistemology.

In the nineteenth century, aspects of Locke's individualism and search for personal happiness were combined with an interpretation of a Kantian view in John Stuart Mill's *Utilitarianism*. This is the view that individuals see happiness, but this happiness is intellectual as well as physical. On this view decisions are made with regard to bringing about the greatest good for the greatest number of people. Now let us return to Freud and look at the ethical implications of his work and see how his view is a natural law theory.

Natural law has been understood here as a view of the nature of the universe and of humanity's place in that universe. The views of one area directly support the views of the other. Thus science and values go together. Science provides the knowledge of what the universe is, how it works and of what persons are. Value theory provides the knowledge of how we fit into that universe and what kinds of limitations must be placed on our behavior to insure that we have a social order that works and that we have sane or rational persons.

Freud began with the individual. This makes sense since he was a physician. But as he tried to understand various forms of behavior he realized that he not only had to understand what a person was but he also had to understand something of the nature of the social order that people lived in, since it was coming into contact with other persons in social situations that led to neurotic behaviors. Freud maintained his view that the individual was the basic building block of society while at the same time acknowledging that social structures had a direct affect on who and what we became. After all, the super ego is primarily social conditioning. But it took Freudian influenced anthropologists to show that the Freudian person was not the basic building block of the social order but was, rather, a product of a social order, an order which has deep roots in our evolutionary past.

There is an interesting parallel here between the concept realist view of observation and the anthropological view of persons. Recall that according to the concept realist position all observation was theory- or concept-laden. That is, we do not just open our eyes and know what we see. We have to learn how to interpret what we see. The parallel is that in the same way an interpretation of an observation is concept-laden, a person is society-laden. How people behave and how they think about themselves is dependent on the structure of the culture they are brought up in. The blueprints for the structure are found in our biological evolution, the social order is the framework of the building and persons are the bricks. It takes all three components to make a culture. Just as, in Kantian language, there cannot be an observation without a concept, there cannot be a person without a social order.

Thus we see how this Freudian anthropological view of persons in the world reflects the concept realist view of science. Just as the atomic chair was the real chair because atomic theory explained how the common sense chair worked, the biological evolutionary anthropological psychological view of the Freudian view is the real person because it takes an understanding of our biological evolution, an understanding of the nature of culture, and an understanding of our unconscious forces to explain the common sense every day behavior of persons.

There is another way to make this point. One of the recurring themes in the philosophical discussions of the nature of knowledge or the nature of truth has been the role of language. Both positivist and concept realist philosophers agree that some formulation of the semantic theory of truth is correct, even if they disagree on what the object of truth is. Thus both Carnap and Sellars, for example, would say that the statement "the snow is white" is true because the stuff in the world we call snow indeed has the visual property we call white. If we used different noises or words to denote these objects and properties then a syntactically correct sentence using those sounds or words would be considered to be a true statement. Thus if that cold white stuff that falls in winter is called mfffty and its color is called brrrty then the sentence " mfffty is brrrty" would be true. This is because of the rules which govern which sounds are used to describe which objects and the rules of how sentences are formed. In other words sentences are true because of the correct uses of the syntax and semantics of the language being used.

In our earlier discussions of Descartes, Locke and Hume, we discussed the privacy of personal sensations in the light of their mind-body dualism. I can feel my pains and describe them but I cannot feel your pains or describe them. This is so because such things are private. Recall also how these philosophers argued that knowledge began with the individual, and in the case of Locke and Hume knowledge began with sense impressions. These impressions are private. Each observer has his own impressions. And each observer uses language to relate these impressions to others. But none of these philosophers address the issue of how we learned that language in the first place.

The issue has become known as the private language issue. The problem here is that on the one hand I use a language to refer to my private thoughts, feelings and impressions. And, presumably, so does everyone else. And because the referents of this language are private there can be no real communication between individuals about these private matters. Indeed, as we have seen, a skepticism regarding whether or not other people have the same kinds of sensations or feelings that I have is warranted. Yet on the other hand, we use this same language to relate publicly observable truths to each other. So, while I can say to someone else that the snow is white and I will be understood, when I say to that person that I have a headache I have no way of knowing if I am being understood since I have no way of knowing if the other person has headaches or, if he does, whether they are anything like the headaches I have.

Thus, on the one hand we have no trouble using language in a public way. And on the other hand we have no trouble using language privately. The question is whether these are two different languages or two aspects of the same language. This can be put in terms a series of questions: If they are two different languages, do they have anything in common? If they are two aspects of the same language, does that mean there is really no such thing as a private language? If this is the case, can we really talk publicly about our private sensations? Or if they are two aspects if the same language does that mean we must accept skepticism in the public realm as well as in the private realm?

The Humean conclusion was that we had to accept skepticism in the public realm as well as in the private realm while the Kantian position would lead to saying that we can talk publicly about our private sensations. But aside from his comments on concepts Kant does not directly address the language issue. But let us take our cue from him. If concepts must have content then we perceive the world in terms of the framework that gives meaning to those concepts. Our thoughts, both public and private are part of Kant's unified manifold. Thus there is a merging of the public and private realms. Since our concepts have content, when we observe other people we take to those observations the full content of the concept of what a person is. We may only know the content of that concept from reflecting on our selves, but when we see another person we know that person has the same kinds of feelings and sensations that we have. But to say that our concepts have content is not enough. We want to know how they come to have content. The answer to this question has two parts. First we shall revisit anthropology and then we shall return to philosophy.

As our ancestors evolved and our brains evolved we became capable of abstract thought and language. The anthropological record clearly shows that there is a biological basis to language since we could not use language until our brains had developed sufficiently. We also know this from linguists such as Noam Chomsky, who has written widely on the subject.[86] Though Chomsky calls his view Cartesian because of the innate factor, after Descartes views on innate ideas, since he does not argue for the innateness of specific ideas but for the capacity to ideate—that the ability to utilize linguistic structures is innate— I have always believed he should have called the book Kantian linguistics. And we know from such psychologists as Jean Piaget that language is learned in social context[87]. If children are not exposed to language they will not learn it.

For the philosophical implications of these points we shall return to the work of Wilfrid Sellars, who attempts to understand the relationship between language and thought, on the one hand, and language and perception, on the other. His concerns have to do with how philosophers have characterized these relationships in the past.

Philosophers such as Descartes, Locke and Hume, because they could not always trust their senses, found it necessary to establish criteria to distinguish appearance or illusion from reality. As we have seen, it was because of such concerns that led these thinkers to make distinctions between the world we sense and the underlying reality. The problem that Sellars sees here is how one can say that something appears to be a certain thing if we don't already know what that thing is supposed to be. For example, under one set of lights a piece of cloth looks orange but under another it looks red. What color is the cloth? Is it red or orange or some other color? To find the answer we must look at the cloth under what we understand to be normal conditions, in sunlight for example. In sunlight the cloth is red. This is because, as Sellars points out "x is red = x would look red to standard observers in standard conditions (Sellars, 1963 147). Standard conditions are those in which things look as they are. But if we can make the distinction between what something looks like and what something is then we have to first understand what that something is. Thus "is" is logically prior to "looks " Another way of making this point is to say that in order for us to make the distinction between appearance and reality we must already have a conception of reality. That is, to make such a distinction we already have to know what would constitute reality and what would constitute an appearance.

The importance of this discussion is that these philosophers all began their inquiries from the standpoint of sensations or private thoughts. When I cannot know for certain if someone else sees the same thing I see, in order to avoid skepticism, I must explain how I can talk about my sensations. Sellars approaches this point by referring to inner episodes. These inner episodes are the private sensations caused by observations as well as thoughts about these observations. The problem comes in trying to show how language is about these inner episodes or sensations. Sellars' point is that for language to be about anything in the world—for language to convey truth—overt speech is about those inner episodes. As Sellars goes on to argue,

> the semantical characterization of overt verbal episodes is the primary use of semantical terms, and that overt linguistic events as semantically characterized are the model for the inner episodes... (Sellars, 1963 188)

So when I say, "the cloth is red" I am publicly reporting a fact, but this public fact began with a private sensation. This process is what makes language an intersubjective process. The reason language becomes the basis for reporting truth is, as Sellars states in his neo-Kantian manner,

> overt behavior is evidence for these episodes is built into the very logic of these concepts, just as the fact that the observable behavior of gases is evidence for molecular episodes is built into the very logic of molecule talk. (Sellars, 1963 189)

The point of this quote is that, given the logic of Descartes, Locke and Hume, their positions are untenable since we cannot begin an inquiry with private sensations, for in order to do so we already have to have a sense of public knowledge. This argument renders the idea of a private language meaningless because in order to speak a private language we would first have to learn a public language. In other words, a private language has the logic of a public language built into its concepts. Thus the whole subjective basis for knowledge is rendered false.

This point is highlighted when we look at the way in which we learn the word "I". It is fascinating to watch children learn to refer to themselves. Once they learn to individuate themselves they begin by referring to themselves by name. Instead of saying "I did it" a child named Bernie would say, "Bernie did it." This is because Bernie hears himself being called "Bernie" and not "I". He hears other people calling themselves "I" so he knows that he cannot be "I". But as Bernie learns how the language works he finally comes to call himself "I". This is because a person cannot understand his own personhood until he also understands the personhood of others. To put this point another way, "the concept of a person is logically prior to that of an individual consciousness." (Strawson, 1963 99)

The way we use language to talk about tables and chairs and grass and snow is the same way use language to talk about feelings or sensations. When I see that Smith in pain I can report the observed fact that he is in pain. And while I may not be able to report on the way Smith feels the pain I will be accurate in reporting the fact that he is in pain. Thus such so-called private experiences are really publicly observable. This same analysis holds for value reports.

We learn terms like "good" and "bad" in the same way we learn terms like "chair" and "table". Since our culture has accepted the Humean separation of fact and value we have come to associate "I like" with "it is good." On the Kantian view the separation of fact and value and the association of like and good is not acceptable. I can like something that is bad and not like something that is good. Let use examples from science, from sports, and from arts.

Above I argued that when we learn such terms as "chair" we also learn to develop the category or concept of "chair". And when we do we also learn to distinguish chairs that do their job well and chairs that do not do their job well. Thus, as we learn what a chair is, we also learn what a good chair is. In this sense, "good" is learned objectively, even if pragmatically. Chairs are designed, at least in part, for a specific purpose—sitting comfortably—thus our understanding of a "good chair" is a chair that meets that criterion. So "good chair" = "comfortable chair", or "good chair" = "chair in which one can sit comfortably."

I am at a football game and am rooting for the home team. We have the ball and the quarterback throws a very long pass that, if caught, will mean a touchdown. But the visiting team intercepts the pass. We boo. We do not like what has happened. But, from the standpoint of evaluating what happened, the player who intercepted the pass made an outstanding play. He did "good" even though I did not like what he did.

When it comes to movies I do not like narration or voice-over. I believe that movies are primarily a visual medium and that a resorting to voice-over means that the director failed at arriving at a visual solution to story-telling. Therefore, he should not have made a film. However, I have a good friend who is a professor of film as well as an award-winning independent film-maker. He argues that film is an audio-visual medium and that voice-over, as long as it does not tell the viewer what is being seen, but adds to the narrative, is permissible. He agrees that a lot of narration in films is redundant. So we argue about Woody Allen films. I cannot watch them because of the narration. He thinks Allen is a genius. When I agree that film is an audio-visual medium and that narration that adds to the story is permissible I can agree that Woody Allen films are well-written and well-directed. But I still do not enjoy watching them. They are good films, but I don't like them.

Next we will imagine a concert where the orchestra is playing contemporary music. Most of the audience finds this music unintelligible and difficult to listen to. They not only do not like it but they also claim it is bad music because it does not have identifiable melodies and pleasant harmonies. But such music can be "good" music because it meets the artistic or aesthetic criteria of the day. One cannot compose today like Bach, Beethoven or Mahler. The forms of those days have been exhausted. The limits of tonality have been reached. Thus the modern day composer must expand the musical language. We might not like it but it is "good" music.

The analogy here between art and knowledge is an important one. Think of a science teacher who claims to be performing an experiment in class. The teacher is not performing the experiment but demonstrating an experiment that was done by a real scientist a long time ago. To compose in the style of the past is to do the same thing. It would be demonstrating how to compose in that style but it would not be art any more than what the science teacher is doing is science. So we see that "like" and "good" are two different notions. "Like" is a personal reaction. "Good" is an objective judgment.

To put this point succinctly, when we separate fact from value we associate "good" with "like". When we associate fact with value we separate "good" from "like".

We learn and use moral language in the same way. We are brought up to think about interpersonal relationships in certain ways and we learn the language that reflects these relationships along with the content of what we learn. Thus, when we say that an action was good or bad we are applying a set of criteria to that action. When we say that killing is wrong we are not just proffering an opinion; we are stating a fact. The statement "killing is wrong" has the same status as "the grass is green." This is because we learn all language in a social context. We learn value language along with object language. This point should be obvious from the preceding discussion. Thus thought and perception are wedded.[88]

Two points need to be mentioned here. The first is that we have subjective reactions to factual situations. We just should not think that those subjective reactions are value judgments. The second point is that in a pluralistic society where different people have learned different values there will be differences as to what is a fact. This does not render such judgments subjective; it just means that more than one set of criteria is being used.

In times of social change we may see old criteria being challenged and attempts made to replace those old criteria with new criteria. Just as there was a scientific revolution when our understanding of the how the physical universe worked changed, we can have moral revolutions when our understanding of what persons are and how they interact changes. To emphasize the point of this discussion, so-called value judgments are not subjective. They are objective in the same way all reporting uses of language are objective. We learn words like "good" and "bad" in the same way we learn words like "table" and "chair". When we use them we apply the appropriate criteria—we apply the appropriate rules governing the use of those words.

The above discussion also applies to the language of feelings. All too often we say that there are no words available to express certain feelings such as love or bafflement. The reason there are no such words is because in our culture we do not value such feelings and we even try to deny their existence. If our culture recognized these feelings we would have words to express them. And we would express them in an objective manner.

It is time to take a breath and see just where we have gotten to. The philosophical issues began in the modern era with the individual as the basic social and epistemological unit. But immediately problems arose with this approach, from the problem of induction to the problem of other minds, to the problem of complete skepticism. Solutions to these problems were proffered, but they ultimately failed because there could never be certain way of knowing that one person knew what the other person knew.

The Kantian approach led the way to a solution. By arguing that one could not separate thoughts from concepts Kant brought out the fatal flaw in the individualist approach. But it took contemporary thinkers such as Sellars and Strawson to complete Kant's work. By showing that individualism is logically dependent on the general, that we cannot have a concept of the individual unless we first have a concept of the general, we show that the individualist approach is based on conceptual confusion. We cannot have a concept of individual persons until we first have a concept of personhood. We cannot have a concept of individual knowledge until we first have a concept of collective knowledge.

This last point ties in with our discussion of Morris in the introduction. His point was that the concept of individualism developed when persons took themselves out of society. But, as we saw in the introduction, persons first saw themselves as part of a social order. By leaving the social order individualism got its start. And then, in the aftermath of the scientific revolution, when the foundations of knowledge had to be reconstructed, the attempt was made using individualism as this new foundation. But this individualistic approach never worked. The major problems facing it could never really be solved without resorting to clever machinations such as instrumentalism in science and custom and habit in epistemology.

But the custom and habit solution led the way back to a new collective solution. Custom and habit are collective, not individual, concepts. Kant took Hume's custom and habit and turned them into the categories of thought. Thus by showing that we think in terms of categories or concepts we can still be empiricists, but we are collective rather than individualistic empiricists, i.e., concept empiricists. Because modern science has used unobservable entities to explain the observable world, and because we acknowledge that these scientific entities—atoms, molecules, forces, ids and egos—are what constitute reality we have come to the position that I have been calling concept realism.

We have seen a parallel argument in this chapter with regard to developments in the social sciences. Freud began as an individualist. His concerns were with individual behavior. But he soon realized that he had to understand the relationship between individuals and the social structures in which they lived. This theorizing led to work in anthropology where we saw how personhood was understood in biological and social terms. Thus we started with the individual but ended up with the culture and the components of that culture. We saw that persons are first and foremost biological beings. This biology is not just the survival and pleasure seeking instincts Freud postulated, though, to be sure, they are part of personhood. Our biological makeup includes our evolutionary history. We are related to the animal kingdom and we have to look for clues to our behavior there as well as to ourselves.

The development of consciousness proved to be a major turning point in our history since it was individual consciousness which eventually allowed us to think of ourselves as individuals apart from our social contexts. But now we have seen that to be an individual is to first be a member of a social order. Thus our friend Timon of Athens, if he had been able to live through all of these changes, would have gone from Timon of Athens, to Timon of the Smith clan, to Timon Smith. And now, if he were to follow the argument and see himself in neo-Kantian Sellarsian terms, or in neo-Freudian Harrisian terms he would start seeing himself as Timon Smith of Athens. He would still be an individual—there is no getting around that—but he would be an individual who knows he belongs to, and gets his identity from, a social order.

Just as individual thoughts are instances of general concepts, just as individual perceptions are concept- or theory-laden, individual persons are products of their biological evolution and social environments. Just as there cannot be a thought without a concept to give meaning to it, there cannot be an individual identity without a social context to give meaning to it.

A good way of summing up the argument about objective and subjective judgments and fact and value is, on the basis of the discussion of this chapter, to acknowledge that values are inherent in facts and facts are inherent in values. Both factual and value claims are objective in the same way.

Now we are in a position to see how to make the connection between the Kantian theories of knowledge and morality. It is not enough to show that we have knowledge through categories and then to claim that moral theory is based on a categorical imperative. We have to take Kant's view that a moral theory must provide reasons for thinking of other people as our moral equals so that we never treat others as means to an end but only as ends in themselves and show that this view can be demonstrated to follow from his views on the nature of knowledge. Thus we can then claim to *know* that others are our moral equals, that we *know* we have moral knowledge.

The way to do this is to return to Kant's notion that knowledge is relative to a category or concept. As we saw in the discussion of language, we learn general truths as we learn specific truths. We learn to apply categories or concepts to particular observations. While we have knowledge of the categories of space and time, of truth, of mathematics, and so on, we also have knowledge of persons as moral agents and as our moral equals. We have such knowledge because we acquire knowledge of persons in the same way we acquire knowledge of everything else. What Kant did not do was to apply his categorical thinking to moral questions.

We learn what a person is, we learn what morality is. So when we look at other persons we *know* we are seeing a moral equal and that we should not treat that person as a means to an end. By separating value from knowledge, our culture has also separated our concept of personhood from the moral dimension, and this separation allows us to think of other persons as objects to be manipulated to further our own ends rather than as moral equals to be treated as ends in themselves. And by using the category of moral personhood, we can answer the fanatic since the fanatic can only de defended by a individualistic approach to persons; by using the collective or categorical approach to recognizing others, the fanatic loses that defense.

People, of course, are individuals and we would not, nor should we want to, deny our individuality. But we must put limits on our individuality if we are going to be moral beings. We can do this by going back to Locke and Adam Smith and developing the notion of the social contract. The main point here, to follow the argument about the nature of knowledge, is that since we acquire knowledge and language through a social process as members of a community we must show how as individuals we can only be moral beings if we see ourselves as members of a community, where each member of that community is the moral equal of everyone else. Just as knowledge is part of a concept or category, people are part a community.

We are individuals but we are born into a social setting. We learn our language and acquire our knowledge through a social process. We learn that we have reason and how to use it by this same process. As we enter the world as an individual who is also a member of a social order or community, we enter into contracts with our equals. It is through this social process that we learn to define ourselves and to realize the limitations of our own individuality and to respect the individuality of others. Some of us become entrepreneurs and start businesses; others are content to be employees. Capitalism, as we have seen, is a development of the individualism of the 17th and 18th centuries. Adam Smith saw markets as relatively small and manageable, which is why the invisible hand could work. But today in a world of multi-national businesses new methods of maintaining the rationality of the market place must be developed. As businesses get bigger, the power of employees must also increase. In keeping with the notions of the invisible hand and of the social contract, workers must enter into a new social contract with employers. Since the businesses are large, the workers must also reflect this size and organize. This brings about the whole notion of labor unions—workers getting together in their own social contract so they can deal with employers on the employers terms. Big begets big. Thus the invisible hand works. New forms of social organization develop to maintain the working of the market place. For big business to oppose the notion of workers' unions would be to oppose the notion of the invisible hand—the rationality of the market place. In our neo-Kantian moral language, for businesses to oppose labor unions would be immoral since it is through these unions that the social contract of the market place is maintained.

If Kant had applied his epistemological categories to his ethical theory he would have developed a natural law theory in which each individual perceives each other individual as a moral equal *and* as an equal member of a community.

We have reached the end of this inquiry. We have shown how a view of knowledge led to a view of science. And we have seen how this view of science works in psychology and related fields. This discussion then led to another look at that view of science. We shall now turn to looking at the implications for ethical theory or natural law theory of the views discussed above. We shall begin with the work of Darwin and then we shall look at the work of Freud.

IMPLICATIONS FOR ETHICS 1
DARWIN

In reading Darwin it is obvious that people are part of nature. This would imply that we must be careful of our natural environment, for without a viable environment we would not be able to survive. In making sense of his notion of the "struggle for existence" we must make sure that we either control our population or increase our food supply. And we see that Darwin's concern was not the individual but the species, so we must think more of how we function in groups to support each other so the group can survive.

For an interesting discussion of the ethical implications of evolution let us turn to the work of biologist C. H. Waddington who, in discussing the nature of ethics, distinguishes between meanings of "ethics". One sense includes "notions as the wickedness of murder or lying, the goodness of loving kindness or truthfulness, and the like."[89] The second sense has to do with how people acquire ethical concepts. This involves not only how children learn but also involves understanding the relation of the child to the external environment. And, finally, we learn how to use knowledge and acquire wisdom. (Waddington 26-27)

We must then learn to pass on ethical information from generation to generation. Waddington sees the process of transmitting ethical information as similar to that of transmitting genetic information, which is why he calls the process "socio-genetic." (Waddington 28) "And just as the content of heredity transmission becomes modified by natural selection, so the content of socio-genetic transmission can be modified by analogous processes, such as the confrontation of beliefs with empirical evidence and so on." (Waddington 29)

Such empirical beliefs must include the point that humans are a part of nature (Waddington 77) and, as such, there can be no omnipotent observer, since we are part of what is being observed. (Waddington 79)

Evolution is not about individual survival but species survival. Of course, if no individual survives, then the species will cease to exist. But the emphasis is on the species, or, in cultural terms, the group. Waddington argues that evolution is not so much about "survival but hereditary transmission,..." he then goes on to argue that

> Biological evolution, then, is carried out by an "evolutionary system" which involves four major factors: a genetic system, which engenders new variation by the process of mutation and transmits it by chromosomal genes; an epigenetic system, which translates the information in the fertilized egg and that which impinges on it from the environment into the characters of the reproducing adult; an exploitive system by which an animal chooses and modifies the environment to which it will submit itself; and a system of natural selection pressures, originating from the environment and operating on the combined result of the other three systems. (Waddington 95-96)

Because of this process "Man, I argue, becomes moulded into an ethical being by his interactions with other members of his social group." (Waddington 100)

This means that mankind has "two heredities, a biological one and a cultural one;..." (Waddington 106) This, in turn, leads Waddington to argue "that the existence of ethical beliefs is a necessary part of the human evolutionary system....we can assign a function to the existence of ethical beliefs, and can therefore utilize the efficiency with which this function is fulfilled as a criterion for deciding between alternative systems of belief we may encounter." (Waddington 173)

Thus ethical thinking is a part of who and what we are as humans because of our combined biological and cultural inheritances. We are biological beings, we are social beings and we are beings capable of using reason in the service of our biological and cultural survival.

The notion of cultural inheritance has been developed in a very different way, but in a Darwinian context by Daniel Dennett who uses a concept derived from the work of Richard Dawkins called "memes" which he defines "as the name or any item of cultural evolution..."[90]

In this context Waddington argues that since adaptability is one of the most important lessons we learn from evolution, "the search for a unified metaphysics remains either an intellectual pastime having no important effects on human action, or it leads belief into the dangerous confinement of a single dimension." (Waddington 193)

Thus any kind of absolutist or fundamentalist belief system, whether in religion, politics or economics must be avoided since fundamentalisms are all based on the concept of an unchanging world view and would not allow us to adapt to changing conditions. To put this point differently, any form of fundamentalism or ideological thinking would be immoral.

This last point is argued for in a different context by Robert Wright in *The Moral Animal*. In discussing different forms of marriage, from monogamy to polygny Wright argues that "...once we've made such choices, once we have moral ideals, Darwinism can help us figure out which social institutions best serve them."[91]

The point here is that there is no clear-cut answer. Different situations, different combinations of factors, can lead to different situations. But the general conclusion holds: the world changes, therefore fundamentalisms cannot offer realistic, workable solutions to real problems. We must be able to adapt to new situations.

IMPLICATIONS FOR ETHICS 11
FREUD

Freud did not directly talk about morality very much. Morality for Freud was, for the most part, the system of values that existed in the social order. But he did try to explain how we came to learn these values and how these values affected us. Some of this issue has already been discussed above in our look at the way in which the unconscious develops and how our unconscious thoughts, which contain our value teachings, become the basis for our behavior. But in a couple of places Freud directly mentions moral issues. In *The Ego and the Id*, in his discussion of the superego Freud talks about how our superego or ego ideal becomes our conscience. The ego ideal is the heir to the oedipus complex "and thus it is also the expression of the most powerful impulses" of the id. (Freud, 1962A 26) Because of the demands of the unconscious on the reality principle of the ego "Conflicts between the ego and the ideal will, as we are now prepared to find, ultimately reflect the contrast between what is real and what is psychical, between the external world and the internal world."(Freud, 1962A 26) This conflict between "the demands of conscience and the actual performances of the ego" (Freud, 1962A 27) is what leads to our sense of guilt. Since the contents of the super ego are socially conditioned we see how our unconscious ego ideal is the product of the social order in which we live. To put this point somewhat differently, our ego ideal is the product of other people. Thus our sense of guilt stems from other people. Which is why Freud can state "Social feelings rest on identifications with other people, on the basis of having the same ego ideal." (Freud, 1962A 27) Freud then goes on to argue that

> Religion, morality and a social sense—the chief elements in the higher side of man—were originally one and the same thing. According to the hypothesis which I put forward in *Totem and Taboo* they were acquired phylogenetically out of the father complex: religion and moral restraint through the process of mastering the oedipus complex itself, and social feeling through the necessity for overcoming the rivalry that remained between the members of the younger generation. (Freud, 1962A 27)

Morality is not just something we make subjective decisions about. The whole concept of morality comes from the kind of biological social beings we are and how we biologically and socially evolve. The biological part of us, our id, "is totally non-moral" our self-aware part of us, our ego, "strives to be moral" and the socially conditioned part of ourselves, our superego "can be supermoral." (Freud, 1962A 44) Thus we see the basis for the example about the conflicts among the three discussed above. What keeps behavior in check is a combination of personal guilt and social constraint. The guilt comes from internalizing the rules of the social order and the constraint comes from the social order acting on those rules. And this is where ethical theory comes in.

> The cultural super ego has developed its ideals and set up its demands. Among the latter, those which deal which the relations of human beings to one another are comprised under the heading of ethics. People have at all times set the greatest value on ethics, as though they expected that it in particular would produce especially important results. And it does in fact deal with a subject which can easily be recognized as the sorest spot in every civilization. Ethics is thus to be regarded as a therapeutic attempt—as an endeavor to achieve, by means of a command of the super ego, something which has so far not been achieved by means of any other cultural activities.(Freud 1969, 79)

This discussion points out that just as we are biological beings who must interact with our physical environments we are also social beings who must interact with our psychical environments. Just as biological survival and reproduction define the kinds of beings we are, so does the fact that we are moral beings. This point gives strength to the point made by Fox that this is the kind of beings we are. We need to survive as a species and we need to survive as individuals. The species always takes precedence over the individual, but there would be no species if there were no individuals. We have biological drives to insure species survival and we develop social or moral constraints to insure individual survival. The drives of one aspect of ourselves—our id—are mediated by another aspect of ourselves—our superego—with a third part of ourselves—our ego—acting as referee. Morality, then, is not really about individual goodness. It is about individual and species survival. Any system of conduct which inhibits this survival is not moral, regardless of how such views are presented. Proof of this statement can be seen in Freud's own time when a socially puritanical and repressive morality led to all of the psychological problems that Freud dealt with. Just because a code of behavior is justified by some appeal to the higher faculty of ourselves or to some external force such as religion, it does not follow that such a code of behavior is moral in the sense it reflects our actual biological and social needs.

This last point best brings out the difference between a naturalistic approach to ethics and an *a priori* approach as we saw in Kant or in religion. In modern Protestantism, which, as we have seen, is tied up with individualism and capitalism, morality was based on individual worth and survival. The main factor in such morality is individual reason. On this point both Locke and Kant would agree. Indeed, one could argue that Kantian reason and Lockean reason were virtually identical. And one could go on to argue that Kant's view of personhood, while much more sophisticated than Locke's, was not all that different in that while Kant's concepts have empirical content, Locke's view of singular distributive terms was not unlike the Kantian position. Both views had the concept of other person in a way that Hume's view lacked.

While Locke's view on morality stayed true to his view of the natural order of things, Kant's view of morality ignored that order and concentrated on reason without context. And this is why we can call Locke a natural law theorist but we cannot do so with Kant. And we can also call Freud a natural law theorist because he places morality in the natural context. But Freud is never explicit about the moral implications of his work. As Philip Rieff states

> What we can learn in reading through what is perhaps the most important body of thought committed to paper in the twentieth century is never comforting. None of the consolations of philosophy or the hopes of religion are to be found in Freud. There are truths in these texts, but no truth; helps but no help. The succession of profound and original insights leaves us more than ever strangers to ourselves. We know more, but we are made to realize how little our knowledge matters. No ultimate advice may be expected from Freud. His is a very intimate wisdom, tailored to this patient and that occasion. Yet he made it clear that we are all, despite the variety of symptoms, very much alike. Therefore, the implications to be drawn from his thought refer to that populous world, made up entirely of latent and manifest patients, in which we all live. No prophet of our destiny, neither Marx nor Darwin nor any other, has spoken with greater import to the human condition in general and yet spoken to it more intimately.[92]

This is so because

> Psychoanalysis is the triumph in ethical form of the modern scientific idea...Freud carried the scientific suspicion of nature into ethics. It was as if, after all the pronouncements of theology and philosophy, after all the indications of experience, we had scarcely begun to understand ourselves. Not only is the external nature examined by the physical sciences basically deceptive, but even more so, Freud insists,

our inner nature—the ultimate subject studied by all the moral sciences—lies hidden. (Rieff 1960, 68-69)

And by discovering this inner self Freud gives us an "ethic of honesty" which would be achieved "by working through the layers of falsehood and fantasy within us to a superior accommodation to reality." (Rieff 1960 315) So, by learning about who and what we are, and by facing those truths, we can finally be in a position to properly understand why we look at the world the way we do, who and what we are and how fit into that world. And Freud's blueprint offers few if any easy explanations. It may not be clearly marked—indeed we make it up as we go along.. The only way we will get our house built is by being relentlessly honest with ourselves, and we do this by stripping away all the comforting beliefs and illusions we have developed over the centuries. For these beliefs and illusions have actually prevented us from ever moving into our new house.

Now there may be no Truth in Freud, as Rieff states, but there are truths. So let us look at the truths we have seen so far and see what implications for a naturalistic ethical theory we can glean from them. The first thing we learn from Freud is that we have to honestly confront ourselves, even if, especially if, we do not like what we find. If we deny anything about ourselves we will not have a clear or accurate picture of who or what we are and will, therefore, develop ethical theories which will make unrealistic demands upon us. And by trying to attain these unrealistic demands we will create all kinds of problems for ourselves. Indeed, one can argue that the source of our neuroses is just this attempt to try to live up to unrealistic demands. Our superegos tell us what kinds of persons we have to be. Our ids try to let our natural drives guide our behaviors while our egos try to mediate the two in a realistic way. But if the ideals are set too high or too unrealistically—in a way in which they cannot be attained—we let our superegos dominate who we think we should be and strive to be something that we cannot be. We repress our true selves. Then this repressed energy tries to assert itself and does so in inappropriate or antisocial ways—in neurotic ways. In the process the ego weakens to the point that we no longer have real self-identities.

This process is a two-way street. On the one hand, we have a bunch of neurotic individuals, while on the other hand we have a sick society. If all members of a society are neurotic then the society will be neurotic. And if the society is neurotic—if the society has unrealistic values—then its members will be neurotic. But if the individuals strive for honesty about who and what they are they will not be neurotic and neither will their society.

While Freud began with the individualistic view we saw that, ultimately, people are a product of the ways in which they have been socially conditioned. So, while people are products of their social environment, that social environment was created by people. All this really says is that you cannot separate individuals from their social context. But if we know what people are and if we know how social orders are created we can change the social order and we can change ourselves. And this is the ethical lesson to be learned from Freud. The first and foremost aspect of ourselves that we have to confront is our sexuality. This does not mean that we just indulge in sex all day long. What it does mean is that we have to acknowledge that we are sexual beings and develop a code of behavior—an ethic—which takes this into account. Such an ethic would involve how we raise our children as well as how we behave towards each other. We would have to be open about sexuality. No more stories about storks and cabbages. When children ask questions we must answer them honestly, albeit in a way they will understand. But even when we are open about our sexuality we still have to live in a social context so we have to develop rules regarding interpersonal behavior. Developing a balance can be difficult. But the main lesson to be learned from Freud here is that on the one hand a society cannot be too free because then people will not cohere into a social unit and no benefits from that social organization will occur. On the other hand, if a society is too strict or too repressive, that society can either destroy itself or direct its energies outward. Thus societies must recognize the instincts and needs of its members and provide outlets for them but must maintain sufficient order so that the society can maintain itself. This illustrates the view that living with other people is like living in between heaven and hell. We need other people to meet our needs, but we have to keep those needs under control in order to keep those other people around.

A good example of this point can be seen in sexual behavior directed towards inappropriate persons, i.e., children and/or other family members. Here is where the lessons of Robin Fox become important. If humans are the kinds of beings who naturally, for biological reasons, shun incest then any social setting in which incest is practiced is clearly a neurotic setting. In other words, by allowing a behavioral pattern which must be seen as unnatural in biological terms to develop we have developed an unnatural social structure. The same holds for adults acting on their sexual desires for children.

What has happened in both cases is that the social order has lost touch with its own roots and has made unrealistic demands on its members. If people engage in incestuous behavior it must be because the social structure is very repressive and does not allow for a normal expression of sexuality. So people have to find hidden but available outlets for their drives. In the case of child sexual abuse we would find not only a highly repressive society but a society which makes such unrealistic demands on its members that those members never properly mature. They stay at an infantile level of psychological development in that their egos have never fully developed to get in control of their ids or superegos so the objects of their sexuality will be at their psychological age level. But since they have chronologically aged they have fully adult sex drives.

Thus by denying our sexuality and by developing a social order that denies who and what we are we create a whole series of problems for ourselves. Also, as we have seen, the kinds of problems that lead to improper sexual behaviors lead to more far reaching problems which, in turn, can destroy the social order. Such issues include overpopulation, too much stress on individualism and losing touch with our physical environments.

Possible solutions to these problems can be found in the evolutionary and anthropological work that has been discussed. Clearly, overpopulation is a major issue. This issue runs through many of the other issues. When the physical environment can no longer support the human population all kinds of problems occur. These problems, as we have seen, include such behaviors as war and infanticide. These lead to increased food production, which, in turn, leads to a serious depletion of resources. And all of this leads to a social breakdown.

One of the most important lessons, if not the most important lesson, we can learn from anthropology is that we must control our populations. There are actually two issues here. Both are implied in Harris' work and the second is made explicit in Draper's work. The first has to do with survival. The second has to do with social structure. Perhaps the best way to make these points is to put them together. When overpopulation begins to create problems such as war or famine, the ways in which people solve these problems leads to another set of problems. These problems arise because of the social structures that are put into place as a result of the first set of problems.

Rigid social structures with clearly defined sexual roles, rigid power structures, and practices such as infanticide all stem from overpopulation. And these practices then lead to a social order which loses touch with its physical environment. The social or moral rigidities that were put in place to deal with the earlier set of problems lead to the kinds of situations that allow incest and child sexual abuse to occur. Without overpopulation, if our numbers were kept down to what could adequately survive on what our environment provides, many of these other problems would never arise. Therefore, value systems which tell us to procreate without limit, on this view, would be considered the height of immorality.

Also implied in this discussion is that we must take care of our physical environment. If we abuse that environment it will no longer be able to support us. Another issue regarding population is important here. This has not so much to do with overall numbers but with the number of people in a group or family. Harris goes on as if the hunter-gatherer way of life is the best way of life there can be. This is so because this way of life affords a good living with lots of leisure time. And it keeps people in harmony with their physical environments so most of the problems that have been discussed in this chapter never arise.

Of course, we can't go back and become hunter-gatherers. We are not going to tear down our cities and ignore many of the advancements that have been discovered over the centuries. But we can learn some of the lessons hunter-gatherers have to teach. First of all, hunter-gatherer groups were fairly small, consisting of perhaps three dozen people. When groups got much larger they would break into two new groups. This is because when groups get too big people become alienated, to use a modern term, and lose their sense of belonging. Also, it is one thing to provide food and lodging for three dozen people; it is another thing entirely to provide for two or three times that number. Another factor here is exogamy. If one group stays too large, and there are few such groups, finding a mate would be more difficult. But with lots of small groups around, finding mates would be easier. This is so both for social or practical reasons and for biological reasons.

Not only is overpopulation a serious problem but so is bigness. However, too small a group can also cause problems. Here I am thinking of the small family unit—the so-called nuclear family—which has developed over the past three centuries. It is called the nuclear family because it represents the nucleus of what a family should be, not a complete family. The complete family would be the extended family—the hunter-gatherer group as depicted by Harris and Draper or any agrarian extended family of the pre-industrial revolution era. The extended families of more recent periods reflect the modern individualistic puritanical ethic and, therefore, represent the same kinds of values we see in today's nuclear family.

The problem with the nuclear family is simple. Because it is too small a unit it has no real control over its own destiny in a large social order. And because it is so small the children in such a family do not become properly socialized. They are at the whim and mercy of their parents' neuroses. In such a small setting, because of the limited and confining structure, if one is not properly disciplined one will never develop a superego. If one is overly disciplined one will develop too strong a superego. In both cases a strong ego will not develop. The implication here is that the "normal" child will be neurotic. He or she will have little or no self-confidence, no real sense of self and will probably be psychosexually immature.

A small family in a large society leads to all the neurotic problems that Freud wrote about. Indeed, the small family in a large setting, with a repressive set of values that put the individual over the group, was the cause of all the problems Freud discovered. In such a setting parents could control and abuse children in a way that would not be available to them in a larger familial setting.

The fact that the so-called nuclear family is breaking down is a sign that it does not work. What is happening, because of remarriages, is that new versions of extended families are starting to develop. For example, Mr and Mrs A, who have two children, divorce. Mr A then marries Ms C and Mrs A marries Mr D. Both Ms C and Mr D had children from a previous marriage. So now the children from all these families start to interact. The problem is that we are still thinking in terms of nuclear families so we haven't as yet made the conceptual switch. But it will come. Instead of calling what is happening the hybrid nuclear family we will soon be calling it the hybrid extended family.

The point here is that we must expand our basic social units while decreasing our larger units. So while we can't tear down our cities and become hunter-gatherers we can change how we identify ourselves. For example in the world today two apparently contradictory things are happening. On the one hand large nations are combining into larger groups. The European Union is one such group and the North American Free Trade Agreement area is another. But even within these areas small groups want to separate. There are the Basque separatists in Spain and there is a movement for the Canadian Province of Quebec to separate from Canada. It is as if we cannot make up our minds. On the one hand we want to join with others and on the other hand we want to break away and assert our independence.

Actually such apparently opposite moves are understandable. One person will not join with another if he sees his identity being threatened by such a union. And since nations or provinces reflect the view of the people who live there, the same kind of reasoning applies. In a political or geographical location where the residents have a strong sense of who they are and where that identification applies to the political entity, those citizens will have no problem in entering into unions with other political entities. But in cases where these identities are weak, or where there are perceived threats to that identity, it will be difficult for such persons to enter into such unions or alliances.

So, in a world where the individual reigns, everything depends on a strong identity. Yet the very conditions which give rise to this kind of individualism lead to individual neuroses. This, as we have seen, is because in an individualistic society, especially a repressive or puritanical one, individuals do not become properly socialized so their identities do not properly develop. And as we have seen the concept of individualism is dependent on the social order. Individualism without a social identification will lead to the break up of the social order. And this will lead to a further eroding of individual identity. Thus extreme individualism as a political or ethical theory is self-destructive.

Let us now tie together all of these loose ends. From the concept realist view of science and from its applications in the psychoanalytic approach to understanding what people are we have learned some very valuable truths. We learned that individual perceptions are concept or theory laden. We learned that individual or self-identity is social context-laden. We learned that scientific theorizing is based on an understanding of a problem or set of problems as they arise in a social or scientific setting. Scientific objectivity is still reflective of the values and concerns of the social order in which science is done. People are reflective of their biological and anthropological origins. To be human is to acknowledge this heritage, this context. So when we do science, especially when we examine ourselves scientifically, we begin with the values and beliefs of the context in which we formulate how we are going to study ourselves. And that context defines what we are going to study. But once we get our studies underway we may discover that things are not what we thought they were. We find that tables and chairs are not solid objects. And we find that we are not the rational self- reliant beings we thought we were.

These conclusions then led to further study. By looking the results of some of these studies we found out some very painful truths about ourselves. But the most important truth is that we will continue to have serious personal and social problems if we ignore these findings. For these findings tell us a great deal about ourselves and about how we should organize our social structures. We need to get away from an extreme individualistic ethic; we need to get away from a puritanical ethic; we need to enlarge the size of our families; and we need to decrease the size of our political identifications. By doing these things we will be acknowledging our biological and sexual heritage and we will create a social and political environment which will allow us to be ourselves. The more we deny who and what we are the more neurotic we become.

But how are we to do this? There are no easy answers. There are a couple of political slogans around that reflect these problems. "Act locally, think globally" is one. This means that if one takes into account larger issues and acts accordingly, the actions of one person can make a difference. So, if I am aware that pollution is a problem I can change my behavior by using my car less and by recycling items that would otherwise end up in the garbage dump. If large numbers of people act this way we will see some change in the overall environment. Such changes will be small and any significant effects will take a long time to see, but this is one way to start.

Since we live in an individualistic culture we can start making individual choices. We can challenge the status quo wherever we can. We can challenge orthodox thinking on economics and politics. We can challenge sexual mores. And as more and more people make such challenges we will see changes in our social structures which will reflect the individual changes. And these changes in social structures will then make it easier for other people to make such changes.

In the political realm the answers are a bit more straightforward, if a bit more difficult to achieve. Modern nations are artificial. Most borders exist because of the results of conquests. But if local separatist movements get started we can return to a kind of city-state where states will develop around large urban areas. This concept comes from the work of urban theorist Jane Jacobs. In a series of books she has shown what it takes to make cities work, how cities evolve, how thriving cities are the basis for thriving agricultural practices and how the whole idea of city states can work.[93] In no way can Jacobs be considered a natural law theorist, but her work uses a naturalistic approach to understanding how cities work. These urban areas are, in a sense, natural artifacts. They are centers of development. And as our political units get smaller our social priorities will change. We will no longer need large armies. And when our militaristic mentality changes we will see changes in attitudes towards social and sexual roles in our society. Remember, in natural law theory it does not matter where one starts because everything is connected.

However, some lessons that individualism has taught us are worth keeping. One of the most important has to do with free expression. As we saw at the beginning of our discussion of concept realism Karl Popper argued that knowledge advances by conjecture and refutation. That means that there has to be a free atmosphere for people to put forth hypotheses, no matter how strange they may sound, nor how threatening to the social value context they may be. For unless ideas can be openly debated a society in crisis will not find any solutions. For the political applications of Popper's philosophy of science see his major political work *The Open Society and its Enemies*[94] in which he takes an extreme individualist position arguing that any form of top-down or bureaucratic or totalitarian society is the enemy of freedom and, therefore, of science. I have always believed that Popper did not always understand the implications of his own work. On the one hand he argued that observation is theory laden, and that he was the person who brought down logical positivism. But his views ended up being not all that different from positivism in that he still believed that science could attain ultimate truth through the process of conjecture and refutation rather than by inductive observation. Thus he did not take the insight about the theory-ladenness of observation to its conclusion.

We have reached the end of this stage in the construction of our house. We began with a look at the major criticisms of Locke, Hume and the positivistic view of science. This led us to Kant, who provided the historical basis for the alternative view of science I call concept realism. We then saw how this view has been used to look at the nature of humanity. We then drew some general conclusions about the implications of this view.

One of the themes throughout these chapters is the notion of change. Another is that our social institutions are, to some extent, products of our choices. The views in chapter three were presented as solutions to problems which arose because of the scientific revolution. The views in this chapter were presented as solutions to problems which arose in the views presented in chapter three. These views are complex and go a long way in answering most of our questions, but problems with this view have arisen in the last quarter century or so.

These problems arise in three areas. First, as we have seen, a great deal of energy has been spent on understanding sexuality and its role in the social order. Since, as we have also seen, biology is not destiny, and that we can choose social relations, the whole notion of our world and our

Natural Law, Science, and the Social Construction of Reality 185

framework of knowledge is, at least in part, constructed by us.

The views in chapter three can be called "modernism" since they reflect what has been known as the modern era. Chapter four dealt with many problems that arose in the modern view of the world. And in the next chapter we will look at the view that has been developing out of this view. This new view of the world is being called "postmodernism" since it follows modernism and because it is a view in progress and, as such, has no complete designation as yet.

The main attribute of postmodernism is to acknowledge that our view of the world is a construct and that it could have been constructed differently. The second attribute of postmodernism is its concentration of constructed notions of gender and sex. If notions of sexuality play a central role in the structure of our social institutions, then by understanding what is involved in sex and gender, we can come to understand more completely how are institutions are constructed so we can reconstruct them.

So, on to chapter five and postmodernism.

Chapter 5

THE POSTMODERN RESPONSE

The last chapter introduced the development of modernism in the 17th century. We saw that the hallmarks of modernism were that the individual was the basic unit of the social order; that individuals came together and in so doing created a social contract; that individualism permeated economics as well as politics so that capitalism became equated with democracy; that reason was seen as the "be all and end all" for solving problems; and that a form of Puritanism permeated the entire individualistic enterprise. This view of the world has certainly had its successes. The modern world has tremendous wealth; there have been tremendous strides in our knowledge of the world; science and technology have given us knowledge to conquer diseases, to help overcome natural enemies, and to enhance our lives.

But, as we also saw, this view of the world has also had its failures. By placing objects or artifacts or symbols before people, people have all too often been misplaced or ignored by modernist social structures. In economic matters this is very obvious. The early modern economic theorists such as Adam Smith and David Ricardo saw capitalism and the developing market economy in a positive way. If the market worked—if the checks and balances of the producer, consumer and laborer worked—if the invisible hand made its presence felt—then the market economy would benefit everyone. But this did not and does not happen. Big interests take over small interests. And when there are problems economists tend to think in abstract terms about the economy.

Adam Smith's view was concerned about everyone in the marketplace. Laborers, consumers and producers had to have equal power for the market to work. Indeed, the market was supposed to serve those who participated in it. But economic decisions always seemed to be made to benefit the abstraction known as the economy instead of the people who participated in it. Thus instead of seeing that everyone had a chance to participate in the economy, economic decisions usually resulted in less participation. This is because the abstraction became more important than the people who made up the economy. So when inflation is rampant, no one asks why. Rather, ideological solutions are put in place which serve the concept of the economy, but not its participants. Such "solutions" usually involve higher interest rates and lower government spending. These moves usually hurt the people at the lower end of the socioeconomic scale—those being hurt by inflation in the first place—more than any one else. If a low wage earner has trouble meeting mortgage payments in an inflationary period, he or she will have even more difficulty in meeting those payments when interest rates rise. And who benefits most from such a policy? The institutions such as banks that control money. Since the bankers and other money handlers are the ones who control the economy, they believe the economy is working correctly when they themselves begin to benefit.

Or look at urban planning. The modern city is an institution of wonder. The modern city is a product of the industrial revolution when people left the land to come to industrial centers to look for employment. We developed transportation systems for getting around these newly developed areas. But soon we started to concentrate on the abstractions again. We had traffic jams, so we had to move more cars. So we built roads to facilitate the movement of cars. But these roads went through established residential neighborhoods and upset the lives of the people who drove the cars. The roads were intended to serve the needs of the people who used cars. Instead, they served the cars and created problems for the people.

The same kind of abstract process took over culture as well. An individualistic culture where people could make their own decisions about what was important to them became a model for mass consumerism, where individualism became a kind of consumer collectivism and where people began to identify with icons rather than develop their own individualism. Indeed, individualism became a kind of icon associationism where one defined one's individualism by which icons one identified with. This process in turn led to style over substance. And as styles changed, so did personal identifications. One had to reflect the current style if one was to be accepted by one's peer group. Thus, symbol, or cultural abstraction, replaced culture.

One of the things that allowed this abstract thinking to be applied to moral questions was the principle of utility, which stated that when choosing a course of action one should choose the alternative which would bring about the greatest good for the greatest number. So abstract thinking coupled with the principle of utility provided a moral justification for acting in that abstract manner. But this manner of thinking leads to a great paradox: while espousing individualism, and while claiming the individual as the basic social unit, but by thinking abstractly and by making decisions in the abstract, individuals were adversely affected. Ultimately this abstract individualism denies the importance of actual individuals.

This process has led to tremendous cultural fragmentation. At one time people read general magazines such as *The Saturday Evening Post* or *Life*. Such magazines had something for everyone: news features, lifestyle columns, fiction, and so on. Now there are virtually no general magazines but lots of highly specialized magazines. So people are less and less aware of other things going on in their culture and know more and more about their own special interests.

This social fragmentation has had serious moral consequences as people find it harder and harder to make connections between different aspects of their lives or between their interests and what is going on in the larger culture. It is as if the world of David Hume as portrayed by Laurence Sterne in *Tristram Shandy* has come true. Everything has become fragmented. Since the automobile has become a major icon of our culture this fragmentation has become very obvious there. John Z. De Lorean's account of his time as an executive at General Motors gives a fascinating account of this. In the late 1950s and early 1960s GM was trying to develop small cars to compete with the smaller imports from Europe that were slowly taking market share away from the North American manufacturers. One such car was the Chevrolet Corvair. This car had a rear engine like some of the European sports cars such as Porsche. The early models had handling problems due to the weight distribution. The cost of fixing the problem would have been $15 per car in 1960 dollars, virtually nothing in a car that cost a couple of thousand dollars. GM had spent thousands of dollars on advertising and legal costs in out-of-court settlements due to accidents with the car. But in the early days management would not spend the $15 per car to fix the problem. As De Lorean states

There wasn't a man in top GM management who had anything to do with the Corvair who would purposely build a car that he knew would hurt or kill people. But, as part of a management team pushing for increased sales and profits, each gave his individual approval in a group to decisions which produced a car in the face of the serious doubts that were raised about its safety, and then later sought to squelch information which might prove the car's deficiencies.[95]

Two points need to made here. One is that the executives would not want an unsafe car for themselves, and perhaps really did not want to build one, but their decisions were made in the context of the abstraction of the "corporation" and the corporation's needs overrode their personal concerns. The second point is that executives were making decisions about areas out of their expertise, further fragmenting the decision-making process. The bottom line though, to use corporate speak, is that these executives ended up building a car that they as individuals would never consider owning. It was being built for another abstraction, "the marketplace". But since the individualism of modernism maintained itself as the main social value, there was no cohesive way to challenge these kinds of actions. Indeed, the people would initially agree with these kinds of decisions since they held the same kinds of values, and thought in the same kinds of structures, as the people who made these decisions.

It was only after dealing with the consequences of these decisions that dissent developed. In an individualistic culture dissent could not become too organized. So we see the proliferation of special interest groups that come and go as issues come and go. Such organization does not lead to coherent political movements. This is also the case since modernist thought tends to be fragmented. Connections between issues are not made. Each issue is seen as an isolated abstraction. So instead of dealing with a set of connected social issues which may have a set of solutions, people look inward and just try to protect themselves from the negative consequences of this fragmentation. Instead of looking to the sources for various social ills, such as increased crime, people build walls around themselves to shut these problems out.

This process is explained in detail by economist John Kenneth Galbraith in his *The Culture of Contentment.*[96] The factors that lead to the downfall of modernist culture are its excesses. By leaving people out of the equation, by seeing things in abstract ways, by not making connections between the different aspects of our culture, we have alienated ourselves from our culture. And this alienation has led to the development of a new postmodern culture. And, as we saw in the preceding chapter on change, the roots of the new order can be found in the old order. The problems that need to be solved, and the ways in which the problems are understood, come from the old culture. It is only by putting these new solutions together that we see we are developing a new cultural paradigm or image.

ORIGINS OF POSTMODERNISM

The roots of understanding the downfall of modernism and the rise of postmodernism can be found in our discussion of concept realism and in the chapter on scientific change. In the discussion of concept realism we saw that facts are concept-laden. The parallel point is that persons are society-laden. We are products of our social environments. The ways in which we are brought up reflect how we think about ourselves. If we are brought up in an individualistic culture we will value individualism. But when we see our social order facing serious problems we will start to formulate solutions which may have the consequences of transforming that social order.

We are seeing in the world today the consequences of this extreme individualism of the modernist world-view. The two points made in the discussion were that an individualistic culture has nothing to hold it together and will disintegrate, and that we have to see individuals in a cultural context in order to understand what it is to be a person. We can see our society falling apart. This is happening partly because of individualistic values triumphing over collective ones. The result of this is that people do not act with other people in mind. That is, we no longer take into account how our actions will affect others. Also, as a direct consequence of this attitude, we tend to deny that we have any responsibility for the consequences of our actions. This point comes out in many ways. My favorite examples have to do with recent court cases. In one case a houseguest was warned not to dive from high places into the swimming pool. He dove off the roof and was severely injured. He sued his hosts and won. In another case a woman bought a coffee from a fast food restaurant, opened it, and held it between her legs as she drove away. The coffee spilled and she was burned. She sued the restaurant for making the coffee too hot and she won. These actions are clearly examples of individualism gone rampant and the breakdown of any meaningful cultural context. It is because of such behaviors that modernism has begun to be challenged. The new paradigm or image that is being developed to replace modernism is currently being called postmodernism. Like all attempts at developing a new paradigm or image, there are many differing models. Along with postmodernism, another alternative paradigm has been developing—feminism. Like postmodernism there are also many differing models of feminism. What I shall do in this chapter is to look at one train of thought which combines postmodernism and feminism. Indeed, the view of feminism that I will present here is an excellent example of postmodern thought. So in the text I will often be referring to feminist postmodernism.

But before we continue we should have some idea as what postmodernism and feminism are all about. The rest of the chapter will fill in the details but some basic definitions are in order here.

As we have seen, modernism is about individualism, a certain model of rational thought and the view that objective knowledge or truth is attainable through the use of the rational methods known as science. As we have also seen, this program has had its failures. Knowledge or truth is context-laden, the uses of rationality have their limitations and individualism ultimately fails. A new paradigm or model of persons in the world, then, will have to offer a view of the connectedness of people, a different model of rationality and a view of science which takes into account the people who undertake scientific investigations and their cultural context. People cannot be left out of the equation. A consequence of this combination of views is that knowledge or truth is not so much discovered but created or constructed out of the materials that are found. In other words scientific truth is as much a human creation or construct as it is something that is found to be the case in the world.

FEMINIST POSTMODERNISM

Feminism is a form of postmodernism in that it reflects many of these concerns. Feminist theory begins from the standpoint that if men and women are to be treated as equals the existent model of persons in the world must be changed. A new paradigm of persons in the world must be developed which reflects feminist concerns. A consequence of this view is that by studying the nature of sexuality and gender the roles of men and women are seen not as biologically determined but as social constructs that can be changed.

This discussion starts with a continuation of the psychoanalytic views presented in the previous chapter. Freud developed a view of persons which reflected the thinking of his day. We saw how his views were developed in different contexts.

We are now going to continue this journey. We will see how psychoanalytic thought is being transformed from a modernist to a postmodernist view of persons. The people whose work we will look at here, like Freud, all theorize from the foundation of clinical work. We begin with a view known as object relations theory and its major theorist D. W. Winnicott.[97]

Object relations theory differs from more traditional psychoanalytic views in a number of ways. The major difference has to do with how infants begin to realize that they are independent beings living in a world that is external to themselves. Freud saw this process occurring as a result of the conflicts between id and superego. Winnicott sees the process somewhat differently. At first, infants have no real sense of self. They don't think of themselves and they see all the objects that they come into contact with as extensions of themselves. Object relations theorists then see infants as becoming aware of the fact that these other objects are not part of themselves. So they begin to experiment to find out what they are. At this point two things happen, according to this view. First, infants start to learn to distinguish external reality from their own imaginations and second, the ego begins to develop. It is the ego that leads the experimentation. It is when the infant runs into parental restrictions that the superego develops.

On this view the ego is stronger than on Freud's view and the ego, or one's sense of self, is based on one's perception of oneself as an object. In other words our sense of self is based more on how we perceive our bodies than on purely psychological phenomena.

The next major difference between object relations and Freud has to do with understanding how children go through the stages of psychosexual development. Freud saw these stages as being determined by biological development. Object relations theory agrees about the oral, anal and genital stages but disagrees about the process being biologically determined. Children go through these stages when the objects—the parts of their bodies—present themselves to the child. The child has to be ready to go through the stage.

The role of the mother is crucial. Winnicott does not expect every mother to be perfect. Rather he talks about "good enough" mothering. The mother has to be good enough to ensure that the child goes through these stages and develops a strong sense of self. Experimentation must be encouraged, but structured. An important implication of this view is that since development is not biologically determined, how boys and girls mature have more to do with social conditions and their own senses of self than with biology.

We are just about ready to buy that new car and to begin reconstructing our new house. What we will find is that all the sales people and architects are women. These new developments in postmodern psychology that we will be looking at here can all be placed in the general category of postmodern feminism. But, one may ask, how can feminism embrace Freud after all the negative things he said about women? The psychology of the early feminist movement is represented by Betty Friedan's book *The Feminine Mystique*.[98] These attempts at "humanistic psychology" emphasized individual choice and development. Maslow laid out the stages one had to go through to become "self-actualized". Carl Rogers laid out similar steps one had to go through to "become a person". Early feminists believed that if they could become self-actualized persons they could break out of the social roles they had been forced into and could then become any kind of person they wanted to become.

Very quickly it was realized that humanistic psychology was not the answer for women. This was the case for a number of reasons among which two in particular stand out. First, humanistic psychology does not take into account the social context in which people function. In a sense humanistic psychology is the highest form of modernism where individuals function on the basis of reason. But no matter how much one could reason, one could not escape the social order in which one functioned. So even if individual women became everything they could become from an individualist psychological perspective, they still would have had difficulty in following through in the social world.

From a theoretical standpoint this is because humanistic psychology only deals with individual development and does not address how people function in the social world, let alone acknowledge the social dimensions of individual personalities. Humanistic psychology, since it places all the emphasis on the individual, cannot account for social action. In other words, there is no social dimension to humanistic psychology. For a fascinating discussion of this issue, see *Surplus Powerlessness* by Michael Lerner.[99] It is as if people act in social vacuums. Lerner's main point is that in a complex society individuals have very little power over things in their lives. But when the powers that be try to convince people that they do have power and that their failings are their own fault, the reality of the powerlessness doubles. We blame ourselves for things beyond our control and do not try to change things that are within our control

It is no mere coincidence that Maslow and Ayn Rand had a mutual admiration for each other's work. Rand saw Maslow's work as the psychological theory she needed to reinforce her political individualism and Maslow saw in Rand's work a model of how self actualized people would function in a socio-political context.

The second reason is that humanistic psychology derives from the one just discussed. One of the most important aspects of postmodernism is its denial of extreme Individualism and an acknowledgement of the need for collective or communal action. Postmodernists in general, and feminists in particular, are concerned with a concept of autonomy that not only recognizes an individual as an individual but that also recognizes others as equals.

The point here is that truly self-actualized persons are psychologically self-sufficient and do not need other people. The point of postmodernist feminism is that we are all connected. Also, Maslow's concept of autonomy is masculine. His concept of the self-actualized person included the notion that such people weren't just self-sufficient, they were self-contained. Jean Grimshaw asks whether this means that self-actualized persons no longer need other people or that we can now enter into relationships with other people based on equal need[100]. Grimshaw argues that Maslow holds the first view while feminism should be concerned with the second view. Thus humanistic psychology is concerned with a masculine as opposed to a feminist view of self-actualization, and therefore must be rejected as a feminist model.

NANCY CHODOROW

But a psychological theory of development and of personality is still needed. So back to Freud we go. Thus we recognize that some form of psychoanalysis is the only acceptable extant psychological theory which has at least some of the conceptual material needed to explain the complexity of human behavior and which can be modified in some significant ways to account for feminist psychology. The problem becomes one of not throwing out the baby with the bath water. Our first architect will be Nancy Chodorow. In *The Reproduction of Mothering: Psychoanalysis and the Sociology of Gender* she begins by stating the obvious: that women mother. They not only bear children but also have the primary responsibilities for raising them. Given the fact that women bear children it appears natural that they would also be the primary caregivers. But women have also participated in varying ways in the paid labor force and have had other social roles as well. Yet they still mother as well. Chodorow wants to know "how do women today come to mother?" The implication here is that by coming to understand how women learn the role of motherhood we will also be asking "how we might change things to transform the sexual division of labor in which women mother."[101]

The main reason for raising questions regarding the role of mothering has to do with how the role of the mother has changed in our generation. As the role of women has changed in how they contribute to the family, so has the role of mothering. During most of history mothering was a job that was integrated with the other jobs that women did. This was especially the case in the extended agrarian family. But as these other jobs were no longer needed, more emphasis was placed on mothering. Instead of mothering being just one of many jobs a woman did, it has become the central job for many women. But with all of the changes that have occurred over the years, women still mother and still want to mother. From a psychological point questions regarding the Freudian "anatomy is destiny" view must be dealt with. And from a sociological point we must try to understand the hows and whys of the ways in which women learn to mother. The term "reproduction of mothering" means that mothers teach their daughters not only how to mother but to want to mother. The mother "reproduces" not only in biological sense by having a daughter but in a psychological and sociological sense by teaching her daughters to do the same kind of job she has done.

Chodorow's point is that

> the contemporary reproduction of mothering occurs through social structurally induced psychological processes. It is neither a product of biology nor of intentional role training. I draw on the psychoanalytic account of female and male personality development to demonstrate that women's mothering reproduces itself cyclically. Women, as mothers, produce daughters with mothering capacities and the desire to mother. These capacities and needs are built into and grow out of the mother-daughter relationship itself. By contrast, women as mothers (and men as not-mothers) produce sons whose nurturant capacities and needs have been systematically curtailed and repressed. This prepares men for their less affective later family role, and for primary participation in the impersonal extra-familial world of work and public life. The sexual and familial; division of labor in which women mother are more involved in interpersonal, affective relationships than men produces in daughters and sons a division of psychological capacities which leads them to reproduce this sexual and familial division of labor. (Chodorow 1978, 7)

The rest of the book provides the evidence and argument to prove this point. Chodorow's strategy is straightforward: first discuss the traditional reasons given for why women mother, show these reasons to be at least inadequate as explanations if not downright wrong and then present her views. The two traditional views that have been proffered to explain the role of woman as mother have been the biological and sociological. The biological view is straightforward. Women give birth and lactate; they have the necessary biological tools to do the job of mothering. The sociological view is also straightforward, and, to some extent, dependent on the biological one. This view sees social roles in terms of how they function in the overall society. Social roles are often seen in terms of division of labor. Men hunt or go to work. Women gather or stay home. The social roles derive from the biological ones in that women take on the mothering role because they are the ones who become pregnant and feed their young. When these two views are combined we get a view which states that since not only was the sexual division of labor essential to hunter-gatherers, but "because it was essential, it has become built into human physiology."(Chodorow 1978, 18).

Such answers make sense in societies where women are pregnant for most of their fertile years. But they do not make sense when women have some kind of control over their fertility. There is no evidence for a biological maternal instinct. If mothering were biologically instinctual then women would not or even could not be in a situation to choose to have or not have children. Just because women *can* get pregnant does not entail that they *must* get pregnant. And even if there is some kind of mothering gene there is no one-to-one correspondence between genes and behavior. Such answers may also have made sense for hunter-gatherer societies. But we no longer live in such societies. Our social organization changes the demands made upon us. If those same theorists looked at our modern urban society first, they may have concluded that there are genes to prevent mothering as well as genes for mothering since we have developed both biological and social controls over fertility. Social organization has a lot to do with this development. We live in a society that allows us the luxury of having research institutions to discover ways of controlling fertility. But if our social organization did not make such demands upon us to limit fertility we would not look for such things.

Chodorow points out that

> It is not enough today to give an evolutionary-functionalist explanation for women's mothering, then, unless we include in our functional account the reproduction of a particular social organization, beyond species survival or unmediated technological requisites. This organization includes male dominance, a particular family system and women's dependence on men's income...The sexual division of labor in which women mother has new meaning and functions, and is no longer explicable as an outcome of biology or of the

> requirement of survival. The evolutionary-functionalist account doers not provide a convincing argument grounded in biology for why women, or biological mothers, should or must provide parental care. (Chodorow 1978, 21)

The point here is that when social organization changes so do the roles that men and women play. The implication of this point is that social organization has a direct effect on biology. While men are men and women are women from a biological standpoint, differing social organizations can lead to differing social roles for men and women. This point was made in chapter two with regard to Patricia Draper's work on the !Kung tribe where different social organization, and in that case, different relationships to the land, led to different social roles. But Chodorow's point is more general in that not only do our social roles change in different social contexts, but our individual psychology changes as well. For as our roles change we come to see ourselves in different ways. With regard to parenting, Chodorow argues that mothering "requires certain relational capacities which are embedded in personality and a sense of self-in-relationship." (Chodorow 1978, 33)

Mothering involves not just the social demand or men's power over women, though, of course, these are determining factors in how mothering is done since they are part of the social organization in which mothering is performed. But from a social psychological perspective a woman cannot mother "unless she, to some degree and on some unconscious or conscious level, has the capacity and sense of self as maternal to do so." (Chodorow 1978, 33) Thus the social organization must see to it that women are not only in a position to become mothers, but also that they will want to. The explanation of this point is the theme of Chodorow's book, and she develops it in the context of object relations theory. The important point that object relations theory makes is that while we are biological beings, and we go through biological stages of development, we are also social beings and we are self-aware beings. Biology initially controls our development, but this development takes place in a social context. Our sense of self develops partly due to the interaction between ourselves and our social environment. Freud maintained an emphasis on individual development and pushed the social context into the background, even after he acknowledged this bio-social-self development process. Object relations theory simply acknowledges the equality of the social context and argues that individual development makes no sense unless we see how it occurs in its proper social context. The most important aspect of our social context is the fact that we form relationships with other people in those contexts. It is in the forming of these relationships that we look for the resolution of our personal conflicts and the satisfaction of our personal needs. These include our psycho-sexual needs. It must be emphasized that we cannot satisfy our needs until we know how to interact with others. Thus the *object* of our desires is the *relationship* we develop with other people and the relationship they develop with us.

Object relations theory builds on the psychoanalytic model by putting our biological development in its proper social context. Because our biological development takes place in a social setting, our own egos must be must stronger than Freud initially thought. For if they were not we would not be able to develop the relationships we do. But, of course, most of who and what we are is unconscious. Another way of putting this point is to say that what we have learned—how we have been brought up—has been internalized and the conscious decisions we make with regard to our social roles and with regard to meeting our personal needs reflect what we have internalized.

It is in this context that Chodorow looks at how girls learn to become mothers.

> The reproduction of mothering begins from the earliest mother-infant relationship in the earliest period of infantile development. This early relationship is basic in three ways. Most important, the basic psychological stance for parenting is founded during this period. Second, people come out of it with the memory of a unique intimacy which they want to recreate. Finally, people's experience of their early relationship to their mother provides a foundation for expectations of women as mothers. (Chodorow 1978, 57)

The mother is the primary caregiver and the infant is totally dependent on her. This is true not only biologically but sociologically. The infant needs the mother to survive biologically and to begin to learn how to become a person and to form relationships. As the infant grows and begins to develop a sense of self and a sense of being in a social world she can assert her own individuality. But this individuality will reflect the experiences she had as an infant.

Freud saw infants as completely narcissistic. The love for the mother that the child develops out of this is also narcissistic in that the child loves the mother because the mother nurtures the child. Out of this kind of relationship, depending on personal experiences, the child can seek two kinds of lovers. One can be narcissistic where the love object is based on one's conception of oneself. Or one can seek a supportive love object, one modeled after the nurturant mother. But, as Chodorow points out, Freud was never able to properly explain how the young woman is supposed to choose a male love object in terms of his being a sexual object. Another sense of love is needed here, a love that is other-directed. Chodorow refers to the work of various object relations theorists here who have developed a sense of "primary love" which explains the experiences of the infant. Even while the infant is still nonverbal she experiences her environment. These generalized experiences become "focused on those primary people, or that person, who have been particularly salient in providing gratification and a holding relationship. These people are the objects of primary love, which is object-directed and libidinal, and which exists in rudimentary form from birth. The hypothesis of primary love holds that infants have a primary need for human contact for itself. Attempts to fulfill this need play a fundamental role in any person's development and eventual psychic makeup." (Chodorow 1978, 64) This is important in that, unlike Freud, object relations theory sees a person's identity as having a twofold origin and orientation. One is the narcissistic which gives the infant a sense of personal unity between the physical and psychical selves. The second orientation develops from the separation of infant from mother and of the object world. The infant starts to see herself in relation to other things and persons in the world. It is out of this development that the child learns that the environment not only affects her but that she can affect the environment. And, in turn, here is where the reality principle develops. The child begins to recognize that the mother is a separate being with needs of her own. But the child still needs maternal love. The recognition of this separation and of experimenting to find ways of satisfying her needs is where the reality principle develops. This is earlier in the development of the child than where Freud saw the reality principle developing. This view is more complex than Freud's because it takes into account not just the child's needs but also the child's perceptions of the world around her and how that world works.

Chodorow goes on to point out that an important aspect of the child's introduction to "reality" is her mother's involvement with other people such as her father and siblings. All these other people help the child to define her own boundaries. This done through the process of recognizing that these people are all separate people and not just extensions of herself or of her mother. By comparing herself to all of these people she starts to develop her sense of social reality. In the context of nuclear families, the father is the important figure here. Because of his involvement with the mother he provides the first barrier between the child and her mother. The child learns to differentiate the father from the mother and both parents from herself and to compare the two with regard to how they interact with her. But it is still the mother who is the primary person in the child's early life.

The importance of showing that differentiation takes place very early on in a child's development, and that the child's sense of a social world begins earlier than Freud hypothesized does not invalidate psychoanalytic theory but revises it and indicates its real subject: "A socially and historically specific mother-child relationship of a particular intensity and exclusivity and a particular infantile development that this relationship produces." (Chodorow 1978, 76) The implication is that if one were brought up in a different social setting and in a different mother-child relationship one would be a different person. One cannot divorce the person from the social context in which the person became that person. It follows that how a child is brought up will determine how the child sees not only herself but what her social role will be and how to play that role. The child comes to define aspects of herself with her mother. And her early relation to her mother will define for the child her sense of intimacy (Chodorow 1978, 77-78). Here all of the standard Freudian factors come into play. The ways in which children's personalities form and how their neuroses may form all stem from this early period. But Chodorow's specific concerns have to do with how children learn their respective gender roles. Her point is that these social roles are instilled almost from birth by the way children are brought up. Boys and girls are brought up differently because of the different social roles they respectively play. Because men and women play different social roles they bring up their sons and daughters to play those respective roles. Thus

> Women's early mothering, then, creates specific conscious and unconscious attitudes or expectations in children. Girls and boys expect and assume women's unique capacities for sacrifice, caring and mothering, and associate women with their own fears of regression and powerlessness. They fantasize more about men, and associate them with idealized virtues and growth. (Chodorow 1978, 83)

Boys are brought up to be men and fathers and girls are brought up to be women and mothers. The social roles that girls and boys take on in later life are *taught* to them and this teaching is virtually unconscious because the parents were raised in the same way. These social roles are embedded in the social structure and are part of the parents' unconscious.

This process is reproduced from generation to generation because the differences in roles are reproduced. Boys are brought up to be men and to play that role in certain ways and girls are brought up to women and to play that role in certain ways. This is so because, given the nature of the social order, the relationships between mother and son and mother and daughter, and between father and son and father and daughter are all different. Since Chodorow's main concern is how girls become mothers, her discussion focuses on the mother daughter relationship. Her point is that girls learn to become mothers from their mothers because the way they are raised leads to "differential object-relational experiences, and the ways in which these are internalized and organized." Chodorow goes on to argue that

> Developments in the infantile period and particularly in the emergence and resolution of the oedipus complex entail different psychological reactions, needs, and experiences, which cut off or curtail relational possibilities for parenting in boys, and keep them open and extend them in girls. (Chodorow 1978, 91)

The import of this is that social roles are learned. Biology, then, is not destiny. And this leads to a semantic distinction between sex and gender. Sex is biological. In this sense men are men and women are women. But gender is sociological. The social roles that men and women play—that is how men and women do their respective jobs—are learned. When social roles are determined by sex then there is no real distinction to be made. But if social roles change then the distinction becomes important. To put this in a schematic form we can say that

Female	Sex
Mother	Gender

So, for example, if a man were to stay home with the children he would be of the male sex but of the female gender with regard to the job he is doing. And if a woman goes to work she will be of the female sex but with regard to her job she will be of the male gender. But if the stay-at-home dad does the parenting job the way fathers and not mothers do it then it can be said that he is of the masculine gender. And if the woman does her job the way a man would it can be said that she is of the masculine gender. Thus there can be all kinds of configurations. So when people want an equal number of men and women on various groups they should talk about sexual parity not gender parity. This issue is discussed at length by historian Thomas Laqueur.[102]

This issue will come up again during our discussion. But now let us get back to Chodorow's work. The important stage of development in children that leads to their sex and gender identities is the oedipal stage. And, of course, how children develop before they reach that stage will play a major role in how they get through that stage and how they will resolve their oedipal complexes. As we have already seen, boys and girls are socialized differently from birth. This different socialization reflects the roles of the parents and, therefore, the gender roles the children will play as adults.

How this socialization is carried out depends on the family structure and on the societal structure in which the family functions. The point here is that even if specific families do not function the way in which most families function the over all social structures of the society will still exert an influence since the people in that family participate in the society at large and have been influenced by it.

The society in which we live can be defined as a patriarchal society in which the patriarch (the father or the male) is not present during much of the childrearing. Thus the female or the mother does most of the rearing. But she does so in the context of a patriarchal or male value structure. The results of this kind of social structure results in clearly defined differences between boys and girls and between men and women, in what their respective social roles will be and in how they relate to the their parents, particularly the parent of the opposite sex. It is this specific kind of upbringing structure that leads to the Freudian oedipal complex where boys focus on their mothers as a sexual object and fear their fathers and where women see themselves as not men. The implication is that if familial and social structure were different not only would the ways in which we raise our children be different, but the ways in which we, and our children, would see our sexuality and gender roles would also be different. In her discussion of the Freudian view Chodorow states that

> we must reject any assumption that what this account describes is natural, self evident, and unintended. To the contrary, it seems to be both consciously and unconsciously intended, socially, psychologically, and ideologically constructed. And...it is not inevitable (Chodorow, 1978 113).

The point here is that children learn their genders and are taught to identify with the appropriate parent. It is through this learning process that girls learn to identify with their mothers, with the roles their mothers play and how their mothers play those roles. The problem for boys is that they go through this same stage but with the mother as the primary parent. Thus the oedipal stage is asymmetric for boys and girls. They both go through the stage, but because they go through the stage differently the outcome for each is different.

A boy is faced with the choice of giving up his penis or giving up the parent of identification, the father. This is a choice because, assuming heterosexuality, the boy can continue to identify with his father if the boy takes on a feminine stance. So he makes his choice easily. He chooses to keep his penis and in so doing his mother becomes identified as a sexual object, which the boy must repress. Depending on how this process gets resolved will depend on whether the boy, as a young man, develops an oedipus complex or not.

A girl, on the other hand, is not confronted with this kind of choice because the parent of identification is of the same sex. A girl's sexual identification with her father is made not at the expense of losing anything with her mother. Rather "a girl develops important oedipal attachments to her mother *as well as* to her father." (Chodorow, 1978 127) These attachments do not replace the pre-oedipal attachments she has made with her mother, but build upon them. Thus "a girl never gives up her mother as an internal or external love object, even if she becomes heterosexual." (Chodorow, 1978 127) Since girls remain attached to their mothers while choosing men as their sexual objects they remain in a "bisexual triangle....They usually make a sexual resolution in favor of men and their father, but retain an internal emotional triangle." (Chodorow, 1978 140)

Chodorow's point is that what occurs during the oedipal stage of development is

> not all one way, nor is it a direct product of biology. It is an object-relational experience in which what is going on among family members is causally important for a child's development. The psychological processes and features of gender personality that grow out of the oedipus complex are grounded in family structure and family relations (Chodorow, 1978 159).

Thus not only do the children have to go through various adjustments with regard to their parents, the parents have to go through various adjustments with regard to their children. Not only do children have to decide which parent to relate to but the parent also has to decide how to relate to the child. How all of these decisions are made will determine how the child gets through the oedipal stage, how the parent will regard the child's sexuality and, finally, how the child will begin to perceive his or her sexuality and gender in the overall context of the society they live in. Because of the role of the mother in our society as the primary parent of both boys and girls, as we saw hinted at in a quote above, boys and girls develop differently with regard to their parents. Boys and girls, women and men, "grow up with personalities affected by different boundary experiences and differently constructed and experienced inner object-worlds, and are preoccupied with different relational issues." (Chodorow, 1978 169)

All of this means a great deal because what Chodorow has revised the whole Freudian notion of sexuality without diminishing its importance. Her revision shows that while we are biological beings, the behavior reflecting that biology is biologically determined but is learned and constructed by our social relationships. The importance of this is that anatomy is not destiny, that we are not bound to certain roles because we are male or female, that we can separate gender from sex and that we can change the structure of our social order. This last point is extremely important because its corollary is that the roles men and women are in today are socially constructed and not biologically determined.

Understanding the importance of the implications of the oedipal stage is crucial. In this Chodorow is at one with Freud. But the way she sees the oedipal process and its implications differs significantly from Freud. So let us look at these implications. Boys and girls are brought to be men and women. As we have seen, boys and girls are brought up differently because of this. The important point is that they are brought up differently in two ways. One is with regard to how they are socialized and taught to take on their respective gender roles. The second has to with the fact that, because of these different gender roles, and because the mother is the dominant parent in our society, boys and girls are brought up differently with regard to how they learn to relate to their different parents.

It is this latter process that is psychologically important. Because the mother is the dominant parent girls are brought up to have a different relationship with their mothers than boys are. Girls maintain their pre-oedipal relationships longer with their mothers than boys do. Girls do not turn away from their fathers but add them to their object world. Girls do not "resolve" their oedipus complexes the way in which boys do since they neither repress nor do they entirely give up their pre-oedipal attachment to their mothers.

All of this means that since girls are brought up to be mothers by their mothers they establish and maintain a bond that mothers do not form with their sons. This makes girls' experiences of "themselves as less differentiated than boys, as more continuous with and related to then external object-world and as differently oriented to their inner object-world as well." (Chodorow, 1978 167) "Feminine personality comes to be based less on repression of inner objects, and fixed and firm splits in the ego, and more on retention and continuity of external relationships... From the retention of pre-oedipal attachments to their mother, growing girls come to define and experience themselves as continuous with others;" (Chodorow, 1978 169) with "greater potential for participation in relational spheres." (Chodorow, 1978 170) And it is from all of this that girls are taught to become mothers, for mothers need to relate in this manner to their children. And, in turn, this is where the whole sense of woman as nurturer comes from for nurturing is a primary aspect of primary aspect of mothering.

The analogous experience for boys is quite different. Because boys are brought up by their mothers but are brought up to be like their absent fathers "Boys come to define themselves as more separate and distinct, with a greater sense of rigid ego boundaries and differentiation. The basic feminine sense of self is connected to the world, the basic masculine sense of self is separate." (Chodorow, 1978 169) This is because

> mothers experience their sons as a male opposite. Boys are more likely to have been pushed out of the pre-oedipal relationship, and to have had to curtail their primary love and sense of empathic tie with their mother. A boy has engaged, and been required to engage, in a more emphatic individuation and a more defensive firming of experienced ego boundaries (Chodorow, 1978 166-167).

And because mothers bring up boys who are sexual opposites boys must learn to develop their masculine gender identification in the absence of the male role model, the father. Thus "Boys are taught to be masculine more consciously than girls are taught to be feminine...Masculine identification, then, is predominantly a gender role identification." (Chodorow, 1978 176)

Gender roles are taught. Girls learn their roles more by

identification with their mothers while boys have to be consciously taught how to be men. Given our previous discussion of modernism, which stressed both individualism and the notion of abstract thought, we can see how important Chodorow's work is in explaining the psychological and sociological foundations of modernism. On the one hand we will see how the individuation and separation of the male can lead to the whole notion of individualism and, on the other hand, we will see how this same process can lead to the kind of abstract thought that we have identified with modernism. Since individualism and abstraction come together so well in capitalist economics, that is where we shall begin.

Let us begin this discussion with a look at family structures, especially with regard to the specific roles men and women play in families. It is a popular view to hold that the family is the basic social unit. Somehow the family is seen as a microcosm of society at large. If one were to read any sociology text one would see this view shown to be false. Societies are made up of a number of social institutions, of which the family is just one. A look at the history of family life shows that family structures have changed significantly over time. Changes in family structures usually reflect other changes going on in the society. For example, for a significant part of the modern era the traditional family was the extended family or clan, usually based in an agrarian setting. Of course there were individual parents but the whole extended family functioned as a social unit and the socialization of children was the responsibility of all of the members of the family, not just the biological parents.

The industrial revolution changed this. As people left the farms to go to the cities to find work, family units became smaller out of economic necessity. Living accommodations in the city were smaller, so the number of people who could live in such a place had to be fewer than on the farm. And not everyone left the farm, so the extended family broke apart. In the city men went to work and women stayed at home with the children, which led to a sexual division of labor that did not exist on the farm. Recall Draper's point in chapter two about how familial structures and division of labor change according to how people relate to the land, or, in this case, the means of production. The point here is that the family is just one of the institutions that constitute society and is as subject to change as any other social institution. In the modern era changes in the family have occurred due to changes in the economy. Thus changes in the means of production, the source of the means of survival or of the wealth of the society are usually the main source of change in familial structures. And changes in familial structures will, of course, reflect the needs of the economic changes.

In today's world when sociologists determine the socioeconomic status of a family, even in a two-income family, it is the man's income and job status that is used to determine the family's status, although as single parent families begin to grow in number this approach will undoubtedly change. The point of this brief discussion of family structures ties in with our previous discussion. We have seen that because of our social and familial structures men and women are brought up to take their place in society. Since their respective places or roles have been defined sexually, men and women are brought up differently. Women's roles are defined in terms of their nurturing roles as wife and mother. But men's roles tend not to be defined in terms of their husbandly or fatherly roles but in terms of their work roles. As Chodorow puts it, "ideology about men and definitions of what is masculine come predominantly from men's non familial roles. Women are located first in the sex-gender system, men first in the organization of production." (Chodorow, 1978 178) She goes on to state that

> Women's role in the home and primary definition in social reproductive, sex-gender terms are characterized by particularism, concern with affective goals and ties, and a diffuse, unbounded quality. Masculine occupational roles and men's primary definition in the sphere of production are universally defined and recruited, and are less likely to involve affective considerations. This nonrelational, economic and political definition informs the rest of their lives. The production of feminine personalities oriented towards relational issues and masculine personalities defined in terms of categorical ties and the repression of relation fits these roles and contributes to their reproduction. (Chodorow, 1978 180)

The importance here is that familial structures are reflective of the society at large and as such insure that children born into the society are properly brought up to take on the roles that society has set out for them. This is why women mother, why they mother the way they do, why women raise their daughters and sons differently, and why sons and daughters relate differently to their mothers. In other words, the family can be seen as a central social unit in that it reflects the society's values and structures and is designed to reproduce those structures and values in the new entrants into that society. But the family cannot be considered the, or even a, central social institution since its job is reflective of the society at large. Mothers bring up their daughters to be mothers—to reproduce themselves in a social sense—because that is their job. That is the job they were brought up to do.

The small family goes hand in hand with capitalism. Capitalism needs a number of kinds of workers. Hierarchical capitalism, the form that is practiced in the world today in large corporations requires different kinds of skills and attitudes for different levels in the hierarchy. Low-level jobs require the ability to work in clearly defined structures and to follow orders. Other level jobs require the ability to take responsibility and make decisions and to give orders. Chodorow points out that families in different socioeconomic classes tend to bring up their children with the values of that class. Her main point is that the nuclear family in which women mother is properly suited to raise children for their role in the hierarchical capitalist world. (Chodorow, 1978 186) And the traits we have seen defined as masculine and feminine reflect the roles of men and women in that hierarchical capitalist world. The repression and denial of the affective in men allow them to conduct business in an objective manner where emotions and other affective considerations are not needed or wanted. Thus they can concentrate on the abstraction of business and make decisions which are good for business but have no relation to other aspects of life, just like the executives discussed by John DeLorean.

Chodorow's interest in understanding why women mother the way they do is to find a way to change things. After all, she is writing from a feminist perspective. At the very least feminism means that women should not only be seen as being equal to men but that they should be able to choose what their place in the world will be. Equality does not come easily. One cannot just declare oneself to be equal. One has to understand where the inequity comes from and develop a counter strategy which will eventually result in equality. Man-woman equality is not possible in a patriarchal system where men control power and are brought up by women to have that power. Thus by understanding how women come to be in that kind of mothering role we can come up with a strategy to change how the social order works. As we have seen, Chodorow accepts the psychoanalytic dynamic of personality but, rightly, criticizes Freud and other psychoanalytic theorists for their portrayal of women. This was not just something that followed from general psychoanalytic theory but was derived from the value structures of the social order in which the theories were formulated.

Thus, by understanding the psycho-social dynamic by which children are brought up one can develop an alternative way of raising children which will, hopefully, result in these children treating each other with greater equality, especially with regard to sex and gender issues.

Chodorow agrees with the basic view of psychoanalysis that the basic personality of a child is pretty well fixed by the age of five. But gender roles are not. Here the crucial stage is the oedipal stage of development. On the traditional view, as we have seen, each parent plays a different role for his/her children. And this role is sex/gender specific. Girls are brought up to be women and boys are brought up to be men. By understanding the roles each parent plays, and by understanding at what stages of development the crucial social conditioning takes place, we can develop an alternative familial structure where the parents take on different roles in terms of what they teach each child and how and when they teach it.

The obvious beginnings of such a model would have both parents taking on equal responsibilities for all children, regardless of sex. If men can be seen to be mothering in a way that women would normally mother, and if women can be seen to be absent and individuating, or if both parents take on more of a mothering role, gender role stereotyping can be avoided. The important point here is that we do not just want *more* parenting; we want a *different kind* of parenting. The crucial stage in the child's development would be at the onset of puberty—the oedipal period—when attitudes towards sexuality become developed. As we have seen, how a child relates to his or her parents at this stage is crucial for the how the child develops attitudes towards his or her own sexuality and gender roles.

If the mother tries to maintain a closeness with her son so he does not see his mother as a possible sex object but as a cross-gender friend of equal status to his father, he may still be able to develop the masculine skills he needs to compete in the business world but he can also develop feminine traits of connectedness. Such a male can be feminine but still be attracted to women. Such a male could be considered a "male lesbian?"[103] Why not? We can construct new socio-sexual categories which actually describe ourselves instead of trying to fit into old categories.

This discussion raises a series of questions. Is it possible for a man and a woman to have a close personal friendship without sex? Why does the marital relationship have to be based on sexual fidelity? Does the sexual bond somehow define marriage? What of other emotionally close relationships?

This may mean a man will not be as cutthroat a capitalist as he could or should be, but he will still be able to survive in the economic jungle. Or, perhaps, if enough men showed feminine traits maybe the capitalist world would become femininized a bit. And if a father develops a closeness to his daughter maybe she will develop enough masculine skills to compete in the capitalistic world without giving up any of her femininity. Or a new economic model might develop which is less abstract and caters more to the social and emotional needs of the society rather than to just the needs of the abstract economy.

The notion of gender as a social construct also raises the question of sex as a social construct. We are all built in certain biological ways. But the ways in which we define male and female and the ways in which react to male and female are social constructions. Why can't men kiss each other the way women can? Why can't men have sexual relationships with other men and why can't women have sexual relationships with other women—even if such persons are not gay or lesbian? Why do we limit our sexuality, especially if we do not limit our gender that way? Questions such as these are discussed in the aptly titled book *Gender Outlaw: On Men, Women, and the Rest of Us* by Kate Bornstein, a woman who was born a man but after three failed marriages realized something was wrong and underwent a sex-change operation. She now has a lesbian as her lover.

In one of the sections of the book is a play she wrote on the subject. One of the characters states that her gender identity has nothing to do with her sexual preference. She says that her gender identity answers the question of personal identity, while her sexual preference tells her whom she wants to be romantically or sexually involved with.[104] When responding to a similar question, another character states that gender is the need to belong—the need to fit in—to be part of something. (Bornstein 195)

The point here is that if gender is a construct so is sex—social gender roles are not biologically determined but socially constructed. Therefore we must do some serious reconstructing of our social order and how we raise our children. Once we understand how this construction works we can deconstruct some of the social edifices that currently exist and reconstruct some new ones. All we need is an understanding of the psycho-social dynamics that come into play in such constructions. And Nancy Chodorow appears to have provided the foundation for such reconstructioning

CRITICISMS OF CHODOROW

But Chodorow's views are not without some serious problems, her critics would say. I don't want to get tangled up with criticisms of a view I am trying to explain before that view has been more completely laid out. But let us step outside the house for a few moments to consider some of the important criticisms of Chodorow's position. In a sentence these criticisms amount to the facts that Chodorow's view is too mother-centered, white middle class and heterosexist. It only looks at how some people develop but certainly does not attempt to explain all mother daughter relationships.

My first response to these points is to say that they are, by and large, correct. Chodorow is working from a limited point of view, but it is not quite as limited as her critics imply. Before I look at the specific issues a couple of general comments should be made. First, Chodorow is working from the standpoint of a sociologist, not a psychologist. This is important since she is looking at the social conditions and structures in which the psychodynamic processes she discusses take place. So while she primarily use a white middle class heterosexual model, she does so because this model represents the dominant value systems of our society. This, of course, does not invalidate the criticisms, but it weakens them. Another point in Chodorow's defense could be that one has to start somewhere. A major criticism of Freud was that he theorized from a too-narrow clinical base as well. This is clearly true, but we need to look at his achievements. My point is rather than shooting Chodorow down for leaving things out, we should see how far we can go with the model she has developed. This approach is in line with the Kuhnian view of developing a new paradigm. Many viewpoints must be considered before we finalize our house plans.

Now let us look at some of the specific points in turn. Chodorow herself addresses the homosexual issue in a series of lectures presented at the University of Kentucky in 1990. She goes back to Freud and argues that his views on women and on homosexuality were not as limited as usually presented. He was aware of all kinds of diversities. But his assumptions in his cultural context, and, perhaps more importantly, the assumptions of his readers and interpreters, limited his views.

Chodorow points out that Freud acknowledged in his writings that there is a continuum between hetero- and homosexualities and that all of us are inherently bisexual. Of this work Chodorow argues that it leaves us with "several potential openings toward more plural conceptions of gender and sexuality."[105] Chodorow continues that because Freud assumed the normalcy of heterosexuality he did not try to explain it, thus "psychoanalysis does not have a developmental account of 'normal' heterosexuality..." and because of this it is either weak or empty to "imply that heterosexuality is not different in kind from homosexuality..." (Chodorow, 1994 132)

Her main point is that, while sexuality is, of course, biological, how it develops has more to do with psychological development and sociological context than with biology alone. And since there is such a diversity of heterosexual forms, from a clinical standpoint "there is no normal heterosexuality." (Chodorow, 1994 62) And if there is no such thing as normal heterosexuality we cannot say that homosexuality is not normal either. Thus, when properly read and revised, object relations theory can account for the psychosexual developments leading to homosexuality as well as to heterosexuality. I have usually looked upon sexuality from a biological point. Sex is biological. How we learn about our sexuality is psychosocial. From a strict and narrow biological standpoint, sexuality is about reproduction. I recall being struck when reading in animal studies with regard to overpopulation that one of results of overpopulation in some animals was homosexuality. So I concluded from this narrow biological standpoint that homosexuality was, in some way, nature's built-in population control. Why any one person is homosexual was another question, one I could not answer. Thus I was quite confused when gay and lesbian couples wanted to have children, and I became even more confused when lesbians actually wanted to get pregnant. The only solution to my problem was to acknowledge that social and cultural forces—the need to be a mother—were stronger than biological forces. I came to this conclusion after reading Chodorow's early work and this view was strengthened by reading her later work. But, while I still maintain this point to some extent, further research has shown that Chodorow was on the right track in that homosexuality does need a category of its own—that sexuality does not have neat borders all through nature.

The original views of natural law had more limiting notions of what was natural. For example, Aquinas states:

> When speaking of man's nature we may refer either to that which is proper to him Or to that which he has in common with other animals. From the first point of view, all sins in so far as they are against reason are also against nature, as Damascene states. From the second, some special sins are against nature, as, for instance, those that run counter to the intercourse of male and female natural to animals, and so are peculiarly qualified as unnatural vices. (Aquinas 94.2)

Thus, since homosexuality is not found in nature it is unnatural, and therefore immoral.

But current knowledge has demonstrated Aquinas' views to be false. In *Biological Exuberance,* Bruce Bagemihl has amassed a wealth of observations showing that homosexual, bisexual and transvestite behaviors exist all through nature, from insects to birds to small mammals to bulls and goats to elephants to whales and gorillas.

As Bagemihl states

> Wild animals often form significant pair-bonds with animals of the same sex. Homosexual pair-bonding takes many different forms, but two broad categories can be recognized: "partners" who engage in sexual or courtship activities with each other, and "companions," who are bonded to each other but do not necessarily engage in sexual activity with each other.[106]

Bagemihl goes on to argue that

> The traditional view of the animal kingdom-what might be called the Noah's ark view-is that biology revolves around two sexes, male and female, with one of each to a pair. The range of genders and sexualities actually found in the animal world, however, is considerably richer than this. Animals with females that become males, animals with no males at all, animals that are both male and female simultaneously, animals where males resemble females, animals where females court other females and where males court other males—Noah's ark was never quite like this! Homosexuality represents but one of a wide variety of alternative sexualities and genders. Many people are familiar with tranvestism or transexuality only in humans, yet similar phenomena are also found in the animal kingdom. (Bagemihl 36)

Thus our traditional categories of male and female do not capture the true diversity of nature. They are limiting constructions which must be radically changed or abandoned if we are to truly construct socio-sexual categories which reflect nature as well as the kind of social order which acknowledges this natural diversity.

The next topic has to do with the white middle-class view of Chodorow's work. The point here made by such thinkers as Patricia Hill Collins and bell hooks is that families not in this mainstream, especially families of color, have very different structures and dynamics and therefore the white middle class analysis of familial structures does not apply to them[107].

There is no doubt of the truth of such claims. But what can be done is to apply a psychoanalytic object relations analysis to such familial structures to see how those structures develop. Then that analysis can be added to the white middle class analysis for a more complete picture of the psychological foundations of our social structures. Also, one can note that Chodorow's analysis can explain the dynamics of middle class families of color, especially if these families have adopted the values of the white middle class. But, needless to say, this issue leaves a hole in our picture. This has to do with the focus on the mother. The dominant parent in our society is the mother. This does not mean that fathers play no role in raising children. But, as we have seen, the dominant parent is the mother. Even in families where a mother is not present, because of the norms of the society which places emphasis on the mother, the idea of the mother is felt, especially in the way everyone plays out their respective social roles.

But Chodorow does address this issue, if only in passing by her recommendations for both parents to take a more active and sharing role in childrearing. By having the father present more the major issue gets addressed. If the father takes on some of the jobs usually done by the mother, and if the mother does some of the jobs usually done by the father, this total focus on the mother will be eliminated.

Another issue regarding the focus on the mother has to do with how women who are not mothers see themselves. In other words how women who are not mothers, whether by chance or choice, see themselves, and are perceived, by a mother-dominant society. This point does not deny that our society is mother-dominant, but raises questions about that dominance. Mardy S. Ireland argues that women who do not have children have difficulty in defining who or what they are.[108] Ireland talks about women who are childless, women who are child**less** and childless-**free** and women who are child-**free**. Child**less** women are traditional women who see themselves as lacking something. The childless-**free** category is transitional where women learn to come to terms with their situation and the truly child-**free** woman has comfortably made this choice. These stages reflect upbringing as well as a changing social context with regard to the changing role of women in our society. And while much of Ireland's analysis of this change appears consistent with Chodorow's position, Ireland also notes the lack of the role of the father in Chodorow's analysis. Ireland suggests joining Chodorow's account of mothering to Lacan's account of fathering for a more complete psychoanalytic view of women's (and men's) psychosocial development.[109]

ELLYN KASCHAK

Now to return to building our house. The next stage also involves some serious criticism of Chodorow's work but it also builds on some of the concepts. Again we see a practicing therapist trying to develop an account of feminine psychology which, while still psychoanalytic in nature, is able to explain the changes that women are going through and still want to go through. The work in question here is that of Ellyn Kaschak. Before I get into Kaschak's work a terminological point must be made about the use of the term "psychoanalytic". This term is not synonymous with the work of Freud, who was, of course, the founder of this approach to psychology. But there have been many developments in psychoanalysis since Freud. We have just seen one of these developments in object relations theory. Kaschak explicitly rejects much of Freud, especially his views on women. But more importantly she rejects the whole male bias that is found at the basis of how psychoanalysis treats the differences between men and women. But, and this is the point I want to stress, by still talking about the different aspects of personality that include the unconscious, one is still, broadly speaking, in the realm of psychoanalysis.

Kaschak formulated many of her concerns as a novice therapist. She realized that, when given assignments dealing with sexuality, assignments which she often questioned, she was told that she was being treated equally and not just as a woman. Her name came up and she was the one to deal with the next case. But while she was being treated equally, she quickly realized that the operational concept of equality was a masculine one. She was being treated equally. She was being treated as if she were a "he" on a staff consisting mostly of "he's".

The problem for her was that in some cases of sexual problems the fact that she was a woman and saw these issues differently than her male colleagues saw them made her realize that while she was being treated equally, it was an inappropriate equality, for it saw problems in only one way—a masculine way. And as a woman who had been socialized to see sexuality differently than men do, she often saw the inappropriateness of the diagnoses and treatments. Kaschak's starting point is to criticize traditional masculine epistemologies. As we have seen, knowledge is not objective. It is value- or context-laden. By excluding the experiences of women, Western epistemology has ignored a whole range of knowledge. It has done so by claiming to be objective and value-free, but has tended to ignore knowledge that does not fit into its framework. Since women are not valued, their knowledge is not valued.

In order to develop a psychology of women one must look at the assumptions of how one gets psychological knowledge. One must look at the epistemological assumptions of psychology. If they are found lacking, one must establish new criteria, based on experiences that are known to be valid, even if—especially if—they were rejected by the previous model. Thus, a feminist approach to epistemology must begin with the experiences of women, both individually and in their social context[110].

This feminist epistemology, and the psychology which will follow from it, must develop a new language since it will be describing things that are not included in the old epistemology or in the old psychology. While Kaschak acknowledges that all behavior and language have cultural influences embedded in them (Kaschak, 1992 29) most of the boundaries or categories we use to classify people and behavior are imaginary. We see this when we look at the same behavior from a different standpoint. Kaschak gives examples of behaviors of various patients. She then asks us to reconsider the behavior if the person were male instead of female, or vice versa, or a person of color instead of white, and so on. The purpose of this exercise is to make us realize the assumptions we take to our observations of behavior. What we label as correct for a man becomes incorrect for a woman. What may be unacceptable for a white middle class woman may be acceptable to a lower class woman of color. The point here is to break down those boundaries and to re-assess our assumptions. Such assumptions not only have to do with class and gender but with assumptions regarding our old friend "anatomy is destiny". If we can accept that behaviors in women and men are acceptable when we previously thought they were not then we can begin to see that gender is a cultural and not a biological concept. "The connection between anatomy and destiny is not inevitable, as Freud suggested, but socially/psychologically constructed and maintained."(Kaschak, 1992 54) It is maintained and enforced by the experience of shame. "Shame is one of the most potent of societal and individual psychological enforcers, putting nothing less than the basic sense of esteem and worth at stake."(Kaschak, 1992 41)

Kaschak here is using shame in a similar but not synonymous way in which Freud uses the concept of guilt. The concept of guilt in Freud, as we saw above, is general, while Kaschak's use of shame is more cultural and gender specific. Shame is used to humiliate, not just with regard to specific behaviors but with regard to one's concept of oneself. Women are brought up to think of themselves as second-class citizens and shame is designed to keep them thinking that way. Thus atypical behavior is kept in check by shaming or humiliating the person in question. The issue then becomes one of understanding how anatomy is not destiny and how this use of shame works so that women can learn to become the persons they want to become. Kaschak points out that since the Freudian model explains established relationships between men and women and how women have been taught to see themselves, his work deserves another look. But this time the look will be through feminist eyes. Kaschak does this by revisiting the Oedipal myth, but now the roles of Jocasta and Antigone will be looked at more carefully. Kaschak's point is that in masculine or patriarchal society women's sexuality is shaped by male concerns; it does not exist on its own. But by looking at how women are portrayed by men, and then by analyzing and reconstructing these roles, we can get a sense of female sexuality.

    Kaschak points out that Freud's look at the Oedipal myth only looks at a third of the play. The other two thirds, and the last third especially, are just as relevant as the first. For this third gives us more insight into the role of women in this myth. And, in turn, this understanding of women gives us a clearer understanding of men and of the relationship between the two. In the play, after discovering what he has done, Oedipus merely blinds himself. I say "merely", for as Kaschak points out, the correct punishment for his crime of incest should have been castration. The point Kaschak makes here is that if he had kept his sight he still would have been able to look upon women. And, of course, being able to do so would have aroused him. By blinding himself he cut himself off from being tempted again. This point is important. Men define female sexuality. Female sexuality exists for men. The inference is that women exist for men. When a man becomes aroused it is because a woman has aroused him. When I was reading this section of the book I thought of the Christians who always tried to reach a state of purity. But these men would find themselves aroused by women. Since they have taken such pains to purify themselves it must be the women who are the temptresses. In this way feminine sexuality became associated with temptation and thereby with the devil. For an interesting theological look at this issue see Elaine Pagels *Adam, Eve And The Serpent.*[111]

    To return to the Oedipal plays, Kaschak points out that it was Jocasta who died for Oedipus' sins, proving that she was not a person in her own right, simply an extension of Oedipus. And in blinding himself, Oedipus did not really do himself much harm as he had Antigone to become his eyes. Thus she became an extension of Oedipus as well. It is in this context that Kaschak points out that Freud himself realized that the last of the taboos to be developed was the one forbidding father-daughter incest (Kaschak, 1992 62.)

    The point here is that in a patriarchal society where male values dominate and women are subjugated, men can use their power over women to make them believe that they deserve to be treated this way. This is how shame works. By being brought up to believe that one is a second class citizen and that one only exists for the first class citizens, anything that would bring one attention or the disfavor of the ruling class must be considered taboo. These taboos must be enforced not only by peer pressure but in an individual way. It must become part of all women's personalities. On a psychoanalytic model this part of the personality must be unconscious. In this context Kaschak asks of the plight of Antigone. Kaschak's point is that Antigone is always presented in terms of some male figure without an identity of her own. This is reflected in Oedipus' blindness, since Oedipus never saw Antigone as a person in her own terms. His blindness can be viewed as both a punishment for the way he used his sight and a comment that he has always been blind. (Kaschak, 1992 75)

Thus Oedipus is not just physically blind, but he is, and always has been, morally blind. And what of Jocasta and Antigone? "Jocasta is known to us only by her relationship to her men. There is absolutely no indication of her relationship to her children other than to the one who became her husband"(Kaschak, 1992 75). The same is true for Antigone. We only know her as the eyes of Oedipus. She does not escape from her father to have her own life. Kaschak calls this situation the Antigone complex. Her point is that Freud was incorrect in trying to see female personality development and female sexuality as a mirror image of male personality development and male sexuality, or as an incomplete male psychology. She acknowledges that Freud knew his account of feminine sexuality was wrong, but he did not offer any alternative. Kaschak suggests that instead of talking about mirror image Oedipal complexes or Elektra complexes we should be talking about Antigone complexes. We can only understand how female sexuality has developed by understanding its role in a male society. Kaschak has a dual point here. One is that women will not be able to resolve their Antigone complexes in a male dominated world. The second point is implicit. In order for women to resolve their complexes the social order must change. The resolution of the Antigone complex will involve: separating from father to return to herself; facing her own vulnerability; developing interdependence and flexible boundaries; developing her own identity as a woman before dealing with men; ceasing to make males central.(Kaschak, 1992 84)

> The purpose of rethinking the Oedipus and Antigone myths is to .."develop a paradigm to aid our understanding of

> current sexual and gender arrangements....Resolution of the Antigone phase is a complex personal, interpersonal, and cultural phenomenon. It involves leaving the stage of possession by the father" (Kaschak, 1992 87).

How to develop this new identity is the next stage. In the current world, women, perhaps more so than men, identify who they are by how they look. This is the case for two reasons. First, as we have seen, in a patriarchal society women exist for men. Women's sexuality is defined by men. Thus women are brought up to appear attractive to men. Women are, at least initially, judged on how they look; men are not. The second reason for this, and the point that explains the first, is that, at least from a psycho-social perspective, we identify more with our bodies. It is our bodies that participate in the social world. It is by appearance we identify people. Thus how we look tells us a lot about who and what we are.

How women dress, how they use makeup, and their overall deportment are all determined by what men expect from women. And, all too often, women, not men, are the biggest critics of how other women look. Kaschak relates this to the Antigone complex in that women are being used as men's eyes. (Kaschak, 1992 94) And, of course, this concern with appearance is what leads to various problems such as eating disorders, depression and general feelings of inadequacy.

What needs to be accomplished is for women to develop a sense of their own identity and their own self-worth. In order to be able to do this, women must first understand how they have developed the kind of self-image they have. Kaschak argues that

> the crucial period for development of women's appearance-based identity extends from the moment of birth, when it is physically based and preverbal, through adolescence, when it is taught and enforced by complex social forces including adults, peers, and society at large through books, magazines, the media, and even the responses of strangers in public....
>
> Developmentally, adolescence is the crucial stage for full emergence and crystallization of this constellation of gendered and embodied meaning. That is, it is in adolescence that this truly becomes a difference that makes a difference.(Kaschak, 1992 90)

Kaschak argues that the physical basis of self-identity for both boys and girls coalesces in adolescence (Kaschak, 1992 91). Now, the issue becomes one of how to change this pattern so that all people can develop more integrated sense of self that is more internally than externally defined. This, of course, has been the issue in all of psychoanalysis, from Freud through Chodorow and Kaschak, but the emphases have been different. Because so much of women's identities are based not just on their own development and needs but on how they are judged by men, a woman's inner development is more complex than that of a man, who does not have to worry about how he appears to other men or to women, at least not to the extent that women have to care about this issue. Kaschak sees this issue not in terms of penis envy or that women are somehow incomplete men. Rather she sees this in terms of women being "invisible beings."(Kaschak, 1992 101) This is so because women, in our society, do not exist as people in themselves, but as adjuncts to men.

In developing her alternative account of how women (and men) should be raised, Kaschak develops her differences with Chodorow. In her discussion of the Oedipal plays, she argues that this whole structure has to be re-examined instead of accepted, as Chodorow does.(Kaschak, 1992 61) In her account of development that we have just looked at, we can see obvious differences between her and Chodorow in that Kaschak sees gender indoctrination as occurring from birth where for Chodorow the pre-oedipal and oedipal periods are the crucial periods when gender structures take hold. But Kaschak takes her critique of Chodorow even further. She begins by asking what Chodorow and others mean by relatedness. Do men and women actually differ in the ways described by Chodorow? Does the association between gender and mothering hold? And will Chodorow's suggestion about parenting work? (Kaschak, 1992 114-115)

Basically Kaschak answers all these questions in the negative. Her basic points are that Chodorow has used an idealized version of the nuclear family, a social unit which is historically recent and which is in the minority. But this kind of gender identification occurs in all forms of family life and has obviously been occurring through the centuries when family structures were quite different. Thus one cannot put the blame on the nuclear family. Next, based on her clinical experience Kaschak argues that more parenting of the kind that Chodorow recommends may even exacerbate the problem rather than solving it, for the gender indoctrination may come from both sources. This is because fathers, more so than mothers, tend to emphasize gender differences (Kaschak, 1992 121-122). Kaschak's point is that this kind of genderization reflects the overall society in which it occurs and that all familial structures in that society will do the same job of cultural indoctrination.(Kaschak, 1992 124)

Finally, Kaschak also argues that men engage in related behavior as well. It is not only women who learn to relate, albeit they do relate to people differently in different contexts. Men relate positively to their wives and to their workmates and teammates. What needs to be done is to change the nature of how people relate.

Kaschak sees the solution of more parenting a bad one. It seems to be a common attitude in our society that if something does not work we should do more of it. The problem is not with who parents but with the social value structure. Here Kaschak's assumes that "more parenting" will be more of the same kind of parenting that has been occurring. But, as we have seen, this is not Chodorow's point. Chodorow wants to see a different kind of parenting. When people act in a social context they act in a relational manner. Different actions reflect different relations. Men and women tend to relate to other men and women differently. The initial point that Kaschak wants to make is that when we act relationally we set up boundaries between ourselves and other people and other things. Men tend to have more extensive and inclusive boundaries than women do. This is because they are brought up this way. Men are brought up to be in control and to own; women are brought up to mother and to be there for men. So the boundaries men set for themselves are greater and more inclusive than the boundaries women set for themselves. Indeed, one could argue that the boundaries of women are not set by themselves but by men, or at least by the male value structure of the social order. But the boundaries that men set for themselves are also defined in terms of that culture. Men do not choose how to set their own boundaries any more than women do. The social order does that for them. Thus Kaschak argues that men have just as much difficulty in individuating themselves as women do. It just that since the dominant values are masculine, it appears that men have stronger egos or self-images than women do.

While men appear to be self-sufficient women are encouraged to think of themselves as connected (Kaschak, 1992 138). This keeps women more invisible and dependent on their relationships. It is this invisibility and connectedness that prevents women from developing a stronger sense of self, a stronger self esteem, which will allow them to break some of this connectedness so they could function in an apparently more independent manner.

But what is thing we call the "self"? As we saw in the opening sections of the book, the concept of individualism is a very recent one. Many societies do not have the same sense of individuation that we have in the west. For example, less industrial cultures think more in terms of the group than the individual. Even modern industrialized societies in other parts of the world, Japan for example, put the culture before the individual. Kaschak argues that the concept of individuation for women in our culture is somewhere in between these two extremes. (Kaschak, 1992 151) On the one hand women are individuals, on the other hand they exist for men and for their children. This dichotomy sets up an unresolvable conflict for women in our society. If they become too independent they are criticized for not doing their jobs. If they become too dependent they cannot function on their own. Thus women are damned if they do and damned if they don't.

The solution to the problem of women's (and men's) sense of self or self-esteem is not just to become more independent or more connected, as Kaschak sees Chodorow's position. (Kaschak, 1992 154) Rather, Kaschak presents the concept of the self-in-context.

> That is, the self is an abstract concept by means of which meaning and consistency are attributed to a person in context. The very sense of self is a metaphor. The emerging sense of self is a set of abstract symbols and, at the same time, an embodiment of the abstract. The sense of self weaves together self-concept and self-esteem in a skein of meaning. Only by keeping the context in view can the developing sense of self and of self-esteem be understood. (Kaschak, 1992 154)

Thus,

> There is not one certain kind of self for all women. Instead there are differences as a function of race and class, differences between women in these groups as a result of unique combinations of experience and unique meanings made of those experiences. And the differences within a woman in different situations depend on the meanings they invoke for her (Kaschak, 1992 155).

The implication for this point is that self-concept—the beliefs we have about ourselves and self-esteem—the feelings and evaluations we have about ourselves—are "not separable any more than the cognitive is ever separable from the affective, or either is from the evaluative: one cannot be expressed without expressing the other." (Kaschak, 1992 156)

What needs to be done is to raise the self-esteem of women. By doing that the self-concept will also be raised. The negative point which must be overcome is that "As long as simply being a woman is judged as less or abnormal, women will suffer from damaged self-esteem." (Kaschak, 1992 162) Now we need to ask how, in a male-dominated society where women are either invisible or where their existence and identities are determined by the male value system, we are going to raise the self-esteem of women.

If I may allow myself another self indulgence which takes us outside our house for a moment, but which is nevertheless tangentially relevant, I have always found it interesting when reading any reformer who talks about changing how other people think without reflecting on how they came to think in the way they do. This not just the case with feminist thinkers but with all reformers or revolutionaries. They have come upon a new way of thinking. And, of course, they want to share their discoveries. But, for various reasons such as the way they have been brought up, most other people do not think the way the reformer does and do not even comprehend this new thinking. This is why the reformers talk about the need to change things. I agree with the conclusion. The problem I have is that, if these people have been able to change how they think, they should be able to share the process they used to make this discovery. All too often reformers talk as if they hold some truth which other people have to be prepared for in order to understand—that they have had a truth revealed to them and now must go on to prepare people so they can accept it. This, of course, is modernism at its worst. Chodorow and Kaschak are not guilty of this kind of thinking, though their writing often appears to reflect this attitude. So when Chodorow and Kaschak talk about changing how children are to be brought up and how we must learn to think about things in a different way they should do so in a more personal and less clinical manner. They should, as part of the new socio-political program, personalize how they made these changes and should not sound as though they are proselytizing.

In order to answer the above question Kaschak talks about how our society classifies problems or decides when a pattern of behavior constitutes a set of symptoms and when these symptoms constitutes a disease. The answer is quite simple. The experts make these decisions. In the case of psychological disorders in the United States it is the American Psychiatric Association which decides what is a disease and what is not. The decisions are actually voted on at membership meetings.

Now this in itself is not necessarily a problem. For example, who decides whether a painting or a piece of music is a work of art? Or who decides when a piece of scientific investigation is worthy of dissemination? In all cases it is members of the group in question. Painters and musicians, and perhaps critics respected by painters and musicians, decide what is art and all academic journals are peer reviewed.

Normally this process is fine. Indeed who else is to judge but the people who have the first-hand knowledge to judge? But problems arise when the existing order is challenged. When Arnold Schoenberg started composing atonal music there was a hue and cry from the traditionalists that because his work did not have a traditional harmonic base it could not be considered music. Yet today music has progressed far beyond Schoenberg's innovations. The same kind of negative response greeted the innovations of Charlie Parker, Dizzy Gillespie and Kenny Clarke, who changed the melodic, harmonic and rhythmic structures of jazz. And the same kind of response greeted such painters as Picasso and Dali. Today they are considered geniuses.

The same problems exist for any innovator. In this context when feminist theoreticians try to challenge standard behavioral categories they are met with hostility from the medical establishment. But in this case the consequences will affect how people are treated. Kaschak's point is that the diagnostic procedure and the classification of disease is "culture bound while assuming universality." (Kaschak, 1992 168) In *Medicine and Culture,* which deals with medical, as opposed to psychological, illnesses, Lynn Payer demonstrates that even in physical medicine different cultures see the same set of symptoms in a different light. Thus in the United States low blood pressure is considered a disease but in England it is not. In the States there is much more surgery than in other countries even though the incidences of the apparent disease and the mortality rates are the same. The point, of course, is that in physical medicine, what constitutes a disease and what constitutes treatment are determined by the culture. Thus many so-called disorders are not disorders or illnesses but "are actually orderly developments stemming from the training to be a woman in this society."[112] The so-called illnesses which affect women in ways they do not necessarily affect men include depression, disconnection and detachment, negative self-image or low self-esteem and personality disintegration[113].

The way to deal with these issues is twofold. One, of course, is to change how women are thought of in our society. This is the aim of the women's movement. But in order to accomplish this end there must be methods available for treating these so-called diseases in a way which treats women in a more positive manner.

An outline of a model for a feminist psychotherapy is the topic of Kaschak's concluding chapter. The important point that must be kept in the forefront of any attempt at feminist psychology is that the reason women suffer from these various diseases is because of the incomplete ways in which women are socialized. Women, in a male-dominated society, are not brought up to become persons but artifacts. Thus we are dealing not just with so-called personality disorders but with an over all social phenomenon. "Feminist change must, by its very nature, be multifaceted involving confrontation with meaning in every sphere" (Kaschak, 1992 210).

Meaning becomes the key concept. "All experience is interrelated and is organized by meaning. Meaning is not a cognitive or an intellectual term, but encompasses thoughts-feelings-behavior or mind-heart-body...The most centrally meaningful principle in our culture's mattering map is gender, which intersects with other culturally and personally meaningful categories such as race, class, ethnicity, and sexual orientation...Feminist therapy involves identifying and changing the personal/cultural meanings explicit and implicit in the unresolved oedipal and antigonal complexes as they are imbedded in each woman's (and man's) most personal experience. (Kaschak, 1992 211)

In relating a case where a woman saw two therapists and got two different reasons for doing something, Kaschak points out that both therapists were looking for "the correct meaning of the experience." (Kaschak, 1992 212) This concern for the truth, the one and only truth brings up the philosophical issue of essentialism. Essentialism has been a part of western thought since its beginnings. Plato and Aristotle were essentialists. Today the positivist view of science, even while acknowledging the fallibility of scientific truths, still clings to the goal of ultimate truth or of discovering the essences or true natures of things. Perhaps one of the most important aspects of postmodernism is its anti-essentialism. For a good discussion of this issue in this context see Diana Fuss, who sees the desire for essentialism as a measure of how much a group has been oppressed. The more one has been oppressed the more one wants to claim one's own views as ultimate truth. I like to put this point as follows: We have to be open minded, but we have to open minded my way and my way only. But, her point is that there is no such thing.

> We are not on a quest for *the* right meaning. Complexities of meaning must be carefully disentangled and disembedded. Part of the feminist therapist's job is to be able to retain this complexity in the service of moving toward greater simplicity by relieving women of the physical/psychological burden that gendered meanings engender. (Kaschak, 1992 213)

So what does all of this mean. First it means that just because an existing social order defines a set of behaviors as symptomatic of an illness does not mean that from another perspective those behaviors could be normal. Or, more importantly here, those behaviors are symptomatic of an illness, but the illness is not of the person who exhibits those symptoms but of the social order that gives rise to those symptoms. An old saw in sociology is that if one person exhibits a certain set of behaviors then that person has a problem. But if many people exhibit those behaviors then they are all reacting to some social phenomenon. In the case of women's behaviors this is clearly the case. Women most likely have never properly fit the role that they have been forced into by patriarchal society.

In a somewhat different context a similar point is made by Donna J. Haraway, who argues that since this is a constructed role it is like being a cyborg. A cyborg is a being that is a combination of natural or biological material coupled with artificial or constructed materials. This partly artificial life form creates an interesting image with which to see the role of women in modern society.[114] We see evidence of this in literature from the beginning of western civilization; witness Oedipus and Antigone. Closer to our time look at what happened in the 18th and 19th centuries when women were not only forced into limited roles as defined by men but were also denied their sexuality.

This point raises the old nature/nurture issue again. One of major consequences of women being forced into invisibility in order to conform to the needs of the patriarchal society, their natural sexuality was denied. More than anything else, I believe, this factor led to many of the problems, as documented by Kaschak, women have been experiencing in our culture. One of the great accomplishments of the woman's movement has been the acknowledgement of female sexuality. The ironic thing is that now that women have been able to acknowledge their sexuality they tend to exhibit it more in the way men would want to see it. Just look at the ways in which women are now dressing with more make up and shorter skirts, thus exposing more of themselves in the very way that men would like to see women dress. For a very different and anthropologically interesting account of why women wear cosmetics see Judy Grahn, who argues that the fact of menstruation was instrumental in many aspects of culture, from women learning mathematics to making the connection between menstrual and lunar cycles. The use of cosmetics, especially red lipsticks and rouges are symbolic of the menstrual blood.[115]

Freud tells us all we need to know about that period. In order for women to become complete persons, to use psychological jargon, they must come to realize that what they have been forced to become is where the pathology lies. But in order to do that, women have to both change themselves and change the world in which they live. Therapeutic models such as the one proffered by Kaschak will go a long way to help the individual woman. And social models such as the one proffered by Chodorow will go a long way in changing the world.

Kaschak obviously has some significant differences with Chodorow's work. I do not want to get into an argument as to whose work is better and whether or not Chodorow could meet Kaschak's criticisms. That would be looking for the one answer. I also do not want to become the kind of sloppy thinker who believes that all points of view can be reconciled. But we can bring together aspects of both to get a clearer picture of how women are treated and brought up in our society. The important point here is that while Chodorow's work is limited to the idealized white middle class family, it nevertheless does reflect the over all male dominated culture. Thus even when other familial structures exist, since those values operate, as Kaschak herself has shown, Chodorow's analysis of the oedipal stage of development is valid and broadly consistent with Kaschak's analysis of the antigonal structure. While Kaschak gives us an excellent therapeutic model, Chodorow gives us a good analysis of the social structure in which that model can be used.

JANE FLAX

So while I don't want to minimalize the differences between the two, I think they complement each other more than perhaps either would acknowledge. When combined, the two bodies of work give us a complex view of women in our society, how they are indoctrinated to be what they are and how to start overcoming that indoctrination. All that we now need is a social context based on a psychoanalytical model. This we get from Jane Flax[116]. I would like to begin my discussion of Flax with a personal anecdote. As a graduate student I wrote a (poorly received) paper arguing that Freud's concepts of ego, id and superego provided a model for epistemology. The id represents some notion of underlying reality, the superego is the cultural structure through which we view the world and the ego is, in some sense, representative of rationality which we use to construct, criticize and rationally investigate the knowledge gained through the filter of the superego. This model is clearly neo-Kantian. The question was whether or not the ego was strong enough to penetrate the shield of the superego. If it could then the underlying reality—the primary qualities of Locke or the noumenal world of Kant—could be knowable. If the ego were not strong enough then all knowledge was at best a social construct. Of course, I did not use the language of social construction in

1971 but that is what I meant. The conclusion I arrived at was that knowledge was embedded in our culture. How a culture raised its children and saw the world were the determining factors in what constituted knowledge. Different cultures would have different knowledge. At that time I was as influenced by Feyerabend and Sellars as I was by Freud. In reading Flax' work I believe I have found not only a kindred spirit but someone who makes the point I was only hinting at in a way I would never have been capable of.

Flax intertwines her discussions of Freud with her discussions of feminist theory and postmodernism, but I would like to try to separate these threads. I will begin with her discussion of Freud. Then before I look at Flax' work in the other areas I will look at some of the feminist implications that have been developed from the work of re-interpreting Freud. Flax begins her discussion of Freud by stating that "For all its shortcomings psychoanalysis presents the best and most promising theories of how a self that is simultaneously embodied, social, `fictional,` and real comes to be, changes, and persists over time." And in addition to revealing much about the "riddle of sex" and how central sexuality is to the formation of the self, psychoanalysis also helps us to understand power in its noninstitutional forms especially with regard to "how relations of domination become woven into the fabric of the self and how desire and domination become intertwined." (Flax, 1990 16)

And with all the negative things Freud said about women, and many other problems with his work, Flax still sees in Freud, when at his best, the foundation of a theory that would account for the complexities of psychological development, for he included in his account all of factors that Flax sees are needed for such an account. Interestingly she finds most followers of Freud less open about the complexities of sexuality than Freud himself was (Flax, 1990 17). (Isn't that always the case with the followers of an innovator.) But Freud is still the person to be reckoned with.

> No subsequent psychoanalytic theory has been able to abandon libido theory and still account for embodiment or to transcend mind-body dualisms. No purely biological theory has been able to account for the interpersonal, cultural and fantasy elements of human experience or mental illness. Although the many inadequacies of instinct theory and Freud's concept of sexuality may tempt us to abandon them, these ideas are still important. They operate as a demand and warning not to succumb to either a dualistic or a simplistically unitary view of the mind-body relation. Freud's

ideas about sexuality and embodiment can thus be appropriated by feminist and postmodern discourse, but they require further analysis by them (Flax, 1990 60).

The main thing that Flax sees lacking in Freud's work is "a feminist consciousness of the power of gender in our social and intrapsychic lives and in our theories about them." (Flax, 1990 18) And, if I may point out, Chodorow and Kaschak present the beginnings of such a consciousness. What Flax really sees as important in Freud is that his work does not fit into the standard rationalist or empiricist models derived from enlightenment or modernist thinking. Psychoanalysis offers a radically new Weltanschauung, although many of its implications have not been explored. It is this new view of persons in the world, to borrow a term from Sellars, that appeals to feminists. By presenting a new view of persons in the world, with new view of gender relations, feminists can develop a truly feminist view of persons in the world as an alternative to the standard masculine modernist view. And this view will be a feminist postmodern view.

The laboratory of psychoanalysis is the clinical session. It is in the clinical session, as we saw in chapter two, that elicits individual truths which form the basis of general theorizing. But, Flax asks, "what is this 'truth'? What is its epistemological grounding and status?"(Flax, 1990 70) Flax believes that Freud did not answer these questions satisfactorily. The reason that she hints at is because Freud's work bridged two worlds. On the one hand, as we have seen, Freud saw himself as a rational modernist; on the other hand Freud's work showed that people are not the rational beings modernism claims. Thus Freud tried to justify his non-modernist conclusions in modernist terms. As we shall see later one of reasons for the appeal of Freud to feminism is that his work opens the door to the kind of post-modern thought that is needed to develop feminism with a proper account of gender relations.

It is in this context that Flax looks at the problems regarding gender analysis in Freud's work. She does this in terms of what she sees as five major or paradoxes in his work. Her point is that these antimonies are all gendered. They are: 1) nature versus culture; 2) other versus self; 3) libido economics versus object relations theory; 4) body versus mind; and 5) patient versus analyst. (Flax, 1990 77) As has been hinted all through this chapter the distinction between nature and nurture or culture is not a viable one. What we often take for nature is really a product of nurture. My own view of the issue, if I may be so bold as to insert it here is that we probably can never know which is which. When we investigate nature we do so in a cultural context. That culture tells us what to look for and how to look for it. So even if we come up an answer that tells us that a certain behavior is biological or in our nature, the way we looked at that behavior reflects our culture. Thus while there may be a true basis of who and what we are in nature, as long as we look for it in a cultural context--and that is the only way we can look for anything since it is the cultural context which gives rise to the questions we want answered—we will never be able to truly separate nature from nurture, even if there really is something to separate, as I have also hinted at above.

Flax' point here is that while Freud's work opens the gates to seeing that biology is not destiny he still argued as if it were. By doing so Freud not only confused nature with nurture but also confused the "culturally constituted demands of family life with those of work." He did this because of his confusion over gender. "In associating women and what they do with nature, Freud transforms a concrete product of social activity into an inevitable consequence of the evolution of civilization..."(Flax, 1990 78) The distinction between the self and others is seen by Flax as examples of the distinctions between oedipal and pre-oedipal as well as between male and female. By positing that boys and girls go through these stages so differently and thereby learning to relate to others differently Freud built on his nature nurture distinction again. "By privileging the oedipal phase and denying the power of the first object relation, Freud participates in and rationalizes an act of repression both typical of and necessary to the replication of patriarchal culture." (Flax, 1990 81)

Freud's position with regard to number 2 explains 3. By seeing girls as he does "Girls remain partially attached to both their oedipal and pre-oedipal objects. Hence the girl never completely resolves her oedipal complex." (Flax, 1990 82) "In Freud's discussion of women's bodily self and how he imagines we experience it, an important displacement occurs: The social construction of gender is fused and confused with biological sex, especially anatomical differences." (Flax, 1990 83) Thus the distinction between nature and nurture is used to maintain these other distinctions. The way in which Freud distinguished between the therapist and patient also reflects this male/female dichotomy. The therapist (male) is in control of the patient (female).

The point of all this is that Freud's views on sexuality, especially in seeing all aspects of sexuality as biological instead of cultural, pervades all his thought. So, on the one hand we have Freud's views on the complexity of personality, which allows for the social construction of gender, while on the other hand we have Freud's views of the biological determination of gender roles. The five antimonies that Flax sees are five instances of the one major antimony in Freud's work. That is why Flax sees the need for a proper feminist analysis of gender in psychoanalytic terms: It will allow psychoanalysis to become the kind of psychological theory feminists need in order to develop a proper view of female psychology which is not seen from a male point of view.

This would be a good place to look at what Flax has to say about Chodorow's work. Flax finds much to agree with in Chodorow's work, but, to be sure, there are some differences. The main areas of agreement are that "without a radical change in child-rearing arrangements, women's status will not be fundamentally altered." And "how intertwined gender is with our core identity and accordingly how difficult it is to change our core selves." Thus "We can begin to understand the sex/gender system as arising out of a series of interacting social relations, including those of families..." (Flax, 1990 164-165) A major problem Flax finds with Chodorow is that she does not place "childbearing and child rearing into a political, economic and social context." And "she does not discuss class and race differences in child rearing and what these imply for a general theory of mothering and social psychology." (Flax, 1990 165)

In this context Flax goes on to list what she sees as the major points feminist writers have made about the nature of families. These points are:

> 1) The sexual division of labor is crucial in understanding women's oppression,
> 2) Understanding the history and dynamics of families is crucial for feminist theorizing,
> 3) Recognizing that families are complex structures and relate to other complex structures such as other social structures and power relations,
> 4) Families are oppressive to women,
> 5) Family structures must be changed to at least minimally allow men and women equal time for child rearing,
> 6) Gender is a creation of social relations first experienced in the family,
> 7) The different roles men and women are in are not natural but are developed in a social context
> 8) Nothing human cannot be changed. Even biology can be affected by social relations. (Flax, 1990 166-167)

From this list Flax concludes that

> A careful consideration of even the best feminist accounts of child rearing, families and gender relations makes it clear that

child-rearing practices and family arrangements are not the originating or sole cause of asymmetric gender relations or identities. An analysis of child-rearing practices cannot explain why women have the primary responsibility for child rearing, only some of the consequences of this fact. In other words, the child-rearing practices or family arrangements that some writers posit as causal presuppose the very social relations we are trying to understand: a gender-based division of human activities and hence the existence of socially constructed sets of gender relations and (the peculiar and in need of explanation) salience of gender itself. (Flax, 1990 167)

While I quote this passage, I am not sure I agree with it, let alone understand it. In a sense I think that Flax has overstated the issue here. As we have seen from the work of Chodorow and Kaschak, and indeed, from Flax herself, we really cannot separate gender issues from the social context that gave rise to them. By asking what gender is, Flax is also asking for an account of the conditions that gave rise to the problems that feminists are identifying. My point, and, I believe the point of Chodorow, Kaschak and Flax is that these issues are not separable, even though from a methodological point of view we can ask specific questions.

So, what is gender? Obviously there is no simple answer. But from the theorists that we have looked at in this chapter, and from some of the anthropological work we looked at in chapter two, we can begin to give some kind of answer. There are two concepts here: sex and gender. For most of our history these two concepts have not been separated. Gender was determined by sex. In that situation the question as to what is gender does not arise for gender does not exist as a separate concept. But today, thanks largely to the women's movement, gender has become separated from sex and has become an issue of its own.

From the theorists we have looked at we see that gender has to do with social roles and sex with biology. Perhaps the question that Flax is asking about gender should be put differently. Clearly the question has arisen because of how the women's movement led to the separation between sex and gender. If women can do things that men have traditionally done, and men can do things that women have traditionally done, we separate gender from sex. But we do this only because of the new separation. If previous societies did not have their social roles split along biological lines, questions regarding the difference between sex and gender would not arise. The question that Flax is asking only exists because the separation between biology and gender exists. So we should be asking not what gender is but why does this separation exist? What I am getting at is that if people had been brought up to do certain jobs in a social structure because of their sex, if people can now be brought up to do any job why do we even need to raise the question about gender?

The point I am hinting at is that our answers will be found in looking at why certain social structures exist. And we got look at why some social structures exist from the anthropologists we looked at in chapter two. If culture, at least initially, is a result of solving problems of group survival in relationship to the physical environment, then social roles will reflect those realities. Draper's work clearly showed how the relationship to the physical environment directly affected social structures. Out of the social structures come the individual social roles. For an interesting account of how, in some ways, the contemporary women's movement developed as a response to changes in men's attitudes, especially with regard to the development of the Playboy mentality, see Barbara Ehrenreich *The Hearts of Men: American Dreams and the Flight From Commitment.*[117]

Now assuming that the kinds of psycho-social development that Freud and the neo-Freudians we are looking at holds in some relative way to these other cultures, we then get the beginnings of a picture of the formation of gender. As cultures solidify their structures people are raised to be members of that culture. One of the factors in how they are raised has to do with what roles they will play as adults. In cultures with clear sexual divisions of labor, we will see what Freud and Chodorow describe: People being raised from day one to learn how to be good members of their culture and to play the roles the culture demands of them. When the culture is not dominated by one sex, but when there is a sexual division of labor, both sexes may be equal as Draper hinted at in her study of the !Kung tribes. But when the culture is dominated by one sex, the problems we have been looking at here arise. But they only arise when the inequalities are perceived as a problem which can be solved.

To put this point another way, people are products of their culture. Yet, culture is a product of decisions that people have made. The initial decisions which led to the formation of the culture may not have been conscious ones, but they were human decisions, nevertheless. For a fascinating look at the whole issue of consciousness, and how people can function on a day-to-day basis without being completely self-aware, see *The Origin of Consciousness in the Breakdown of the Bicameral Mind* by Julian Jaynes.[118] As people continue to live under the conditions that gave rise to the culture, children are brought up to be good members of the culture. The structures behind this upbringing, as described by Freud and

Chodorow, of course, are unconscious. And the children who are brought up in the culture have as part of their unconscious, the roles that they will play.

Only when we reflect on our culture and look at the relationships between biology and social roles do we distinguish between sex and gender. The question we need to ask here is Why does this reflection lead to this conclusion? The answer has to do with how cultures function. When things are working well no one looks by definition there are no problems. This view would be reinforced by how we are culturally conditioned. It is only when problems arise do people start to investigate the culture. The initial investigations may be very basic. But before long people begin questioning the very foundations of the culture.

This is what has been happening with regard to the women's movement. Women were no longer fitting in to the culture. They wanted to know why. The answers they have been coming up with all have to do with being forced into cultural roles as defined by biology. But their analysis shows that this forced role no longer makes sense, if, indeed, it ever did. One way of advancing their arguments is to make a distinction between biologically determined roles and social structures. It is because of these social structures and attitudes that people are brought up the way they are. But by distinguishing between what people are and what they can be they identify a problem which can then be investigated in the hope that a solution will be found. By separating sex from gender the problem gets defined. Thus gender is not really a thing to be defined but a statement of a problem which has to be solved. And, of course, how one defines the problem will determine how one will look for a solution as well as what will count as a solution.

This discussion raises another issue. Just when does something become a problem? If women have treated a certain way for so long why do they, all of a sudden, start to demand changes? The answer obviously has to do with the way in which society has been changing and with the way women are being educated. The point here is that if knowledge is contextual, a change in context will give rise to a new set of problems. An excellent example of this from the history of science, as we saw in chapter four, is Mendel's discovery of the laws of genetic inheritance. When he made his discoveries they were ignored. The reason for this was that the rest of biology was not interested in such questions. Some thirty-five years later his work was rediscovered and its importance was recognized. For a discussion of this issue see François Jacob .

What we have been looking at in this chapter is a set of variations on what the problem is and how to go about solving it. The defining of the problem has come from women who have been excluded from male society. The reasons for this exclusion are complex and have to do with the history of the culture and how the cultural institutions work to keep people in their culturally defined places. But as changes occurred in the culture people were able to reflect on the cultural structures. As the culture changed some of the roles in the culture changed. But the role of women did not change. It was too well entrenched. This is why women who saw the need to change also saw the need to explain not only why the changes should occur, but they had to show how and why their roles were what they were. Only with a contextual analysis like this could they offer a program of change. For the program of change, as we saw from our discussion of change in chapter three, has to be presented in such a way as it is seen to be solving problems in the original culture.

By relying on the work of Freud as a starting point the proverbial two birds are being killed with one stone. One is that psychoanalysis provides the most powerful model of human development. And two, who is more male centered than Freud? So by using psychoanalysis to both formulate and solve the problem of sexual inequality, women are appealing to the male structure of the society by formulating the problem in terms men can understand while using the most powerful tool available for their own purposes.

And what is the problem? The problem is why are women still being treated as invisible members of our society whose function is to serve men? The answers, as we have seen, require us to understand how cultures work and how people are brought up in those cultures to play the roles the culture demands of them. Thus Chodorow's analysis of family structures and Kaschak's analysis of how entire lives are engendered provide the beginnings of the formulation of the problem and of the solution. Both would agree that different methods of child-rearing are needed, even if they disagree on what those methods are to be. Both agree that solutions to the problem have to be stated in psychosexual terms. And both would agree that we cannot change individuals unless we can change social structures. But since people are products of social structures we need an analysis of how people are affected by their social structures so they can begin to change them from within. Flax' work gives some over all direction to these concerns.

The next question that has to be asked is how we formulate the problem. Perhaps this is what Flax meant when she asked for the need to explain what gender is. The formulation of the problem is found in feminism. But there are many different varieties of feminism. This should come as no surprise, since there are many possible ways of formulating the problem, and even more possible solutions. But that is what feminism or feminisms are all about: Defining and redefining the problem so that possible solutions can be found. An interesting analogy presents itself here. Until now we have been looking at the issue from the standpoint of individual psychodynamics in a cultural context. Perhaps the most important part of psychoanalysis is not its model of human development but its method of therapy. The model of psychological development in psychoanalysis serves the therapeutic model. Feminism, in developing alternative models of individual development do so in order to develop a new model of social structure. This new structure can be likened to a therapeutic model. In other words this new model will be the cure that women are looking for. So while we are developing individual models of development we are also developing social structure models of development. We are not only doing psychoanalysis to individuals; we are doing it to the whole social structure.

CAROL GILLIGAN

Before going on with this narrative we must take a look at the origin of the study of how children acquire moral concepts. The initial work on the subject was done by Swiss psychologist Jean Piaget. See his *The Moral Judgment of the Child*.[119] This work was developed by Lawrence Kohlberg, who argued that there are definite stages of moral development in children. "The child can internalize the moral values of his parents and culture and make them his own only as he comes to relate these values to a comprehended social order and to his own goals as a social self.".[120] Kohlberg undertook a study of 72 boys in age groups 10, 13 and 16, half from lower-middle and half from upper-middle income brackets. (Kohlberg 197) He gave the boys moral dilemmas which they had to solve. Based on the variety of statements received he and his associates defined six stages of moral development, which Kohlberg broke down into three stages of moral levels. The breakdown is as follows:

Level 1. Pre-moral level
Stage 1. Punishment and obedience orientation (Consequences for actions determine right and wrong)
Stage 2. Naive instrumental hedonism (satisfaction of one's own needs defines what is good)

Level 2. Morality of Conventional Role-Conformity
Stage 3. Good boy-nice girl orientation (What pleases others is good)
Stage 4. Authority maintaining morality (maintaining law and order, doing one's duty is good)
Level 3. Morality of Self-Accepted Moral Principles
Stage 5. Morality of agreements and democratically determined law (society's values and individual rights determine right and wrong)
Stage 6. Morality of individual principles of conscience (right and wrong are a matter of individual philosophy according to universal principles)

Now let us take another look at the plans for our house and see how some of the ideas just discussed have been developed. We will now look at the work of Carol Gilligan, a professor of education who noticed that men and women reacted differently with regard to questions about themselves and about questions of morality. Gilligan describes this as difference of voice. Noticing this difference led her to also notice the differences between men's and women's developments. She wanted to understand the relationship between women's development and their different moral voice. Though this concern led to her work Gilligan is clear to state that the different voice she hears is characterized not by gender but by theme and that its association with women is an empirical observation. Gilligan recognizes that these different voices arise in different social contexts. Her interest is "in the interaction of experience and thought, in different voices and the dialogues to which they give rise, in the way we listen to ourselves and to others, in the stories we tell about our lives."[121]

In order to do this she set up three studies, all dealing with moral issues. The studies were done in interviews. Gilligan's concern was to see how people differed in how they spoke and reacted to the issues. These differences would reflect differences in how people saw the issues, how they dealt with moral conflict and how they made their moral choices. The three studies are the college student study, the abortion study and the rights and responsibility study. In her work Gilligan acknowledges the influence of Nancy Chodorow. I read Gilligan's work as an empirical study which demonstrates that Chodorow's position of boys and girls being raised differently leads to different conceptions of their places in the world. Gilligan shows this difference in how boys and girls, men and women, think about themselves in regard to making moral choices.

Part of the background of Gilligan's work is the Piaget-influenced work of Lawrence Kohlberg, whom we met earlier. Kohlberg was Gilligan's teacher. The Piaget-Kohlberg view of moral development is based on how boys develop. Thus Kohlberg argues that boys' moral reasoning is superior to that of women because it goes beyond the stages of women's moral reasoning in that men's moral reasoning tends to use abstract principles applied to specific cases while women's moral reasoning tends to remain situational. Gilligan sees in Kohlberg's work a great paradox, "for the very traits that traditionally have defined the 'goodness' of women, their care for and sensitivity to the needs of others, are those that mark them as deficient in moral development." (Gilligan, 1982 18) This is so, Gilligan states, because of Kohlberg's (and Piaget's) views of morality are based on the study of men's lives. But when we study women's lives we see a different conception of moral thinking, one based on the understanding of "conflicting responsibilities" and of fairness to all persons involved in the conflict.(Gilligan, 1982 19)

These two different conceptions of moral reasoning come through clearly in one of Kohlberg's studies. A dilemma is set and eleven-year-olds were asked to resolve it. Gilligan takes two representative answers, one of a boy and one of a girl. The dilemma is that a man named Heinz has no money but his wife is sick and may die if she does not get her medication. Since Heinz cannot afford the medication, the question is whether or not he should steal it. This is a dilemma since stealing is wrong, but so is letting someone die.

The eleven-year-old boy, Jake, answers that in this case it is permissible to steal the medicine because human life is worth more than money and that the druggist can make up the money from other customers. Jake also recognizes that Heinz will be breaking the law but that the judge should give him the lightest possible sentence. Jake sees the law as man-made and subject to error. "Yet his judgment that Heinz should steal the drug, like his view of the law as having mistakes, rests on the assumption of agreement, a societal consensus around moral values that allows one to know and expect others to recognize what is 'the right thing to do'." (Gilligan, 1982 26)

Gilligan sees this mode of reasoning as mathematical in nature—'sort of like a math problem with humans'—Jake set the problem up like an equation with a straightforward solution. "Since his solution is rationally derived, he assumes that anyone following reason would arrive at the same conclusion and thus a judge would also consider stealing the right thing for Heinz to do." (Gilligan, 1982 26-27) Gilligan points out that Jake is aware of the limits of logic and when asked if there are right and wrong answers to moral problems, Jake responds by saying that there can only be right and wrong judgments.

The eleven-year-old girl, Amy, gives not only a very different answer but a different kind of answer than Jake did.

> Well, I don't think so. I think there might be other ways besides stealing it, like if he could borrow the money or make a loan or something, but he really shouldn't steal the drug—but his wife shouldn't die either. (Gilligan, 1982 28)

When asked why Heinz should not steal the drug, Amy's answer has nothing to do with the law but with the effect that the theft could have on the relationship between Heinz and his wife.

> If he stole the drug, he might save his wife then, but if he did he might have to go to jail, and then his wife might get sicker again, and he couldn't get more of the drug, and it might not be good. So, they should really just talk it out and find some other way to make the money. (Gilligan, 1982 28)

Gilligan sees Amy's answer as reflecting the moral dilemma in human, not in abstract mathematical terms. Amy's answer reflects her understanding of the continuing nature of the relationship. Thus

> it would be wrong to let her die because "if she died, it hurts a lot of people and it hurts her." Since Amy's moral judgment is grounded in the belief that, "if somebody has something that would keep somebody alive, then it's not right not to give it to them," she considers the problem in the dilemma to arise not from the druggist's assertion of rights but from his failure of response. (Gilligan, 1982 28)

Two issues arise here. One is that the original interviewer had difficulty in understanding Amy's answers so he kept repeating his questions. This repetition led to Amy losing confidence in her answers. But this issue is really symptomatic of the main issue, which is that men and women, boys and girls, think differently about moral issues. The interviewer does not understand this difference, which is why he keeps repeating his questions. His views are based on the same kind of assumptions that Jake's answer were based on, which is why he had no trouble understanding Jake's answers. But since he does not share Amy's assumptions about the nature of moral judgments, he does not understand her. The point that Gilligan makes here is that

> these two children see two very different moral problems—Jake a conflict between life and property which can be resolved by logical deduction, Amy a fracture of human relationship that must be mended with its own thread.(Gilligan, 1982 31)

Gilligan goes on to argue that while Kohlberg asks, "What does he see that she does not?" he does not ask the equally valid question, "What does she see that he does not?" Such a question, for Kohlberg, lies outside the moral domain. (Gilligan, 1982 31) Had he asked this question Kohlberg may have learned about another approach to solving moral dilemmas. Jake's solution involves hierarchical ordering while Amy's solution involves a network of connections which is sustained by a process of communication (Gilligan, 1982 32).

In another part of the study Kohlberg asked eight-year-olds to describe a situation in which they were not sure about the right to do. Jeffrey described a situation in which his mother gave him a task to do but he wanted to play with his friends. His response was to say that he thinks about his friends and he thinks about his mother and then he thinks about the right thing to do. He knows what the thing to do is "Because some things go before other things." Karen describes a situation where she has a lot of friends but can't play with all of them. Because they are all friends they will have to take turns. If someone is alone she will play with that person. When asked what she thinks about when making the decision she answers "Um, someone all alone. Loneliness." (Gilligan, 1982 32-33) Thus Jeffrey thinks hierarchically while Karen thinks in terms of a network of relations.

Gilligan sees these two views as different but complementary while Kohlberg's criteria of moral reasoning see the method the girls use as inferior to the method the boys use since it does not reach the proper stage of abstraction. To gain some insight into these differences Gilligan returns to Jake and Amy. But this time they are asked to describe themselves. Jake describes himself as "perfect." When asked for specifics Jake states his name and age, where he lives, what his father does, that he doesn't believe in crime except if your name in Heinz, and that he finds school boring. He then says that he doesn't know to describe himself. He doesn't know how to read his personality. When asked to say how he would describe himself, he relates what he likes and what his achievements have been. Amy begins by asking what the question means. She then goes on to say that she likes school and wants to be some kind of scientist, that she wants to do things and she wants to help people. That is the kind of person she is, or at least tries to be. When asked why she is the kind of person who wants to help others she states that the world has lots of problems and that everybody should try to help somebody. (Gilligan, 1982 33-34)

Gilligan points out that by "Describing himself as distinct by locating his particular position in the world, Jake sets himself apart from that world by his abilities, his beliefs and his height." And while Amy also lists her likes, wants and beliefs, "she locates herself in relation to the world, describing herself through actions that bring her into connection with others (Gilligan, 1982 35). Gilligan goes on to argue that Jake sets up his self-image in terms of how he measures up to his ideal of personal perfection while Amy sees her self-image in terms of an ideal of care. "While she places herself in relation to the world and chooses to help others through science, he places the world in relation to himself as it defines his character, his position and the quality of his life." (Gilligan, 1982 35)

This difference of ideals becomes even clearer when each person was asked about how they understood responsibility. When asked how to resolve a conflict between responsibility to oneself and to others Jake answered that "You go about one-fourth to the others and three-fourths to yourself." When asked Why? He answered that the most important thing is yourself. And when asked what responsibility means Jake said "It means pretty much thinking of others when I do something....because you have to live with other people and live in your community...." When Amy was asked the same questions she first answered that conflict resolution would depend on the situation. It would depend on who the other person is and how much responsibility you have towards that other person. When asked why, she said that people are more important than things, "but if it's somebody that you really love and love as much or even more than you love yourself, you've got to decide what you really love more, that person, that thing, or yourself." And when asked what responsibility means Amy said "That other people are counting on you to do something and you can't decide, 'Well, I'd rather do this or that.'" (Gilligan, 1982 35-37) From this discussion Gilligan argues that again Jake uses his mathematical model from which a formula yields a solution. He begins with his responsibility to himself and then considers the extent to which he is responsible to others. "Responsibility in his construction pertains to a limitation of action, a restraint of aggression, guided by the recognition that his actions can have effects on others, just as theirs can interfere with him." While we see Amy responding "contextually rather than categorically....To her, responsibility signifies response, an extension rather than a limitation of action. Thus it connotes an act of care rather than the restraint of aggression."(Gilligan, 1982 37-38)

What we see here are excellent examples of Chodorow's concepts of separateness and connectedness as well as excellent examples of Kaschak's views of how views of the world and their place in are gendered from birth. While Gilligan is careful to point out that her work was not designed along gender lines, her analysis of Kohlberg's work clearly shows that boys and girls are brought up to think differently about themselves and their relations to others. Here we clearly see Chodorow's concepts of separation and connectedness at work. In this context Gilligan refers to Claire, another woman who was involved in the study. Claire was interviewed twice; once when she was a high school senior and later at the age of twenty-seven. As a student Claire does not have a good sense of who she is. She is still developing her identity. She finds herself caught between who she is and how other people perceive her. The need to make a decision about what to do after graduation forces her to look at herself and learn to make decisions for herself. This leads her to change her thinking from the abstract "what is right" to the particular "what is right for me."

> I'm trying to tell you two things. I'm trying to be myself alone, apart from others, apart from their definitions of me, and yet at the same time I'm doing just the opposite, trying to be with or relate to—whatever the terminology is—I don't think they are mutually exclusive. (Gilligan, 1982 53)

Thus "Claire is caught...between a responsiveness to others and to herself." (Gilligan, 1982 53) When asked about Heinz' dilemma she responds much the same way that Amy did. Claire believes that Heinz should steal the drug because he should have done anything to save the life of his wife. And while the druggist had a legal right to refuse to give Heinz the drug which he could not pay for, Claire sees the druggist as having a moral responsibility to show compassion and not refuse.

When interviewed five years later Claire now sees things somewhat differently. She subsumes law in terms of responsibility. "Judging the law now in terms of whom it protects, she extends her ethic of responsibility to a broader vision of social connection." The result of this change as far as Kohlberg is concerned is to lower her score on his scale of moral development since her view moved further away from his standards of abstraction. Her response to this is to be somewhat confused, but she at least sees that she has moved. While her views are less certain, they have more direction (Gilligan, 1982 55). She now sees Heinz' dilemma as a contrast between the wife's life and the druggist's greed. She sees the druggist's preoccupation with profit as both a failure of understanding as well as a failure of response. In doing so she shifts from talking about a hierarchy of rights to talking of a web of relationships.

> Perceiving relationships as primary rather than as derived from separation, considering the interdependence of people's lives, she envisions "the way things are" and "the way things should be" as a web of interconnection where "everybody belongs to it and you all come from it "(Gilligan, 1982 57).

Claire goes on to describe morality as "'the constant tension between being part of something larger and a sort of self contained entity' and she sees the ability to live with that tension as the source of moral character and strength." (Gilligan, 1982 57) We see in this discussion that men and women, because they are socialized differently, develop very different views of what morality is. Since our society's values are male values where women are devalued, women's moral reasoning is devalued. The irony here is that, since women have been given the job as primary caregivers by men, one would think that men would value women's views on morality, especially since women are brought up in context of male value structures to be the primary teachers of morality. Thus, since women are given the job of primary caregivers and as primary teachers of morality on male terms one could argue that the view of morality that women have developed is superior to the view that men have developed. Women could argue that male abstract reasoning is fine for doing mathematics or science, or for doing politics or waging war, but not for moral reasoning. The kind of reasoning portrayed here would not lend itself to saying that it is a superior kind of reasoning. But it is reflective of a different view of persons in the world. Gilligan sees the problem as one of interpretation.(Gilligan, 1982 62)

Men's and women's respective views of morality and of self concepts are incommensurable. Since men's values dominate our society women's values are at best devalued or ignored; women are made invisible. In her discussions of Jake's views Gilligan often referred to the violence inherent in them. This was evident in how he separated himself and saw laws as protecting himself from others. To put this comment in perspective, recall both Locke and Freud. In reading Jake's views of individualism I thought immediately of Locke's view of the world. Jake could have been paraphrasing Locke. This shows how accurate Locke's description of modern society was and, in turn, how influential that description has been in the development of modern society.

Freud, of course, talked about violence and war as a result of the unresolved oedipal complex. This, as we saw, was a consequence of individualistic values in a repressive society. Jake's comments could have come from a case study of Freud. This shows how accurate Freud was in explaining this aspect of behavior. For an interesting literary look at this conflict of values, see the *Xenogenesis* trilogy by Octavia E. Butler. The trilogy consists of three novels: *Dawn, Adulthood Rites* and *Imago*. While this is a science fiction story it is really about two different models of human thought; the hierarchical and the non-hierarchical. The problems of humans, such as wars, are the direct result of hierarchical thinking. The aliens do not have such conflicts because they are a non-hierarchical culture. The theme of the trilogy is that the only way humanity will survive is if it becomes absorbed by a non-hierarchical culture. Of course, the aliens represent the non-hierarchical thinking of women. Thus if humanity is to survive it must adopt these feminine values.

Now let us look at how women responded to Gilligan's studies of moral decision- making. While she used three issues, one will suffice. I have chosen the abortion issue because I think it illustrates most strongly Gilligan's points about how women reason about moral issues..

In her earlier work Gilligan noticed two dominant themes in women's accounts of moral reasoning. One was the unwillingness of women to make moral judgments. Gilligan saw this as stemming from the women's reluctance to judge rather than from any uncertainty as to their rights to make such judgments (Gilligan, 1982 66). The second theme, a development of the first, was that making a choice or a judgment often involved women in some conflict between her right to make the choice or judgment and her accepted role which would be to defer such choices or judgments to others, especially if the choice involved something a woman wanted for herself when her role demanded self sacrifice. (Gilligan, 1982 70) This conflict clearly arose when making the choice to have or not have an abortion.

One could put this point in Chodorow's and Kaschak's terms of the invisibility of women and the way in which their roles are not valued by the male value structure. While women are given certain roles, those roles, and the ways in which they are carried out, are not valued by the male system, they are nevertheless given moral responsibilities, especially in regard to caring for others. Thus it becomes difficult to make decisions for themselves, for when it comes to themselves they are supposed to be invisible. How women deal with these conflicts was the subject of the abortion study. In the study twenty-nine women were interviewed. Their ages ranged from fifteen to thirty-nine and they were diverse with regard to social class and ethnic background (Gilligan, 1982 71).

As Gilligan points out, in its simplest form, the decision to have an abortion centers on the self. The concern is with survival. "The woman focuses on taking care of herself because she feels that she is all alone. From this perspective should is undifferentiated from would, and other people influence the decision only through their power to affect its consequences." (Gilligan, 1982 75) In this context, as the answers of two of the respondents show, is the question of whether or not the decision was the right one would only arise if the decision would bring out a conflict in her own needs. (Gilligan, 1982 75) But in making the decision the woman in question is able to make a truly adult choice.

At this stage of moral development the abortion decision is often seen in terms of self-sacrifice. The woman chose to have an abortion not because it was the easy thing to do but because it was the hard thing to do. A woman may have wanted the child but found herself alone and not in a position to be able to raise a child, so she makes a sacrifice in not fulfilling the social role of mother because she knows she is not in a position to be a good and responsible mother. Other women, who are more aware of themselves and their situations see the abortion decision in somewhat different terms. They are concerned with truth. They raise such concerns as whether the decision is selfish or responsible, moral or immoral. These questions lead the women to rethink the concept of responsibility, juxtaposing it with how other people think.

In raising these questions women separate the voice of self from the voices of others and ask whether or not it is possible to be responsible to herself and also be responsible to others. It is in this context that concepts of women as individuals start to develop. Individual women can come to see themselves as capable of making such decisions. Concepts such as self-sacrifice and care and of weighing how others are affected will still enter the decision making process. But now such women see that they have obligations to themselves as well as to others. Thus the "different moral voice" that Gilligan elicits in her work shows women grappling with their role as caregiver where the need to always put others first come first comes into conflict with their own individual needs. An analogy here is a point in airline safety. When a mother is traveling with a baby, or if anyone is traveling with someone who needs to be looked after, they are told to first make sure of their own safety and then to look after their charges. For example, if the cabin becomes de-pressurized, the caregiver should make sure she has her oxygen mask on first. Then she will be in a position to care for her charge. But if she tries to get the oxygen mask on the baby first, she may die in the process, and then she will not be able to help anyone else. Thus morality is a combination of self-preservation and obligation to others, where obligations are met without any thought for receiving anything in return.

Though this discussion of Gilligan only deals with parts of her book, all of her important themes are present here. The important point of her work is that she found that women and men reason differently about morality and about self-image and that these modes of thinking are connected. Gilligan's work led to a careful study of this thinking process to which we now turn.[122] I shall refer to this work as Belenky et al.

This study, based on interviews with 135 women from different backgrounds, 90 of whom were college students and 45 were involved with some family agency, describes "the ways of knowing that women have cultivated and learned to value, ways we have come to believe are powerful but have been neglected and denigrated by the dominant intellectual ethos of our time." (Belenky et al, 1986 vii) The study examines "women's ways of knowing" and describes "five different perspectives from which women view reality and draw conclusions about truth, knowledge and authority. We show how women's self concepts and ways of knowing are intertwined." (Belenky et al, 1986 3)

Building on, but not copying, Perry's schemata Belenky et al grouped the women's ways of knowing into five categories: Silence; received knowledge; subjective knowledge; procedural knowledge; and constructed knowledge. Silent women see themselves as having no voice and are at the whim of external authority. At the received knowledge stage women see themselves as capable of accepting received knowledge and of reproducing knowledge gained from authorities, but not as capable of producing their own knowledge. The subjective knowledge stage sees women as trusting their personal intuitions as a source of knowledge. The procedural stage sees women as learning and applying objective techniques for obtaining and using knowledge. Finally, the constructed stage sees women viewing knowledge as contextual and learn to value all modes of learning. (Belenky et al, 1986 15)

Belenky et al realize that this list may not be exhaustive, that similar categories can be found in men's thinking and that they used a very small sample. But their results provide both interesting and valuable information as well as a model for understanding women's "different" voices. The "voice" imagery became very important in this study for it came to stand not just for a person's point of view but it reflected different aspects of women's lives and their respective experiences and developments. Women would talk about such things as "being silenced," "speaking up," "not being heard," "words as weapons," and so on. These speech metaphors differ in kind from visual metaphors such as "standing at a distance to remove oneself from the object of study." "Unlike the eye, the ear requires closeness between subject and object. Unlike seeing, speaking and listening suggest dialogue and interaction." (Belenky et al, 1986 18) This difference is important for many of the dominant value concepts in our society are visual, not aural. For example we talk of 'blind justice" or "blind or double blind" testing in science. Belenky et al's point here is that visual-based knowledge is more highly regarded and more objective and speech-based knowledge. Visual metaphors are closer linked to mind and intellect than are aural metaphors. But women kept using the aural metaphors. Thus "voice" became the unifying theme of the book. (Belenky et al, 1986 18-19)

We shall now look at each of the five stages of voice development in women. Women who felt the least self-confident and the most controlled by others described their situation as one of silence. They were silenced by those around them. They saw words being used to separate and diminish people and felt that they could be punished for using words. Women in the survey said that they deserved to be hit for mouthing off or that even if they did speak no one would listen. (Belenky et al, 1986 24-25)

These "silent women" develop language but "they do not cultivate their capacities for representational thought. They do not explore the power that words have for either expressing or developing thought." Thus these women find themselves "cut off from others in a world full of rumor and innuendo." (Belenky et al, 1986 25) Such women have no confidence in their own abilities if they even believe they have abilities and do not even learn from their own experiences. (Belenky et al, 1986 26) They accept authority blindly and see this obedience "as being of utmost importance for keeping out of trouble and insuring their own survival, because trying to know 'why' is not thought to be either particularly possible or important." (Belenky et al, 1986 28) These women also accept strict sex-role stereotyping, which, of course, reinforces their powerlessness. "Men are active and get things done, while women are passive and incompetent." (Belenky et al, 1986 29)

Belenky et al believe that individuals who grow up to see

themselves as "deaf and dumb" "are raised in profound isolation under the most demeaning circumstances..." (Belenky et al, 1986 34) Women who function at the received knowledge stage acknowledge listening as a means of acquiring knowledge. Words become *central* to the knowing process." (Belenky et al, 1986 36) What they hear in the words of others is "concrete and dualistic. Things are right or wrong, true or false, good or bad, black or white. They assume that there is only one right answer to each question, and all other answers and all contrary views are automatically wrong." (Belenky et al, 1986 37) The major result of this is that received knowers still their own voices so they can hear the voices of others. They also "have a literal faith that they and their friends share exactly the same thoughts and experiences. They relish having so much in common and are unaware of their tendency to shape their perceptions and thoughts to match those of others." (Belenky et al, 1986 38)

Since women functioning at this stage of development are capable of hearing and understanding they "have faith that if they listen carefully enough they will be able to do the 'right thing' and will get along with others." (Belenky et al, 1986 45) In contrast to the "silent women" who talk in terms of "I want," "I feel," "I had to" and "they made me" received knowers talk in terms of "should" or "ought." (Belenky et al, 1986 46) And because they believe that knowledge originates outside of the self, they are dependent on others for their knowledge. An implication of this is that such women are also dependent on others for their identities. They strive to be what they believe other people expect them to be. (Belenky et al, 1986 48)

The next level of development is the stage of subjective knowledge where women develop their inner voice. They learn that external authorities cannot always be trusted and, in turn, learn to trust their own inner voice or their own "gut." And while the development of this inner voice is a major development, this stage of subjective knowing it is still authoritarian and dualistic. Things are still black and white, right or wrong, only the authority that is now listened to is the inner self instead of an outer authority. "Truth now resides within the person and can negate answers that the outside world supplies." (Belenky et al, 1986 54) This step in learning to listen to one's inner voice is a major step because it acknowledges that external authorities have failed. And since, in our society, most external authorities are male, by taking this step women acknowledge that the male authoritarian world has failed them. (Belenky et al, 1986 57-58)

Belenky et al point out that many of the women they saw at this stage of development or higher had originally experienced themselves as outside or at the bottom of the power hierarchy. In their eyes, the public world was controlled by men, the experts with the credentials and the clout, those who seemed to know what they were talking about and could argue others down. They described the public truth these experts held as remote, mysterious and inaccessible (Belenky et al, 1986 60).

By acknowledging this point and by relying more on their own experiences, and on the experiences of other women like themselves and in affirming their maternal or nurturing aspects they were able to develop confidence in themselves. By learning to trust their own experiences they transformed their lives. (Belenky et al, 1986 60-61) In developing their sense of self, women at this stage of development often see themselves not so much in a positive view. They would not say "I am so and so." Rather they would say what they are not. "I am not like my father," "I am not like my teacher." This often turns into a view that appears to be a "go it alone" attitude but is really a "go it without men" attitude since these women are rejecting this failed authority. (Belenky et al, 1986 79)

If it is true that women tend to define themselves in terms of their relationships, as we have argued based on the work of Chodorow and Gilligan, then it is not surprising to find that when traditional relationships or structures breakdown the result would be expressed in negative terms. "No matter what their pasts were, most subjectivist women found it difficult to reflect upon or even describe themselves clearly." (Belenky et al, 1986 81) While they knew what they were not and what they were rebelling against, as yet they did not know who they were in positive terms. What these women tended to do was to listen. Given the unsettled sense of an ever-changing self, it is not surprising that observation and listening serve an important function. They are the primary means they have available for articulation and differentiation of self.

To some extent listening to others is self-serving. It is a way of learning about the self without revealing the self; however, good listeners draw others to them. "Subjectivist women value what they see and hear around them and begin to feel a need to understand the people with whom they live and who impinge on their lives" (Belenky et al, 1986 85-86). Belenky et al are not sure why some women then make the move from the subjective stage of knowing to the next or procedural stage of knowing, but they do give some common sources. First, and perhaps most important, is that the women's old ways of knowing were challenged. (Belenky et al, 1986 88) Other factors may include being a situation where one is forced to make decisions about oneself, such as a student having to decide what courses or career paths to take, or in coming into conflict with what one wants and with what one's subjective knowledge tells one.

One of the students interviewed for the survey was at the subjectivist stage when she entered college. A counselor forced her into making some personal decisions. Another student took an art history course thinking it would allow her to maintain her subjectivist approach but was forced to justify her reactions. "It wasn't enough to stand in front of a painting and go 'wow!' Wow does not make a paper." (Belenky et al, 1986 89) The demands of the situations these students were in led them to develop their analytical skills. "They have learned that truth is not immediately accessible, that you cannot 'just know'. Things are not always what they seem to be. Truth lies hidden beneath the surface, and you must force it out. Knowing requires careful observation and analysis." (Belenky et al, 1986 93-94)

The world of procedural knowledge is more complex than the world of subjective knowledge. The women in question learned that there is more than one way to look at something. Instead of assuming that everyone in a similar situation thinks the same way and sees things the same way, these women have learned that there are many ways to look at something and many ways to think about things. They have progressed past the dualistic modes of knowledge and have acknowledged the complexity of the world. "They are interested not just in what people think but in how people go about forming their opinions and feelings and ideas." (Belenky et al, 1986 97) And this "how and why" leads to what Belenky et al call "connected knowledge." Such knowledge involves understanding as well as just knowing. This is crucial. "Understanding involves intimacy and equality between self and object, while knowledge implies separation from the object and mastery over it." (Belenky et al, 1986 101) This involves the attempt to understand things from different points of view. When dealing with other people it means trying to understand things from the other person's standpoint.

The concept of empathy is at work here. When we truly connect with other people we learn to empathize with them; to see or feel about things they way they see or feel. For an interesting discussion of degrees of empathy in a feminist psychoanalytical context see Diana Tietjens Meyers.[123] Belenky et al define these two different epistemologies. Separated knowing is based on impersonal or so-called objective procedures for discovering truth while connected knowing discovers truth through care. When speaking of connected knowing "we refer not to any sort of relationship between the self and another person but with relationships between knowers and objects (or subjects) of knowing (which may or may not be persons). (Belenky et al, 1986 102) This does not mean that knowers enter into some kind of relationship with inanimate objects the way they do with other persons. But it does mean that knowledge of such objects comes from how people come into contact with such objects, with what roles such objects play in the lives of the knowers. It also involves learning how other people relate to the same objects.

Connected knowers have to learn to develop procedures for gaining access to other people's knowledge. This can be accomplished by trying to share another person's experiences. Of course one can never be certain that one knows what another knows, but one can come close. One person can learn to trust another person and come to believe what the other person says. Person A will become interested in the life of person B and in so doing come to realize that the form or pattern of how person B thinks is more important than any one specific thought. Once person A understands, however imperfectly, person B's thinking process, person A will be able to know how and what and why person B knows. And, of course, the process works in reverse. By learning about how each other thinks, empathy will develop between A and B, and the mutuality of A and B's knowledge will yield a richer knowledge of what they both know. This process yields even richer rewards when done across many people (Belenky et al, 1986 119).

Once this level of connectedness has been achieved we reach the final level of Belenky et al's stages of development, the stage of constructed knowledge. In reaching this stage women learn to speak in their own voices and must "'jump outside' the frames and systems authorities provide and create their own frame." (Belenky et al, 1986 134) In so doing they must construct their own worlds and their own knowledge; their own epistemology. The first step in doing this is to integrate knowledge one knows with knowledge one has gained from other sources, including other authorities. This integrating process is the process by which they begin to construct a new empathic world-view.

One quickly learns that truth is always contextual and that the context is largely determined by how people react and interact in the context. Thus, in a sense, the context is also constructed. When one knows that one is in a constructed context and had as much to do with constructing that context as anyone else, the role of previous authorities becomes diminished if not eliminated. This does not mean that constructed knowledge is totally subjective. We passed the subjective stage a long time ago. But it is not objective in the traditional sense either, for we have passed that stage as well. Constructed knowledge is a new category of knowing, one that leaves the traditional subjective/objective dualism behind.

Our house example will be helpful here. I want to move to a new house. I can proceed in a number of ways. I can buy an existing house; I can have a house built that is based on an existing plan but with some modifications; or I can design my own house. If I design my own I can start with an existing plan and modify it to meet my needs within the limitations of the existing plan or I can start from scratch. If I start from scratch I also have various options. I can work with existing plans as a start and then come up with my own variation or I can sit down and think through what I want my house to do. What purposes or functions must my house have? What sizes do I want the rooms? What kinds of rooms do I want? Where do I want the rooms situated, especially in relation to each other? What kinds of construction materials do I want to use? In other words, I am really asking about how I live.

This house will end up looking like no other house in town or anywhere else since it reflects how I live and not how anyone else lives. But since I live in a world with other people and am connected to other people my house will be recognizable as a human house and not seen as an alien dwelling. The house plans are subjective in the sense that they reflect my thinking but the house plans will exist in the world for anyone to see, so, in a sense, they are objective. Other people can use these plans, or modify them to suit personal needs. Thus I take things that are in the world, make decisions about how I relate to them, look at how I relate to them in the context of what is important to me and the people around me and then I make my decisions. These decisions are not made in isolation since my plans have to be realized. The way I plan my house must reflect the realities of construction materials and techniques. I do not create the world. I do not create how I think about things. But, given the context in which I function, I come to a point where I create how I understand and relate to the world. And my knowledge of the world comes from this understanding and relating.

To use another analogy let us look at buying a car. I am a licensed racing driver, so I want a car with certain handling abilities, but I also want a good everyday car. After comparing what I want in a car with what was available I make a choice. The car is very close to my ideal, but it is not 100% of my ideal. I would love to make some changes and have communicated some of my concerns to the manufacturer. I would like the seats designed a bit differently; I would like fabric instead of leather available for the interior; and I would like a different brand of tires. If cars were easy to design and assemble, I could construct my own. I would be using designs and materials available in the world but I would be using them my way.

The point is that the desire to know and the criteria used to determine what knowledge is come from how we interact with the world and other people in the world. In other words, human relationships, or cultural patterns, are the starting points of epistemological inquiry. And since how we relate to people also reflects the kinds of persons we are, which in turn reflects how we were brought up, concepts of personhood become central to epistemological inquiry. "We know what we are" could be the slogan of constructed knowers.

In constructed knowledge, distinctions such as objective/subjective, fact/value, pure/applied become meaningless. Knowledge, no matter how specialized and apparently separated from us, comes out of who and what we are and how we live.

We have just taken a very long and interesting ride through some largely uncharted terrain. So let us see where we have gone and where this trip may lead. First we saw how social roles are socially constructed. They are not determined by biology, even though they were once thought to be so determined and though, to some extent, biology still plays some part: women still become pregnant and men still do the impregnating. And basic cultural forms dealing with survival are a result of how we biologically interact within our physical environments. We saw that our lives are engendered from the moment we are born but that the crucial stages in what this engendering will mean for our later lives are just before and during the onset of puberty: The pre-oedipal and oedipal stages of development. In this way biology also plays a part since the onset of puberty is a stage of biological development.

Then we saw how this engendering leads to men and women learning to think differently about how they relate to the world and to other people and how they think differently about these relations. We also saw how these different ways engenderment leads to a different understanding of how the world works. Thus people in different social roles—in different genders—have a very different understanding of the world. They have different knowledge of the world and they have a different way of justifying that knowledge. Different social roles, different engenderment, leads to different epistemologies.

As women mature they go through various stages of individual development and empowerment. The important point here is that because women are brought up to play certain social roles their individual development may be impeded. Thus some women may stay in the silent stage through their lives, some may stay in the subjective stage, and so on. Because of the different ways men and women are socialized and engendered, and because the dominant value structure of our society is reflected in the male view of world and of how persons relate to that world, women's views of the world and of how persons relate to the world are devalued. This is one of the main reasons that women can remain in the silent or subjective stages of knowing. This is one way that women are made invisible.

Some of the implications of this account of women's development have far-reaching implications for psychology, sociology, epistemology and politics. It would be interesting for a team of psychologists and sociologists and even anthropologists to trace the relationships between the Freudian stages of biological development with the Chodorow-Kaschak-Flax-Gilligan-Belenky et al stages of psycho-social development. Questions to be investigated would have to do with how the way children are brought up relates to how they mature. Why do some women develop to the stages of constructed knowledge and others do not? Does this development, or lack of development, have anything to do with how children are raised from birth? And if so, at what stages of biological development do various psychological or sociological practices have the desired, or not desired, effects? What kind of alternate psycho-social structure would be more efficacious in raising more constructed knowers? And since we know that men can be engendered with feminine characteristics and that women can be engendered with masculine characteristics we must also look into how such results are achieved.

The point of all this investigation, as the astute reader will have guessed, is to learn how to develop the beginnings of a new social paradigm, and to develop a new theory of natural law, in which women and men would be equal. In developing this new paradigm of persons in the world, to combine the language of Kuhn and Sellars, we also have to develop new evaluative techniques. For example, on the Kohlberg scale of moral development, abstract moral reasoning is considered higher than the connected or constructed knowing that women tend to exhibit. But on the Belenky et al scale, this abstract reasoning is lower on the scale. A parallel point that should be made here has to do with concepts of autonomy. As discussed above, modernism is based on a kind of autonomy that results from the individual being the basic social unit. The basic social unit in postmodern feminism would appear to be some group or culture or community. The kind of autonomy that the constructed knower has is along the lines advocated by Grimshaw.

At this point we may be in a better position to answer the question Flax posed with regard to understanding just what gender is. In addition to what was stated above, gender is not just about who does what but about how something is done. We can talk about men being of the feminine gender and women being of the masculine gender because of how they think and act. Thus, when we talk of a man being of the feminine gender we mean that this man thinks about moral issues in a way that Gilligan shows women tend to think about moral issues. We mean that this man has gone through his developmental stages the way a woman would have gone through them and he has become a constructed knower. Conversely, a woman who achieves male-like autonomy and learns to function, say, in the corporate world on men's terms, has been brought up in a way that she has gone through her developmental stages much the way a man would have developed.

Thus sex and gender must be separated, even if, at some later date we recombine them in a manner suggested by Bornstein's work. And we separate them in a given cultural context, with a given understanding of psycho-sexual-social development which reflects how things are conceived and acted upon. These differing conceptions of how persons function in the world lead to the challenging of the old paradigm and the development of a new one.

We have here a clash of paradigms. The two views are not directly comparable. It makes no sense to try to argue, at least at this stage of our discussion, which is better. The point is that we are trying to develop a new paradigm of persons in the world. The Kohlberg model is based on the principles of modernism. The model presented here is based on what I have been calling postmodern feminism. Whether or not this new paradigm will be able to replace the old one, and how this might occur, will be discussed later. Before we are in a position to do that we must try to complete the new paradigm of persons in the world.

But before we move on I want to take a very brief look at the role of feelings or emotions in this view of the world. The modern male view of the world often denigrates women's decision-making as emotional. We can see how this view is reflected in the Kohlberg-Gilligan dispute where the contextual thinking women use is looked upon as inferior to the abstract thinking men use. This is because such thinking is thought to be emotional or based on feelings instead of being based on logic. But, as we have shown, this judgment is unacceptable. And in some ways the emotional or feeling or contextual decision making associated with women may be a superior mode of reasoning.

In our discussion of positivism we only mentioned feelings or emotions in passing. The psychological theory of behaviorism which is based on positivistic epistemology either denies the existence of feelings by arguing that such things are simply learned responses, or it says that feelings or emotions can be seen as by-products of behavior. In our discussion of concept realism we only mentioned feelings or emotions in passing as we looked at the impossibility of Protestantism private languages. Thus the language we use to describe feelings or emotions is learned publicly just the way language which describes overt behavior is learned. The implication of this point is that feelings and emotions are real and can play a part in the explanation of behavior. There has been a lot of work done on this theme. Most of it addresses the positivist view in trying to demonstrate that emotions or feelings are intensional, i.e., about something, and can therefore be included in the explanation of behavior. For example, we can say that a person acted in such and such a way because of fear, whether or not there really was something to be feared. For a thorough discussion of this point see Patricia S. Greenspan, *Emotions and Reasons.*[124]

What are emotions or feelings? In a sense I am using the terms imprecisely as synonyms. Introductory psychology books explain emotions in terms of the autonomic nervous system. Thus there is a physical basis to emotions. This is also consistent with the psychoanalytic view of persons in that persons are first and foremost biological entities. Thus the ability to experience emotions is built into what we are. I like to characterize emotions as warning signals. Our biological mechanisms, which include our senses, warn us of possible dangers. We enter a strange situation and the hair on our neck rises. We become apprehensive. We carefully check out the environs. Only when we feel we are safe do we move on. Or consider our physical reactions on receiving extremely good or bad news. In the case of good news we feel elated or almost intoxicated. In the case of bad news we feel depressed or as if we are in shock. The physical and the psychological are clearly intertwined. And we feel certain things when we are with other people, ranging from love to fear to loathing. In a sense we pick up "vibes" from other people. Whether these are subliminal or subconscious observations, or the reception of some kind of electrical energy emitted by the person's brain or nervous system, we do receive these feelings and act on them.

The emotion is what we feel. The emotion is a biological or psychological state and the feeling is our cognition of it. Since it seems unnecessary to distinguish between a state of being and the awareness of that state I use emotion and feeling somewhat synonymously. The point is that such feelings are real. They are part of our world; they are part of what we are. To deny our emotions would be to deny a part of ourselves. But, of course, we can be mistaken about our feelings. We can feel fear when there is nothing to be afraid of and we may not feel fear when we should beg to be afraid, or we can misinterpret something and feel a false fear. So when we feel an emotion we must check it out to see what it is and if it is a correct response to the situation. Thus reason can and must be used to investigate our emotions. Let us say we enter a new situation. It can be as mundane as going to a party with the expectation of meeting a new partner or as frightening as returning home to find our home has been broken into. Or it can be any new situation. Wherever or whatever the situation is we enter with certain expectations, however amorphous these expectations are. We react to what we see in terms of these expectations. These expectations, of course, are somewhat based on our own past experiences and the role that such situations play in our society.

So here I am at a party hoping to meet a new lover. I meet various people but do not feel that any of them for me. Do I know this for certain? No, for I have not reached that level of investigation. But can I assume I am right? Probably, since the reactions I am having to these people fit in with past experiences, when I felt a certain way about someone before I discovered she was not for me. I feel this way about this person. Therefore she is not for me. Of course I can be wrong since I have not given her a real chance. She may be on party behavior and is masking her feelings. But then I can argue to myself that anyone who has to do that will not be for me anyway.

Emotions are not rational, but we can use rational methods for investigating the validity of our feelings. Emotions are real and must be included in our accounts of behavior and in our accounts of personhood. To deny the role of emotions in behavior is to deny an important aspect of what it is to be a person.

We are now ready to continue with developing our new paradigm of persons in the world. In the next chapter we look at how postmodern feminism looks at science.

Chapter 6

POSTMODERN SCIENCE AS SOCIAL CONSTRUCT

Now that we have some idea as to what a feminist postmodern person is like, we need to see what kind of science or epistemology this person would develop. I say "science or epistemology" since, from an historical perspective, science grew out of epistemology but epistemology is still used to critique science. This is so because traditional epistemology was concerned with discovering the truth *and* the conditions which allow us to say that so and so is true. Today science concerns itself primarily with the search for what is true while epistemologists concern themselves with the criteria of truth. Unfortunately, scientists do not take heed of what epistemologists or philosophers of science have to say because scientists believe that their method is self correcting and they do not need conceptual criticism of their methods.

Yet the conceptual foundations of science are found in the philosophy of science. As earlier chapters have shown, the assumptions underlying what science is leads to how science is practiced. Thus, for a complete understanding of what science is, how science is done and why it is done that way, external or conceptual criticisms of science are necessary. The question that arises here is whether science would have developed differently if women had a more central role in its practice. This question is addressed by Sandra Harding in *The Science Question in Feminism*, who points out that since the mid-1970s there have been serious feminist criticisms of science.

> The radical feminist position holds that the epistemologies, metaphysics, ethics, and politics of the dominant forms of

science are androcentric and mutually supportive; that despite the deeply ingrained Western cultural belief in science's intrinsic progressiveness, science today serves primarily regressive social tendencies; and that the social structure of science, many of its applications and technologies, it modes of defining research problems and designing experiments, its ways of constructing and conferring meanings are not only sexist but also racist, classist, and culturally coercive. In their analyses of how gender symbolism, the social division of labor by gender, and the construction of individual gender identity have affected the history and philosophy of science, feminist thinkers have challenged the intellectual and social orders at their very foundation.[125]

Harding goes on to state that these critiques of science can be seen as calling for a "moral, social and political revolution" (Harding, 1986 10) which will lead to a new view of science which will be more progressive. This revision of science must begin with an understanding of the role that gender plays in our social system and in the social system of science. As we have seen in previous chapters, our lives are engendered. We are brought up to be men and women and along with these sexual identities come our social and individual identities. Men and women are brought up differently; they are socialized differently; their views of the world and their place in it are different. Harding's point, reflecting the work of Gilligan, Chodorow and Kuhn, is that not only is this engendering a social issue but it also affects what science is, how science is done and how scientific theories are culture-laden. In order to understand how science is engendered we must first understand how engendering works. In the previous chapter we saw how it works in a social context. Harding will show us how it works in the laboratory.

To accomplish this, Harding identifies five points to be dealt with. First is the issue of whether or not the presence of women in science will make a difference as to what is studied or how it is studied. The second point parallels issues we saw in the previous chapter dealing with the social sciences. There we saw how male-dominated social sciences worked to keep women in their assigned social roles. It was women social scientists and therapists who challenged this approach. Can women show how the so-called hard or natural sciences are guilty of the same kinds of limitations or abuses? The third point follows from the first two. If men and women, because of how they are socialized, would approach science differently, and would yield different knowledge or define different problems and research programs, what sense does it make to talk about pure science as opposed to theory or culture-laden science? The fourth issue deals with bringing other kinds of criticism to science. Science must be "read" in the same way a literary text is read so that the way science is done—the ways in which problems are defined and research programs are planned—can be shown to be cultural and gender-laden. The fifth point is that out of these critiques a feminist epistemology or philosophy of science may emerge. But then can there be a feminist philosophy of science, or will there be many feminist views, since feminists come from all different cultural and socioeconomic backgrounds? And if there can be a unified feminist philosophy of science can it be wedded to the existing view of science or will this (or these) feminist views be incommensurable with the male view?

Harding begins her inquiries by pointing out that the culture of science is isolated from the rest of culture. Scientists are not usually exposed to psychoanalysis, literary criticism or other critical approaches to different aspects of life or other modes of knowledge gathering. And because natural scientists, especially those of the positivist view we met in chapter three, ignore the history, sociology and philosophy of science, criticisms of science from these other disciplines are ignored by these scientists as well. Yet, by criticizing science from an external perspective, one which includes gender criticism, Harding hopes to develop a view of science which is more naturalistic than the positivist view since her view will include the social context in which science works and will look at how science and its social context interact and influence one another.

The converse of this point is that non-scientists do not look to science for solutions to problems in other areas. Thus institutions such as religion, even though science has demonstrated the falsity of their world-views, continue to play a major role in people's lives.

In addition to the separation of fact from value, the main reason that scientists have separated themselves from the rest of the culture is that physics is used as a paradigm of science. Physics is the science that best suits the laboratory environment where hypotheses can be tested with controlled experiments in a controlled environment. Thus the real world has no place in physics, in spite of the fact that the problems physicists try to solve originated in the real world. But this aspect of physics is often ignored in describing what science is and how it works. This point is crucial. Scientists say they provide explanations of why things behave the way they do. But as we saw in the above chapters, and as Harding argues, the concepts used in explanations are learned socially and require social interpretation in the same way that explanations in the social sciences do. "The social meanings that explanations in physics have for physicists and for the 'man and woman in the street' are necessary components of these explanations, not scientifically irrelevant accidents.... An explanation is a kind of social achievement." (Harding, 1986 45)

Harding's point here is that because of its isolated nature, physics should not be used as a paradigm of science. Perhaps physics, with all its successes, is the anomaly. Perhaps the messiness of the social sciences, where social context is obvious, should be the paradigms of scientific method. If this were the case such issues as the way gender affects how science is done would be more obvious and we would quickly abandon the notion of science as a pure objective undertaking. This point about physics being the paradigm of science underscores the points made in chapter one about how positivistic social scientists appear to leave people out of their equations and just concentrate on abstractions such as "society" and "the economy."

To emphasize this Harding shows that the ways in which science is done clearly reflect social values and social institutions. Referring to the work of various historians she shows that science developed along class and social structural lines. While science is presented to the world as a value-free enterprise, the actual practice is anything but value-free. The values that pervade the scientific enterprise are not just the values of a society that lead scientists to formulate their problems and research programs, but the structural values of the society are reflected in how science is structured. One of the factors at work is the "cultural stereotype" (Harding, 1986 63) of women. Women are relegated to such gender-specific jobs as homemaking and childrearing. Science is presented as a masculine undertaking, so women are not encouraged to become scientists. But even when women study science, for the most part, when they enter the profession it is in subordinate positions, positions which reflect the overall role of women in the culture.

> What it means to be a man is, in part, to share in masculine control of women. Men's individual and collective needs to preserve and maintain a defensive gender identity appear as an obstacle to women's accumulating status within science. In other words, masculine gender identity is so fragile that it cannot afford to have women as equals to men in science. (Harding, 1986 64)

The point here is that in order to understand how science is practiced and why it is practiced that way, one must look not only at the so-called scientific method but also at the social structures the scientific enterprises functions in. If women are systemically kept out of science this practice must follow social practices of how women are treated in the society at large. And in order to understand the relation between the two practices the systematic study of gender becomes central to understanding both how the social order works and how science works. Harding shows how the practice of natural science is androcentric. She begins with biology because various findings in biology have a clear implication for the social sciences; these findings are in turn used to support the sexist views that underlie their practices.

Because of the sex bias of science many aspects of social life, particularly of women, are either not studied or are distorted. For example, most Western sociology tries to emulate the scientific method of physics and studies outward public behavior and ignores the emotional lives of persons. In so doing we get distorted views of social life. For example, by focusing on marriage, most studies talk about the social function of marriage and of the roles of the partners. These roles are often understood in biological terms. That is, biology is not only associated with gender, but, given the deterministic nature of scientific explanations, the association between sex and gender is often presented as determined. But if one were to look at how individuals see marriage, one would probably get very different descriptions of that marriage from the man and woman. In a very real sense, because of the difference in how men and women are socialized and because of the differences in how they approach their respective social roles, men and women would give very different reasons as to why they married and what the marriage was all about.

Because the investigations tend to be done from a scientific or masculine bias, the descriptions given tend to reinforce the differences between men and women from a male perspective. This point becomes important when findings in biology are applied to explanations of social roles. Harding points out that biologists claim that the intersection of two areas of biology creates a powerful argument for the view that social roles are biologically determined (Harding, 1986 92-93). These areas of biology are evolutionary studies and neuroendocrinology. Neuroendocrinologists claim to be able to identify the biological determinants of behavior and evolutionary theorists claim to show how human behavior had to develop the way it did. Together they provide a strong argument for biological determinism of social roles. If either view is shown to be incorrect then the connection between them cannot hold. And this is what Harding sets out to do. She does this by clearly showing how these biases operate in the practice of these sciences.

Harding quotes from various anthropological sources to show

that "even the earliest observations by Westerners, who presumed they had found humans untouched by Western development, were in fact observations of groups who had already been forced to adapt to the cultural patterns of the West." (Harding, 1986 96) The descriptions of various hunter-gatherer groups were done in such a way that both the Western and androcentric biases were present. The very descriptions of hunter-gatherer life are made without reference to the role of women in those societies. For example we are always told that man the hunter invented weapons since weapons were needed on the hunt. But one could make just as strong an argument that women invented tools since they were needed to prepare the foods they gathered.

The important point that Harding makes here is that it appears that only men seemed concerned with categorizing gender. Because of this "it is reasonable to believe that the selective focus on purported sexual sameness across species and sexual differences within species is not only questionable but also a distinct consequence of androcentrism." (Harding, 1986 100)

What holds in anthropology and evolutionary theory also holds in neuroendocrinology where theorists are quick to use their findings to support the views that social roles are biologically determined. Here Harding raises this question: while it is obvious that there is a lot of bad science out there, is this bad science as usual in the Kuhnian sense or can we see a development of good science? Practicing scientists might respond that they are practicing good science and that if they have presented false views the methodology of science will eventually show this. But as we have seen, this is not necessarily the case since all science is value- or culture-laden many cultural biases will not be tested for since they make up the criteria for what will be tested and how it will be tested. So do we throw out the proverbial baby with the bath water? No. But we must develop alternative views and make explicit gender biases when they are active in any kind of scientific theorizing.

The question this approach raises is whether this alternative view of science will be a feminist science or whether it will be gender neutral. Harding's argument would appear to eliminate the notion of a neutral science since all inquiry is theory- or culture-laden. But we can develop new ways of looking at things. If gender parity is ever achieved perhaps scientists will learn to formulate problems in different ways or even consider different problems as the proper subject matter of science. But Harding raises certain points which appear to put a roadblock in the way of developing this new science. One of the problems is that there is no unified view that could be called feminist postmodernism. There are many

Natural Law, Science, and the Social Construction of Reality 265

such views. Also, in her discussion of Kuhn Harding shows that there are problems in how one would go about formulating an alternative view of science. And thirdly, Harding discusses how many feminist postmodernists have turned to African or other less modern societies to look for models of how this new science will be structured. I will look at each of these points in turn.

One of the hallmarks of modern science has been its homogeneousness. Modern science tries to bring explanations of all different kinds of things under the same rubric. But postmodernism is not homogeneous. It acknowledges all kinds of differences. Even within the women's movement there are significant differences as to how to achieve sexual and gender parity. In other words there is no essential definition of "woman" and hence nonessential definition of "feminism" or of "feminist postmodernism." There are many feminisms and many feminist postmodernisms. There are two main reasons for this situation.

One reason for this diversity of views is that, at the beginning of any new movement, or of any new research program—at the onset of a period of revolution in science—there are many possible solutions. So it is with political and social change. There are many models available and different people are proffering all of them as possible solutions to the problems confronting women in our society. The second reason is that since any undertaking is culturally laden, the apparent solutions to the problem arise out of the same cultural and theoretical context that the problems came from. Thus the conceptual equipment used for solving the problem contains the concepts which led to the problem. So a great deal of conjecturing must go on before coherent research programs can be developed.

A main factor exacerbating the problem is the individualism of the original situation. One of the hallmarks of modernism is individualism. Individuals put forward their concerns which may be of a personal nature and turn these concerns into political issues. The slogan was "make the political personal," but too many people have made the personal into the political. Eventually, some of these issues will be dealt with. But as long as postmodernism works on a culture-laden view, which it must, there will always be numerous possible solutions to numerous different problems. Thus essentialism, or homogeneity of thought, which postmodernism denies, indeed has its own problems. To put this point in terms of the analogy used in the discussion of scientific change, instead of having two houses to compare, we will have many, and more than one alternative house may be available to move into. One of the areas that feminist postmodernists have turned to for possible solutions has been to non-modern cultures such as hunter-gatherers or cultures where it appears sex and gender roles are not as clearly defined as they are in modern Western society, or societies which appear to live in closer harmony with their physical environments. Recall the discussion of the !Kung above. The point here is that feminist postmodernists are looking for models in which persons are not separated from their environments. Or, to put this point in epistemological terms, modern Western epistemology separates the knower from the known while other cultures see themselves as part of the known. A correlation to this epistemological point is that Western separation goes hand in hand with its individualism. So feminist postmodernists are also looking for models with greater sense of community or interconnectedness. This, of course, emulates an important aspect of what has been identified as feminine in the works of Gilligan and Chodorow: how women are socialized to be social beings. The point here is to develop a model where the culture, the persons and the epistemology are inseparable. (Harding, 1986 171) Developing this model will go a long way towards dealing with many of the issues identified by feminist postmodernists with regard to separation of sex from gender and of the cultural and epistemological consequences of that separation.

An important method of dealing with these issues is in looking at modern science as a text to be deconstructed. What this means is that we have to look at science with a critical eye just as we would look at anything else. We must not take the experts' words for things. We must challenge their expertise and their perspective. In a sense, this is what the previous chapters have partly done. In those chapters I tried to show how a particular train of thought develops into the basis of a whole conceptual framework or of the foundation of a view of how the world works and of the roles of persons in that world. In so doing, I also tried to show how these views have been criticized and how each criticism led to another view, and so on. This chapter is a continuation of that process.

One of the points made in defense of modern science is its success. Yet one could argue that many other explanatory schemes were just as successful in their own contexts and on their own terms. Science explains how the world works; so do a lot of other competing explanations from witchcraft to various folk beliefs. We must show that science, in many ways, is just like these beliefs. Science, in a sense, is the mythology of the modern era and Copernicus, Newton, Descartes, Locke Hume and Kant are its folk heroes.

> We are not expected to be any more critical of the ability of science to make justifiable claims about the reality hidden

beneath appearances than are African villagers of their inherited views of the world around them. The scientific world-view was initially adopted as a result of critical thinking (among other reasons), but that is not why most people hold these beliefs today. Critical thinking is not a characteristic of Western thinking just because it is Western; nor is folk thought uniquely characteristic of non-Western thinking. (Harding, 1986 208)

The point here is that modern science is believed because it is part of our culture, not because it is better than some other explanation scheme. If science were accepted or believed by most people because of reason, we would not see the range of beliefs we see in our society where people accept science but also hold ancient and medieval views of many aspects of the world and see no contradiction in doing so. In a society where we can go to the moon and explain the nature of matter in atomic terms and still talk of sunsets and accept medieval theologians as experts on the place of persons in the world, we can see that critical thinking is something that does not get a lot of use. Science, for all its successes, has become just another aspect of our culture and sits alongside ancient mythology, folklore and medieval theology as part of our overall belief system.

By understanding this point we do not have to be dazzled by scientific expertise. We can challenge the way science is done and the role it plays in our culture, and we can develop alternative explanation schemes which will reflect a feminist postmodern cultural perspective. We will do this by looking at the attempts of feminist scholars to do epistemology and science. Let us begin by asking what characteristics this new science will have. In order to answer this question we have to review some of the hallmarks of masculine modernist science. As we have seen in earlier chapters, the old view of science saw truth in abstract way, divorced from everyday life, and the world was understood in terms of such contrasts or dualisms as culture/nature, mind/body, reason/emotion, public/private, and so on. We also saw problems with these kinds of contrasts when we discussed the notion of category mistakes. To review that point, these are statements that appear to be well-formed and grammatically correct but which are in fact nonsense. The example used above was "The subway car gave birth to twins." Subway cars are not the kinds of things that can give birth so the sentence is neither true nor false.

Let us look at some other examples. I can say that my boss is incompetent. Because of the way in which we contrast things, the implication exists that my boss could be competent. All he needs is some proper training and direction. But what if, after all the training and direction, he still cannot do the job. We cannot call him incompetent because of the implication of competence. We have to say that the category of competence, whether applied in the positive or negative aspect, does not or cannot apply to my boss. The point that the postmodernist makes here is that the kind of contrast that is embedded in modernist logic is a mistake. If it is not a logical or meta-logical mistake then it is a cultural mistake. To use another example, in a recent psychological profile the testee is asked if he or she is an extrovert or an introvert. Since these terms name opposite tendencies or character traits they are seen as opposites so we can only be one of these things. But persons are more complex than that. I can be very outgoing and be the life of the party but I can also be quiet, self-analytical and inward looking. So when someone asks me if I am an introvert or an extrovert I answer "yes!"

To return to Harding's list above, she points out that the first of each group is identified with good science and with maleness and the second member of each group is identified with feminism and bad science. Thus a feminist postmodern science will not be abstract but will be grounded in everyday experience and in human relationships and will not be dichotomous in the way modern science is. Let us now turn to some feminist postmodern epistemologists and scientists.

A primary aspect of both the philosophy of science and of science is logic. Logic is the science of inference and, as such, sets out the rules of what can be inferred or argued and how an argument can proceed. Logic is seen as an abstract, albeit objective, set of rules or principles which guide reasoning. In order for an argument to make sense the reasoning must be internally consistent and the various rules of inference must be followed. Many of these are similar to rules and principles found in mathematics and some thinkers have argued that since the logical procedures are found in mathematics, logic is conceptually prior to mathematics, and, therefore, mathematics is just a branch of logic. The point of this approach is to make logic an abstract procedure to be followed, regardless of the subject matter or context. The rules of logic rule all other forms of discourse. But logic itself has gone through various stages of development. Some of these were influenced by developments in other areas of endeavor. While logic may strive for abstract objectivity, it is just as contextual as any other form of knowledge. One can trace the history of logic, and its external influences, in much the same way that one can trace the history of any scientific concept.

So our question becomes one of looking at how the use of logic in specific contexts reflects the over all values of that context and of seeing how we can develop a feminist post modern logic. In doing so I shall follow the work of Andrea Nye, who argues that there is no one logic, "but only men and logics, and the substance of these logics, as of any written or spoken language, are material and historically specific relations between men, between men and women, and between them and objects of human concern."[126] Logic is a human invention; it can be, and has been, modified or reconstructed by humans.

Nye develops this point by presenting a critique of the history of logic. She begins with Parmenides. Nye states that logic and poetry are usually considered opposites: poetry is used to express emotion while logic is passionless. Yet logicians have demonstrated a passion for their subject. And Parmenides presents his views on logic in a poem. So, right from the outset, logic could not be divorced from emotion, no matter how hard various theoreticians tried to do so. In his poem Parmenides is concerned with truth and with being. But he soon comes to see, as shown by the rigors of logic, that one cannot choose between what is and what is not, for there is no "is not." Rather, one must seek the correct way of discovering what is. And the nature of what *is* is "a well rounded sphere, uniform and not admitting of degrees, homogeneous and not subject to any death or destruction." (Nye, 1990 12) Thus what is, or truth, is uniform, absolute and eternal. Nye points out that Parmenides passionately searched for this truth, which he could hold "tightly in the embrace of logical necessity." (Nye, 1990 13)

This homogeneous truth manifests itself in interesting ways. Parmenides saw persons monistically. Persons were not bodies and minds but the physical body thought. But more interesting, and of far more concern to feminist postmodernists, was how Parmenides took this view to men/women issues. Since homogeneousness was more desirable than separation or fragmentation, heterosexuality was looked upon as an evil necessity for the propagation of the species, but not something to be desired. Men and women are different and must be separated. "Love between men is preferable to love between men and women because it does not involve any mixing." (Nye, 1990 15) This logical truth that Parmenides sees is a corrective to the natural philosophies which existed before he wrote. Older views of the world have a feminine divinity at the centre of the world with "nature ordered in natural cycles of growth and decay, sexual reproduction as a kind of natural immortality, the regular and reciprocal cycles of family life as the basis of social and natural order..." (Nye, 1990 17) While the Greeks, as demonstrated in Parmenides' work, saw a supreme force outside of natural life as the creator. Order was a matter of law, not of nature. And as such, men ruled women.

The point here is that the view of logic that developed in Parmenides and grew in Western civilization reflected the cultural views of the creators of this logic. The belief in an enduring eternal creator led to the development of a logic which allowed this conclusion to stand. Thus rather than logic leading the Greeks to their views of the place of persons in the world, their views of the nature of the world and of the place of persons in the world led to their views on logic.

This is seen more strongly in Plato. Two issues are at work in Plato's views on logic. One was that Parmenides' logic was too limiting. It did not allow for speculative discourse since one could not talk about what is not. This lack led to people playing games with language and logic. These "game players" became known as sophists and were seen as using language and logic to confuse people. The second point is that this confusion took place in a society that was changing and becoming more complex. People like Socrates and Plato who preferred the old ways of society saw a need to reform speech so that these old values could be used to restore order. As Nye puts it, Plato saw the sophists "as enemies of truth" who needed to be exposed. (Nye, 1990 31) Plato saw in Parmenides that if something was not the case it belonged to the category of "what is not" and could not be talked about. This view of discourse was seen as much too limiting since one could state things that were false. Thus Plato made an important distinction between "what is not" and "what is not true". "A predication is true not depending on whether it is, or says that something is, but on whether what it says is the same or different from what is." (Nye, 1990 27) But Plato agreed with Parmenides about the nature of truth which became preserved in Plato's forms.

Plato took Parmenides' law of non-contradiction and added to it his views on how we can talk about truth and falsity. The implication of this combination is that it allows users of arguments to divide discourse and to set up categories which can be used to control the direction of arguments. A good example is the question, "have you stopped beating your spouse?", where the question demands a certain answer. To give a different answer is to break the rules of discourse. The point that Nye emphasizes here is that Plato is the one who is dominating the discourse. One can now use logic not only to persuade someone else of the truth of the matter but one can also now direct and control the discourse so that how one speaks of something will control what one can believe about that thing. By establishing a higher existence Plato also provided the authority for the arguer. Thus a view of logic is developed in order to establish a way of looking at the world that has moral authority. Logic becomes the handmaiden of politics.

For our feminist postmodern sensibilities this is important for, as Nye points out, the personae in Plato are men.

> The interchanges that the Stranger's logic was to structure took place as part of exclusively male institutions...As with Parmenides, the mixing or mingling of the sexes still has no place in logic. Logical discussion is between men. But logic place is no longer an impotent mystical flight from a material feminine reality to metaphysical Being. The terms set in the Sophist are for an alternate male society, outside the household, away from women, away from birth and death and heterosexuality in a new public space reserved for men. (Nye, 1990 36)

Nye sees this trend developing for the worse in Aristotle. Aristotle begins his logical studies by criticizing Plato. His point is that since Plato's substance is other-worldly, and since one can start an argument anywhere and then use logic to one's ends, one can prove anything. The concept of truth is lacking in Plato's logic. What Aristotle wants to do is ground logic in knowledge so that reasoning can produce new knowledge. But, as Nye points out, Aristotle's logic was designed for the Athenian institution of debate and this logical technique became used as a debating tool rather than a method to used in the search for truth. (Nye, 1990 42). "The debates for which Aristotle's logic was a handbook were not between a few leisured aristocrats disinterestedly contemplating eternal truths, but between men intent on winning and preserving power, privilege and wealth."(Nye, 1990 43) And when used in legal contexts winning, not the pursuit of truth, became the goal.

In this context Nye discusses Aeschylus' *Orestes* drama. Nye shows how logic is used to acquit a guilty person. Orestes is charged with matricide. But since the court rules that the only true blood line is between father and son, killing the mother is not killing a person of one's own blood. So while Orestes is guilty of murder it is of a lesser degree than of killing someone of his own blood. The point here is that since there is no mention of the context of the crime, nor of the principles of morality involved in the crime, but only the use of logical technique, any notion of justice becomes lost in the legal arena. "In the new courts, success depended not on guilt or innocence, but on cleverness and dexterity in argument."(Nye, 1990 45) In his *Politics*, Aristotle argues that non-Greeks did not have the reasoning abilities of Greeks, and he argued the same for slaves, workers and women, or anyone who did not participate in rational debate, as defined by the aristocracy. Thus Logic was used as a tool of the aristocracy to limit who could be considered a person who could participate in Greek society. "In this way the scientist's, the Greek's, the master's, the male's perceptions are elaborated into necessary truth." (Nye, 1990 59)

Nye continues this line of argument with a look at Stoic logic. Because of political developments in the development of the Hellenic empire, narrow definitions of who was Greek could no longer be accepted. In order to deal with the different but equal views of all the Hellenic peoples, logic had to be altered. The Stoics, whose thought dominated this period, rejected Platonic form and Aristotelian substance and established a logic that was to be the "grammar of the cosmos." (Nye, 1990 66) This was accomplished by looking at the functions of language as a conveyor of truth. In studying language the Stoics made distinctions between sign, meaning and referent. This breakdown of how language worked overcame specific dialects and allowed logic to stand on its own, independent of any specific language. (Nye, 1990 67) But in doing so, logic lost touch with its subject matter and became even more abstract so that logic users became even more adept at manipulating the rules of logic for their own ends. And this left ordinary people, workers, slaves and women even further away from being able to participate in the affairs of the society.

Nye emphasizes this last point with regard to the status of women. She argues that since the Stoics held the same views about biology as Aristotle, they also saw the role of the woman in reproduction to be minor and passive. The semen is the active element in reproduction. Nye concludes this chapter, which she titles "Logos Spermatikos" by pointing out that

> Regardless of physical conquest, regardless of which monarch, potentate, emperor, or ruling party is in control, in an autonomous dissemination of meanings that mimics the creation of God, language is now capable of generating its own cosmos, the cosmos of sexist, racist, ethnocentrist culture. (Nye, 1990 79)

This line of argument is continued with a look at two medieval logicians, Abelard and Ockham. Abelard's work builds on the work of the Stoics. The concept of Logos in the medieval Christian world became Christ, thereby giving a divine foundation for logic and for the view of the world and of persons in the world which was derived from that logic.

"Now there was no need to intuit the spermal order of the universe; instead truth came first-hand in the word of God, and any tampering with that truth by the human mind could only be a distortion." (Nye, 1990 86) While Nye acknowledges Abelard's real contributions to logical theory she still emphasizes the world view implicit in that logical theory by showing how Abelard used logic. This comes out clearly in his dispute with Heloise. The story of how Abelard seduced Heloise is well-known. The way he rejected her afterwards is not as well-known. Heloise responded to Abelard's position, accusing him of being incapable of love, of being only concerned with himself, and with forcing her into a life for which she had no vocation. Abelard's response ignores Heloise's substantive points but just reinforces his position. He speaks to "'enlighten' her so that she will do what he wants, what the Church wants, what God wants,...He makes clear the purpose of his logic: it is meant to regain his and the Church's power and control over Heloise." (Nye, 1990 99)

Nye concludes the chapter on Abelard by pointing out that his logic was never meant to probe the weak points in medieval thought but to strengthen it against attacks that Heloise and others would bring against the established view. But things are somewhat different with William of Ockham, whom Nye likens to the 20th century's Vienna Circle, drawing political, social and cultural parallels. But, more importantly, Nye sees Ockham's attempts to consolidate medieval logic as the basis for later developments in both logic and theology, especially with regard to the development of Protestantism.

Ockham's project was to reform language so that theological concepts would be easier to express and so that all levels of discourse, from that of popes and priests to all believers would be improved. Ockham argued that logic is not a language but a *metalanguage* to be used to correctly order the concepts used for ordinary discourse. This can be seen in the Ockham-influenced teachings of Martin Luther. "Convinced like Ockham of the absolute freedom and omnipotence of God, driven by the sense that sin was permanently embedded in his and other men's souls, he turned the logic that God could save even a sinner, if he wished, into dogma." (Nye, 1990 119) We are not saved by what we do but by God's grace. We can earn God's grace through faith. With the development of the printing press, bibles became available to everyone and, along with the absolutist logic, teachings became dogma. And, of course, the role of women was affected.

At first it appeared that Luther's teachings would be liberating for women since he gave women credit for playing an honorable if subordinate role in life. But women still could not be considered worthy of divine grace. And, not coincidentally, this was the time of the witch-hunts. As Nye points out, the campaign against witches was expressed in a fundamentalist logic. This fundamentalism was reinforced by literal readings of scripture, since there was no papacy or clerical hierarchy to interpret scripture. Heresies must be eliminated with zeal. Faith was everything. And it was an absolutist faith. Any woman not under the control of a man was suspected as a witch for she was not living a proper life.

Nye does not claim that Ockham was responsible for the witch-hunts. But she does argue that his logic provided a way thinking which allowed these attitudes to develop.

> If Ockham's logic is the logic of a world in which God's will is supreme, it can also become the logic of a world willed by men. The functional science purged of value and quality that begins to develop in the seventeenth and eighteenth centuries makes possible the realization of that possibility. It would be the twentieth century before logic is fully adapted and a logical idiom formulated in which the last vestiges of spoken words have disappeared, leaving only the formulae of manipulation. (Nye, 1990 121)

Now it is to Gottlob Frege that we turn. Frege's concern was to unify knowledge. In order to do so he believed that an objective logic had to developed. This logic had to be independent of everyday language since everyday language is subjective and imprecise. Logic had to be more like mathematics. One could never develop a true account of knowledge with the imprecisions and subjectivity of language. In mathematics one can express generalities with precision. This is done with use of functions. So Frege tried to develop a logic that used mathematical functions. These functions would express a constant relationship between a subject and predicate so the expression, regardless of context, would always have the same truth value. For example, we know that John Doe is human. We also know that humans are mortal. Therefore, using Aristotelian logic, we can conclude that John Doe is mortal.

But this conclusion is only about John Doe. How can this conclusion be expressed in mathematical terms? Instead of saying that John Doe is mortal we turn the sentence around and say that "Mortality is a characteristic of John Doe." This formulation makes mortality a property of the subject rather than just a contingent fact about a particular person. Frege's point here is that by functionalizing speech we eliminate its subjective or psychological aspects and stick to the reportage of fact. In other words one could eliminate all private aspects of life and use this new logical or mathematical language to report about the public world of verifiable truth. Frege makes a major distinction between *sense* and *reference*. Reference is objective and concerns the relation between a word and what the word stands for. Sense is subjective and has to do with the context and the private concerns of the observer. The goal here is to develop a language with reference but without sense. And this is where Frege ultimately fails, since sense cannot be entirely eliminated from language.

As Nye points out, as long as there is a speaker there is intensionality. "Words do not stand alone like formulae in an account book, they also express what is thought and believed even when that thought is limited to the simple yes or no of bivalent logic." (Nye, 1990 144) And when this intensionality is made explicit, such as in a sentence where personal belief is expressed, formal substitution fails. "The sense of words in language will not stay still, cannot be fixed or counted on, or counted in the way mathematical quantities can be counted." (Nye, 1990 144) While Frege failed at separating sense and reference and therefore failed in setting up his objective mathematical language, his work inspired many others to continue the task. We see Frege's influence in the work of Russell and in the work of the logical positivists, whom we met earlier.

The point here is simple. One cannot divorce the knower from the known. And one cannot divorce the context in which the knowing takes place from what becomes known. The knower and the context are imbedded in the language used to express what is known. To attempt to rid language of the knower and the context is to also eliminate what is known. Nye takes this point further since she is concerned with how the history of logic has excluded women. Women have been excluded from the world of logic because of their gender roles. As Nye has shown, logic developed in the male arena of power and control. Men then used their logic to define women's thinking patterns as illogical and therefore of lesser value than the thinking processes of men. And logic is used, in conjunction with functionalist sociology, to show that women belong in their inferior roles.

As was argued above, the old view of the world is crumbling and a new order is being developed. Here I have looked at a postmodern feminist order. It seeks equality of the sexes by rejecting male-dominated logic and by challenging the view that sex and gender are synonymous. Because of their differing social roles, men and women are socialized differently. That is why they think differently. As Nye points out men may speak more powerfully than women do, but women read more critically than men do. They learn to look more at context rather than just at the image.

Nye's point is not to abandon logic but to abandon some of the claims made about logic. Logic is not the be-all and end-all of thought and knowledge. Knowledge requires knowers who know in contexts. To deny the knower and the context is to deny knowledge.

In my discussion of the origins of modernism I argued that modernistic thinking leads to abstraction in thought and that this abstraction leads to eliminating people and their concerns from discourse. For example, we think of the Economy but in formulating policy we ignore the effects of the policy on individuals who will be on the receiving end of the policies. In Nye's work on logic this point is emphasized. By concentrating on the abstraction at the expense of the people and the context they are in, most of Western thought, whether Ancient, Medieval or Modern has exhibited this point. No wonder we are finally in a position to reject this kind of thinking. And no wonder this rejection of abstraction is being led by women.

Now that we have seen that logic is not some super-scientific way of thinking, but just another way of thinking, we are in a position to look at alternative views of what science is. I will begin with an alternative view of evolution written from a women's perspective. The roots of this position, though, come from the work of Professor Sir Alister Hardy whom we met in chapter four, who argues that because of certain physical characteristics, humankind must have spent a significant part of our early evolution in an aquatic environment. This point should not come as a surprise since, according to traditional evolutionary thinking mammals are descendants of sea creatures. If times were hard on the land it would be natural for mammals developing on land to move towards the sea to find food and shelter. After all humans are good swimmers.

But the main evidence for this aquatic view has to do with the ways in which human hair has developed. The virtual loss of and the configuration of the remaining body hair, is consistent with swimmers and other water living mammals. Head hair has not disappeared since the head would be out of the water and the hair provided protection from the sun. Hardy also notes the sleek shape of human body in relation to other apes. This sleekness allows for better movement in water. And Hardy, following the work of Professor Wood Jones, also attributes human's erect posture as a result of wading and swimming.

This view of evolution is significantly developed by Elaine Morgan, whom we also met in chapter four. Recall the traditional view of human evolution. It has humans developing in the jungle or on the plains with men very quickly becoming the hunters. Little mention is made of women in the role of human evolution. Morgan's purpose in the book is twofold. Her main concern is to develop an account of the role of women in human evolution. She is able to do this with help from the aquatic hypothesis. Morgan develops this hypothesis beyond Hardy's initial views. In the course of her argument, Morgan takes on the hunter myth as well as all those theorists who revel in mankind's violent nature. By looking at the role of women in human evolution we get a more complex view of human social as well as biological evolution. And we see that some of the ways in which we evolved biologically have to do with how women adapted their childbearing and child rearing to the aquatic environment.

The traditional "man as hunter" view of evolution not only ignored the social role of women, but nowhere in that view is women's contribution to biological evolution mentioned. This is a glaring omission since it is women who give birth and contribute at least half of the gene pool to the next generation. So how women adapted to the new environment is extremely important in understanding overall human evolution, especially if women underwent more changes than men did because of their biological role in childbearing and childrearing. Morgan also emphasizes the shape of the female breast and buttocks as additional evidence in favor of the aquatic hypothesis. As Morgan points out, chimps and other apes do not have large breasts. So why did human women develop large breasts? The traditional answer has been that large breasts are a sexual stimulus. And while this may be true, it does not answer the question of how such breasts first evolved. Morgan argues that the sexual stimulus argument is essentially circular made by male centered theorists who say something like "I find this attribute sexy: therefore it must have evolved in order that I might find it sexy." (Morgan, 1971 30) But the biological question is never dealt with. The question that should have been asked is what purpose this development has in feeding the young. In other words, the question of the shape of a woman's breast should be understood in terms of the function of the breast and not in how men perceive the breast. This is a question that male theorists do not ask. Morgan finds the answer in the aquatic state. She asks us to imagine an anthropoid family in the water when the baby get hungry. Feeding the baby in the water does not work because the waves interfere with the feeding. But, sitting on the rocks and letting the baby reach for the breast does not work because things have changed.

> There isn't any fur. If you let your head lie in the crook of her arm, the milk is high up out of reach. You have to hoist your torso into an erect position, and try to balance your head and

somehow keep your lips clamped to this chimpanzee sized nipple of hers, and you don't think it's easy. Your arms are too short to go around her waist, and if you scrabble around trying to get a purchase on something, there's nothing there but a faintly corrugated surface of slippery wet ribs...So you really need two things: you need the nipple brought down quite a bit lower, and you need a lump of something less bony, something pliant and of a convenient size for small hands to grab hold of while you lie on her lap and guide your lips to the right place. Or, alternatively, guide the right place to your lips. And since you are what evolution is all about, what you need you ultimately get. You get two lovely pendulous dollopy breasts, as easy to hold on to as a bottle, and you're laughing. (Morgan, 1971 31-32)

Morgan finds additional evidence for this view in the fact that the only other mammals who have similarly-shaped breasts are aquatic: these are the class of mammals known as sea cows. (Morgan, 1971 33) Other evidence can be found in our current bodies. The webbing between our thumbs and first fingers and under our arms is a vestige of our aquatic past. Humans are also the only mammals with the shape of nose we have. Water would have entered the nose of any other apes that tried to swim under water given the shape of their nostrils. The shape of our nose protects us (Morgan, 1971 38-39). Another piece of evidence is our tear ducts. Living in a salt-water environment without the ability to properly digest salt water could be problematic. If our ancestors ingested a lot of sea-water there would have to be a way for the body to get rid of the excess salt. Various sea birds use their tear ducts to do this. Knut Schmidt-Nielsen demonstrated this with a study on cormorants in 1956. (Morgan, 1971 45) The process was also discovered in the Malacolemys terrapin and in other amphibious creatures from sea lizards to the marine iguana in the Galapagos Islands. Morgan states:

> Up to now no one, not even Darwin has offered a convincing explanation of the origin and purpose of human tears. I would suggest that the only weeping birds are marine birds, and the only weeping crocodiles, snakes, lizards, turtles, and mammals are marine crocodiles, marine snakes, marine lizards, marine turtles, and marine mammals, it is surely not beyond the bounds of reason to suppose that the only weeping primate was once a marine primate. (Morgan, 1971 47)

So now that we have some very good evidence to accept the fact that a significant part of our evolution was in the water, Morgan then raises interesting questions regarding sex and sexuality. Sex has to do with biology while sexuality has to do with social organization. Clearly the two are related. The most important question about sex has to do with the fact that all other apes and land living mammals have sex from the rear while humans have frontal sex. The only other mammals that have frontal sex are marine mammals such as whales and dolphins. This point just adds to the conclusion regarding our aquatic past. But this biological evolutionary adaptation changed many aspects of human social and psychological lives.

The upright position of aquatic humans led to overall changes in anatomy. "When she began to stand upright, the normal quadruped 90-degree angle between her spine and her hind legs had become 180-degrees and this had displaced some of her abdominal internal organs, resulting" in bringing the vagina forward. (Morgan, 1971 52)

In addition to bringing it forward the vagina was also pushed farther into the body cavity. This, as Morgan points out, is a normal marine adaptation. But with this female adaptation also comes a male adaptation. Morgan raises two points here. One is that Homo Sapiens has the largest penis of all primates and the other has to do with the change from rear to frontal sex. The answer to penis size relates to both of these issues. In rear-approach sex the vagina is at the surface and easily penetrated. In frontal sex the vagina is internalized. Thus in order to reach the new internalized vagina from the front the male had to have a longer penis. But frontal sex has led to other problems, especially when our ancestors left the sea to return to land. In order to properly appreciate the problem Morgan takes us on a wide-ranging discussion of the issue of human aggression. This discussion has a dual purpose. One is to counter the popular view of humans as an aggressive or violent species. The other is to show that some of our aggressive tendencies have their roots in the biological changes made while we were aquatic which did not always work well when we returned to the land.

The literature on aggression is fairly well known and includes the works of Robert Ardrey, Konrad Lorenz and Ashley Montagu. All of the literature, regardless of the position taken on how violent or non-violent humans are, accepts to one degree or another the "man as hunter" hypothesis, seeing humanity evolving on the plains or in the jungle with man the hunter, or the "Tarzan Hypothesis" as Morgan calls it, as the correct view of human evolution. While they may disagree as to how violent humans can be, they all accept the fact that aggressive tendencies come along with the view of man the hunter. However, while humanity did go through a hunter-gatherer stage, as we have seen from the work of Marvin Harris, the Tarzan hypothesis is clearly wrong. What Morgan does is to take a feminine sensibility to the issue. She formulates the issue differently and comes up with a different way of looking at the issue.

Morgan begins this discussion by asking us to think about average people in their daily habitat. Are they violent? Is that window cleaner a violent predator? Is the postman ready to attack his customers? Or think of an army at war. Here Morgan makes four points about war.

> 1) War is by no means an activity which involves the majority of the species.
> 2) It is not part of our primitive heritage. Stone-age humans did not wage war.
> 3) Other animals can act in warlike manners but usually in abnormal or pathological conditions.
> 4) If one were to visit soldiers in war one would not find them seething with rage wanting to kill. You would have found the postman, the window cleaner and your neighbor. (Morgan, 1971 62-63)

Morgan's point here is that the "one kernel of truth behind this bloodthirsty reputation men have tagged onto themselves...is that somewhere along their evolutionary path they have mislaid a very valuable piece of behavioral machinery."(Morgan, 1971 63-64) This piece of behavioral machinery, according to Morgan, was lost when humans made the change to frontal sex and left the water where it worked and moved back onto the land where it created problems. To see this issue in perspective let us look at the behavior of a variety of animals at play and in a fighting situation. As Morgan points out, "in most species conflict between two animals of the same kind invariably stops short of slaughter. The fight goes on until one of the combatants gives in, and either retreats or gives a signal of submission. The effect of this appeasement gesture is immediate and automatic. And so it needs to be, because more often than not the appeasement gesture renders the appeaser totally helpless." (Morgan, 1971 64) Such appeasement signals involve baring the neck or some other vulnerable part of the body. But this does not work with humans. Some such signals work, but they cannot be counted upon. These signals appear to work all through the animal kingdom but they broke down in humans. Using evolutionary thinking, Morgan states that for such a mechanism to have been bred out of the species there would have to have been a time when such a mechanism would have acted against rather than for species survival. For the answer she takes us back to the sea coast of Pliocene Africa when we first left the sea.

Morgan asks us to imagine this aquatic ape adapting to living on land. Remember that all land mammals practice rear sex. So when a female presents herself as ready for sex but presents her front the male gets confused. He is receiving mixed messages. He is being aroused but the frontal presentation the female makes is identical to an appeasement position where she is baring her vulnerable parts. So while he is aroused he is also being warned off. Morgan argues that males had to be able to overcome reacting to the appeasement position. The males who would succeed at this would be the males "whose behavioral mechanism was very slightly defective." (Morgan, 1971 77) And it is this slight defectiveness that allows humans to kill one another. But this does not mean that humans are intrinsically violent.

One of the arguments that the Tarzanists make is to compare humans to closely related animals who exhibit violent behavior and argue that this is where we inherit our violent tendencies from. Morgan argues that such views are based on serious mistakes, the most serious being that the model used, the baboon, is further removed from humans than other apes such as gorillas and orangutans, which are virtually non-violent. If we are to use evolutionary arguments we should at least be accurate. Of course, one of the problems of studying human behavior is that we take our assumptions about who and what we are and manage to find support for those assumptions in nature. Morgan has made different assumptions about human nature in general and about the role that women have played in human evolution in particular, and has come up with a different view of human culture. Perhaps the most important aspect of Morgan's work is to acknowledge the importance of women in the history of human evolution. Without some of the developments women underwent it is highly likely that humanity would not have survived the Pliocene.

Mainstream science has not acknowledged Morgan's work, and she has in fact been ridiculed. But as Daniel Dennett points out in his work on the philosophical implications of Darwin's work, *Darwin's Dangerous Idea: Evolution and the Meaning of Life*

> During the past few years, when I have found myself in the company of distinguished biologists, evolutionary theorists, paleo-anthropologists, and other experts, I have often asked just to tell me, please, exactly why Elaine Morgan must be wrong about the aquatic ape theory. I haven't yet had a reply worth mentioning, aside from those who admit, with a twinkle in their eyes, that they have often wondered the same thing. There seems to be nothing *inherently* impossible about

the idea; other mammals have made the plunge, after all (Dennett, 1995 244).

And Richard Ellis, in his *Aquagenesis: The Origin and Evolution of Life in the Sea,* acknowledges the plausibility of the aquatic view since water has always been a crucial aspect of human evolution[127].

Clearly, in rejecting Morgan's work, one can see Harding's view of a male dominant science at work.

But because of the importance of women, and by focusing on women instead of men, we start to see a different picture of early humanity than the one presented by men in their image. To develop this new picture we now turn to the work of Donna Haraway, a biologist by training, who became interested in questions of methodology and of feminist concerns about the nature of science as voiced by Harding. By studying how primates have been studied, Haraway has chosen an area that falls between a hard science like physics or biology and a soft science like sociology.

Haraway begins her work with a discussion of the philosophical themes underlying her work. She reiterates some of the points made by Harding with regard to the ways in which "race, sexuality, gender, nation, family and class have been written into the body of nature in western life sciences since the eighteenth century."[128] She then discusses how fact and fiction are intertwined in popular culture. Her point is that so-called fiction is about human action and is therefore based in fact and facts are constructed out of social contexts. While fact and fiction are not identical they are clearly related. The main difference that Haraway sees is that fiction is an active form while fact refers to something already complete. A fact is understood as something unchangeable while fiction is in then process of occurring. But, for Haraway, science is a narrative process or a form of story telling: "Scientific practice is above all a story-telling practice in the sense of historically specific practices of interpretation and testimony." (Haraway, 1989 4)

These points about the narrative nature of science are important because a crucial aspect of feminist postmodernism, as we have seen in our discussions in the previous chapter and thus far in this chapter, is to show that science is indeed a culture-laden undertaking. By showing how various cultural assumptions are at work in science one can show that the findings are not absolute truth but culturally relative truth. By altering our cultural position or by altering our cultural assumptions we may not only arrive at different conclusions or with a different set of facts, but we may also realize that we were asking the wrong questions in the first place. Thus a new science—a new narrative—will develop. Haraway underscores these points by arguing that, "primatology is about an Order, a taxonomic and *therefore* political order that works by the negotiation of boundaries achieved through ordering differences." (Haraway, 1989 10) These boundaries are established by cultural norms and practices and involve the dualisms of *sex/gender* and *nature/culture* (10). Haraway's point is that "natural sciences, like human sciences, are inextricably within the processes that give them birth. And so, like the human sciences, the natural sciences are culturally and historically specific, modified, involved." (Haraway, 1989 12) Thus it makes sense to ask what the concerns of scientists are, what their methods are and how what they do is different from religion or ethnography (Haraway, 1989 12). "The place of the detached eye of objective science is an ideological fiction, and a powerful one. But it is a fiction that hides—and is designed to hide—how the powerful discourses of the natural sciences really work." (Haraway, 1989 13)

The book is called *Primate Visions* partly because Haraway's task is to present a variety of these visions of primate studies and to show how all of them reflect the cultural biases of the studiers and how these studies and studiers changed. She begins her study by calling primatology a Judeo-Christian science which places animals and man in a relationship that reflects the biblical story, and she says that many primatologists look upon their studies as recreating the Garden of Eden. (Haraway, 1989 9) She states that early primatologists such as G.V. Hamilton and Robert Yerkes presented primate life in idyllic human family terms (Haraway, 1989 23). In the chapter titled "Teddy Bear Patriarchy in the Garden of Eden" Haraway argues that Carl Akeley, who designed the African exhibit at The American Museum of Natural History presented this teddy bear view of human families in his primate exhibit. "Akeley thought in African Hall the visitor would experience nature at its highest moment of perfection. He did not dream that he crafted the means to experience a history of race, sex, and class in New York City that reached to Nairobi" (Haraway, 1989 27). Thus the whole exhibit is nothing but teddy bear science. It is not truth. It is not an accurate depiction of nature. It is a cultural idealization which was "dedicated to preserving a threatened manhood: exhibition, eugenics and conservation"(Haraway, 1989 55).

A couple of the more recent studies are worth looking at, beginning with studies undertaken for *National Geographic* magazine. Haraway places the magazine in its political and cultural context, reminding the reader that the prominence of the magazine began in 1898, the year of the Spanish-American War, when Alexander Graham Bell became president of the NGS (National Geographic Society). The war enhanced the importance of geography for United States citizens, and articles in the magazine after the war stressed the benefits of colonialism, geography, and the commercial possibilities of America's new possessions. Committed to forging a national society from the scattered local branches and creating a broadly popular magazine, Bell brought in his future son-in-law, Gilbert Grosvenor, as assistant editor. With little sympathy for professionalism, Grosvenor, who set policy until 1954, had the task of increasing circulation. Under his son Meville Bell Grosvenor, his policies have essentially remained in force into the 1980s. (Haraway, 1989 157)

Haraway goes on to argue that this highly successful venture was not about the *"popularization"* of science but that Grosvenor "stressed *participation* in doing science, in a nineteenth century sense...The professional geographers initially fought the changes, but they lost, retiring to form another scientific geographical society" (Haraway, 1989 157).

Thus *National Geographic* reflected the biases of the editors and sponsors and could in no way be considered a an unbiased scientific reporting magazine. It showed nature, but in a nice way that people in their living rooms could relate to, a way that reflected the values of the white, middle class readers of the magazine.

And it manipulated readers with regard to gender issues. To be a scientist meant to be a man. National Geographic used women in scientific roles, turning science and scientists into household figures while propagating the male teddy bear view of nature. (Haraway, 1989 158) But it is the partnership with Gulf Oil in the 1980s that really comes under criticism. NGS used the work of such very credible women scientists as Jane Goodall, Dian Fossey, and Shirley Strum and cast them in the light of benign mother. At that point in time—and even today—the idea of woman as scientist was at best an oxymoron if not an outright absurdity. But woman as mother or as educator was and is acceptable. In the NGS and Gulf Oil co-produced TV specials we saw a development of the male view of nature where nature is female and has to conquered or controlled by man. But now there is a woman scientist explaining this view of nature to us, which, given the political and historical context, makes the male view of nature more acceptable to us. Haraway's take on this is that "Animals are non-white and have to be looked after, says the white mother". (Haraway, 1989 135-136) And this is the case because "Race and gender are the major contentious products of 'human family' discourse" (Haraway, 1989 196).   The next vision Haraway looks at the development of physical anthropology and the hunter image. Most of us are familiar with the notion of "man the hunter" discussed briefly in chapter four. The evolutionary theory which explains this vision is that man evolved in the forest as the environment changed from living in the trees to hunting on the ground. Man had to develop an erect posture to see his prey. But in the post-World War Two period it was important to be anti-racist. The main figures here are Theodosius Dobzhansky and Sherwood Washburn. In 1944 Dodzhansky presented a paper entitled "On Species and Races of Living and Fossil Man" which argued that fossils show that all men are descended from the same source and that the concept of race is scientifically nonsense. He and Washburn then worked out an account of the fossil record and how it explained the evolution of man. Washburn saw the issue of evolution in terms of adaptive behavior. In a sense Washburn worked backwards from a then-current view of man as hunter to show how the newly emerging human fossil record could account for the necessary changes from ape to man the hunter.

The point here is that again we see science being used for cultural purposes in a specific cultural political context. Washburn's scientific humanism provides

> An account of human nature that evaded history, relegating it to the recent laminar residues of the geological scale. "Man" was self made, and yet "human nature" was safely unchangeable by history. The moment of origins, the boundary between nature and culture, and the operation of constraints were the chief objects of this scientific narrative (Haraway, 1989 220).

Now that we have seen a variety of primate visions, and therefore a variety of views of what science is, we can see where these visions lead us. The obvious point is that science is a cultural undertaking which reflects the values and concerns of the culture in which it is practiced. This does not always mean that culture-laden science is bad science, but it does mean that the picture of the world that a particular view of science paints will always be an incomplete picture because of how science is done in that particular context.

By externally criticizing science, and by looking at various scientific images from the standpoint of other, alternative, images, Haraway, using something like the Sellarsian model discussed in chapter two, shows how cultural assumptions work in the scientific enterprise. In doing so, she shows us important points that have been omitted from these scientific images of man in the world, to use the Sellarsian term. Haraway's second point is that by eliminating women's images or visions from the scientific enterprise we have developed images of the world which are at best incomplete and possibly misleading with regard to the nature of the world.

On the one hand, postmodernism argues that knowledge is a human construct. On the other hand, postmodernists acknowledge that the world we live in is a real world. The very important point here is that while our understanding of the world is a construct, it is one made out of materials found in the world and not just in our imaginations. While we may never achieve a purely objective view of the world, since all our observations will reflect some cultural framework, we can try to overcome the most obvious assumptions or prejudices which are built into that framework. Thus we have to be careful as to how we conceptualize our problems and we must be clear on how our conceptualizations lead to how we collect data and what kinds of data we collect. (Haraway, 1989 308)

We can achieve this clarity by challenging our assumptions from both an internal and external standpoint. We have to realize that primatology, and all science, is a sexualized enterprise which represents the sexual divisions of labor and values within the culture where the studies are being done. Secondly, we have to realize that our own criticisms of other images reflect our values and concerns. And we have to realize that the so-called feminist enterprise can also be practiced by men. Just because a woman does something does not make that task feminist, and just because a man does it does not make it anti-feminist. The feminist postmodern approach is a method which can be used by any and all practitioners as long as all practitioners realize that their respective practices reflect a value structure. Haraway's point is that in doing science we must not omit the feminine.

Since I spent a great deal of time on scientific methodology in earlier chapters I would like to make some connections between Haraway's view of science and some of the people discussed above, namely Popper, Kuhn and Sellars.

Popper's main point is that one has to be able to state the kinds of evidence that would count against one's hypothesis before undertaking any experiments so that such negative data would not be discounted by the experimenter. This is the basis for the whole notion of scientific criticism. In his political writings Popper equates the critical aspect of science with democracy. Science can only flourish in a democratic society because that is the only kind of society where criticism is not only acceptable but necessary (Popper, 1945). Haraway would certainly agree with this point, even if her notion of democracy is different than Popper's.

Haraway would certainly agree with many points of both Kuhn

and Sellars. Indeed, one could argue that they set the stage for the postmodern analysis of science. They were the ones who argued that all observation is context-laden and that one cannot achieve a truly objective view of the world. We will always be looking at the world through some conceptual framework or paradigm—we will always we looking through the window of a specific house.

Haraway has shown that many of these previous frameworks or houses were incomplete: they omitted the feminine perspective and therefore presented an incomplete view of that framework. Without the feminine perspective the scientific house could never be completed and even the parts that have been built may need restructuring.

Perhaps the strongest point about the nature of science is that made by Sellars when he claimed that science is the judge of what exists and what does not exist. Since science is about explaining the world we live in, as long as we realize that all science is contextual, within that context, I think Haraway would agree with this point. After all, she is a biologist and studies cell structure, specializing in the microorganism *Mixotricha paradoxa*. The study of such an organism is mediated by the kinds of technology we use to study it; but in her studies of biology Haraway sees not only "extraordinary biological architectures and mechanisms", but she also finds that "Biology is an inexhaustible source of troping. It is certainly full of metaphor, but it is more than metaphor"[129]. Haraway said this in an interview published in *Feminist Science Studies: A New Generation*, an anthology which will be the basis of the following discussion.

We study the world both literally and figuratively. We construct our new scientific houses both literally and figuratively. We live in the world and we study the world. But we are part of that world and so by studying it we also study ourselves, and by studying ourselves we come to better understand how we study the world. So to complete our postmodern house we need the feminist as well as the male architect. By looking at how women actually function in the world of science we will see how this feminist touch affects how our new house will be built. The basis of this discussion will be the above-mentioned anthology, *Feminist Science Studies,* a book is in four parts. The first part deals with women who work across traditional borders—women who came to science through women's studies or who came to women's studies from science—and continue to work in both areas. The second section deals with women within the sciences. The third section deals with changing science-teaching methods. And the fourth looks to the future.

The dual theme of the book is that science must be made relevant to people in the world and that by bringing feminist concerns to the world of science this relevance can be accomplished. As we have seen, by making science specialized and abstract we divorce our knowledge of how the world works from our experience of the world. The main problem with this approach is that we divorce ourselves from our own knowledge and we think about ourselves in an abstract manner. This is why so many of our social science theories, from behaviorism in psychology to monetarism in economics to Kohlberg's work on how we learn moral concepts, we treat people in the abstract. These views deny everything that we say is important about being human. Yet, because of the commitment to abstract knowledge we accept such conclusions. We also continue to teach science in this abstract manner and then wonder why people do not want to study science.

This process of abstraction is not limited to science but is also prevalent in art. Without going too far off on a tangent I would like to mention a couple of parallel points.

Classical music was part of the so-called pop music scene of its day. Jazz was the pop music of its day. But as each musical form became more complex and as composers and performers pursued their musical interests they often left their audiences behind. Part of the problem is that the audiences did not try to keep up with developments in music. The other part of the problem was that the performers did not attempt to educate their audiences. So the art form, which is supposed to communicate to the audience, and the audience, who is supposed to understand what goes on in the music, become divorced from each other.

Music tends to be taught from a technical standpoint. Of course, in music, as in science, technique is important. But technique should not be taught or used as an end in itself. Technique is a means to an end. In jazz drumming the master of technique as an end in itself is Buddy Rich. Many people love his solos because of their technical showmanship. But the solos are devoid of musical content and context. The master of musical drumming is Max Roach, who structures his drum solos to the song structure. He has all the technique needed to play but he uses that technique for musical ends (*Rich versus Roach* CD, Mercury MG20448).

The point here is that the same process occurs in science. Science, as Kuhn showed, is taught after the fact, as if the rational technique was used throughout, when in fact the process of science can be a messy one requiring creativity on the part of the scientist. By teaching science in this abstract manner students lose all sense of discovery and they lose all sense of the role of the scientist as a creative problem solver. Problems of science, after all, come from our questioning of how the world works. Thus science should be taught from a standpoint of what the problems were and how and why the problems were solved. In this way we can see the relevance of the scientific enterprise to our everyday lives, even when this science is extremely complex.

Another way of making this last point is that both science and art are context-laden problem solving undertakings. In each case there are criteria for what counts as art or science and in each case we can examine a work—a painting—a musical performance—a poem—an experiment—to see if the work brings us new knowledge or new understanding of the subject area. Art and science both provide knowledge and understanding of the world, albeit in different ways and about different aspects of the world. But there is a creative aspect to science and a technical aspect to art. Science has subjective processes and art has objective standards.

But, as I argued in the discussion of concept realism, pure science is where the practical solutions come from. And innovation in the arts is also the result of experimentation. Pure science and abstract art need not be abandoned but there has to be more communication between the scientist and the artist and the public. If art and science are to flourish, we must use the democratic model of trial and error, of free discussion. But consumers of art and science must also know what the experiments are about so the criticism will be valid.

The theme of part three of *Studies*, and where I shall begin this discussion, is that the authors of the introduction to this section point out that the contributors "have developed an effective critique of science and feminism, and constructed ways to integrate this critique into education in the sciences and women's studies" (Weasel et al, 2001 139). The main themes running through this section are the need to integrate studies from different sources and to understand that everything in life, including science, is gendered. Once we understand how the genderization of a subject operates—from excluding women to making the subject artificially abstract—we can change how that subject works. And the best way to do that is to change how it is taught, from relating the subject, no matter how abstract, to how and why the problems arose in the first place, to showing how this abstract subject connects with other subjects that students are knowledgeable about.

One such curriculum involves "linking women's studies and physical sciences and engineering" in the hope that these links will "foster constructive bridges that will bring together students, faculty, and subject matter from women's studies and the physical sciences and engineering"

(Weasel et al, 2001 173).

For teaching, many authors and educators found that participatory learning works well in these interdisciplinary contexts (Sharon Kinsman in Weasel et al, 2001 198). Ultimately the point of all this interdisciplinary teaching is because

> The making of science is not separate from the making of society. Scientific practices are not just any kinds of doings, they are material-discursive intra-actions with intertwined epistemological and ontological significance. The making of what we call "science" and what we call "society" are mutually constitutive, not because they impact one another, but because the constitutive intra-actions do not honor the arbitrary boundaries we construct between one and the other (Karen Barad in Weasel et al, 2001 241).

This approach to teaching science comes out of the experiences of many women who entered the sciences and felt out of place. The first section of *Studies* has such chapter headings as "Proud to be an Oxymoron" and "Resident Alien." The point here is that many women who went to study science because of questions they had about everyday life were often confused by the abstract nature of how science was studied. This confusion led to looking at the relationships between what they were studying and why they wanted to study it. When their expectations were not met they realized that the culture of science had to be changed (Angela Ginorio in Weasel et al, 2001 17). One scholar was even asked, "What are you, a *Chicana* or a scholar?" (Weasel et al, 2001 18). Obviously it was bad enough for a woman to want to be a scholar, but a *Chicana*?! Such comments clearly show the limited categories we use to think about the world.

The second point that women scholars make is that they feel like outsiders in the men's world of science because of how things are done. Women tend to want to integrate information from different sources, while the dominant (male) model of science tends to be abstract and highly specialized. This is why these women think of themselves as oxymorons and aliens. These points are well put by Caitilyn Allen, holder of a joint appointment in natural science and women's studies. "Over the years, it has become clear to me that the two disciplines not only study different subjects, but they do so in fundamentally different ways. My position offers me the opportunity to gather up and unite these disparate perspectives" (Weasel et al, 2001 22). Jan Clarke went from biology to sociology because she needed a political and social context to make sense of biology and then she found that "by no means were all the methods of lab research directly transferable to social research...—people simply do not cooperate with a researcher in the same way chemicals and plant roots conform to scientific method" (Weasel et al, 2001 37). Martha P. L. Whitaker took years to realize that "the tools of hydrology and women's studies need not be mutually exclusive...Each discipline can benefit from the other" (Weasel et al, 2001 49), but in doing so they will be transformed.

And the point of all this is that "feminist theory, because of its multidisciplinary approach to gender and emphasis on variation" can improve not only the animal studies that J. Kasi Jackson does, but all sciences. Armed with this multidisciplinary approach, women scientists focused their energies on issues that were either purposely overlooked by traditional scientific methods or by the social context of how science was done. Three areas stand out here: women's health issues such as breast cancer, the proper role of parenting, and various environmental issues.

Recall the discussion above regarding the cultural context of medicine. The focus of the feminist approach is to make science more relevant to the people it is supposed to serve instead of focusing on how the experts see things. As we know the so-called expert all too often knows everything there is to know about a subject but has no clue as to why that body of knowledge exists. There is no sense of history and no sense of the original problems that gave rise to that study. Thus the medical expert sees a condition and offers a solution. This solution may cure the disease or it may not, but, given the status of knowledge in the field, that particular approach is considered to be the thing to do. In practicing science or medicine in this way no regard is given to the specific concerns of the patient. Another parallel here is the Kohlberg-Gilligan dispute. Most doctors follow the abstract method of applying a general principle to a problem without taking into account the specific situation.

In her studies of how breast cancer has been treated, Bonnie Spanier found that the social context of how science was practiced had a direct bearing on treatment. Spanier is a microbiologist and found that even in that field she "found the imprints of a sexist belief system—of one sex naturally dominant over another, of hierarchy and centralized control as natural arrangements—...For biology at the macro and micro levels, cultural beliefs about natural difference and about 'sex' reinforced reductionist tendencies and a cult of simplicity in science to produce the distorted idea that genotype dictates phenotype, that biology is destiny" (Weasel et al, 2001 263).

In breast cancer treatment this attitude led to a whole set of practices which were questionable. One involved genetic screening. If a woman had a certain gene that suggested she would get breast cancer the best treatment would be a radical mastectomy even before any cancer appeared, although the cancer rate for people with this gene was in the 15% range (Weasel et al, 2001 264). Or hospitals had genetic counselors to advise patients on possible forms of treatment, but all too often these counselors worked in an "ideological context that makes genetics the center of disease analysis and solutions predisposes genetic counseling toward using genetic tools" (Weasel et al, 2001 265). Thus the analyses given by these counselors are anything but value neutral. Another factor is that so much research is funded by drug companies that some of the possible treatments that will be advised can be influenced by the state of what kinds of research are funded and by whom. Thus even business practices can influence medical decisions because of how the world of science and research is structured (Weasel et al, 2001 269).

Spanier has argued for possible treatments to be counseled in context of the patient's needs and not the needs and perspectives of the medical profession of the pharmaceutical industry.

Concerns similar to those raised with regard to how the medical profession operates have been asked about to how the scientific community regards the environment. Valerie Kuletz has done work on attitudes towards nuclear waste. She found a fundamental difference between how local and indigenous groups and government and scientific groups view nature. "Fundamentally, the most important difference between these two groups concerns objectivity: whether one holds an intersubjective view of nature, or whether one 'objectifies' nature, making an epistemological separation between subject and object, self and others, nature and culture" (Weasel et al, 2001 323-324).

Kuletz investigated the high rates of cancer among indigenous peoples of the American Southwest, areas of nuclear weapon testing and nuclear waste disposal. All too often the scientific community or their government spokespeople saw no relation between the nuclear waste and the high levels of cancer because the two could not be "scientifically" correlated (Weasel et al, 2001 324). This was the case because the government wanted it that way and because there could be more than one possible explanation. Thus the explanation chosen reflected the concerns of the group making the decisions.

This point recalls the discussion of causality in chapter three. How do we know when something causes something else? What is a cause, what conditions must exist for us to say we know that A causes B?

As long as there are a variety of factors involved, anyone can massage the data to one's advantage. And one can do this because of how we objectify nature. This last point is made in a different context by John Passmore in *Man's Responsibility For Nature*, where he argues that the *Old Testament* way of looking at the world has nature existing for our exploitation. "By the time the Genesis stories were composed—in Mesopotamia—man had already embarked on the task of transforming nature. In the Genesis stories man *justifies* his actions"[130]. As we have seen in our discussion of the rise of Protestantism along with capitalism, the pursuit of property and wealth, and working the land, were considered good. When we put all these things together—religion, capitalism, and then objectifying of nature—it is no wonder that our concerns for people come last. Of course, the whole project of the feminist analysis of science is to show that science is not objective in the way in which scientists claim since the scientists have a direct interest in what they are doing.

Scientists should be concerned not with objectifying nature but with trying to better understand how we are interdependent with nature so we can protect ourselves and our environment. And these points become even more important when discussing the last issue, the so-called scientific approach to motherhood.

As Jacquelyn S. Litt points out in *Medicalized Motherhood: Perspectives from the Lives of African-American and Jewish Women*, the term "scientific motherhood" dates from 1842 but really took on significance in the 1920s, when mothers started using doctors more regularly[131]. Litt defines scientific motherhood or medicalization as "the process through which biomedical interpretations of conditions have acquired cultural legitimacy, eclipsing (or at least pushing aside) other perspectives, such as custom, religion, and traditional knowledge, on human problems and conditions. Throughout the twentieth century, the domain of medicine expanded to include mothering practices, as well as childbirth, old age, death, child development, sexuality, appearance, alcohol use, and eating problems as requiring the intervention of medical experts and frames of reference" (Weasel et al, 2001 276).

Litt goes on to argue that by the 1930s "scientific motherhood had been institutionalized as the province of professional medicine, particularly pediatrics and obstetrics" (276). Thus mothers ran to doctors for any and all issues and came to accept their views, even when this advice contradicted their own experience. The best example of this was the routine for feeding children by the clock, regardless if they were hungry or not (Weasel et al, 2001 279).

The point here is that mothers have knowledge which they get from interacting with other mothers and with their children. By relying on so-called specialist advice, even when they know the advice is wrong, mothers become separated from their traditional communal and social roles. And as we saw above, they become separated from their own knowledge.

Now we don't want to throw out the proverbial baby with the bathwater. We can certainly accept new knowledge. Indeed, a central argument of this book has been that we *must* accept new knowledge, and that this new knowledge then changes our understanding of the world, which will in turn lead us to change our values and practices. But the postmodern feminist position about this new knowledge is that we should not simply take the expert's words for anything. We, as the people affected by this knowledge, must have a say in its applications. Thus we must look at where the knowledge comes from, how it is to be used, and how it will change us. Instead of letting expert knowledge control us, we must in control of the uses of this knowledge.

By arguing that knowledge—and science is knowledge that is demonstrable—is something that arises out of our cultural contexts, we say that all knowledge is context-laden and that the contexts come from our culture. Thus knowledge is something that we construct. So as we remodel our old house, we use new knowledge but we get to choose how to use it. We do this by following what the authors of the introduction to this section lay out as the six basic principles of postmodern feminist science.

> 1. *Our scientific theories and practices must be grounded in the awareness that life is interdependent and that we are inextricably part of that life.*
> 2. *As women, we must be restored to our rightful place as active subjects.*
> 3. *Research, development, and use of science and technology must be ethical and not cause harm.*
> 4. *Liberatory, feminist sciences must work to identify, respect, and protect boundaries.*
> 5. *We must acknowledge men's role in reproduction and facilitate their responsibilities and involvement in child rearing.*
> 6. *Feminist activists, scientists, and academics must work cooperatively for liberatory social change. They must also stay connected to the communities and take their lead from people likely to benefit from, or be impacted by, the outcomes of their work* (Weasel et al, 2001 254-256).

Natural Law, Science, and the Social Construction of Reality 295

Thus science is part of our cultural context and not something that is separate from it. To use the house analogy again, we are in the process of transforming or reconstructing our house as we acquire new materials and new understandings of how to use those materials. The view of science that has developed in the modern era has been as if we have built a laboratory in the back yard and go there to perform experiments divorced from our everyday life and then come to our old house and try to live in the old way but with this new knowledge being added on. Since we do not really understand this knowledge we must rely on the experts who developed it to tell us how to use it. Thus we lose control over our homes and of our day-to-day to lives. Postmodern feminism, by providing a conceptual and gendered account of how science works has been attempting, to show how the experts reflect not an objective truth but a very narrow view of truth which only reflects the concerns of some of the people.

Now we must look at how this analysis translates into a natural law theory. Recall that natural law theory is a view of the world in which facts and values are combined, or where our understanding of the natural order—our fact or knowledge base—supports our moral and ethical systems—how we fit into that natural order. This postmodern feminist analysis of science has shown that science arises out of our daily concerns. Two things are involved if science to make sense—if science is to explain what we want explained in terms that reflect the world we live in. One is that science can certainly use sophisticated techniques for doing its job but, the second is that we as citizens of the culture who want things explained must do our parts in keeping up with developments in knowledge so that we are not controlled by the so-called experts. This does not mean that everyone will be an expert on everything. That is impossible. But it does mean that if we want to have control over our lives we have to have at least some way to make sense of what the experts tell us. The analysis of knowledge that this feminist view gives us is that as consumers of knowledge we have a responsibility to maintain a level of understanding at least at the conceptual level. We must all have a sense of what the problems are and how the experts go about finding solutions to those problems, and a sense of how we will use that knowledge in our everyday lives. If science is done in a way which reflects our day-to-day concerns, even if it becomes very technical, we will have at least a conceptual understanding of the science and how to use it. Thus, on this view, science does not become an abstraction removed from our daily lives. Yet science may very well be complex.

As we saw in our discussion of science in the neo-Kantian

context of Kuhn and Sellars, science is a value-laden problem solving enterprise. The feminist analysis of science agrees with this but takes it a step further by showing that the values that lead to science come from our community and that how we do science is constructed out of the materials of the community. These constructions are limited by the nature of the materials at hand and our understanding of them. As we gain new knowledge and/or new understandings of our knowledge, our understanding of the world we live in will change. We are constantly reconstructing our house. But we get to choose how to reconstruct it. And we will now make sure that the house has a feminine touch, which was clearly lacking in our earlier houses.

Above I made a reference to the relationship between art and science. Let me develop that a bit here. The point is that on the old view of science the experts told us what was discovered and what it meant. In societies where fact and value were separated people could or could not accept these pronouncements, so people lived in all kinds of houses. In some cases the same house would be partially reconstructed from different periods. So on the one hand a person would accept an ancient view of how the world came to be while accepting up-to-date scientific explanations of various phenomena from the germ theory of disease to modern genetic theory to the possibility of extraterrestrial life, not realizing that these different views were incompatible with one another. But perhaps it wasn't important to people that some rooms in their houses were lit by electricity while other rooms were lit by candles.

The analogy between art and science is about the relationship of knowledge and evaluation. Art is not science and science is not art, yet each uses materials and methods from the other. To illustrate this point let us look at three hypothetical situations any one of us can find ourselves in.

We attend a concert of 18th century music. One of the works listed is unknown to us. According to the program notes the conductor was on a trip to Austria to finalize the estate of an uncle who had just died. Among the uncle's papers was an old manuscript dated from the 1730s. It appeared to be a concerto. Upon playing it the conductor decided it was not great but a worthy addition to the repertoire. Upon listening to the piece at the concert, we concur. The work is not great but it could be considered a lesser work of art of the mid-baroque period.

After the intermission the conductor admits to a hoax. The piece was not by his ancestor but by a composition student. The conductor thought it such a good rendering of the baroque style that it deserved to be performed. Upon hearing this piece of news, our evaluations of the music change. It can no longer be seen as a work of art, no matter how minor.

Natural Law, Science, and the Social Construction of Reality 297

The next concert in the series presents music of contemporary Canadian composers. Most of the music sounds discordant and harsh. Indeed, one could say the music was unmusical. Why would anyone want to compose such noise and why would anyone want to call it music?

The next event we are all attending is a lecture on understanding the nature of space travel and the possibility of the Earth having been visited by aliens. The lecture is incomprehensible because of all the mathematics being used. How can a non-scientist understand such talk when the subject is of general interest to all of us?

In all of these cases, in order to appreciate what is going on, the audience member needs specialized knowledge of the field in question. In order to properly appreciate the music or to understand the science, one needs knowledge of music or of science. In this sense one can see at least a superficial similarity between art and science: one needs to know about the field to understand developments in the field. But the similarities go deeper than that. The same kinds of techniques and reasoning processes which go into the understanding of science also are needed for the understanding of art.

The important point here is that as users or consumers of science and of art we have a responsibility to understand the subject matter if we are to properly appreciate and use it. I can listen to abstract, dissonant music because I understand what the composer was concerned with. I don't have to like it but I cannot just dismiss it as noise.

Thus the analysis that the postmodern feminist position provides is that by combining fact and value—indeed by showing that values are facts and that facts are value-laden—we also do away with the old distinction between pure and applied science. We saw that these distinctions had to be abandoned in our discussion of neo-Kantian philosophy. But now we not only get rid of them but we place some responsibility on the non-expert to have an understanding of science (and art) so that we all can make better decisions on how to live our lives and how to restructure our houses.

Thus, the postmodern feminist analysis of knowledge breaks down the separation of knower and known. It becomes a natural law theory because our values and knowledge of the world are clearly intertwined. Our understanding of the natural order leads directly to how we should behave in that natural order—our knowledge of the natural order tells us what kinds of behaviors are natural. Morality and knowledge are intertwined.

And what will some of these moral views be?

First, to repeat the point I have just made, non-experts have a responsibility to maintain an understanding of developments in knowledge.

Second, the two main reasons for the development of the feminist analysis of knowledge are that for women to attain equality with men the male dominant social structure had to change, and that the feminine understanding of knowledge had to be made part of the whole picture. In doing so, many issues become transformed or reconstructed, so that this new world will be quite different from the old one.

Third, since we now know that both sex and gender are constructs we can make choices about our behavior in ways that were not previously open to us.

Finally, we must constantly maintain an awareness of others in our lives, for the main point that the first three lead up to is the that of connectedness. No person is an island, to paraphrase John Donne. Just as knowledge is connected—what we know about one thing relates to what we know about something else—we are connected. We all share roles in a social order. This sharing of roles and this interconnectedness create the community and form the basis of the relationship between what we know, why we want to know it, and how we use what we know.

This last point can be put in neo-Kantian terms. Recall the discussion in chapter four about the concept of "person". I argued, using Sellars' notion of distributive singular terms, that if we learned the concept of "person" to mean "moral equal" we would be able to develop a moral theory that answers the fanatic because this concept of a person is not solely based on individualism but on the fact that individuals are members of a community. Postmodernist feminism has shown just how much we are part of a community.

Thus, by making all these connections, postmodern feminism is indeed a natural law theory.

Chapter 7

CONCLUSIONS

We have come a long way. We started by defining natural law as a moral theory in which we began with an understanding of the natural order of things—our knowledge base—and by understanding what persons are and how they fit into the natural order. Another way of putting this is that our values and knowledge are connected. Our understanding of the world forms the basis of our values and our values lead us to investigate the world.

In the past, natural law theory was seen as an absolute view of morality. In discovering the natural order and our place in it we had absolute knowledge of morality—our place in the natural order and the kinds of behaviors that were natural and moral and those that were unnatural and therefore immoral.

But as we have seen, our knowledge base has changed, and with it our values. When our knowledge base changes—when our understanding of what is natural changes—our views of what is moral must also change. I have tried to show how new views of natural law developed as ways of resolving problems that arose with earlier views. Thus Aquinas' view was undermined by the development of individualism and by developments in science. Locke developed a view of natural law based on individualism and on an understanding of the new science. This view, in turn, led to a view of science which divorced fact from value. Kant addressed these issues to show that this distinction was not viable and a neo-Kantian view developed which showed how knowledge and values are intertwined. In looking at this we saw how modern science with its dependency on theorizing could develop, and by acknowledging the role of our concepts in formulating our knowledge of the world, we realized that our concepts, were at least to some extent our own constructs. And we also saw that by ignoring the gender issue, all previous views of knowledge were seen to be inadequate at best. These points led to the development of the postmodern view of natural law.

Now, if people really were logical and well-informed as to all these developments in science and moral theorizing we would all be adherents of postmodernist natural law theory. But people are not always logical or well-informed of new developments in knowledge. Old views are still held, side by side with new views. Thus, to use our house imagery, even though they have added scientific improvements to their homes, many people still maintain medieval values. One obvious reason for this state of affairs is that culture marches on despite changes. So even though we develop new knowledge, and we even incorporate this new knowledge into our everyday lives, we do not let this knowledge change our lives. Just because we can now drive a car instead of riding a horse we do not necessarily see that our values have to change. The car just takes the place of the horse. But, of course, the car changes how we relate to the world and to other people, so our values should change. And, over time, as the car becomes more important to us, some of our values change. But, we still manage to maintain old views since we see no obvious reason to change those old views. This is one reason why we can live in our scientific houses while still holding some medieval beliefs.

The intellectual reason for this is quite obvious, but needs elucidating since many of us are not aware of the apparent contradictions we accept in our daily lives. The main reason for this situation is that beginning in the 18th century with David Hume and the separation of fact from value, and with philosophers and scientists saying that they only deal in fact and have nothing to say about values, such old institutions as the church stepped back in and declared that they had much to say on values. Thus, since the scientific and philosophic communities abandoned their responsibilities to look at the value implications of their work, they allowed the discredited church to enter through the back door to reclaim the moral sphere. And since the church, whether Catholic or Protestant, represented a form of natural law theory in which their value system reflected a view of the natural order, that earlier view of the world also crept back in, so that we started to accept the findings of science on specific issues but not as a view of the natural order.

So today we live in a world which accepts all views together. We have religious people who reject the claims of science and medicine, we have religious people who reject the world view of science yet use modern inventions and medicine, we have people who try to combine two opposing views by arguing for some kind of scientific creationism, and we have non-theistic people who accept the world view of science and who try to develop moral views that reflect this scientific view of the world.

Thus we venerate Einstein and the Pope, without seeing any conflict. Yes, Einstein did say that God did not play dice with the universe. But what he meant was that science will discover laws of nature that make sense. He was arguing against quantum mechanics as the basis of reality because of the randomness of the behavior of quanta.

Now, if the argument of this book is sound, if new bodies of knowledge lead to new values, then we should be adapting a postmodern view of the world. But since people are not always rational—a view defended by postmodernists—we live in a pluralistic world with all of these views still being used. What I will now do is apply all of these views to a set of issues that students are concerned about using a rubric (which can be found in the Appendix) for evaluating ethical theories and for justifying one's decisions. Then I will look at the implications of applying a post-modern view of natural law to a range of issues.

This rubric begins by stating what one proposes to do and by proposing the opposite. We will provide the necessary information relevant to that decision, and then we will evaluate the information in terms of the different ethical theories. In the final assignment, students justify one view over another. Remember, a theory is an explanation, so an ethical theory must provide an explanation of why we should or should not behave in specific ways. The class discussion may begin with an apparently trivial issue so students can see that the manner in which we argue for a trivial issue is the same for the way we would argue for a more serious issue and also that the apparently trivial issue may not be so trivial when we look into what is involved in making the decision. The issue here is: "Should I get out of bed today?" (See Appendix, Rubric 1.)

All the views basically say that we should get out of bed in the morning and do what we are supposed to do. But they say this for different reasons. Some say we must get out of bed so we can fulfill our functions in society, some say we do so out of duty, some say we must do so because not doing so would lead to consequences we may not be prepared to accept. Thus all the theories, with their differing explanations of why we should act morally, provide different reasons for getting out of bed.

Now when applied to the general issue of sexuality, a specific question could be one accepting the naturalness of homosexuality or of bisexuality. Or we could ask something about having a sex-change operation. In class the most asked questions are about understanding sexual diversity. Most students seem quite accepting of different behaviors but they don't always understand them. So let put as our proposal whether or not we should accept homosexuality as a natural, and therefore moral, form of behavior. (See Rubric 2.)

On this issue we see that the different theories yield somewhat different views, with some theories being adaptable to changing knowledge. This is especially true of the views that are based on some form of principle instead of a specific view of what is natural. Specific definitions of what is natural must be completely abandoned when new knowledge shows that the old view of natural is false, as we see with the view of Aquinas. But general principles can be adapted and contextualized as our knowledge changes. Thus the contributions of Kant and Mill are still applicable in a postmodern constructivist context, even if these principles are applied in ways that Kant or Mill could not have conceived of in their time. Thus specific definitions cannot be adapted but general principles can. But, as we have seen in our discussions of the development of knowledge, in new contexts, these old principles become transformed into new versions, especially when they are called upon to make decisions about issues that did not exist when the they were first formulated. For a good example of such an issue, many students today are concerned about issues concerning globalization and the changing roles of governments and the rising new roles of the corporate sector. So for the third issue which will be charted, let us put forward the proposal that globalization, in combination with free trade, is a good thing.. (See Rubric 3.)   Again we see that while all views appear to agree on the issue they do so for different reasons.

Now that we have seen how to apply the different moral theories I would like to return to my main argument which was that each successive view was developed to solve problems in earlier views, so that the prevailing moral view should be the feminist postmodern view. I shall begin by looking at how this view is actually applied. Next I will apply it to another controversial issue. Then I will explore two other areas of application: sexuality and rights. Finally, I will come to some general conclusions about the kind of social order that is implied in this feminist postmodern view.

As we have just seen the actual results of most of the different moral theories we have looked at are similar but the reason for those conclusions are very different. And if the reasons for behaving in a specific manner differ, then, depending on the issue or the context, the conclusions—the actual course of action to taken—can differ. When I read my postmodern natural law paper at the International Medieval Congress in 2002 someone in the audience commented that no matter what the case, strychnine kills. Of course it does. But different theories of how the body works and different theories of how the poison works would explain how strychnine works very differently. And in philosophy, as in science, the explanation of why something is the case is more important than the actual description of the case. And eventually, the different explanations will lead to a different description of what happened.

This is the process of the feminist postmodern view of moral theory. Since this view explains things differently it will eventually also describe things differently. By looking at how decisions affect the people involved in the process this view contextualizes morality. It does not abandon general principles but applies them differently depending on the context. A legal example captures this process nicely. If our legal process were purely utilitarian we would judge an action by its consequences. So if I bring a shotgun into class and shoot it at the wall, I may be charged with disturbing the peace or vandalism. But I would not be asked if I were aiming at anyone for intent is not an issue. If I hurt someone but was not intending to do so, on utilitarian grounds I would be charged with whatever level of harm I had done. The fact I did not intend to harm anyone is irrelevant on strict utilitarian grounds. But thanks to Kant, motive and intent enter the picture. On strict Kantian grounds what I set out to do and why are issues. Of course consequences play a role, but only in terms of intent.

When we combine these views we allow for mitigating circumstances. If I did not set out to harm anyone but did so, I would be charged with a lesser crime than if I set out harm someone. If I set out to harm someone and missed, on this combined view, I could be charged with attempted harm. And if I am found guilty, certain mitigating circumstances could be a factor in how I am punished. Thus on the combined Mill-Kant view specific circumstances can enter the picture. Indeed, one can argue that the legal systems in most Western countries reflect some combination of absolute principle (Kant) and concern with consequences (Mill). When we modify both views as we did in chapter four we allow for mitigating circumstances in line with a person's motives and intent. We evaluate the consequences in terms of the motive and intention.

On the feminist post-modern view we also take the context into account. What might be acceptable behavior in one context may not be in another. We are more concerned about the specific effects of the action on the people we are involved with, thereby limiting the context. Thus we do not entirely abandon moral principles such as consequences, intent and motive. We simply contextualize them. Instead of saying, "Killing is wrong", we now discuss not only the reasons killing is bad, but also who killed whom and why, and then we can punish, or not punish the killer depending on a host of factors involved in the specific situation. A good example of contextualizing killing is the issue of euthanasia or mercy killing.

This is a complex issue and can take up an entire book on its own. But my purpose here is not to definitively resolve the issue but to show how the feminist postmodern view approaches the issue and this approach significantly differs from other approaches.

Aquinas would approach the issue in an absolutist manner. Only God has the power of life and death. Thus mercy killing is still killing and is wrong. Many religious-based groups today who oppose both abortion and euthanasia state they there should be no interference in life from conception to natural death. This statement would appear to imply not getting any medical help for an illness since medical help implies an interference in the natural process. Apparently, proponents of this view allow interference to maintain life but do not allow interference to bring about the cessation of life.

A combined Mill-Kant view may allow for limited euthanasia in specific cases where the case is terminal and where the person affected gives his or her consent. Under this description euthanasia becomes a form of assisted suicide where the terminally ill person wants to end his or her own life but is unable to do so. Since suicide may be acceptable—in most jurisdictions it is legal—aiding someone in this manner may be considered acceptable since the intent is not to murder but to aid someone in their suicide. The consequences of actual suicide and assisted suicide would be the same: the death of the terminally ill person. As long as the motive is pure—there are no personal gains to be made—the consequences are evaluated in terms of the motive and intention.

The feminist postmodern view would be to first ask the people involved how they saw the situation. The terminally ill person may want to be aided in her suicide. Our doctor may be willing to participate in this. But the issue is not just between the doctor and the patient. It also involves the people close to the patient. How do they feel? While the doctor and the patient do not necessarily have to agree with what everyone says, what they say has to be taken into account, because what they say, and why they say it, constitute part of the context in which the decision is to be made. Thus consequences, motive and intent are not abandoned but they come into play after the context is defined and not before, which is why in different contexts the same apparent behavior may be evaluated differently.

Now that we have looked at an issue involving death, let us look at one involving life, namely sexuality. In our discussion of feminist thought we spent a great of time talking about sexuality and gender and how both are social constructs. Now that we have an understanding of how sex and gender are constructs we can look at moral issues concerning sexuality.

Sexuality has many dimensions. One of them is the focus on the physical, on the body. With the development of feminism there came a development of feminist spirituality with attempts at re-creating beliefs in the Goddess and various other views such as Wicca. Thus we see attempts at historical recreation from a feminist perspective in the works of Gerda Lerner and Merlin Stone.[132] For a fictionalized version of these views, see *The Mists of Avalon* by Marion Zimmer Bradley, where Avalon was a matriarchal community that worshipped a goddess but the kingdom was destroyed by the evil King Arthur and male-dominated Christianity. These are interesting attempts to take what is essentially the male modernist model and transform it into a female model. In the old dualistic models, people concerned with spirituality tended to deny the body. They became ascetics or at least withdrew from daily life to pursue their purification. This led to all kinds of problems. For example, a man who tries to attain spirituality absents himself from the company of women. But if a woman should enter his domain, he will probably, in a purely biological manner, respond to her. Since he has sincerely worked at spiritual purification this arousal must clearly be the woman's fault. And given the views of good and evil within early Christianity, it was believed that it must be the devil's work. Thus female sexuality became associated with the devil. Because men did not understand the biology of sexuality, woman became the evil temptress, the devil incarnate. Eve becomes responsible for the Fall Of Man. It wasn't the fact that Adam took the first bite of the forbidden fruit, it was the fact that Eve tempted him that man saw as important. "I did it but the devil (in woman's guise) made me do it."

Now all these attempts at feminine spirituality are interesting, but they really do nothing more than turn the old male modernist model into a feminist modernist model. But such attempts at feminist spirituality are modernist and accept an objective world-view with a Goddess instead of a God. These views, however, are not consistent with a true constructivist postmodernism. But the fact that they exist is not surprising given the discussion above about how culture marches on regardless of new developments in knowledge. To continue with the house analogy, as long as we are still in the process of restructuring the house, we will continue to use features of the house which may in fact be outmoded and which belong to a different paradigm but which are nevertheless still serviceable.

Feminist postmodernism is the view that our social order is a construct and that our knowledge of the world derives from how we are brought up in that social order. The defining characteristic of this view is that interpersonal relationships define the nature of the world and from these relationships we define our values. Thus fact and value are intertwined. Knowledge is about how we interact with each other and with our physical environments. We can develop some kind of metaphysical explanation of how the world works, but such a view would still have to be directly tied to our world. We must speculate about the nature of the universe—to ask questions is to be human—but we have to be careful about what we claim to *know* and what we claim to *believe*. Postmodern feminist philosophy of science, as we have seen, sees knowledge as a social construct derived from our social interactions. And, as we have seen the scientific background that gave rise to feminist postmodernism is a materialistic one. Thus the kind of spirituality that is talked about is not truly postmodern. Perhaps, instead of calling the materialist view of science "scientific or concept realism" we should call it "social construct realism." But in any case, it is a realist or materialist view of the world and of persons. Thus the question should become "How can we transform modernist questions of spirituality into post-modernist questions about materiality?"

One way in which we can do this is to find things that are analogous to the separation of mind and body or spirit and body. In traditional dualist philosophies such as that of Descartes the mind was the name given to the thinking part of ourselves. But if we acknowledge that thinking is a brain process then we don't need to postulate a mind. But we can focus on the intellect, and on the relationship between the intellect and the emotions.

Emotions are more basic than intellect. As I like to put it, I laugh, therefore I think. We experience emotions of all kinds from awe to fear to love to lust. And then we reflect on those emotion in terms of their meaning and significance, if we need to act on them, and if so, how. When we see how the intellect works we work on honing our intellectual skills. As we saw in chapter three, if we hone them too much we develop a view of the world that denies the very things that make us human. So we have to use our intellect to insure we don't overuse it. We must not deny the importance of emotions. They are a big part of what makes us human and, as we saw, they play a big part in feminist ethical theory. The ways in which we set up our social relationships has a lot to do with our emotional needs. The way we analyze and reconstruct those relationships involves the intellect. But since we need social interaction and social organization we also need emotion.

Philosophy is one of the best ways to develop our intellectual skills. It is about analyzing concepts, ideas, and emotions. It lets us explore the world of reason and allows us to use reason to solve practical problems. So instead of going to a monastery and trying to purify myself to attain some spiritual truth, I should go to the library or bookstore and read and think and converse with others on abstract topics. Topics should be explored to the limits of reason, but when a conclusion has been reached or when a chain of reasoning has reached its end, we must then reflect on the relevance and on the context of our conclusions to see if they are practical.

As we have seen since science is a social construct, the social order must have a say in the kinds of things that science explores. This does not imply an anti science attitude. But it does mean, as the main argument of this book has shown, that how science is done reflects social values and that the findings of science affects our values. Thus our values must guide science and we must be aware of how science can lead to the changing of our values. Science does not operate in a vacuum. But science is also an excellent way in which to attain great use of our intellect.

The important point here is that if we accept a material view of persons then intellectual pursuits are one possible replacement for so-called spiritual pursuits. But since we do not separate the intellect from the body the way old views separate mind from body, pursuing so-called spirituality would on a materialistic view of persons imply that instead of spirituality we should be pursuing sensuality. Our senses are our contact with the world. We learn about the world through our senses. So to properly appreciate the world we should learn to heighten our sensory experiences. Instead of cutting ourselves off from the world we should dive in and engage in the world. We use sight to see what is there, but we also use sight to learn to see nature more clearly, to see how closely we are connected to nature, to appreciate art, to be more critical of how we see things. We use our sense of taste to tell us what we are eating. So we can use our sense of taste to really appreciate good food. We use the sense of hearing to communicate and listen for danger. But we can also use our hearing to appreciate really good music as well as the sounds of nature. We use the sense of smell to help us appreciate good food and to warn us dangers. So we can cook with more fragrant seasonings and use scents in more aesthetically pleasing manners. And finally there is touch, perhaps the most sensual of all. We touch all kinds of things, from fine materials to sculptures to other people. We should learn to touch carefully and sensually..

And this last comment brings us back to sexuality. If we are truly biological beings, then sexuality is a major part of who and what we are. So we should be able to really enjoy physical pleasures. And we should not forget the intellect. We first react to things sensually, but then we reflect on these experiences and use our intellects to learn how to increase our pleasures.

The subject of sexuality has a number of dimensions to it. On the one hand, there is simply learning how to appreciate the physical aspects of sexuality. On the other, there are the various social constrictions we place on sexuality. But the previous attitudes, as we have seen, are nothing more than social constructs, so they can be changed. We must use our intellects to see how we can change our sexual institutions.

The most obvious sexual institution that can be changed, and indeed is changing, is marriage. Some form of marriage will always be with us as long as we identify ourselves as individuals and want an individual mate. But the real questions are about why we marry. Through most of history the purpose of marriage has been to insure a stable environment for the raising of children. Since Christianity put so much emphasis on the soul or spiritual side of life as they understood it, sexuality was seen as an impediment to attaining a proper level of spirituality or religiosity, but Christianity also recognized the Old Testament commandment to be fruitful and multiply. This is where the notion of the main purpose of sexuality is reproduction comes from—if one cannot be pure, one should at least marry and have children.

With the beginnings of capitalism the need for women to be virgins became important to insure that the first born, the heir, was in fact the offspring of the landowner and not someone else. This economic and social need led to the development of virginity as a moral imperative, especially within puritanical Protestantism. But as we have seen Protestantism and capitalism go hand in hand.

Today with proper means of birth control and of determining paternity, none of the old restrictions on pre-marital sexuality make sense. And other factors are also changing the face of marriage. One is that people marry and choose not to have children. Another is that people with children get divorced. With people living longer, and with social conditions changing rapidly, what sense does it make to say people must stay together for life? Now there is great pressure to allow gays and lesbians to marry. Gays ands lesbians also want to have children. As we saw in our discussions of sex and gender, all kinds of possibilities are available to us in redefining sex and gender, and different forms of marriage is one aspect of these changes.

But if marriage is changing so drastically, should the role of sex in marriages also change? Because of concerns of parentage, and the ways in which religion has tended to see sexuality, sexual fidelity has become the hallmark of marriage. Adultery is one of the main reasons for divorce. But if we are sexual beings and the role of sex in our lives is open to reconstruction, then questions about the role of sex in marriage become relevant. Of course, such questions are not entirely new. Recall the various attempts at redefining marriage in the 1960s with such notions as open marriage. These experiments failed. But one of the reasons they failed is that they were tried in a culture that was not really prepared do deal with the consequences of such behavior, no matter how good it sounded on paper. I have no answers to these questions, but the way the discussion has been going, these questions need to be asked.

Now let us turn our intellects to looking at how our attitudes and values with regard to sexuality in a more general way can change. If sexuality is fluid and such concepts as man and woman, male and female, are not fixed, then we can make all kinds of choices about sexuality that were never open to us before. We can recognize homosexual behavior as normal. We can acknowledge that there may be good biological explanations for the concept of a woman being born in a man's body, or a man being born in a woman's body. We know there are people who do not have the XX or XY chromosome pairs; there are people with a third chromosome. How these differences are expressed is up to us. If we accept Chodorow's notion of "sexualities" then there is no one correct way to look at the issue.

So why do we have to limit socially acceptable sexual behaviors in our societies today. Why can't traditionally heterosexual men have sexual relationships with each other or why can't traditionally heterosexual women have sexual relationships with each other? If sex is a form of emotional expression then why can't there be all kinds of sexual behaviors? And, to return to the marriage issue, why can't there be a sexual expression of strong emotion between close friends?

To put all of these questions a bit differently, if we change how we understand sexual behavior and sexuality in general, we can also change how we understand the social roles of sexual behaviors and of sexuality in general. How these changes will occur is an open question, and if they will occur is also an open question. But, given our discussions of sex and gender as social constructs, these questions clearly arise. And, as we continue to explore these issues, even more questions will arise.

The last issue I want to discuss here is that of rights. Rights are usually contrasted with privileges. Everyone has rights, while privileges are only available to some people. Rights are usually discussed in an individualistic context, for it is usually held that only individuals have rights. As we saw in chapter three, the extreme individualist view of persons and of politics—known today as libertarianism—is indefensible on two grounds. First, as we saw in our discussion of Locke, rights develop as a result of a social contract which creates a community. It is the terms of the contract—the community—which bestows rights on individuals. Even if one argues that humans have inalienable rights, these rights can only be exercised in the context of a social contract. To put this point differently, persons living in isolation do not need rights. Robinson Crusoe does not need rights. If there are no other people there are no restrictions on one's behavior, so the issue of rights does not arise.

The second reason that the individualistic view is indefensible is that the notion of the individual is dependent upon a social order. We are born into a community and we learn to become individuals. We see this in how children are raised, in how we acquire language and in how we acquire our concepts, including the concept of individuality.

So if extreme individualism is a non-starter what about rights what about the notion of rights for individuals in a communal society? Here, the notion of rights is usually discussed in terms of the individual freedoms a society allows its members. Such rights can be the right to free speech, the right to assembly, the right to legal counsel, the right to make money, and so on. There are two models here. One would be a top-down regime with power concentrated at the top where such rights exist at the whim of the ruler. The second model would be a democratic society where rights are seen as integral to the political structure. The basic principle behind such an approach is the Lockean social contract. The principles of individual rights could be enshrined either in a constitution or in common law, as long as the practices are consistent. The British traditions deal with these questions effectively. This approach is essentially utilitarian and raises issues with regard to the relationship between the individual and the state as well as issues with regard to the notion of group or collective rights. Such questions can be answered, and, for the most part, societies such as England, Canada, and the United States manage fairly well, though major issues do exist. There are two major examples of problems with this approach. One can be seen in the various civil rights movements where certain groups of people have been systemically discriminated against, and in political movements to recognize that, as a person born into a society, one can expect certain rights, including the right to be able to participate in the society. The issue here is that of welfare policy. Should people, who, through no fault of their own, be supported at the poverty level so they can participate in the society?

The answers to these questions are not obvious. They depend on how the relationships between the individual and the society are defined. Does a society consist simply of individuals, or does a society determine who *is* an individual? For example, in Canada a Charter of Rights and Freedoms was amended to the Constitution in 1982. This amendment caused as many problems as it solved. Canada is a triple nation with both English and French populations, as well as an indigenous native population. The thinking was that if every individual had the same rights, tensions among these different peoples would be solved. But this was not the case since the French population and the native population did not want individual rights, they wanted collective rights. They wanted rights because they belonged to a particular group. All French speakers should have the right to get government services in their own language not because they are individuals who speak French but because they are part of the founding French culture which must be protected and preserved.

Fortunately the courts and Parliament have understood this and Canada recognizes collective rights in a way that England and The United States do not. But this notion of collective rights fits nicely into the postmodern view of culture. One main notion of the feminist postmodern view is how we are interconnected. How we construct our society determines how we view moral issues. The main point here is that this view sees social interactions as a form of interconnectedness. Yes, we are all individuals, and yes, we are all members of a group. We have rights because we are part of the group but we exercise those rights as individuals. Thus the distinction between the individual and the group becomes undermined since the individual is not entirely separable from the group. And each group—each community—can define the relationships as they see fit.[133]

Thus, the question of rights in a feminist postmodern society, like all other issues, is completely redefined because the very nature of who and what we are has been redefined. Many of the questions that feminist postmodernism ask do not have definitive answers because we are constantly reconstructing our societies. As long as we keep asking questions we can never have definitive answers.

Now we have reached the end of this journey, but, like all intellectual journeys, it never really ends. But let us sum up where we have been and how we got there, so we can get a sense of where this journey may continue in the future.

We began by defining natural law as an ethical theory in which facts and values are intertwined. We saw how Plato and Aristotle were natural law theorists. And we developed the view of Thomas Aquinas who is considered to be the most important natural law theorist. Then we saw problems with all these views. After discussing the nature of change we presented the view of John Locke as the first answer to the problems in Aquinas's view. We then saw how problems developed with Locke's view and presented a Kantian view as a means of solving those problems, but saw how problems developed in this approach also. Finally we presented feminist postmodernism as a solution to those problems.

One irony in this narrative is that people today use Aquinas to support various theological views in an absolutist manner, while Aquinas wrote the way he did because of new knowledge. He, in effect, was updating Catholic theology from an Augustinian Neo-Platonic view to a neo-Aristotelian view. And it is reflecting on the notion of changing knowledge and changing values that led to the development of the contemporary constructionist model of knowledge. To put this point in Aquinian terms, we are given reason with which to understand the natural order and our place in that order. But by using that reason, by continuing to ask questions, we come to the conclusion that Aquinas' conclusions are false and that any attempt to defend an absolutist position is immoral on natural law terms.

Next I argued that if we are truly rational, we should all accept the postmodern feminist view, since it is the most developed. Just as we no longer use Newtonian theory to explain the behavior of matter since the development of quantum mechanics, we should no longer use earlier theories to explain why we should behave in specific ways. Moral theory, at least on natural law theory grounds, develops in the same way as scientific theory. New theory presents an explanation of phenomena that solves problems raised by earlier explanations.

But since people are not completely rational, and since our cultures just carry on regardless of individual rationality, we see various views at work at the same time. Eventually, perhaps, the latest view will prevail. We have many unanswered questions. Perhaps when some of these questions, especially with regard to sexuality and how sexuality pervades all our social relationships, are answered, and those answers start to transform our cultures, will we consciously begin to apply our new theory in a consistent manner.

However, regardless of how the future unfolds, natural law theory is alive and well.

Appendix

RUBRIC 1

Proposal	Should I get out of bed today?	Should I stay in bed today?
Relevant data	I have two classes and I need to be there to understand the material. I have a part-time job to get to after school and I need the money since my rent is due	I am not feeling well and need the extra sleep. I can get the class notes from someone. Or I can ask to see the professor. I will sleep in but I will try to get up for the job
Plato	Since Plato's view of justice is that everyone fulfill their function in society I would be obligated to get out of bed and get to school. I should have thought ahead and not stayed out so late last night	Unless I am dying, or unless my presence would be detrimental to the running of the school or the job, I must get there

Aristotle	Similar to Plato. I must fulfill my purpose or function in society. Thus I must get out of bed. I should have partied with more moderation last night. Thus I could have partied and still met my purpose today	Unless I am dying or my presence would be detrimental I must get there
Aquinas	Similar to Aristotle. I have a purpose to fulfill. I should not have partied last night. What I did was not within my function	My function in life is to meet my obligations. I must get up
Locke	Since I entered into a contract to attend school and since the professor is the other contractee and is expecting me to be there I must be there to uphold my end of the bargain	Unless something serious is preventing me from getting up I must meet my contractual obligations
Kant	I have a duty to be in school. If I do not get there I will be acting in a manner that would break the universality of my obligation. I would also be treating school as a means to an end rather than an end in itself	Unless something serious is preventing me from getting up I must meet my moral obligations

Mill	What would be the consequences of not getting up? If they are not severe then perhaps I can stay in bed. But if I need to learn what is taught in school today and I miss it I will pay the consequences by failing the course. And I cannot afford to lose my job which can happen if I don't get to work on time.	If I can make up the notes and still understand what is going on perhaps I can afford to miss class today. But I'd still better get to work because I need the money and I cannot afford to get fired.
Kant-Mill combined	My duty is expressed in terms of motive and intent, which is how the consequences are measured. If I miss class and fail the course I can make it up. If I miss work and get fired I can plead to get rehired. In both cases since I am sincere in wanting to pass and in wanting to work the prof and the boss may go easy on me. but whom am I kidding. There are no real extenuating circumstances. I would be fooling myself if I thought so. I'd better get myself in gear and get to school	If there are real extenuating circumstances and if my prof and boss are understanding, they may accept a good excuse for missing. But since the negative consequences far outweigh any benefits I would get by staying in bed I'd better get myself in gear and get to school and to work

| Gilligan | Similar to the last view except now by looking at the context I must also see how this view affects people around me. what will my room-mate think? What will my classmates think? What will I think of myself if I screw up? Forget the big picture. Bring things down to size. When it comes down to looking at myself in the context of my friends, classmates and coworkers and my prof and boss, if I sleep in I would look like the jerk I am. Time to get up and start acting liking a responsible person | Unless I don't care about the people around me and how my actions affect them, or unless there is some serious extenuating circumstance, I'd better get up and get to school. |

Rubric 2

Proposal	Homosexuality is natural and is therefore moral behavior	Homosexuality is unnatural and is therefore immoral behavior
Relevant data	According to recent studies we know that homosexuality exists all through nature from insects to fish to mammals to apes. Thus it should be accepted as normal in humans	The primary function of sexuality is reproduction. Sexual behavior which cannot result in reproduction is considered unnatural and immoral
Plato	Homosexuality was considered natural in ancient Greece due to either environmental or congenital causes. Plato wrote on the subject in various dialogues, especially the *Symposium*	While homosexuality was considered natural it was confined to specific periods in a man's life-in teens and old age. In between men were supposed to have a family.
Aristotle	Similar to Plato.	Similar to Plato.
Aquinas	Would be opposed to the acceptance of homosexuality on the grounds of its unnaturalness. According to knowledge available to him homosexual behavior did not exist in nature and was therefore unnatural in humans	Accepts the view that homosexuality is unnatural and therefore immoral both because of the primary function of sexuality and because he believed homosexuality did not exist in nature

Locke	Does not address the issue directly but his views on moral issues reflected the protestant puritanism of his day. However one could argue that his notion of the social contract could be updated to acknowledge changes in knowledge	Would likely accept this view given his protestant puritanical outlook but could be persuaded to change given acceptable data
Kant	Does not address the issue directly but he would initially say that such behavior would not be moral. However if we just apply his imperative then one could properly justify such behavior since it would be between consenting adults who would respect each other's concerns	Would perhaps initially accept this view but if the categorical imperative is used by two consenting adults to ensure that each person's concerns are addressed and that each person treats the other as an end Kant may reject this negative position
Mill	Mill did not address this issue directly but was concerned about consequences and about human happiness. So if two consenting adults, fully aware of the consequences of their actions, agreed to participate in such behavior mill would most likely accept such behavior	Mill does not address this behavior directly and was more concerned with intellectual pleasure than with physical ones but if people were aware of the possible consequences of their actions and were prepared to accept them, then Mill would most likely reject this negative proposal

Mill-Kant combined	This view which combines the notions of motive and intent with consequences would accept this proposal as long as the consenting adults knew what they were doing, why they were doing it and were prepared to accept the possible consequences. This view would also be influenced by relevant data so the claim above would be relevant and would let this view accept the naturalness of homosexual behavior	This view would reject the negative proposal on the grounds that new knowledge has rendered this claim false and that if consenting adults knew what they were doing and why and were prepared to accept the consequences
Gilligan	Clearly from the discussion of feminist ethics sexuality or sexualities of all stripes are considered natural. Thus homosexual behavior is moral. Consenting adults still have to be concerned with motive and intention and must be prepared to accept the consequences of their actions	The feminist position would clearly reject this negative proposal since it views all sexualities as normal

RUBRIC 3

Proposal	Globalization along with free trade is good as it brings down protective trade barriers, frees capital for new investment and creates new jobs.	Globalization along with free trade is bad as it takes power away from individuals and sovereign states and gives it to international corporations who are not accountable to anyone thus taking any principle except that of short term profit out of the discussion
Relevant data	One of the reasons for the great depression of the 1930s was trade barriers. Trade opens up economies. Also for countries which produce more than they can use, and for countries which don't produce enough trade is the only way to correct these imbalances. The free the trade the better off everyone will be	Nothing wrong with free trade but the current agreement takes too much power away from local governments in puts the power in the hands of the private companies that do the trading. Sovereignty gets lost and multi national companies are not accountable to anyone. Jobs may get created in developing countries but they are not permanent. We have seen evidence of sweatshops and exploitation of workers in the name of competitiveness. Free trade is a good idea but the current approach to it is flawed.

Plato	Plato does not address this issue, of course, but even in his day there was some trade. Plato's main concern would be whether or not the trade allowed everyone to fulfill their proper function in society. If trade allowed things to function smoothly he would be in favor	Plato does not address this issue but even in his day there was some trade. If one segment of society took too much power so that the state could not function efficiently and that people could not fulfill their proper functions he would be opposed
Aristotle	Aristotle does not address this issue but may be in favor of free trade as long as the state ran smoothly and that people fulfilled their functions	Aristotle does not address this issue but would be opposed if people were unduly exploited by others. This would upset the mean of politics and would prevent each person from achieving a good life
Aquinas	Aquinas does not address this issue. Trade in itself is not a bad thing as long as things are done properly	Aquinas does not address this issue but he was concerned about exploitation. Given the Christian view of usury being a sin, and of undue exploitation, if companies were treating workers in an unfair or unchristian manner he would be opposed to free trade

Locke	Locke was a good capitalist. He would be in favor of free trade as long as the traders entered into a proper social contract that was enforceable. Indeed, one could argue that this free trade view, spearheaded by the corporate sector is the last gasp of Lockean modernism	Locke was a good capitalist. He would be in favor of free trade if it were done according to an enforceable contract. But if people were exploited and did not have proper access to legal recourse he would be opposed.
Kant	Kant did not address this issue but as long as the traders treated everyone as ends in themselves and not as means to an end his position could accept free trade	Kant did not address this issue but as long as the traders treated everyone as ends in themselves and not as means to an end his position could accept free trade
Mill	Mill did not address this issue but if the consequences both to the individuals affected by trade and those employed by the companies were treated properly and consequences to the over all society were good then mill could accept free trade	Mill did not address this issue but if companies exploited people by having the workers endure negative consequences and if contrary to what the people said the over all society did not benefit mill would be opposed to free trade

Kant-Mill combined	This view would look at whether or not the free trade actually benefited everyone without negative consequences. If this was accomplished this view could support free trade	This view would look at whether or not the free trade actually benefited everyone without negative consequences. If workers were being treated as means to an end and/or if only a select group benefited from these policies at the expense of others then this view would oppose free trade
Gilligan	This view is about community and interactive support for one another. If trade accomplishes this then this view could support it	This view is about community and interactive support. If people are harmed or exploited or if one group benefits at the expense of another group this view would be opposed to free trade

NOTES

1. Passerin d'Entrèves, Alexander. *Natural Law: An Introduction to Legal Philosophy*. New Brunswick, New Jersey: Transaction Publishers, 1994. 13

2. Cornford, Francis M. Trans. *The Republic of Plato*. New York and London: Oxford University Press, 1968. 175-176

3. Aristotle. *De Anima. The Basic Works of Aristotle*. Edited by Richard McKeon. New York: Random House, 1941. 537

4. Copleston, Frederick. *History of Philosopy*. New York: Doubleday Image, 1962. 81

5. Aristotle. *Nicomachean Ethics. The Basic Works of Aristotle*. Edited by Richard McKeon. New York: Random House, 1941. *928*

6. Aquinas, Thomas. *Summa Theologica*. London: Blackfriars, 1963. Translation led by His Eminence Michael Cardinal Browne and the most Reverend Father Aniceto Fernandez. 1a 2ae Question 94, articles 1 and 2

7. Durkheim, Emile. *Suicide*. Translated by John A. Spaulding & George Simpson. New York: The Free Press, 1979

8. Morris, Colin. *The Discovery of the Individual 1050-1200*. Medieval Academy Reprints For Teaching. Toronto: University of Toronto Press, 1987

9. Wallau, Heinrich Wilhelm. "Gutenberg", *Catholic Encyclopedia* (www.newadvent.org/cathen/07090)

10. Butterfield, Herbert. *The Origins of Modern Science 1300-1800*. New York: The Free Press, 1965. 13, 17, 16.

11. Newton, Isaac.*Newton's Philosophy of Nature*. Edited by H.S. Thayer. New York: Hafner, 1965. 26-27

12. Nikiforuk, Andrew. *The Fourth Horseman: A Short History of Plagues, Scourges, and Emerging Viruses*. Toronto: Penguin, 1996. 56

13. Kuhn, Thomas *The Structure of Scientific Revolutions*. Chicago: University of Chicago Press, Phoenix Books, 1962

14. Lakatos, Imre and Musgrave, Alan eds. *Criticism and the Growth of Knowledge*. Cambridge: Cambridge University Press, 1970 See also *Paradigms and Revolutions* edited by Gary Gutting, Notre Dame: Notre Dame University Press, 1980

15. Feyerabend, Paul. *Against Method*. London: Verso. 1975

16.Strawson. P.F. *The Bounds of Sense,* London: Methuen, 1966, 11

17. Sellars, Wilfrid. "Philosophy and the Scientific Image of Man" reprinted in *Science, Perception and Reality*, London: Routledge and Kegan Paul, 1963

18. Highwater, Jamake. *The Primal Mind,* New York: New American Library, 1981

19. Hallendy, Norman. *Inuksuit*, Vancouver, Douglas & McIntyre, 2000

20. Descartes, René. *Discourse on the Method of Rightly Conducting the Reason and Seeking Truth in the Sciences*, commonly known as *The Discourse on Method*, available in many editions

21. Wurzbach, Natascha, ed. *The Novel in Letters*, London: Routledge and Kegan Paul, 1969. My discussions are also influenced by Ian Watt's *The Rise of the Novel*, Hammondsworth: Penguin Peregrine editions, 1970.

22. Locke, John. *An Essay Concerning The True Original, Extent and End of Civil Government*, in Barker, Sir Ernest, *Social Contract*, London: Oxford University Press, 1960

23. Locke, John. *An Essay Concerning Human Understanding*, in *The Empiricists*, Garden City: Dolphin Books, Doubleday & Company, abridged by Richard Taylor, 1961.

24. Barker, Sir Ernest. "Introduction" to *Social Contract*, London: Oxford University Press, 1960, viii-ix

25. Weber, Max. *General Economic Theory*, in Collins, Randall, ed., *Four Sociological Traditions*, New York: Oxford University Press, 1994, 48

26. Randall, John Herman Jr. "What Isaac Newton Started" in Thayer H.S. ed., *Newton's Philosophy of Nature: Selections From His Writings*, New York: Hafner Publishing Company, 1953. ix-x.

27. Newton, Isaac. *Optics*, in Thayer op cit 99

28. Newton, Isaac. *Philosophiae Naturalis Principia Mathematica*, in Thayer op cit 3

29. Hume David *An Inquiry Concerning Human Understanding*, edited by L.A. Selby-Bigg, Oxford: The Clarendon Press 1967, 12

30. Russell, Bertrand. *Sceptical Essays*, London: Allen & Unwin, 1956, 18-19

31. Russell, Bertrand, *Introduction to Mathematical Philosophy*, London: Allen and Unwin, 1919

32. Strawson, P. F. "On Referring", *Mind*, vol. LIX, no. 235, July, 1950. Russell's and Strawson's papers can both be found in *Classics of Analytical Philosophy* edited by Robert R. Ammerman, New York: McGraw Hill, 1965

33. Hempel, Carl G. "The Theoretician's Dilemma: A study in the Logic of Theory Construction," reprinted in Hempel, *Aspects of Scientific Explanation and Other Essays in the Philosophy of Science*, New York: The Free Press, 1965

34. Wittgenstein, Ludwig. *Tractatus Logico-Philosophicus*, translated by D.F. Pears and B.F. McGuinness, London: Routledge and Kegan Paul, 1963. For the Vienna Circle, see especially the work of Rudolf Carnap, *The Logical Syntax of Language*, New York: Harcourt Brace and World, 1937. See also A.J. Ayer. *Language Truth and Logic,* New York: Dover Publications, 1952

35. Pavlov, Ivan. *Conditioned Reflexes*, London: Oxford University Press, 1927. For a brief summary of this experiment see "It's Not Just About Salivating Dogs" in *Forty Studies That Changed Psychology*, ed by Roger R. Hock, Englewood

Cliffs: Prentice Hall, 1992

36. Watson, John B. *Psychology From the Standpoint of a Behaviourist*, Philadelphia: J.P. Lippincott, 1919

37. Skinner, B.F. *Science and Human Behaviour*, New York: MacMillan, 1953

38. Hume, David. *An Enquiry Concerning the Principles of Morals,* in Steven M. Cahn and Peter Markie eds. *ETHICS: History, Theory andContemporary Issues* New York: Oxford University Press 1998, 258

39. Bentham, Jeremy. *An Introduction to the Principles of Morals and Legislation*, Cahn 319

40. Mill, John Stuart. *Utilitarianism* Cahn 347

41. Narveson, Jan. *Morality and Utility,* Baltimore: Johns Hopkins Press, 1967

42. Hare, R.M. *The Language of Morals*, Oxford: Oxford University Press, 1964 and *Freedom and Reason*, Oxford: Oxford University Press, 1965

43. Eddington, Arthur. *Nature of the Physical World*, Cambridge: Cambridge University Press, 1928

44. De Santillana, Giorgio. *The Crime of Galileo,* Chicago: University of Chicago Press: Phoenix Books, 1959; Pietro Redondi, *Galileo Heretic,* translated by Raymond Rosenthal, Princeton: Princeton University Press, 1983 and Dava Sobel, *Galileo's Daughter,* Harmondsworth: Viking, 1999

45. Popper, Karl. "Three Views of Human Knowledge" in *Conjectures and Refutations*, London: Routledge and Kegan Paul, 1965 and Wilfrid Sellars "Scientific Realism or Irenic Instrumentalism" in *Philosophical Perspectives*, Springfield: Charles C. Thomas, 1967

46. Skinner, B.F. *Walden Two*, Saddle River: Prentice Hall, 1976

47. Sellars, Wilfrid. "Empiricism and the Philosophy of Mind", reprinted in *Science, Perception and Reality*, London: Routledge and Kegan Paul, 1963

48. Chomsky, Noam. "Review of *Verbal Behavior*" in *Language*, Volume 35, 1959, 26-58

49. Skinner, B.F. *Verbal Behaviour*, Acton: Copley Publishing Group, 1991

50. Smith, Adam. *The Theory of Moral Sentiments,* in Heilbroner, Robert L. ed. *The Essential Adam Smith,* New York: W.W. Norton & Company, *1987, 66*

51. Smith, Adam. *The Wealth of Nations* in Heilbroner, 169

52. Kant, Immanuel. *Prolegomena to Any Future Metaphysics*, translated by Lewis White Beck, Indianapolis: Bobbs-Merrill, 1950, 8

53. Kant, Immanuel. *Critique of Pure Reason*, translated by Norman Kemp Smith, Toronto: MacMillan, 1965, B20

54. Kant, Immanuel. *Critique of Practical Reason* , translated and edited by Mary Gregor, Cambridge, Cambridge University Press 1997 5:45

55. Kant, Immanuel, *Critique of Judgment,* translated by James Creed Meredith, Oxford: Oxford University Press, 1969

56. Kant, Immanuel. *Foundations of the Metaphysics of Morals*, translated by Lewis White Beck, Indianapolis: Bobbs-Merrill Co, 1959, 5

57. Koenig, Bernie. "Response to Wilson" *Dialogue*, XXVII, 1988 357-360

58. Darwin, Charles. *The Origin of Species*, New York: Mentor, 1958

59. Haeckel, Ernst, (imola.wcc.Hawaii.edu/kruppBIOL101)

60. Mayr, Ernst. *What Evolution Is.* New York: Basic Books, 2001, 30

61. Margulis, Lynn. *Symbiosis in Cell Evolution*, New York: W H. Freeman 1981

62. Hardy, Sir Alister. "Was Man More Aquatic in the Past?" *The New Scientist*, 17 March, 1960

63. Morgan Elaine. *The Descent of Woman,* New York: Stein and Day, 1971

64. Gay, Peter *Freud: A Life for our Time.* New York: W.W. Norton, 1988

65. For a philosophical discussion see "Unconscious Belief" by Arthur Collins, *Journal of Philosophy*, LXVI, 20, 1969

66. Breuer, Josef and Freud, Sigmund. *Studies in Hysteria*, translated by Alix and James Strachey, London: Hogarth Press, 1956, 101

67. Freud, Sigmund. "A Note on the Unconscious", 1912; "The Unconscious" 1915, both translated by Cecil M. Baines and published in *General Psychological Theory*, edited by Philip Rieff, New York: Collier Books, 1963, and *The Ego and the Id*, translated by Joan Riviere, revised and edited by James Strachey, London: The Hogarth Press, 1962A

68. Freud, Sigmund. *A General Introduction to Psychoanalysis*, translated by Joan Riviere, New York: Washington Square Press, 1960, 312

69. Freud, Sigmund. "The Passing of the Oedipus Complex", 1924 and "Female Sexuality", 1931, reprinted in *Sexuality and the Psychology of Love*, edited by Philip Rieff, New York: Collier Books, 1963, 180

70. Freud, Sigmund. *Totem and Taboo*, translated by James Strachey, New York: W.W. Norton, 1962B

71. Freud, Sigmund. *Civilization and its Discontents*, translated by Joan Riviere, revised by James Strachey, London: The Hogarth Press, 1969

72. Freud, Sigmund. *Beyond the Pleasure Principle*, translated by James Strachey, New York: Bantam, 1959

73. Sherwood, Michael. *The Logic of Explanation in Psychoanalysis,* New York: Academic Press, 1969

74. Jung, Carl. *Memories, Dreams and Reflections*, translated by Richard and Clara Winston New York: Vintage, 1965 and *Analytical Psychology: Its Theory and Practice*, London: Ark, 1968

75. Horney, Karen. *New Ways in Psychoanalysis*, New York: W.W. Norton, 1966

76. Fox, Robin. *The Red Lamp of Incest*, New York: E.P. Dutton, 1980, ix

77. Fox, Robin. *Encounter With Anthropology*, New York: Dell Laurel editions, 1975, 276

78. Harris, Marvin. *Cannibals and Kings: The Origins of Culture,* New York: Random House, 1977

79. Montagu, Ashley. *The Nature of Human Aggression,* New York: Oxford University Press, 1976. Montagu's work was a response to those who argued that aggression and warlike behavior are parts of human nature. See Konrad Lorenz, *On Aggression,* New York: Harcourt Brace and World, 1963. See also Robert Ardrey, *African Genesis,* New York: Atheneum, 1961, *The Social Contract: A Personal Inquiry into the Evolutionary Source of Order and Disorder,* New York: Atheneum, 1970 and *The Territorial Imperative: A Personal Inquiry into the Animal Origins of Property and Nations,* New York: Atheneum, 1966.

80. Draper, Patricia. "!Kung Women: Contrasts in Sexual Egalitarianism in Foraging and Sedentary Contexts" in *Toward an Anthropology of Women,* edited by Rayna R. Reiter, New York: Monthly Review Press, 1975. This is the tribe portrayed in the film *The Gods Must be Crazy.*

81. Popper, Sir Karl. *The Logic of Scientific Discovery,* translated by the author with the help of Dr. Julius Freed and Lan Freed, New York: Harper and Row, 1965. For a later discussion of the topic see Popper's *Objective Knowledge,* Oxford: Oxford University Press, 1972 and for later developments of this issue see Wilfrid Sellars, op cit 1963 and Paul Feyerabend, op cit 1978

82. Rudner, Richard. "The Scientist Qua Scientist makes Value Judgments", *Philosophy of Science,* 20, 1953. For the argument that these value judgments are pragmatic in nature see James Leach, "Explanation and Value Neutrality", *The British Journal for the Philosophy of Science,* 19, 1968.

83. Sellars, Wilfrid. *Science and Metaphysics: Variations on Kantian Themes,* London: Routledge and Kegan Paul, 1968

84. Popper, Sir Karl. *Conjectures and Refutations,* London: Routledge and Kegan Paul, 1965

85. Wittgenstein, Ludwig. *Philosophical Investigations,* translated by G.E.M. Anscombe, Oxford: Blackwell, 1963

86. Chomsky, Noam. *Syntactic Structures,* The Hague: Mouton, 1957, *Cartesian Linguistics,* New York: Harper and Row, 1966, and his review of Skinner's *Verbal Behaviour.*

87. Piaget, Jean *The Language and Thought of the Child,* translated by Marjorie and Ruth Gabain, London: Routledge and Kegan Paul, 1959

88. For an empiricist approach to the issue see Renford Bambrough, *Moral Scepticism and Moral Knowledge,* London: Routledge and Kegan Paul, 1979.

89. Waddington, C. H. *The Ethical Animal,* London: George Allen and Unwin, 1960 25

90. Dennett, Daniel. *Darwin's Dangerous Idea: Evolution and the Meaning of Life,* New York: Touchstone, 1995, 342

91. Wright, Robert. *The Moral Animal,* New York, Vintage, 1994, 102

92. Rieff, Philip. *Freud: The Mind of the Moralist*, London: Victor Gollancz, 1960, x

93. Jacobs, Jane. *The Death and Life of Great American Cities.* New York: Random House, 1961, *The Economy of Cities*, New York: Random House, 1969 and *Cities and the Wealth of Nations*, New York: Random House, 1984

94. Popper, Sir Karl. *The Open Society and its Enemies*, London: Routledge and Kegan Paul, 1945

95. De Lorean, John Z and Wright, J. Patrick. *On a Clear Day You Can See General Motors: John Z. De Lorean's Look Inside the Automotive Giant*, Grosse Pointe, Michigan: Wright Enterprises, 1979, 56

96. Galbraith, John Kenneth. *The Culture of Contentment*, Boston: Houghton Mifflin, 1992

97. Winnicott, D. W. *Psychoanalytic Explorations*, edited by Clare Winnicott, Ray Shepherd and Madeleine Davis, Cambridge: Harvard University Press, 1992

98. Friedan, Betty. *The Feminine Mystique*, New York: Dell, 1964. In this book the individualist psychology of Maslow was seen as the model that women needed to break out of their old roles. The work of Maslow that is cited by Friedan is *Motivation and Personality*, Harper: New York, 1954. See also Maslow's *Toward a Psychology of Being*, New York: Van Nostrand, 1968, and Carl Rogers, *On Becoming a Person*, Boston: Houghton Mifflin, 1961.

99. Lerner, Michael. *Surplus Powerlessness*, Oakland: The Institute for Labor and Mental Health, 1986

100. Grimshaw, Jean. *Philosophy and Feminist Thinking*, Minneapolis: University of Minnesota Press, 1986

101. Chodorow, Nancy. *The Reproduction of Mothering: Psychoanalysis and the Sociology of Gender*, Berkeley: University of California Press, 1978 4

102. Lacqueur, Thomas. *Making Sex: Body and Gender From the Greeks to Freud*, Cambridge: Harvard University Press, 1990

103. Zita, Jaquelyn N. "Male Lesbians and the Postmodernist Body", *Hypatia*: vol 7, no. 4 Fall 1992

104. Bornstein, Kate. *Gender Outlaw: On Men, Women, and the Rest of Us*, New York: Vintage, 1995 191

105. Chodorow, Nancy. *Feminities, Masculinities, Sexualities: Freud and Beyond*, Lexington: University of Kentucky Press, 1994, 32

106. Bagemihl, Bruce. *Biological Exuberance: Animal Homosexuality and Natural Diversity.* New York: St. Martin's Press, 1999, 20

107. Collins, Patricia Hill. *Black Feminist Thought: Knowledge, Consciousness, and the Politics of Empowerment*, New York: Routledge, 1991, and bell hooks, *Talking Back: thinking feminist: thinking black*, Toronto: Between the Lines, 1989

108. Ireland, Mardy S. *Reconceiving Women: Separating Motherhood from Female Identity*, New York: The Guilford Press, 1993

109. Lacan, Jacques. *The Four Fundamental Concepts of Psychoanalysis,* translated by Alan Sheridan, New York: W.W. Norton & Company, 1981. Ireland also suggests E.R. Ragland-Sullivan, *Jaques Lacan and the Philosophy of Psychoanalysis,* Chicago:University of Illinois Press, 1987

110. Kaschak, Ellyn. *Engendered Lives: A New Psychology of Women's Experience.* New York: Basic Books, 1992, 28

111. Pagels, Elaine. *Adam, Eve And The Serpent, New York,* Random House: New York, 1988

112. Payer, Lynn. *Medicine and Culture,* London: Penguin, 1988, 170

113. Ehrenreich, Barbara and English, Deirdre. *Witches, Midwives and Nurses,* and *Complaints and Disorders: The Sexual Politics of Sickness,* New York: The Feminist Press, 1973, provide an interesting history of how the medical profession has treated women.

114. Haraway, Donna J. "A Cyborg Manifesto: Science, Technology and Socialist-Feminism in the Late Twentieth Century," in *Simians, Cyborgs, and Women: The Reinvention of Nature,* New York: Routledge, 1991

115. Grahn, Judy. *Blood, Bread, and Roses: How Menstruation Created the World,* Boston: Beacon Press, 1993

116. Flax, Jane. *Thinking Fragments: Psychoanalysis, Feminism & Postmodernism in the Contemporary West,* Berkeley: University of California Press, 1990

117. Ehrenreich, Barbara. *The Hearts of Men: American Dreams and the Flight From Commitment,* New York: Doubleday Anchor Press, 1983

118. Jaynes, Julian. *The Origin of Consciousness in the Breakdown of the Bicameral Mind,* Toronto: University of Toronto Press, 1976

119. Piaget, Jean. *The Moral Judgment of the Child,* New York: Simon & Schuster, February 1965

120. Kohlberg, Lawrence. "How Moral are You?" in Hock, Roger R. *Forty Studies that Changed Psychology,* Englewood Cliffs: Prentice Hall, 1992 196

121. Gilligan, Carol. *In a Different Voice: Psychological Theory and Women's Development,* Cambridge: Harvard University Press, 1982, 2

122. Belenky, Mary Field, Clinchy, Blythe McVicker, Goldberger, Nancy Rule and Tarule, Jill Mattuck. *Women's Ways of Knowing: The Development of Self, Voice and Mind,* New York: Basic Books, 1986

123. Meyers, Diana Tietjens. *Subjection & Subjectivity: Psychoanalytic Feminism and Moral Philosophy,* New York: Routledge, 1994

124. Greenspan, Patricia S. *Emotions and Reasons,* New York: Routledge, 1993. For a discussion of the components of feelings or emotions and how our perceptions of situations lead to actions see Justin Oakley, *Morality and the Emotions,* New York: Routledge, 1993

125. Harding, Sandra. *The Science Question in Feminism,* Ithaca: Cornell University Press, 1986, 9

126. Nye, Andrea. *Words of Power,* New York: Routledge, 1990, 5

127. Ellis, Richard. *Aquagenesis: The Origin and Evolution of Life in the Sea,* New York: Viking Press, 2001

128. Haraway, Donna. *Primate Visions: Gender, Race, and Nature in the World of Modern Science*, New York: Routledge, 1989, 1

129. Haraway, Donna. in Mayberry, Maralee, Subramaniam, Banu, & Weasel, Lisa. *Feminist Science Studies: A New Generation*, New York: Routledge, 2001 81 All other references to this work will be to Weasel et al.

130. Passmore, *Man's Responsibility for Nature: Ecological Problems and Western Traditions*, London: Macmillan, 1974, 7

131. Litt, Jacquelyn S. *Medicalized Motherhood: Perspectives from the Lives of African-American and Jewish Women,* New Brunswick, NJ, University Press, 2000

132. Lerner, Gerda. *The Creation of Patriarchy,* Oxford: Oxford University Press, 1987. See also Merlin Stone, *When God Was a Woman*, Harcourt, 1979, and various works on women and religion by Barbara Walker.

133. This discussion is based on Michael Ignatieff, *The Rights Revolution*, Toronto: Anansi 2000

BIBLIOGRAPHY

Aquinas, Thomas. *Summa Theologica.* London: Blackfriars, 1963. Translation led by His Eminence Michael Cardinal Browne and the most Reverend Father Anticeto Fernandez.
Ardrey, Robert. *The Territorial Imperative: A Personal Inquiry into the Animal Origins of Property and Nations,* New York: Atheneum, 1966
Ardrey, Robert. *African Genesis,* New York: Atheneum, 1961
Ardrey, Robert. *The Social Contract: A Personal Inquiry into the Evolutionary Source of Order and Disorder,* New York: Atheneum, 1970
Aristotle. *The Basic Works of Aristotle.* Edited by Richard McKeon. New York: Random House, 1941.
Bagemihl, Bruce. *Biological Exuberance: Animal Homosexuality and Natural Diversity.* New York: St. Martin's Press, 1999
Bambrough, Renford. *Moral Scepticism and Moral Knowledge,* London: Routledge and Kegan Paul, 1979.
Belenky, Mary Field, Clinchy, Blythe McVicker, Goldberger, Nancy Rule and Tarule, Jill Mattuck. *Women's Ways of Knowing: The Development of Self, Voice and Mind,* New York: Basic Books, 1986
Bentham, Jeremy. *An Introduction to the Principles of Morals and Legislation*
Bornstein, Kate. *Gender Outlaw: On Men, Women, and the Rest of Us,* New York: Vintage, 1995
Breuer, Josef and Freud, Sigmund. *Studies in Hysteria,* translated by Alix and James Strachey, London: Hogarth Press, 1956
Butterfield, Herbert. *The Origins of Modern Science 1300-1800.* New York: The Free Press, 1965.
Cahn, Steven M. and Markie, Peter. eds. *ETHICS: History, Theory and Contemporary Issues* New York: Oxford University Press 1998
Carnap, Rudolf. *The Logical Syntax of Language,* New York: Harcourt Brace and World, 1937 Ayer, A.J. *Language Truth and Logic,* New York: Dover Publications, 1952
Chodorow, Nancy. *Feminities, Masculinities, Sexualities: Freud and Beyond,* Lexington: University of Kentucky Press, 1994
Chodorow, Nancy . *The Reproduction of Mothering: Psychoanalysis and the Sociology of Gender,* Berkeley: University of California Press, 1978
Chomsky, Noam. *Cartesian Linguistics,* New York: Harper and Row, 1966
Chomsky, Noam. "Review of *Verbal Behavior*" in *Language,* Volume 35, 1959
Chomsky, Noam. *Syntactic Structures,* The Hague: Mouton, 1957
Collins, Arthur. "Unconscious Belief" in *Journal of Philosophy,* LXVI, 20, 1969
Collins, Patricia Hill. *Black Feminist Thought: Knowledge, Consciousness, and the Politics of Empowerment,* New York: Routledge, 1991
Copleston, Frederick. *History of Philosophy.* New York: Doubleday Image, 1962.
Darwin, Charles. *The Origin of Species,* New York: Mentor, 1958
De Lorean, John Z and Wright, J. Patrick. *On a Clear Day You Can See General Motors: John Z. De Lorean's Look Inside the Automotive Giant,* Grosse Pointe, Michigan: Wright Enterprises, 1979
De Santillana, Giorgio. *The Crime of Galileo,* Chicago: University of Chicago

Press: Phoenix Books, 1959
Dennett, Daniel. *Darwin's Dangerous Idea: Evolution and the Meaning of Life*, New York: Touchstone, 1995
Descartes, René. *Discourse on the Method of Rightly Conducting the Reason and Seeking Truth in the Sciences*, London: Penguin, 2000
Draper, Patricia. "!Kung Women: Contrasts in Sexual Egalitarianism in Foraging and Sedentary Contexts" in *Toward an Anthropology of Women*, edited by Rayna R. Reiter, New York: Monthly Review Press, 1975
Durkheim, Emile. *Suicide*. Translated by John A. Spaulding & George Simpson. New York: The Free Press, 1979
Eddington, Arthur. *Nature of the Physical World*, Cambridge: Cambridge University Press, 1928
Ehrenreich, Barbara and English, Deirdre. *Witches, Midwives and Nurses*, New York: The Feminist Press, 1973
Ehrenreich, Barbara and English, Deirdre. *Complaints and Disorders: The Sexual Politics of Sickness*, New York: The Feminist Press, 1973
Ehrenreich, Barbara. *The Hearts of Men: American Dreams and the Flight From Commitment*, New York: Doubleday Anchor Press, 1983
Ellis, Richard. *Aquagenesis: The Origin and Evolution of Life in the Sea*, New York: Viking Press, 2001
Feyerabend Paul. *Against Method*, London: Verso, 1975
Flax, Jane. *Thinking Fragments: Psychoanalysis, Feminism & Postmodernism in the Contemporary West*, Berkeley: University of California Press, 1990
Fox, Robin. *Encounter With Anthropology*, New York: Dell Laurel editions, 1975
Fox, Robin. *The Red Lamp of Incest*, New York: E.P. Dutton, 1980
Freud, Sigmund. "Female Sexuality", 1931, in *Sexuality and the Psychology of Love*, edited by Philip Reiff, New York: Collier Books, 1963
Freud, Sigmund. "The Passing of the Oedipus Complex", 1924, in *Sexuality and the Psychology of Love*, edited by Philip Reiff, New York: Collier Books, 1963
Freud, Sigmund. *Civilization and its Discontents*, translated by Joan Riviere, revised by James Strachey, London: The Hogarth Press, 1969
Freud, Sigmund. *The Ego and the Id*, translated by Joan Riviere, revised and edited by James Strachey, London: The Hogarth Press, 1962
Freud, Sigmund. "The Unconscious", 1915, in *General Psychological Theory*, edited by Philip Rieff, New York: Collier Books, 1963
Freud, Sigmund. "A Note on the Unconscious", 1912, translated by Cecil Baines, translated by Cecil M. Baines, in *General Psychological Theory*, edited by Philip Rieff, New York: Collier Books, 1963
Freud, Sigmund. *A General Introduction to Psychoanalysis*, translated by Joan Riviere, New York: Washington Square Press, 1960
Freud, Sigmund. *Totem and Taboo*, translated by James Strachey, New York: W.W. Norton, 1962
Freud, Sigmund. *Beyond the Pleasure Principle*, translated by James Strachey, New York: Bantam, 1959
Friedan, Betty. *The Feminine Mystique*, New York: Dell, 1964.

Galbraith, John Kenneth. *The Culture of Contentment,* Boston: Houghton Mifflin, 1992
Gay, Peter *Freud: A Life for our Time.* New York: W.W. Norton, 1988
Gilligan, Carol. *In a Different Voice: Psychological Theory and Women's Development*, Cambridge: Harvard University Press, 1982
Grahn, Judy. *Blood, Bread, and Roses: How Menstruation Created the World,* Boston: Beacon Press, 1993
Greenspan, Patricia S. *Emotions and Reasons,* New York: Routledge, 1993.
Grimshaw, Jean. *Philosophy and Feminist Thinking,* Minneapolis: University of Minnesota Press, 1986
Haeckel, Ernst, (imola.wcc.Hawaii.edu/kruppBIOL101)
Hallendy, Norman. *Inuksuit*, Vancouver, Douglas & McIntyre, 2000
Haraway, Donna. *Primate Visions: Gender, Race, and Nature in the World of Modern Science*, New York: Routledge, 1989
Haraway, Donna J. *Simians, Cyborgs, and Women: The Reinvention of Nature,* New York: Routledge, 1991
Harding, Sandra. *The Science Question in Feminism,* Ithaca: Cornell University Press, 1986
Hardy, Sir Alister. "Was Man More Aquatic in the Past?" *The New Scientist*, 17 March, 1960
Hare, R.M. *The Language of Morals*, Oxford: Oxford University Press, 1964
Hare, R.M. *Freedom and Reason*, Oxford: Oxford University Press, 1965
Harris, Marvin. *Cannibals and Kings: The Origins of Culture,* New York: Random House, 1977
Hempel, Carl G. *Aspects of Scientific Explanation and Other Essays in the Philosophy of Science*, New York: The Free Press, 1965
Highwater, Jamake .*The Primal Mind,* New York: New American Library, 1981
Hock, Rroger R. ed. *Forty Studies That Changed Psychology*, Englewood Cliffs: Prentice Hall, 1992
hooks, bell. *Talking Back: thinking feminist: thinking black,* Toronto: Between the Lines, 1989
Horney, Karen. *New Ways in Psychoanalysis*, New York: W.W. Norton, 1966
Hume David *An Inquiry Concerning Human Understanding*, edited by L.A. Selby-Bigg, Oxford: The Clarendon Press 1967
Hume, David. *An Enquiry Concerning the Principles of Morals*
Ignatieff, Michael. *The Rights Revolution,* Toronto: Anansi 2000
Ireland, Mardy S. *Reconceiving Women: Separating Motherhood from Female Identity,* New York: The Guilford Press, 1993
Jacobs, Jane. *Cities and the Wealth of Nations*, New York: Random House, 1984
Jacobs, Jane. *The Economy of Cities*, New York: Random House, 1969
Jacobs, Jane. *The Death and Life of Great American Cities.* New York: Random House, 1961
Jaynes, Julian. *The Origin of Consciousness in the Breakdown of the Bicameral Mind,* Toronto: University of Toronto Press, 1976
Jung, Carl. *Memories, Dreams and Reflections*, translated by Richard and Clara

Winston New York: Vintage, 1965
Jung, Carl. *Analytical Psychology: Its Theory and Practice*, London: Ark, 1968
Kant, Immanuel. *Critique of Pure Reason*, translated by Norman Kemp Smith, Toronto: MacMillan, 1965
Kant, Immanuel. *Critique of Practical Reason*, translated and edited by Mary Gregor, Cambridge, Cambridge University Press 1997
Kant, Immanuel. *Foundations of the Metaphysics of Morals*, translated by Lewis White Beck, Indianapolis: Bobbs-Merrill Co, 1959
Kant, Immanuel, *Critique of Judgment*, translated by James Creed Meredith, Oxford: Oxford University Press, 1969
Kant, Immanuel. *Prolegomena to Any Future Metaphysics*, translated by Lewis White Beck, Indianapolis: Bobbs-Merrill, 1950
Kaschak, Ellyn. *Engendered Lives: A New Psychology of Women's Experience.* New York: Basic Books, 1992
Koenig, Bernie. "Response to Wilson" *Dialogue*, XXVII, 1988 357-360
Kohlberg, Lawrence. "How Moral are You?" in Hock, Roger R. *Forty Studies that Changed Psychology,* Englewood Cliffs: Prentice Hall, 1992
Kuhn, Thomas *The Structure of Scientific Revolutions*. Chicago: University of Chicago Press, Phoenix Books, 1962
Lacan, Jacques. *The Four Fundamental Concepts of Psychoanalysis*, translated by Alan Sheridan, New York: W.W. Norton & Company, 1981
Lacqueur, Thomas. *Making Sex: Body and Gender From the Greeks to Freud*, Cambridge: Harvard University Press, 1990
Lakatos, Imre and Musgrave, Alan eds. *Criticism and the Growth of Knowledge.* Cambridge: Cambridge University Press, 1970
Leach, James. "Explanation and Value Neutrality", *The British Journal for the Philosophy of Science,* 19, 1968
Lerner, Gerda. *The Creation of Patriarchy,* Oxford: Oxford University Press, 1987
Lerner, Michael. *Surplus Powerlessness,* Oakland: The Institute for Labor and Mental Health, 1986
Litt, Jacquelyn S. *Medicalized Motherhood: Perspectives from the Lives of African-American and Jewish Women,* New Brunswick, NJ, University Press, 2000
Locke, John. *An Essay Concerning The True Original, Extent and End of Civil Government*, in Barker, Sir Ernest, *Social Contract,* London: Oxford University Press, 1960
Locke, John. *An Essay Concerning Human Understanding*, in *The Empiricists*, Garden City: Dolphin Books, Doubleday & Company, abridged by Richard Taylor, 1961
Lorenz, Konrad. *On Aggression,* New York: Harcourt Brace and World, 1963
Margulis, Lynn. *Symbiosis in Cell Evolution*, New York: W H. Freeman 1981
Mayberry, Maralee, Subramaniam, Banu, & Weasel, Lisa. *Feminist Science Studies: A New Generation*, New York: Routledge, 2001
Mayr, Ernst. *What Evolution Is*. New York: Basic Books, 2001
Meyers, Diana Tietjens. *Subjection & Subjectivity: Psychoanalytic Feminism and*

Moral Philosophy, New York: Routledge, 1994
Mill, John Stuart. *Utilitarianism*
Montagu, Ashley. *The Nature of Human Aggression,* New York: Oxford University Press, 197
Morgan Elaine. *The Descent of Woman,* New York: Stein and Day, 1971
Morris, Colin. *The Discovery of the Individual 1050-1200.* Medieval Academy Reprints For Teaching. Toronto: University of Toronto Press, 1987
Narveson, Jan. *Morality and Utility,* Baltimore: Johns Hopkins Press, 1967
Newton, Isaac. *.Newton's Philosophy of Nature.* Edited by H.S. Thayer. New York: Hafner, 1965.
Nikiforuk, Andrew. *The Fourth Horseman: A Short History of Plagues, Scourges, and Emerging Viruses.* Toronto: Penguin, 1996
Nye, Andrea. *Words of Power,* New York: Routledge, 1990
Oakley, Justin. *Morality and the Emotions,* New York: Routledge, 1993
Pagels, Elaine. *Adam, Eve And The Serpent, New York,* Random House: New York, 1988
Passerin d'Entrèves, Alexander. *Natural Law: An Introduction to Legal Philosophy.* New Brunswick, New Jersey: Transaction Publishers, 1994
Passmore, *Man's Responsibility for Nature: Ecological Problems and Western Traditions*, London: Macmillan, 1974
Pavlov, Ivan. *Conditioned Reflexes,* London: Oxford University Press, 1927
Payer, Lynn. *Medicine and Culture,* London: Penguin, 1988
Piaget, Jean. *The Moral Judgment of the Child*, New York: Simon & Schuster, February 1965
Piaget, Jean *The Language and Thought of the Child,* translated by Marjorie and Ruth Gabain, London: Routledge and Kegan Paul, 1959
Plato. *The Republic,* translated by Francis M. Cornford. New York and London: Oxford University Press, 1968.
Popper, Sir Karl. *Objective Knowledge,* Oxford: Oxford University Press, 1972
Popper, Sir Karl. *Conjectures and Refutations*, London: Routledge and Kegan Paul, 1965
Popper, Sir Karl. *The Open Society and its Enemies,* London: Routledge and Kegan Paul, 1945
Popper, Sir Karl. *The Logic of Scientific Discovery*, translated by the author with the help of Dr. Julius Freed and Lan Freed, New York: Harper and Row, 1965.
Popper, Karl. *Conjectures and Refutations*, London: Routledge and Kegan Paul, 1965
Redondi, Pietro. *Galileo Heretic,* translated by Raymond Rosenthal, Princeton: Princeton University Press, 1983
Rieff, Philip. *Freud: The Mind of the Moralist*, London: Victor Gollancz, 1960
Rudner, Richard. "The Scientist Qua Scientist makes Value Judgments", *Philosophy of Science*, 20, 1953
Russell, Bertrand, *Introduction to Mathematical Philosophy,* London: Allen and Unwin, 1919
Russell, Bertrand. *Sceptical Essays*, London: Allen & Unwin, 1956

Sellars, Wilfrid, *Philosophical Perspectives*, Springfield: Charles C. Thomas, 1967
Sellars, Wilfrid. *Science and Metaphysics: Variations on Kantian Themes*, London: Routledge and Kegan Paul, 1968
Sellars, Wilfrid. *Science, Perception and Reality*, London: Routledge and Kegan Paul, 1963
Sherwood, Michael. *The Logic of Explanation in Psychoanalysis*, New York: Academic Press, 1969
Skinner, B.F. *Walden Two*, Saddle River: Prentice Hall, 1976
Skinner, B.F. *Verbal Behaviour*, Acton: Copley Publishing Group, 1991
Skinner, B.F. *Science and Human Behaviour*, New York: MacMillan, 1953
Smith, Adam. *The Theory of Moral Sentiments*, in Heilbroner, Robert L. ed. *The Essential Adam Smith*, New York: W.W. Norton & Company, *1987*
Smith, Adam. *The Wealth of Nations* in Heilbroner
Sobel, Dava. *Galileo's Daughter*, Harmondsworth: Viking, 1999
Stone, Merlin. *When God Was a Woman*, New York: Harcourt, 1979
Strawson, P. F. *Mind*, vol. LIX, no. 235, July, 1950
Strawson. P.F. *The Bounds of Sense*, London: Methuen, 1966
Waddington, C. H. *The Ethical Animal*, London: George Allen and Unwin, 1960
Wallau, Heinrich Wilhelm. "Gutenberg", *Catholic Encyclopedia* (www.newadvent.org/cathen/07090)
Watson, John B. *Psychology From the Standpoint of a Behaviourist*, Philadelphia: J.P. Lippincott, 1919
Watt, Ian. *The Rise of the Novel*, Hammondsworth: Penguin Peregrine editions, 1970
Weber, Max. *General Economic Theory*, in Collins, Randall, ed., *Four Sociological Traditions*, New York: Oxford University Press, 1994
Winnicott, D. W. *Psychoanalytic Explorations*, edited by Clare Winnicott, Ray Shepherd and Madeleine Davis, Cambridge: Harvard University Press, 1992
Wittgenstein, Ludwig. *Tractatus Logico-Philosophicus*, translated by D.F. Pears and B.F. McGuinness, London: Routledge and Kegan Paul, 1963
Wittgenstein, Ludwig. *Philosophical Investigations*, translated by G.E.M. Anscombe, Oxford: Blackwell, 1963
Wright, Robert. *The Moral Animal*, New York, Vintage, 1994
Wurzbach, Natascha, ed. *The Novel in Letters*, London: Routledge and Kegan Paul, 1969
Zita, Jaquelyn N. "Male Lesbians and the Postmodernist Body", *Hypatia*: vol 7, no. 4 Fall 1992

Index

Abelard, Peter 13, 272-273
Aeschylus 271
Aquinas, St. Thomas 5-9, 11, 17, 21, 48, 91, 213, 299, 302, 304, 312
Akeley, Carl 283
Arendt, Hannah, i
Aristotle, 3-4
Augustine, 5-6
Austen, Jane, 116
Bagemihl, Bruce, 213-214
behaviorism, 83, 102-106, 122-123, 256, 288
Belenky, Mary Field, 247-252, 255
Bell, Alexander Graham, 283
Bentham, Jeremy, 86
Bernard of Cluny, 13
Bernheim, H., 123
Binkley, Robert, ii
Bornstein, Kate, 211, 256
Bradley, Marion Zimmer, 305
Brentano, Franz, 121
Breuer, Josef, 123
Bridgeman, Percy, 101
Brown, Harvey, v
Butterfield, Herbert, 15
Butler, Octavia E., 241
capitalism, 19, 54-55, 58, 65, 109, 116, 170, 175, 187, 209, 293, 308
Chance, M.R, 138
Charcot, 123
Chodorow, Nancy, ii, 195-216, 221-224, 228, 230, 232-236, 238, 243, 245, 250, 266, 309
Chomsky, Noam, 105-106, 163
Clarke, Kenny, 225
Collins, Patricia Hill, 21
Copernicus, Nikolas, 11, 15-16, 24, 34-35, 102, 26
Copleston, Frederick, 4
Cornford, Francis M., 3
cultural materialism, 44
Dali, Salvador, 225
Damiani, Peter, 13
Darwin, Charles, 70, 117-121, 134, 137, 141, 159, 171, 173, 176, 278,

Dawkins, Richard, 173
de Laclos, Choderlos, 116
de Lorean, John Z., 189
de Lorris, Guillaume, 13
de Meun, Jean, 13
Defoe, Daniel, 65
Dennett, Daniel, 173, 281
Descartes, Rene, 19, 51-52, 61, 104, 106, 111, 161, 163-164, 266, 306
distributive singular term, 153, 298
Dobzhansky, Theodosius, 285
Donne, John, 298
Durkheim, Emile, 10
Eddington, Arthur, 101
Ehrenreich, Barbara, 234
Einstein, Albert, 301
Ellis, Richard, 282
emotivism, 96
fact-value distinction, 81-82
falsifiability, 29, 32, 150
Feyerabend, Paul, 31-39, 41, 46
Flax, Jane, 228-233, 236, 255
Fossey, Dian, 284
Fox, Robin, 134-141, 146-147, 175, 178
Frege, Gottlob, 274-275
Freud, Sigmund, 20, 117, 120-141, 144-147, 159-161, 168-169, 171, 173-178, 181, 192-193, 195-196, 198-201, 203, 205, 209, 212, 216-219, 228-232, 234, 236, 245, 255
Friedan, Betty, 19
Fuss, Diana, 226
Galbraith, John Kenneth, 190
Galilei, Galileo, 11, 16, 24, 27, 33-36, 39, 44, 102
Gay, Peter, 121
Gilbert, Gustave, i
Gillespie, Dizzy, 225
Gilligan, Carol, 237-247, 250, 255-256, 260, 266, 291
Golding, William, 133
Goodall, Jane, 284
Goody, Jack, 136

Grahn, Judy, 227
Greenspan, Patricia S., 257
Grimshaw, Jean, 195
Grosvenor, Gilbert, 284
Grosvenor, Meville Bell, 284
Haeckel, Ernst, 119
Hallendy, Norman, 45
Harding, Sandra, 259-268, 282
Hardy, Sir Alister, 120, 276
Haraway, Donna J., 227, 282-287
Hare, R.M., 93-95, 115
Harris, Marvin, 141-147, 169, 179-180, 280
Helmholz, R.H., 121
Hempel, Carl, 80
Henry V111, 14
Highwater, Jamake, 44
Hodgson, Bernard, v
hooks, bell, 214
Horney, Karen, 134
Hume, David, 2, 25, 66-71, 76, 79, 83, 86-88, 90, 93-94, 97, 106, 111-116, 153, 155, 158, 161-165, 168, 176, 184, 189, 266, 300
hypothesis-theory distinction, 102
instrumentalism, 101-102, 168
Inuit, 45
Ireland, Mardy S., 215
Jacob, François, 119, 235
Jacobs, Jane, 183
Jaynes, Julian, 234
Jung, Carl Gustav, 134
Kant, Immanuel, 2, 19, 25, 34, 38, 64, 93, 106, 111-117, 121, 124-125, 133, 147-148, 153-155, 158, 160-165, 167-171, 176, 184, 266, 299
Kaschak, Ellyn, 215-228, 230, 233, 236, 23243, 245, 255
Kepler, Johannes, 16
Kohlberg, Leonard, 237
Kuhn, Thomas, 21-32, 35-39, 41, 64, 70, 118, 120, 212, 255, 260, 264-265, 286, 288, 296
Lacan, Jacques, 215

Laqueur, Thomas, 203
Lavoisier, Antoine, 23-24
Lee-Jarvis, May, v
Leibniz, Gottfried, 111
Lerner, Gerda, 305
Lerner, Michael, 194
Litt, Jacquelyn S., 293
Locke, John, 2, 19, 25, 51-53, 55-66, 69-70, 83, 90-91, 97, 106, 116, 130, 153, 155, 160-161, 163-164, 170, 176, 184, 228, 245, 266, 299, 310, 312
Luther, Martin, 11, 14-15, 273
Mach, Ernst, 101
Margulis, Lynn, 120
Marx, Karl, 108, 176
materialism, 44
McBain, Ed, 159
Mendel, Gregor, 118-119, 235
Meyers, Diana Tietjens, 251
Mill, John Stuart, 86, 88-90, 95,121, 153, 160, 302-304
Montagu, Ashley, 143, 279
Morgan, Elaine, 120, 276-282
Morris, Colin, 11
Narveson, Jan, 92
neo-Kantian, 28, 105, 121,
Newton, Isaac, 11, 16-17, 21, 25, 27-28, 33,39, 52, 59-62, 67, 70, 86, 91, 111, 114, 116, 266, 312
Nikiforuk, Andrew, 18
Nominalist, 12
Nye, Andrea, 269-276
Pagels, Elaine, 218
Parker, Charlie, 225
Parmenides, 269-271
Passerin d'Entreves, Alexander, 1
Passmore, John, 293
Pavlov, Ivan, 83-84
Payer, Lynn, 225
Piaget, Jean, 163, 237, 239
Picasso, Pablo, 225
Plato, 2, 6, 11-12, 17, 21, 39, 64, 90, 226, 270-272, 312
Poe, Edgar Allen, 159

Poincaré, Henri, 101
Popper, Sir Karl, 29-30, 32, 37, 102, 102, 148, 150, 152-153, 184, 286
positivism, 29, 74, 81, 97, 102, 109, 148-149, 152, 155, 157, 184, 256
Priestley, Joseph, 23
private language, 162, 164, 257
Protestantism, 53-55, 58-59, 175, 257, 273, 293, 308
psychoanalysis, 120-122, 124, 125-126, 128, 134, 176, 195, 210, 212, 216, 221, 229-230, 232, 236-237, 261
Ptolemy, 15
Puccetti, Roland, iii
Randall, John Herman Jr., 59
Rand, Ayn, 194
Reiter, Rayna R., 145
Rich, Buddy, 282
Rieff, Philip, 176-177
Roach, Max, 282
Rogers, Carl, 194
Rudner, Richard, 149
Russell, Bertrand, 68, 72-73, 93, 275
St. Anselm of Canterbury, 13
Sartre, Jean-Paul, 131
Scheele, C.W, 23
Schoenberg, Arnold, 225
Sellars, Wilfrid, 38-41, 102, 105, 148-149, 153-156, 161, 163-164, 168-169, 229-230, 255, 285-287, 296, 298
Shepher, Joseph, 135
Simenon, Georges, 159
Skinner, B. F., 83, 85, 104-106
skepticism, 68-70, 162, 164, 167
Smith, Adam, 106-109, 170, 187
Smith, William Robertson, 129
social contract, 52-53, 55-58, 65-66, 69, 107-108, 116, 170-171, 187, 310
Spanier, Bonnie, 291
Sterne, Laurence, 69, 189
Stone, Merlin, 305
Strawson, P.F., 34, 73, 93, 165, 168
Strum, Shirley, 284
theory, definition of, 156-157
Thompson, Philip, 138
utilitarianism, 90-93, 95, 109, 160
van den Haag, Ernest, I, ii
Vienna Circle, 81, 273
Waddington, C.H., 171
Washburn, Sherwood, 285
Watson, John, 83-84
Watt, Ian, 116
Weasel, Lisa H. 283
Weber, Max, 54-55, 58
Wilhelm Wallau, Heinrich, 14
William of Ockham, 272-274
Winnicott, D.W., 192-193
Wittgenstein, Ludwig, 81, 93, 154
Wolff, Christian, 111
Wright, Robert, 173
Wurzbach, Natascha, 52